ANIMAL RIGHTS

CASS R. SUNSTEIN

STEVEN M. WISE

RICHARD A. POSNER

PETER SINGER

CORA DIAMOND

GARY L. FRANCIONE

RICHARD A. EPSTEIN

JAMES RACHELS

LESLEY J. ROGERS

GISELA KAPLAN

DAVID J. WOLFSON

MARIANN SULLIVAN

DAVID FAVRE

CATHARINE A. MacKINNON

ELIZABETH ANDERSON

MARTHA C. NUSSBAUM

Edited by

CASS R. SUNSTEIN *and*
MARTHA C. NUSSBAUM

ANIMAL
RIGHTS

Current Debates and New Directions

OXFORD
UNIVERSITY PRESS

20 19 18 17 16 15 14 13 12 11

ACKNOWLEDGMENTS

We are especially thankful to Dedi Felman and Stacey Hamilton for their extraordinary help and support with this project. Special thanks too to Ellen Ruddick-Sunstein, whose interest in the topic helped to inspire this book.

Chapter 3, "Ethics beyond Species and beyond Instincts: A Reply to Richard Posner," copyright © Cambridge University Press.

Chapter 4, "Eating Meat and Eating People," by Cora Diamond, is printed here with the permission of Cambridge University Press. The Walter de la Mare poem entitled "Titmouse" appears in this chapter courtesy of the Literary Trustees of Walter de la Mare and the Society of Authors as their representative.

Material appearing in chapter 5, "Animals—Property or Persons?," by Gary Francione, is drawn from *Introduction to Animal Rights: Your Child or the Dog?*, by Gary Francione. Copyright © 2000 by Temple University. All Rights Reserved.

Chapter 14, "Beyond 'Compassion and Humanity': Justice for Nonhuman Animals," by Martha Nussbaum, is a version of Nussbaum's Tanner Lecture No. 3; it is published prior to the appearance of Tanner volume 25, by courtesy of the University of Utah Press and the Trustees of the Tanner Lectures on Human Values.

CONTENTS

PART II: NEW DIRECTIONS

CONTRIBUTORS

ELIZABETH ANDERSON is Professor of Philosophy and Women's Studies at the University of Michigan, Ann Arbor. She is the author of *Value in Ethics and Economics* and various articles on value theory, democratic theory, philosophy of law, and feminist epistemology and philosophy of science.

CORA DIAMOND is Kenan Professor of Philosophy and University Professor Emerita at the University of Virginia. She is the author of *The Realistic Spirit: Wittgenstein, Philosophy and the Mind* and the editor of *Wittgenstein's Lectures on the Philosophy of Mathematics, Cambridge, 1939*. A collection of her essays, *Ethics: Shifting Perspectives*, is forthcoming.

RICHARD A. EPSTEIN is James Parker Hall Distinguished Service Professor of Law at the University of Chicago and the Peter and Kirsten Bedford Senior Fellow at the Hoover Institution.

DAVID FAVRE is Professor of Law, Michigan State University, DCL College of Law, and has been involved with legal animal issues for more than twenty years as a board member of the Animal Legal Defense Fund. He has taught property law since 1977 and wildlife law since 1983.

GARY L. FRANCIONE is Professor of Law and Nicholas deB. Katzenbach Distinguished Scholar of Law and Philosophy, Rutgers University. His writings include *Introduction to Animal Rights: Your Child or the Dog?* (2000), *Rain Without Thunder: The Ideology of the Animal Rights Movement* (1996), and *Animals, Property, and the Law* (1995). Francione has taught animal rights law for over 20 years and, with Anna E. Charlton, was the co-director of the Rutgers Animal Rights Law Clinic.

GISELA KAPLAN is a full professor in the Centre for Neuroscience and Animal Behaviour at the University of New England, where she conducts research on the behavior of avian, primate, and other species. She has an active interest in the ethics of research on animals, having chaired university Animal Ethics Committees and served on related advisory bodies, and her laboratory conducts postgraduate research in animal welfare.

CATHARINE A. MacKINNON is Elizabeth A. Long Professor of Law at the University of Michigan Law School and long-term visitor at the University of Chicago School of Law. Raised on a farm in Minnesota, she works for equality rights for women domestically and internationally as a teacher, writer, lawyer, and activist.

MARTHA C. NUSSBAUM is Ernst Freund Distinguished Service Professor of Law and Ethics at the University of Chicago, appointed in the Philosophy Department, Law School, and Divinity School. Her most recent book is *Hiding from Humanity: Disgust, Shame, and the Law* (2004).

RICHARD A. POSNER is a federal circuit judge and also teaches at the University of Chicago Law School. He has written extensively on the intersection of legal, economic, and philosophical issues, as in his book *The Problematics of Moral and Legal Theory* (1999).

JAMES RACHELS taught philosophy at the University of Alabama at Birmingham. His writings include *Created from Animals: The Moral Implications of Darwinism* (1991), *Can Ethics Provide Answers?* (1997), and *The Elements of Moral Philosophy* (4th ed., 2002).

LESLEY J. ROGERS is a full professor in the Centre for Neuroscience and Animal Behaviour at the University of New England, where she conducts research on the behavior of avian, primate, and other species. She has an active interest in the ethics of research on animals, having chaired university Animal Ethics Committees and served on related advisory bodies, and her laboratory conducts postgraduate research in animal welfare.

PETER SINGER's best-known book is *Animal Liberation*, first published in 1975. His other books include *Practical Ethics, Rethinking Life and Death,* and *One World.* He is currently Ira W. DeCamp Professor of Bioethics at Princeton University.

MARIANN SULLIVAN is the deputy chief court attorney at the New York State Appellate Division, First Department. She is a former chair of the animal law committee of the Association of the Bar of the City of New York and a member of the animal law committee of the New York State Bar Association.

CASS R. SUNSTEIN teaches at the University of Chicago and is the author of many books, including *Designing Democracy* (Oxford University Press, 2001).

STEVEN M. WISE is president of the Center for the Expansion of Fundamental Rights, Inc. He has taught Animal Rights Law at the Harvard, Vermont, and John Marshall law schools, and in the master's program in Animals and Public Policy at the Tufts University School of Veterinary Medicine. He is the author of *Drawing the Line: Science and the Case for Animal Rights* (2002) and *Rattling the Cage: Toward Legal Rights for Animals* (2000).

DAVID J. WOLFSON is a corporate attorney in New York City and a Lecturer on Law in animal law at Harvard Law School for the spring term 2004. He also co-taught an animal law reading group at Yale Law School and is an adjunct professor at the Benjamin N. Cardozo School of Law. He is the author of a number of articles on animal law and a member of the animal law committees of the Association of the Bar of the City of New York and the New York State Bar Association.

ANIMAL
RIGHTS

CASS R. SUNSTEIN

INTRODUCTION

What Are Animal Rights?

DOGS, CATS, AND HYPOCRISY

There are nearly 60 million domestic dogs in the United States, owned by more than 36 million households. In at least half of these households, the family dog receives a Christmas present. Millions of dog owners celebrate their dog's birthday. If a family's dog were somehow forced to live a short and painful life, the family would undoubtedly feel some combination of rage and grief. What can be said about dog owners can also be said about cat owners, who are more numerous still. But through their daily behavior, people who love those pets, and greatly care about their welfare, help ensure short and painful lives for millions, even billions of animals that cannot easily be distinguished from dogs and cats. Should people change their behavior? Should the law promote animal welfare? Should animals have rights? To answer these questions, we need to step back a bit.

Many people think that the very idea of animal rights is implausible. Suggesting that animals are neither rational nor self-aware, Immanuel Kant thought of animals as "man's instruments," deserving protection only to help human beings in their relation to one another: "He who is cruel to animals becomes hard also in his dealings with men."[1] Jeremy Bentham took a quite different approach, suggesting that mistreatment of animals was akin to racial discrimination:

The day may come when the rest of the animal creation may acquire those rights which never could have been withholden from them but by the hand of tyranny. The French have already discovered that the blackness of the skin is no reason why a human being should be abandoned without redress to the caprice of a tormentor. . . . A full-grown horse or dog is beyond comparison a more rational, as well as a more conversable animal, than an infant of a day, or a week, or even [a] month, old. But suppose the case were otherwise, what would it avail? The question is not, Can they *reason*? nor, Can they *talk*? but, Can they *suffer*?[2]

John Stuart Mill concurred, repeating the analogy to slavery.[3]

Few people accept that particular analogy; many people find it offensive. But since the early 1990s, the animal rights question has moved from the periphery and toward the center of political and legal debate. The debate is fully international. In 2002, Germany became the first European nation to vote to guarantee animal rights in its constitution, adding the words "and animals" to a clause that obliges the state to respect and protect the dignity of human beings.[4] Notwithstanding its apparently growing appeal, the idea of animal rights has been disputed with unusual intensity. Advocates of animal rights seem to think that their adversaries are selfish, unthinking, cruel, even morally blind. Those who oppose animal rights seem to think that the advocates are fanatical and even bizarre, willing to trample on important human interests for the sake of rats and mice and salmon.

The goal of this book is twofold. First, we aim to bring some new clarity to the animal rights debate—to show what underlies these disagreements, largely by concentrating less on abstractions and more on concrete issues in law and practice. Throughout, our focus is practical, not merely theoretical. What, if anything, should human beings be doing that they are not doing now? Second, we aim to chart some new directions for both practice and theory. In part I, contributors focus on issues that are currently contested and on some current "frontiers" issues. Part II goes well beyond current disputes to chart out some new directions for both theory and practice. By identifying those new directions, we hope to provide some guidance for many years to come.

The goal of this introduction is to give some sense of the lay of the land—to show the range of possible positions and to explore what issues, of theory or fact, separate reasonable people. My principal claim is that in at least some sense, almost everyone believes in animal rights. The real question is what that phrase actually means.

ANIMAL WELFARE AND ANIMAL RIGHTS

Those who want to change human practices with respect to animals fall into two different camps. Some people insist on the protection of *animal welfare*.

Others seek *animal rights*. Animal welfare advocates argue for stronger laws preventing cruelty and requiring humane treatment. The American Society for the Prevention of Cruelty to Animals is committed to this basic approach. By contrast, animal rights advocates oppose any and all human "use" of animals. They invoke the Kantian idea that human beings should be treated as ends, not means—but they extend the idea to animals, so as to challenge a wide range of current practices. These include the use of animals in rodeos, circuses, zoos, agriculture, hunting, and scientific experimentation. People for the Ethical Treatment of Animals and the Humane Society of the United States are committed to this basic approach.

Many of the goals of animal welfare groups receive broad popular approval. Civilized nations prohibit cruelty to animals, and vigorous enforcement of existing prohibitions would do a great deal. On many topics, animal welfare advocates and animal rights advocates are happy to join forces to urge further reforms. Consider a few examples. At greyhound tracks, dogs live in small cages, stacked on top of each other, for eighteen to twenty-two hours each day. Older greyhounds, and those who can't run very fast, are usually killed or sold to laboratories. More than 20,000 are put to death each year. Racehorses are very popular, but when they aren't able to race any longer, they tend to end up at the slaughterhouse, usually at a young age. About 75 percent of racehorses, or 100,000, are slaughtered every year. With respect to the use and abuse of animals, all this is just the tip of the iceberg. Billions of animals are killed every year for food, and many spend their short lives in cages or in other appalling conditions.

When animal suffering is clearly involved, the choice between animal welfare and animal rights might not greatly matter. And in a sense, those who believe in animal welfare also believe in animal rights, at least if we define animal rights to mean "protection against suffering." Any effort to prevent suffering will call for rights of a certain sort. But there are large differences between those who seek animal welfare and those who seek animal rights. If suffering is the focus, scientific experimentation and meat eating might be acceptable if suffering is minimal.

Let us turn, then, to the sorts of rights that animals might have. It will be useful to ask why one might, at any particular point, conclude that the interest in animal rights has gone "too far"—why, in short, one might draw a line between one possible stopping place and another.

WHAT ANIMAL RIGHTS MIGHT ENTAIL

The Status Quo

If we understand "rights" to be legal protection against harm, then many animals already do have rights, and the idea of animal rights is not terribly controversial. Of course some people, including Descartes, have argued that animals lack emotions and that people should be allowed to treat them however they choose. But to most people, including sharp critics of the animal rights movement, this position seems unacceptable. Almost everyone agrees that people should not be able to torture animals or to engage in acts of cruelty against them. And indeed, state law includes a wide range of protections against cruelty and neglect. We can build on state law to define a simple, minimalist position in favor of animal rights: *The law should prevent acts of cruelty to animals.*

In England, France, Germany, the United States, and many other nations, anticruelty laws go well beyond prohibiting beating, injuring, and the like, and impose affirmative duties on people with animals in their care. Omissions may count as cruelty; so too for overworking or underfeeding animals, or for depriving them of adequate protection. Owners must offer adequate sustenance and shelter. The law of New York may be taken as representative. In that state, anyone who has impounded or confined an animal is obliged to provide good air, water, shelter, and food. People who transport an animal on a railroad or in a car are required to allow the animal out for rest, feeding, and water every five hours. Those who abandon an animal, including a pet, face criminal penalties. Indeed it is generally a crime not to provide necessary sustenance, food, water, shelter, and protection from severe weather. Like most states, New York forbids using an animal for work when it is not physically fit.

If taken seriously, provisions of this kind would do a great deal to protect animals from suffering, injury, and premature death. But animal rights, as recognized by state law, are sharply limited and for two major reasons. First, enforcement can occur only through public prosecution. If horses are being beaten at a local farm, or if greyhounds are forced to live in small cages, protection will come only if the prosecutor decides to provide it. Of course prosecutors have limited budgets, and animal protection is rarely a high-priority item. The result is that violations of state law occur frequently, and there is no way to prevent those violations. The anticruelty prohibitions are, in this respect, in sharp contrast to most prohibitions protecting human beings, which can be enforced both publicly and privately. For example, the prohibitions on assault and theft can be enforced through criminal prosecutions, brought by public officials, and also by injured citizens, proceeding directly against those who have violated the law.

Second, the anticruelty provisions of state law contain large exceptions. They generally do not regulate or ban hunting. (It is not permissible to deprive domestic animals of adequate food and shelter, but it is permissible to chase and to kill wild animals.) They generally do not apply to the use of animals for medical or scientific purposes, nor to the production and use of animals as food. Because the overwhelming majority of animals are produced and used for food, the coverage of anticruelty laws is actually very narrow.

Enforcing Existing Rights

Some people are concerned about these limitations on the effectiveness of anticruelty laws. The least controversial response would be to narrow the "enforcement gap." Reforms might be adopted with the limited purpose of stopping conduct that is already against the law, so that the law actually means, in practice, what it says on paper. Here, then, we can find a slightly less minimalist understanding of animal rights. On this view, representatives of animals should be able to bring private suits to ensure that anticruelty and related laws are actually enforced. If, for example, a farm is treating horses cruelly in violation of legal requirements, a suit could be brought, on behalf of those animals, to bring about compliance with the law.

In a sense, this would be a dramatic proposal. But it is simpler and more conventional than it appears. Of course any such animals would be represented by human beings, just like any other litigant who lacks ordinary (human) competence; for example, the interests of children are protected by prosecutors, and also by trustees and guardians in private litigation brought on children's behalf. Many of those who believe in animal rights want to build on this idea. Their proposed step does seem modest. Why would anyone oppose an effort to promote greater enforcement of existing law, by supplementing the prosecutor's power with private lawsuits? Perhaps the answer lies in a fear that some or many of those lawsuits would be unjustified, even frivolous. Perhaps animal representatives would bring a flurry of suits, not because of cruelty or neglect or any violation of law, but because of some kind of ideological commitment to improving animal welfare. If this is a genuine risk, it might make sense to respond, not by banning those lawsuits, but by forcing those who bring frivolous ones to pay the defendants' attorneys' fees.

We are not yet in the most controversial territory. Many of those who ridicule the idea of animal rights believe in anticruelty laws, and they might well support efforts to ensure that those laws are actually enforced.

Regulating Hunting, Science, Farming, and More

But many animal rights advocates go further. They focus attention not only on the enforcement gap, but also on the areas where current law offers little or no protection. They urge that the law should regulate hunting, scientific experiments, entertainment, and farming to ensure against unnecessary animal suffering. It is easy to imagine a set of initiatives that would do a great deal here, and indeed European nations have moved in just this direction. There are many possibilities here.

A state might, for example, require scientists to show, in front of some kind of committee or board, that experiments on animals are actually necessary or promising, and also that the animals involved will be subjected to minimal suffering. If dogs or chimpanzees are going to be used to explore some medical treatment, it would be necessary to ensure that they be decently fed and housed. Similar controls might be imposed on agriculture. If cows, hens, and pigs are going to be raised for use as food, they must be treated decently in terms of food, shelter, and overall care. European nations have moved in just this direction. It would, on this view, be permissible to kill animals and use them for food, but it would not be permissible to be indifferent to their interests while they are alive. So too for other animals in farms, even or perhaps especially if they are being used for the benefit of human beings. If sheep are going to be used to create wool clothing, their conditions must be conducive to their welfare.

Notice that we remain in the domain of animal welfare, though the protection of welfare would certainly require legally enforceable rights. And here things become far more controversial. Partly the controversy may arise because of sheer ignorance, on the part of most people, about what actually happens to animals in, for example, farming and scientific experimentation; probably greater regulation would be actively sought if current practices were widely known. And partly the controversy is a product of the political power of the relevant interests, which intensely resist regulation. But serious questions might be raised about some of these regulatory strategies, for the simple reason that the interests of animals and the interests of human beings are in some conflict in this context. Here as elsewhere, additional regulation would be costly and burdensome. It is possible to fear that regulation of scientific experiments on animals would lead to less scientific experiments on animals—and hence to less in the way of scientific and medical progress. If farms are regulated, the price of meat will increase, and people will be able to eat less meat. Hence it is necessary to balance the gain to animal welfare against the harms to human beings.

Any such balancing must depend, in part, on values—on how much weight we assign to the relevant interests. But to make a sensible assessment, it would be helpful to know a great deal about the facts as well. One of the most important disputes, in the domain of scientific experimentation, is whether and to what extent the relevant experiments really hold out a great deal of promise for medical progress. If we are speaking of perfumes and hair dyes, the claim for imposing suffering on animals seems weak. But if scientists are able to develop treatments for AIDS and cancer, the claim is much stronger. Now some animal rights advocates urge that even if the gains from a certain practice are very large, experiments are not justified. We do not, after all, allow scientists to experiment on human beings, even human beings with serious disabilities, simply because medical advances might be significant. Utilitarians might not find it easy to explain why we impose barriers in cases of this kind. But those who think that human beings should be treated as ends, and never as means, might urge that there is a fundamental difference between animals and people here. They might also urge that it is excessive, or fanatical, to ban experiments that impose a degree of suffering on rats or mice if the consequence of those experiments is to produce significant medical advances for human beings (and ultimately nonhuman animals as well).

Eliminating Current Practices, Including Meat Eating

Now let us begin to explore some quite radical suggestions. Suppose that we continue to believe that animal suffering is the problem that should concern us, and that we want to use the law to promote animal welfare. We might conclude that certain practices cannot be defended and should not be allowed to continue, if mere regulation will inevitably be insufficient—and if, in practice, mere regulation will ensure that the level of animal suffering will remain high. To make such an argument convincing, it would be helpful to argue not only that the harms to animals are serious, but that the benefits, to human beings, of the relevant practices are simply too small to justify the continuation of those practices. Many people who urge radical steps—who think, for example, that people should not eat meat—do so because they believe that without such steps, the level of animal suffering will be unacceptably severe.

To evaluate an argument of this kind, there is no choice but to go area by area. Consider greyhound racing. Many greyhounds live in miserable conditions, and many of them are put to death after their racing careers are over. For those who object to animal suffering, the preferred step would be to ensure that greyhounds are allowed decent lives—and to hope that the racing industry is compatible with that goal. But if it is simply impractical for law to ensure that greyhounds live minimally decent lives, some people would argue that greyhound racing should be abolished.

Of course, the largest issue involves eating meat. Some people would agree that meat eating is acceptable if decent treatment is given to the animals used for food. Such people do not object to killing animals; what troubles them is suffering. But if, as a practical matter, animals used for food are almost inevitably going to endure terrible suffering, then perhaps people should not eat meat.

Some utilitarians make an interesting objection to steps of this kind. They say that the inevitable result will be to ensure that fewer animals exist. Perhaps it is objectionable to protect animals through measures that reduce the total number of animals. Perhaps it is better for animals to have lives, even difficult ones, than not to have lives. Those who disagree think that it is important for animals to have good lives—not to ensure that there are as many animals as possible.

However this issue might be resolved, the basic argument—forbidding certain practices as the only feasible way to avoid widespread suffering—raises a host of questions, including many of fact. Shouldn't it be possible to reduce the level of suffering in scientific experiments by, for example, requiring animals to be adequately sheltered and fed? Why couldn't farms generally give their animals decent lives, as many farms now do? It would also be valuable to ask some factual issues. If vegetarianism were widespread, would human health be undermined (as many contend) or improved (as many also contend)? After the factual questions are resolved, disputes will remain about the weight to be given to the various interests.

The Question of Animal Autonomy

Of course some people would go much further. They would focus not only, and perhaps not mostly, on the relief of suffering. Their agenda is far broader. On one view, animals have rights in the sense that they should not be subject to human use and control. Notice that this is not a Bentham-inspired point about the prevention and relief of suffering. It is instead a suggestion that animals deserve to have a kind of autonomy. And the suggestion goes well beyond the view that animals should be seen as ends rather than means. Many people who use chimpanzees in entertainment or zoos, or who use horses for showing or riding, do not consider the relevant animals to be mere means to human ends. But those who think that animals should not be subject to human control tend to object to all of these uses. They want all or most animals to be able to make their own choices, free from human control.

This claim raises many questions. For one thing, it is not clear whether and how this position might be applied to companion animals. Dogs and cats, among others, have been bred specifically for human companionship, and many of them would not fare well on their own. Perhaps those who believe in animal autonomy would also accept the idea that people can substantially control animals who have been bred to live with them. Perhaps the autonomy argument would apply only to wild animals—forbidding human beings from hunting, trapping, and confining them.

But what if certain practices, such as confinement in zoos or other facilities, can be undertaken in a way that is consistent with animal welfare? What if some animals would do well, or best, under human control? Nature can be very cruel, after all, and many animals will live longer lives with human beings than in the wild. Of course longer is not necessarily better. But we could imagine that many lions, elephants, giraffes, and dolphins could, in fact, have better lives with human assistance, even if confined, than in their own habitats. If this is so, it is not simple to see what sort of response might be made by those who believe in animal autonomy. Perhaps autonomy advocates disagree on the facts, not on the theoretical issue, and think it highly unlikely, in most cases, that wild animals can have decent lives under human control.

ARE ANIMALS "PROPERTY"? ARE ANIMALS "PERSONS"?

I have not yet mentioned the ongoing debate over the status of animals as "property." This is one of the most vigorous debates of all.[5] What underlies this debate?

There is no single answer. Perhaps those who insist that animals should not be seen as property are making a simple and modest claim: Human beings should not be able to treat animals however they wish. Their starting point seems to be this: If you are property, you are, in law and in effect, a slave, wholly subject to the will of your owner. A table, a chair, or a stereo can be treated as the owner likes; it can be broken or sold or replaced at the owner's whim. Many people think that, for animals, the status of property is devastating to actual protection against cruelty and abuse.

On this view, a central goal of the animal rights movement—eliminating the idea that animals are property—can be taken in a modest way, as an effort to remove a legal status that inevitably promotes suffering, and in that sense it is a small part of the animal welfare agenda. But the goal can be taken far more ambitiously, as an effort to say that animals should have rights of self-determination, or a certain kind of autonomy. Hence some people urge that certain animals, at least, are "persons," not property, and that they should have many of the legal rights that human beings have. Of course this does not mean that those animals can vote or run for office. Their status would be akin to that of children—a status commensurate with their capacities. What that status is, particularly, remains to be spelled out. But at a minimum, it would seem to entail protection against torture, battery, and even confinement (except for purposes of human self-defense).

There is, however, an underlying puzzle here. What does it mean to say that animals are property and can be "owned"? As we have seen, animals, even if owned, cannot be treated however the owner wishes; the law forbids cruelty and neglect. Ownership is just a label, connoting a certain set of rights and perhaps duties, and without knowing a lot more, we cannot identify those rights and duties. A state could dramatically increase enforcement of existing bans on cruelty and neglect without turning animals into persons, or making them into something other than property. A state could do a great deal to prevent animal suffering, indeed carry out the central goals of the animal welfare program, without saying that animals cannot be owned. We could even grant animals a right to bring suit without insisting that animals are persons, or that they are not property. A state could certainly confer rights on a pristine area, or a painting, and allow people to bring suit on its behalf, without therefore saying that that area and that painting may not be owned.

It might, in these circumstances, seem puzzling that so many people are focusing on the question of whether animals are property. We could retain the idea of property but also give animals far more protection against injury or neglect of their interests. Or we could say that animals are not property, as children are not property, but still give human beings a great deal of control over them, as parents have control over their children. What, then, are the real stakes in the debate over whether animals are "property"? Perhaps it is thought necessary to destroy the idea of ownership in order to make, simply and all at once, a statement that the interests of animals count and have weight independent of the interests of human beings. Perhaps it is thought that rhetoric matters, and that the idea of "property" fits poorly with how people should behave toward or think about other living creatures. On this view, the debate over whether animals are property is really a debate over a set of more specific issues, involving a wide range of possible goals of those who believe in animal welfare or animal rights.

WHICH ANIMALS HAVE RIGHTS?

There is an obvious question in the background. We have seen that animals might have rights in a minimal sense or in a much larger sense. But people do not see all animals in the same way. They might agree that human beings should protect the interests of dogs, cats, horses, and dolphins; they are unlikely to think the same about ants, mosquitoes, and cockroaches; rats, mice, and squirrels seem to be an intermediate case. It is often objected, to those who believe in animal rights, that their position would lead to truly ludicrous conclusions—to the (ridiculous?) suggestion that people cannot kill ants or mosquitoes, or rid their houses of rats and cockroaches.

Those who emphasize suffering have a simple answer to this objection: Everything depends on whether and to what extent the animal in question is capable of suffering. If rats are able to suffer, then their interests are relevant to the question of how, and perhaps even whether, they can be expelled from houses. At the very least, people should kill rats in a way that minimizes distress and suffering. These claims should not be taken as radical or extreme; many people already take steps in just this direction. On this view, if ants and mosquitoes have no claim to human concern—if they can be killed at our whim—it is because they suffer little or not at all. Here we have some empirical questions about the capacities of creatures of various sorts. And utilitarians should certainly be willing to engage in a degree of balancing. If human beings are at risk of illness and disease from mosquitoes and rats, they have a strong justification, perhaps even one of self-defense, for eliminating or relocating them.

Those who emphasize animal rights have a more complicated task. They tend to urge that animals should be given rights to the extent that their capacities are akin to those of human beings. The usual emphasis here is on cognitive capacities. The line would be drawn between animals with advanced capacities, such as chimpanzees and dolphins, and those that lack such capacities. Undoubtedly a great deal of work needs to be done on this topic. But at least an emphasis on the capacity to think, and to form plans, seems to provide a foundation for appropriate line drawing by those who believe in animal rights in a strong sense.

THE PLAN

With this general background, let us turn to the essays in this book. The goal of part I explores contemporary debates. Steven Wise begins the analysis by outlining the various obstacles to the recognition of animal rights. He argues that the legal system should recognize such rights "one step at a time." He also argues that animals should have rights if they have something that Wise calls "practical autonomy." Drawing on scientific evidence, he suggests that many animals have abilities that should qualify them for rights.

Richard Posner is highly skeptical of Wise's claims, and also of the claims made by Peter Singer, the most well known advocate of animal rights. Posner urges that theoretical arguments are not of much use. He also contends that on pragmatic grounds, people are not likely to want to give rights to animals. Posner concludes with the suggestion that some rights would be damaging to animals themselves. Peter Singer responds directly to Posner, arguing that human beings have the ability to go "beyond instinct," and that theoretical arguments for rights, of the kind that Posner disparages, can in fact be persuasive. Cora Diamond responds directly to Singer's approach to animal rights. She urges that Singer's attack on "speciesism" mischaracterizes the moral issues at stake. She contends that if people are to be on the side of animals, it must be for reasons different from those used by Singer and others who object to the current human use and mistreatment of animals.

Gary Francione and Richard Epstein continue the debate about whether animals count as property, but from a different direction. Francione argues that our current practices are entirely inconsistent with our moral judgments. In Francione's view, most human beings believe, in fact, that animals should not be made to suffer. Nonetheless, human beings make animals suffer, often for little or no reason. Surveying our practices in connection with meat eating, science, and entertainment, Francione argues that our own moral judgments call for radical change. Richard Epstein sharply disagrees. He believes that animals should continue to be treated as property. He thinks that a form of speciesism is, in fact, justified. In his view, many social gains come from the practices that Francione deplores, and there is no adequate reason for dramatic changes from what we now do.

James Rachels turns to the vexing question of what lines should be drawn. What makes some kinds of animals more worthy of protection than others? After reviewing the most popular theories of moral standing, he concludes that the whole business of line drawing is misguided and that the distinctions between species made in the U.S. Animal Welfare Act are unjustifiable. He urges that the appropriate protection of animals should depend in large part on what their capacities are. Lesley Rogers and Gisela Kaplan offer another perspective on the difficulties in deciding to which species we should extend rights. They discuss the available and up-to-date scientific evidence for awareness of self, theory of mind, complex memory, planning actions, complex communication, and intelligence in animals. In so doing they point out that, despite the infancy of research in these areas, we already know that some species of birds perform as well as, or even better than, apes when tested in certain tasks and so too do domestic dogs. Brain size is also considered in relation to cognitive ability and social behavior. Here too birds show us that smaller brains can process information very efficiently. These and other anomalies caution us against ranking species according to performance on a single task or on a single set of criteria and to be mindful of attributing higher value to one set of characteristics than another.

Part II turns to new directions, beginning with three essays exploring novel developments in law and policy. We begin with some practical issues. David Wolfson and Mariann Sullivan explore the use of animals for food. They argue that this is the central issue in animal rights, and that both advocates and critics of animal rights have often neglected that issue. Wolfson and Sullivan provide a concrete sense of the extent of the problem and of what should be done about it. David Favre goes much further. He argues that animals should, in an important sense, be allowed to own themselves, and he explores what this would mean in practice. Cass Sunstein turns to a much-disputed question: Should animals be allowed to sue? He urges that, at a minimum, suits should be permitted, on animals' behalf, to ensure compliance with existing law.

The book ends with new theoretical departures. Why, Catharine Mac-Kinnon asks, is it necessary for animals to be like people to be protected from them or to be entitled to their own lives? As women are used as sex, she argues, animals are used as food. She uses a reading of John Steinbeck's play *Of Mice and Men* to caution that love for beings with less power can do them in, despite the good intentions of the powerful. Critical of standard liberal approaches to theorizing rights based on sameness to dominant groups and standards, she advocates analyzing the situation of animals on their own terms, however difficult.

Elizabeth Anderson explores some tensions among animal welfare, animal rights, and environmental ethics. She observes that those who believe in animal welfare can accept animal experimentation, to which animal rights advocates object; she also demonstrates that those who believe in environmental ethics might support the hunting of deer and rabbits when this is necessary to protect ecological well-being. She argues that there is a plurality of values here and that an understanding of the relevant values helps to resolve hard cases. Martha Nussbaum applies the capabilities approach, which she and Amartya Sen developed, to the question of animal rights. Nussbaum criticizes the view, associated with Kant and his followers, that mistreatment of animals does not raise questions of justice. She also objects to utilitarian approaches, urging instead that the claims of animals should be rooted in an understanding of what sorts of capabilities animals have. Such an understanding, she contends, would require large-scale changes in current practices.

Many of the essays in this book will be controversial—perhaps because they defend the status quo, perhaps because they ask people to act very differently from how they now do. Whatever one's ultimate conclusions, there can be no question that the relationship between human beings and nonhuman animals is now being fundamentally rethought. We hope that this book will contribute to that rethinking.

NOTES

1. Immanuel Kant, *Lectures on Ethics*, trans. Louis Infield (New York: Harper Torchbooks, 1963), at 240.
2. See Jeremy Bentham, *The Principles of Morals and Legislation*, chap. XVII, section IV [–1781] (Amherst, NY: Prometheus, 1988), at 310–311.
3. Bentham's ideas were challenged by many critics. See John Stuart Mill, "Whewell on Moral Philosophy," in John Stuart Mill and Jeremy Bentham, *Utilitarianism and Other Essays* 228, 252 (Alan Ryan ed.; New York: Penguin, 1987). Whewell argued that "to most persons" Bentham's theories will "not [be] a tolerable doctrine" and that our only duties can be to those who are like us. Id. (quoting Whewell) (internal quotation marks omitted). Mill replied: "It is 'to most persons' in the Slave States of America not a tolerable doctrine that we may sacrifice any portion of the happiness of white men for the sake of a greater amount of happiness to black men. It would have been intolerable five centuries ago 'to most persons' among the feudal nobility, to hear it asserted that the greatest pleasure or pain of a hundred serfs ought not to give way to the smallest of a nobleman. According to the standard of Dr. Whewell, the slavemasters and the nobles were right. They too felt themselves 'bound' by a 'tie of brotherhood' to the white men and to the nobility, and felt no such tie to the negroes and serfs. And if a feeling on moral subjects is right because it is natural, their feeling was justifiable. Nothing is more natural to human beings, nor, up to a certain point in cultivation, more universal, than to estimate the pleasures and pains of others as deserving of regard exactly in proportion to their likeness to ourselves. These superstitions of selfishness had the characteristics by which Dr. Whewell recognizes his moral rules; and his opinion on the rights of animals shows that in this case at least he is consistent. We are perfectly willing to stake the whole question on this one issue. Granted that any practice causes more pain to animals than it gives pleasure to man; is that practice moral or immoral? And if, exactly in proportion as human beings raise their heads out of the slough of selfishness, they do not with one voice answer 'immoral,' let the morality of the principle of utility be for ever condemned." Id. at 252–253.
4. John Hooper, "German Parliament Votes to Give Animals Constitutional Rights," *Guardian* (London), May 18, 2002, p. 2.
5. See Steven Wise, *Rattling the Cage* (New York: Perseus, 2001).

PART I

CURRENT
DEBATES

1

STEVEN M. WISE

ANIMAL RIGHTS,
ONE STEP AT A TIME

THE OBSTACLES

An advocate for legal rights for nonhuman animals must proceed one step at a time, as progress is impeded by physical, economic, political, religious, historical, legal, and psychological obstacles.

Physical Obstacles

The physical obstacles are enormous. In the United States, more than 10 billion nonhuman animals are annually slaughtered just for food. The number triples for the rest of the world. Tens of millions are annually consumed in biomedical research, hundreds of millions more by hunting and entertainment; for clothing, fur, and leather; and through numerous other human activities. More than 300 mammals and birds die each time your heart beats.

Economic Obstacles

Political scientist William Lee Miller has written, "Suppose today some dominant industry, built into the lives and fortunes of a great many people—to a degree of the whole nation—were found to be morally repugnant; what difficulties there would be in extracting it from the nation's life!"[1] Huge industries are involved in raising, using, processing, and killing those billions of nonhuman animals. Miller was writing of the enslavement of blacks in the antebellum United States. This human slave trade could be immensely profitable.[2] Slavery historian David Brion Davis sets out some of those details:

> After decades of research, historians are only now beginning to grasp the complex interdependence of a society enmeshed in slavery. There were shifting interactions among West African enslavers, sellers and European buyers: European investors on the slave trade, who ranged from small-town merchants to well-known figures like the philosophers John Locke and Voltaire; wealthy Virginian and Brazilian middlemen who purchased large numbers of Africans off the slave ships to sell to planters; New Englanders who shipped foodstuffs, timber, shoes and clothing as supplies for slaves in the South and the West Indies; and finally, the European and American consumers of slave-produced sugar, rum, rice, cotton, tobacco, indigo (for dyes), hemp (for rope making), and other goods.[3]

The interdependence of our society, enmeshed in the use of nonhuman animals, dwarfs nineteenth-century slave society. Then it was possible to avoid complicity. Today nonhuman animal products are so omnipresent that one cannot live and not support the abuse of nonhuman animals. For example, the blood of a slaughtered cow is used to manufacture plywood adhesives, fertilizer, fire extinguisher foam, and dyes. Her fat helps make plastic, tires, crayons, cosmetics, lubricants, soaps, detergents, cough syrup, contraceptive jellies and creams, ink, shaving cream, fabric softeners, synthetic rubber, jet engine lubricants, textiles, corrosion inhibitors, and metal-machining lubricants. Her collagen is found in pie crusts, yogurts, matches, bank notes, paper, and cardboard glue, her intestines used in strings for musical instruments and racquets, her bones in charcoal ash for refining sugar, in ceramics, and in cleaning and polishing compounds. Medical and scientific uses abound. And there is much more.[4]

What Miller concluded in the context of human slavery is true of nonhuman animals now: "When a pecuniary interest has that magnitude, it is a formidable opponent indeed. Rationalizations are supplied, positions are softened, conflict is avoided, compromises are sought, careers are protected, life goes on."[5]

Political Obstacles

In 1999, law professor Richard Epstein insisted, "There would be nothing left of human society if we treated animals not as property but as independent holders of rights."[6] Epstein exaggerates. Humans would have plenty left. But any industry, such as the meat or biomedical research industries, that depends upon inflicting bodily harm might be severely affected if the animals upon which they depend were given a legal right to bodily integrity.

Turn again to human slavery. Britain's eighteenth- and nineteenth-century slave trade centered on newly enriched Liverpool, in whose ship bottoms rode more than half of Europe's slaves.[7] Alarmed by rising abolitionist voices, Liverpudlians composed a ditty:

If our slave trade be gone, there's an end to our lives,
Beggars all we must be, our children and wives;
No ships from our ports their proud sails e'er would spread,
And our streets grown with grass, where the cows might be fed.[8]

Hand in glove with West Indian planters, Liverpool's members and witnesses argued in Parliament that their slavers were men "of impeccable characters," that the trade itself was not cruel. The Middle Passage, they claimed, was "one of the happiest periods of a Negro's life." It was crazy to think men "whose profit depended on the health" of slaves might harm them. The slavers did the Africans a favor; if they "could not be sold as slaves, they would be butchered and executed at home." Parliamentary fellow travelers argued that slaving was "not an amiable trade but neither was the trade of a butcher an amiable trade, and yet a mutton chop was, nevertheless, a good thing." Abolition would destroy Africa. One member of Parliament rhapsodized that slaves appeared so happy he often wished to be one.[9] Prime Minister Pitt summed up the slaving arguments: "The blood of these poor negroes was to continue flowing; it was dangerous to stop it because it had run so long; besides, we were under contract with certain surgeons to allow them a certain supply of human bodies every year for them to try experiments on, and this we did out of pure love for science."[10]

Abolition, on the other hand, would ruin Britain and its colonies, throw thousands of sailors out of work, and destroy its seafaring training ground. It would cripple British seapower. And all would be for naught, for if Britain abolished its slave trade, other nations would fill the vacuum and steal Britain's profits. Abolition would send many of Britain's "most loyal, industrious, and useful subjects" emigrating to America.[11] Liverpool's sailmakers, bakers, and gunmakers petitioned Parliament to keep slavers sailing. To whom would they sell their sails, biscuits, and guns?[12] Abolitionists were advised to direct their energies toward alleviating the plight of the poor and young chimney sweeps.[13] Britain eventually did the right thing, if not always for the right reasons. Within thirty years, British slavery was gone.

Doomsayers were not confined to Britain. In 1832, the future president of the College of William and Mary, Thomas Roderick Dew, wrote, "It is in truth the slave labour in Virginia which gives value to her soil and her habitations—take away this and you pull down the atlas that upholds the whole system—eject from the state the whole slave population . . . and the Old Dominion will be a 'waste howling wilderness'—the grass shall be seen growing in the streets, and the foxes peeping from their holes."[14]

21

Miller points out that, before the Civil War, American slave owners "were a major and very powerful part of the population, strategically located, from the outset in the highest places."[15] Because five of the first seven presidents of the United States owned slaves, for fifty of the first sixty-four years of the nation's life, the president was a slaveholder. For twenty-eight of its first thirty-five years, the Speaker of the House of Representatives had slaves. The president pro tem of the U.S. Senate was always a slaveholder, as were the majority of every presidential cabinet and the U.S. Supreme Court up to Bull Run. Washington, Jefferson, Jackson, John Marshall—slave owners all.

Some may shift uncomfortably at comparisons between human and nonhuman slavery. They shouldn't. The first definition of *slave* in the *Oxford English Dictionary* is "one who is the property of, and entirely subject to, another person, whether by capture, purchase, or birth: a servant completely divested of freedom and personal rights."[16] International law has, for most of a century, defined *slavery* as "the status or condition of a person over whom any or all of the powers attaching to the right of ownership are exercised."[17]

Philosopher Isaiah Berlin claimed that when a human stops me from doing what I want, I've lost some liberty. When my liberty has been reduced "beyond a certain minimum, I can be described as being . . . enslaved."[18] Sociologist Orlando Patterson characterizes a slave as "the ultimate human tool, as imprintable and as disposable as the master wished."[19] David Brion Davis argues that slavery is just a branch of property law that "starts with the power of one individual over another."[20]

Writers often compare human slaves to nonhuman animals. "The truly striking fact about slavery," Davis writes, is the "antiquity and almost universal acceptance of the *concept* of the slave as a human being who is legally owned, used, sold, or otherwise disposed of as if he or she were a domestic animal. This parallel persisted in the similarity of naming, branding, and even pricing slaves according to their equivalent in cows, camels, pigs, and chickens."[21] Legal scholar Roscoe Pound said that, in Rome, a slave "was a thing, and as such, like animals could be the object of rights of property."[22] Barry Nichols, an expert in Roman law, says in Rome, "The slave was a thing. . . . he himself had no rights: he was merely an object of rights, like an animal."[23] Rome's initial regulation of the treatment of slaves "took the same form as our legislation for the protection of animals. The master might be punished criminally for abuse of his powers, but the slave could not himself invoke the protection of the law."[24] This was true in slaveholding Virginia.[25] And Mississippi.[26]

Religious Obstacles

Genesis says God granted humans dominion "over the fish of the sea, and over the fowl of the air, and every living thing that moveth upon the earth."[27] The Old and New Testaments, St. Paul, St. Augustine, and St.

Thomas Aquinas stitched into the fabric of Judeo-Christian doctrine the idea that nonhuman animals had been created for humans.[28] Twentieth-century Christian theologian and Oxford don C. S. Lewis thought a Christian vivisectionist might therefore justify torturing a chimpanzee to death on two grounds. He might admit he was a speciesist. This is why neuroscience professor Robert Speth argues that apes can never have legal rights: "apes are not humans," and "humanity is our species and . . . our first and primary obligation is to ourselves."[29] Or a vivisectionist might declare humans preeminent, created in the image of God, superior to every other, following God's ordering of the universe.

Religion need not obstruct animals' rights. That it often does should come as no surprise. Religion has often been indifferent, sometimes hostile, toward human rights.[30] The major Western religions, well formed centuries before human rights appeared, long ignored them. The Atlantic slave trade was thoroughly dominated by Christians. Jews enslaved gentiles, Africans, and other Jews.[31] The Islamic slave trade may have equaled the Atlantic slave trade.[32] American slave supporters trumpeted God's imprimatur on slavery from Genesis to Paul. Baptist minister Thornton Stringfellow argued that slavery had received "the sanction of the Almighty" and the "control of the black race, by the white, is an indispensable Christian duty."[33] Even the American Civil War did not strangle the claims of some Orthodox Jews and Christian biblical scholars that human slavery was "an ordinance of God."[34]

Religious faith can blind adherents to facts. Listen to the verdict of Galileo's inquisitors: "We say, pronounce, sentence, and declare that you, Galileo . . . have rendered yourself in the judgment of this Holy Office vehemently suspected of heresy, namely of having held and believed the doctrine which is false and contrary to the Sacred Scriptures that . . . the earth moves and is not the center of the world."[35] Evolutionary biologist Ernst Mayr has written, "No educated person any longer questions the validity of the so-called theory of evolution, which we now know to be a simple fact."[36] On the cusp of the June 2000 announcement that the human genome was pieced together, David Baltimore, president of the California Institute of Technology and winner of the Nobel Prize in medicine, wrote, "It confirms something obvious and expected, yet controversial: our genes look much like those of fruit flies, worms, and even plants. . . . the genome shows that we all descended from the same humble beginnings and that the connections are written in our genes. That should be, but won't be, the end of creationism."[37]

Judges freely admit that religious beliefs may be illogical or inconsistent.[38] They must respect the right of all to believe what they wish. But secular law soars beyond belief. A human-nonhuman animals hierarchy constructed before science was born, before rights were invented, for which no objective evidence exists, that allows a believer to do as he pleases with Creation, seems a bit unfair to Creation. We can believe in hierarchy. We can believe the universe was made just for us. Hierarchy and a major sense of entitlement are not insurmountable problems. The problem occurs when we treat those whom we believe lie beneath us as slaves. Religion once sustained human slavery. It was wrong then. When it blindly sanctions the slavery of every nonhuman animal, it is wrong now.

Historical Obstacles

The idea that everything existed for the sake of humans was a core belief of the highly influential ancient Stoics, first in Greece, then in Rome, and was found in Old Testament law codes and other ancient law. A designed universe formed the core of the immensely influential "great chain of being." Rational humans occupied the topmost rungs reserved for corporeal creatures. Lesser Creation was aligned below them. It wasn't just that nonhuman animals occupied lower rungs, but that we differed so fundamentally that we were incomparable.[39] Nonhumans were literally made for us. Savage beasts fostered our courage and trained us for war. Singing birds existed to entertain us. Cows and sheep kept our meat fresh. Lobsters fed us and provided us with exercise by cracking shells that doubled as nifty models for body armor. Lice made us adopt clean habits.[40]

In the fifth century, St. Augustine, who thought Christ a Stoic in the way he viewed nonhuman animals, fused the animal-related teachings of the Hebrews and the Stoics, and folded them into Christianity.[41] A century later, Byzantine emperor Justinian injected these teachings into his immensely influential legal codes. From there it was absorbed into the legal writings of continental Europe, taken up by the great lawyers, judges, and commentators of English common law, and received nearly whole in America.[42] That is why this idea remains at the root of what the law says we in the West can do to nonhuman animals today.[43]

Indeed, C. S. Lewis thought, "The only rational line for the Christian vivisectionist to take is to say that the superiority of man over beast is a real objective fact, guaranteed by Revelation, and that the propriety of sacrificing beast to man is a logical consequence." The world, he demanded they argue, conforms "to a hierarchical order created by God and really present in the universe whether any one acknowledges it or not."[44]

Most ancient Stoics thought animals had life, sensation, and impulse, but lacked emotions, reason, belief, intentionality, thought, and memory apart from the present.[45] Seneca thought nonhuman animals able to grasp just what they sensed. In his stable, Seneca said, a horse "is reminded of the road when it is brought to where it starts. But in the stable it has no memory of it however often it has trodden. As for the third time, the future, that does not concern dumb animals."[46]

Many nonhuman animals may live only in the world they sense, just as Seneca thought. Every human infant probably lives in that perceptual world, though scientists don't agree for how long. Thousands of humans never develop beyond it and thousands return. But millions of nonhuman

ANIMAL RIGHTS, ONE STEP AT A TIME

animals also live at least partially in conceptual worlds, unchained to the present, not connected to their senses, able to think.

Legal Obstacles

The legal problem is simple and stark. Generally, law divides the physical universe into persons and things. Things are the objects of a person's rights. A person is the subject of rights and can exercise virtually unlimited rights over many things and, to a severely limited extent, other persons.[47] Law professor and legal writer Roscoe Pound called legal persons "the unit of the legal order."[48] A button buys nothing in the United States. The dollar is the unit of currency. Throughout Western history, nonhuman animals have been things, buttons that buy nothing in a legal system. So once were human slaves and women and children.[49] Daniel Defoe wrote:

> Nature has left this tincture in the blood,
> That all men would be tyrants if they could.[50]

Humans are tyrants over things because they can be. Personhood is the legal bulwark that protects everybody, every personality, against human tyranny. Without it, one is helpless. Legally, persons count; things don't.[51] Until, and unless, a nonhuman animal attains legal personhood, she will not count.

Psychological Obstacles

Finally, there are psychological obstacles. In ignorance, occasionally in defiance, of the facts, millions believe nonhumans lack every important mental ability; they are made for humans, and this was how the universe was designed. Therefore they can be legitimately viewed as legal things, and not persons. Beliefs are personal, subjective, often unprovable, and illogical. They dictate what we think is possible.[52] What we see may depend upon what we believe can *be* seen.[53] Law ignores the impossible. Nonhuman animals are invisible to civil law today because for centuries lawyers and judges have not believed that nonhumans could possibly have rights.

Sophisticated judges know they decide cases under the influence of their beliefs. "When I say that a thing is true," declared Oliver Wendell Holmes, Jr., "I mean that I cannot help believing it."[54] Moral judgments are influenced by intuition, experience, and emotions.[55] Judges approach their work with different visions of law and justice constructed from their different beliefs hammered in the unique crucible that is each of their lives.[56] For Holmes, some beliefs are kin to liking beer.[57] Perhaps one man "cannot help" but believe that he can enslave others of another race, gender, religion, nationality, or species, while another "cannot help" but believe that he can't. Such beliefs "can not be argued about," Holmes said, "and therefore, when differences are sufficiently far reaching, we try to kill the other man rather than let him have his way."[58] This is the stuff of revolution, scientific, social, political, and Holmes, wounded three times in the American Civil War, knew it firsthand.

The psychological obstacles are well illuminated again by human slavery. Slave historian David Brion Davis writes:

> Today it is difficult to understand why slavery was accepted from pre-biblical times in virtually every culture and not seriously challenged until the late 1700s. But the institution was so basic that genuine anti-slavery attitudes required a profound shift in moral perception. This meant fundamental religious and philosophic changes in views of human abilities, responsibilities and rights.[59]

William Miller, one last time:

> Thinkers and statesmen and leaders and realistic politicians of all stripes believed that American slavery could not be ended—not by deliberate human action. Those who supported slavery belligerently asserted that it could not be done; those who deplored slavery sorrowfully granted that it could not be done; those who had unsorted mixtures of opinions—the great majority, let us guess—felt that it could not be done, and did not want to hear about it.[60]

OVERCOMING THE OBSTACLES

Avoiding Speciesism

I began my first Animal Rights Law class at the Harvard Law School by hanging a sign on the classroom door upon which my daughter, Roma, had scrawled, "No pigs." This replicated the sign hung on the doorknob of the Harvard Law School classroom in David Mamet's children's book *Henrietta*.[61] Henrietta was a pig. Having "aspired to the Law" as a piglet, she applied to Harvard Law School.[62] Summarily rejected, she haunted its lecture halls until she was barred as a nuisance with the "No Pigs" sign hung from doorknobs. But Henrietta had the great fortune to aid the university's near-sighted president, who couldn't see she was a pig. She so impressed him she was admitted to the law school and at the end of the story, she ascends to the U.S. Supreme Court.

Mamet's book is an allegory about racism and sexism. But it's also about speciesism. Coined nearly thirty years ago by the British psychologist Richard Ryder, *speciesism* is defined by the *Oxford English Dictionary* as "discrimination against . . . animal species by human beings, based on an assumption of mankind's superiority."[63] It is a bias, arbitrary as any other. That is why even the English philosopher R. G. Frey, who opposes rights for nonhuman animals, "cannot think of anything at all compelling that cedes all human life of any quality greater value than animal life of any quality."[64]

Since Linnaeus invented the system of biological classification we use today, humans have assigned themselves to their own family, *Hominidae*, the taxonomic classification just above genus *Homo*. We placed even our closest cousins, the chimpanzees and bonobos, into another family. But genus and family should be irrelevant to entitlement to legal rights. It's what one is, not who one is, that should count. To avoid speciesism, we must identify some objective, rational, legitimate, and nonarbitrary quality possessed by every *Homo sapiens* that is possessed by no nonhuman that should entitle all of us, but none of them, to basic liberty rights. But none exists. However, I identify a quality, which I call "practical autonomy," that I argue is sufficient to entitle any being, of any species, to basic liberty rights.

One Step at a Time for Legal Rights

I believe that legal rights for nonhuman animals will be achieved one step at a time. Their most basic rights must be recognized first. What are they? What nonlawyers think of as one legal right is usually a bundle. During World War I, law professor Wesley Hohfeld untied these bundles.[65] He thought a *right* was an advantage conferred by legal rules upon a legal person. One legal person always has a legal advantage (that's the right). Another legal person bears a corresponding legal disadvantage. Like low- and high-pressure systems on a weather map, neither exists alone, and Hohfeld defined them in relationship to each other.[66]

Hohfeld set out four kinds of legal rights.[67] One is the "liberty." That lets us do what we please, but has little practical value because no one need respect it. The second is the "claim." It commands respect. Your claim can constrain my liberty, as I have a duty to act, or not, in certain ways toward someone with a claim.[68] It's not agreed whether someone has to be smart enough to assert a claim to have one. He probably doesn't.[69] But to be safe, I won't argue that nonhuman animals are entitled to claims, because there probably aren't any nonhumans smart enough to assert one. Many humans aren't either. A person can use a "power" to affect another's legal rights; the power to sue is perhaps the most important.[70] It's not clear whether someone has to be smart enough to assert a power in order to have it, either. She probably doesn't. But to be safe, I won't argue that nonhuman animals are entitled to powers, either. Last, an "immunity" legally disables one person from interfering with another.[71] Claims say what we should not do; immunities what we cannot legally do. I may kidnap you, but I can't enslave you because human bondage is prohibited under domestic and international law. Persons are simply *immune* from enslavement.[72] Rational arguments cannot be made that one must be smart enough to assert an immunity to have one, for by definition immunities don't need to be asserted. Such immunities as freedom from slavery and torture are the most basic kind of legal rights. It's these to which nonhuman animals, like human beings, are most strongly entitled, and immunity rights are likely to be achieved first.[73]

One Step at a Time for Law

I use a "round hole, square peg" theory of legal change. The round hole is our legal system, which treats nonhuman animals as rightless things. The square peg is the potential legal rule that nonhuman animals are persons entitled to basic legal rights. To attain these rights, one must either square the hole or round the peg.

The common law—that jewel of English-speaking jurisprudence—is ideal for peg rounding. Massachusetts Supreme Judicial Court chief justice Lemuel Shaw, perhaps the most prominent nineteenth-century American common law judge, said it consists of a "few broad and comprehensive principles, founded on reason, natural justice, and enlightened public policy, modified and adapted to all the circumstances of all the particular cases that fall within it."[74] It can accommodate highly disparate visions of what law is, some of which may be incommensurable with any other vision.

This idea is standard to constitutional interpretation. For example, Professor Philip Bobbitt envisions interpreting the U.S. Constitution in six ways, each of which he argues is equally "true" if interpreted in an internally consistent manner; each is incommensurable with every other.[75] The six are historical (looks to the framer's intentions), textual (relies on the Constitution's words as commonly understood), structural (inferring rules from the way in which the Constitution sets up its structures), doctrinal (applies rules from precedent), ethical (gets rules from the morality of the citizenry as reflected in the Constitution), and prudential (balances costs and benefits of rules).[76]

Common law judges with "formal visions" inflexibly marinate their decisions in the past. They think judges should decide the way judges have decided because judges have decided that way. The most formal of these judges—I call them "precedent (rules) judges"—think it better that law be certain than right. They see the common law as a system of narrow and consistent rules that they can glean from judicial decisions, then more or less mechanically apply. They resemble some judges who interpret the U.S. Constitution in textual, doctrinal, prudential, even historical ways.[77] Precedent (rules) judges aren't stubborn or lazy or brainless. They value, or think a legal system should value, stability, certainty, and predictability. Here is a startling example of how a precedent rules court recently dealt with a case involving the shooting death of a dog. In June 2001, the Wisconsin Supreme Court refused to change the law that forbids the human companion of a dog from obtaining emotional distress damages when her companion nonhuman is unlawfully killed before her eyes.[78] A policeman had illegally shot her dog. The court said:

> At the outset, we note that we are uncomfortable with the law's cold characterization of a dog . . . as mere "property." Labeling a dog "property" fails to describe the value human beings place upon the companionship that they enjoy with a dog. A companion dog is not a

fungible item, equivalent to other items of personal property. A companion dog is not a living room sofa or dining room furniture. The term inadequately describes the relationship between a human and a dog. . . . Nevertheless, the law categorizes the dog as personal property. . . . To the extent this opinion uses the term "property" in describing how humans value the dog they live with, it is done only as a means of applying established legal doctrine to the facts of the case.[79]

These judges did not believe that "property" properly describes a companion nonhuman. Yet because prior judges believed it, they felt obliged to condone the anachronism. This comes close to a position once taken by the English House of Lords: Once articulated, the common law can be altered only by legislation.[80]

"Precedent (principles) judges" look to a different past. For them, prior decisions lay down not narrow rules, but broad principles, and judges needn't confine themselves to the specific ways in which judges have applied those principles. Like precedent (rules) judges, they resemble judges who interpret constitutions in textual, doctrinal, and prudential ways. But they operate at higher levels of generality. If justice demands a rule be changed, they may use established principles to reconstruct the law in ways that might have astounded the earlier judges.[81]

"Substantive judges" reject the past as manacle. Their legal vision starts with social considerations, moral, economic, and political.[82] Law, they believe, should express a community's present sense of justice, not that of another age.[83] Courts should keep law current with public values, prevailing understandings of justice, morality, and new scientific discoveries. Principles and policies live and die, and when they die, they should be buried. Substantive judges want to know *why* judges once decided a certain way and whether these reasons still make sense. They don't want issues just settled, but decided correctly, and they will change the law to get it right.

Substantive judges who try to peer into the future are "policy judges." They seek to predict the effects of their rulings and think law should be used to achieve important goals, such as economic growth, national unity, or the health or welfare of a community. They resemble judges who use a prudential modality of constitutional interpretation.

"Principle judges" value principles and right when deciding cases.[84] They borrow these principles from religion, ethics, economics, politics— almost anywhere—and these may range from representative democracy to the maximization of wealth to two critical legal principles: liberty ("the supreme value of the Western world") and equality ("far and away the most important").[85] Most judges, especially in the United States, are either precedent (principles) judges or principle judges, which every judge should be when confronted with the seminal question: Who is entitled to legal personhood?[86]

Meeting the Law on Its Own Terms

In 2000, U.S. circuit judge Richard Posner, perhaps the leading scholar-judge in the United States, reviewed my book *Rattling the Cage: Toward Legal Rights for Animals* in the *Yale Law Journal*. In that book I set out some of the arguments I make here. Posner found it "not an intellectually exciting book."[87] But he did "not say this in criticism. Remember who Wise is: a practicing lawyer who wants to persuade the legal profession that courts should do more to protect animals."[88]

This was a uniquely perceptive observation. In arguing for the basic legal rights of nonhuman animals, I rely upon the first principles of Western law: liberty and equality. These are hoary enough to be enshrined in the Declaration of Independence: "We hold these truths to be self-evident, that all men are created equal, that they are endowed by their Creator with certain unalienable Rights, that among these rights are Life, Liberty, and the pursuit of Happiness." French revolutionaries demanded *liberté* and *égalité*. Abraham Lincoln placed them at the forefront of the Gettysburg Address: "Four score and seven years ago, our fathers brought forth upon this continent a new nation, conceived in liberty and dedicated to the proposition that all men are created equal." They live in article I of the Universal Declaration of Rights: "All human beings are born free and equal in dignity and rights."

Equality demands that likes be treated alike. Equality rights therefore depend upon how one rightless animal compares to another with rights. An animal might be entitled to basic equality rights, even if she isn't entitled to liberty rights, because she is "like" someone with basic liberty rights. Liberty entitles one to be treated a certain way because of how one is constructed, especially one's mental abilities. Since World War II, nations agree that the liberty to act as one pleases stops somewhere; they don't always agree where.[89] But some absolute and irreducible degree of bodily liberty and bodily integrity are everywhere considered sacrosanct. If we trespass upon them we inflict the gravest injustice, for we treat others as slaves and things.[90] We may not enslave. We may never torture. Yet these sacred places are the front-line in the battle for the rights of nonhuman animals.

One important aspect of liberty is autonomy and self-determination. For C. K. Allen, one prominent legal writer:

> The essential difference between person and thing seems to lie in the quality of *volition.* Animate creatures clearly possess some kind of motive-power which corresponds with the human will; it may be a very strong force indeed—thus if we wish to attribute to a man a particularly obstinate will, we compare him to a mule. But it is not a kind of will which is recognized by law; it cannot in modern societies, involve the creature which exercises it in any consequences of right or liability. Nor do we attribute to the creatures what is closely akin to

this volitional capacity, that is, the power of reason. Hence a thing has been defined (as having a) "*volitionless* nature."[91]

Purposeful though it may be, Allen implies a mule's will is unrecognized in law because it stems from instinct, the antithesis of volition. The mule has a will. He just can't control it. Whether we call it self-determination, autonomy, or volition, if a being has it, she is entitled to basic liberty rights. Things don't act autonomously. Persons do. Things can't self-determine. Persons can. Things lack volition. Persons don't. Persons have wills.[92]

Philosophers often understand autonomy, which includes self-determination and volition, as Kant did two centuries ago. I call Kant's "full autonomy." Nonhuman animals, and probably children, act from desire, Kant believed.[93] Fully autonomous beings act completely rationally, and their ability to do that demands they be treated as persons.[94]

Kant is not the only philosopher to try to knit hyperrationality into the fabric of liberty.[95] The most honest concede what philosopher Carl Wellman calls a "monstrous conclusion": a great many human beings don't make the cut.[96] Most normal adults lack full autonomy. Infants, children, the severely mentally retarded or autistic, the senile, and the persistently vegetative never come close. Were judges to accept full autonomy as prerequisite for personhood, they would exclude most humans. Yet these complex autonomies are the sort to which primatologist Frans de Waal refers when he claims apes, smart and cultured as he knows they are, can never have legal rights. He thinks rights nonsense unless accompanied by responsibilities of a kind they, and millions of humans, can never shoulder.[97]

Judges decisively reject Kant's notion of autonomy. Events on Leap Day 2000 in the United States show how wrong de Waal and Kant are. A six-year-old Michigan first-grader smuggled a handgun into school and shot a classmate to death. The county prosecutor issued this statement: "There is a presumption in law that a child . . . is not criminally responsible and can't form an intent to kill. Obviously he has done a very terrible thing today, but legally he can't be held criminally responsible."[98] The child couldn't be sued civilly, either.

Isaiah Berlin explained that, for Kant, "Freedom is not freedom to do what is irrational, or stupid, or wrong."[99] But in courtrooms liberty rights often mean freedom to do the irrational, stupid, even the wrong. That is why judges routinely—though not always—honor nonrational, sometimes irrational, choices that may even cut against a decision maker's best interests.[100] Self-determination may even trump human life.[101] The determination of Jehovah's Witnesses to die rather than accept blood transfusions is nonrational. Yet judges accept them. The mentally ill are not usually confined, against their wishes, unless they are dangerous to themselves or others.[102]

Judges who deny personhood to every nonhuman animal act arbitrarily.

They don't *say* they do, of course. Instead they use legal fictions, transparent lies they insist we believe that allow them to attribute personhood to humans lacking consciousness, sometimes brains, to ships, trusts, corporations, even religious idols.[103] They pretend these have autonomy. Legal scholar John Chipman Gray couldn't see any difference between pretending will-less humans have one and doing the same for nonhuman animals.[104] Because legal fictions may cloak abuses of judicial power, Jeremy Bentham characterized them as a "*syphilis* . . . [that] carries into every part of the system the principle of rottenness."[105]

A fair and rational alternative exists: Most moral and legal philosophers, and just about every common law judge, recognize that less complex autonomies exist and that a being can be autonomous if she has preferences and the ability to act to satisfy them. Or if she can cope with changed circumstances. Or if she can make choices, even if she can't evaluate their merits very well. Or if she has desires and beliefs and can make at least some sound and appropriate inferences from them.[106]

In *Rattling the Cage*, I called such lesser autonomies "realistic." I now think "practical" better describes them.[107] "Practical autonomy" is not just what most humans have, but what most judges think is *sufficient* for basic liberty rights, and it boils down to this: A being has practical autonomy, and is entitled to personhood and basic liberty rights, if she

1. can desire;
2. can intentionally try to fulfill her desire; and
3. possesses a sense of self sufficiency to allow her to understand, even dimly, that she is a being who wants something and is trying to get it.[108]

Consciousness, but not necessarily self-consciousness, and sentience are implicit in practical autonomy.

But human newborns, fetuses, even ovums, sometimes have legal rights even though they lack all autonomy. This might be explained as resulting from legal fictions or sheer arbitrariness. But it might also have something to do with autonomy. They may not have it now, but it's believed they have the potential. And if they have the potential, we should treat them as if they have it now.

But the potential for autonomy no more justifies treating someone as if she has autonomy any more, and probably less, than does the fact that one's potential for dying justifies treating her as if she were dead.[109] Philosopher Joel Feinberg thinks allocating rights based on potential is simply a logical error. Potential autonomy gives rise to potential rights. Actual autonomy gives rise to actual rights.[110] And even the potentiality argument fails to explain how the common law can grant basic rights to adult humans who never had autonomy, and never will. — *mentally disabled*

Isaiah Berlin wrote, "If the essence of men is that they are autonomous beings . . . then nothing is worse than to treat them as if they were not autonomous, but natural objects, played on by causal influences at the mercy of external stimuli."[111] The same is true for any being who meets the requirements for practical autonomy. She is entitled to basic liberty rights. Because much of the world, certainly the West, links basic liberty rights to autonomy, and because autonomy is often seen as the foundation of human dignity, in *Rattling the Cage*, I called basic liberty rights "dignity rights."[112] But remember, an animal may be entitled to equality rights even if she lacks practical autonomy.

A SCALE OF PRACTICAL AUTONOMY

Professor Donald Griffin is the father of the scientific discipline of cognitive ethology, which investigates and compares mental phenomena among animals. He knows how elusive firm conclusions about mental abilities can be and finds it helpful to think in terms of probabilities: What are the chances an animal feels or wants or acts intentionally or thinks or knows or has a self?[113] The more certain we are that the answer to any of these questions is "yes," the closer is the probability to 1.0. If "no" is certain, the probability is 0.0. If we think the answer impossible to know, or it's possible, but we just don't know, the probability is exactly 0.50.

Griffin gives Kanzi, a bonobo whose astonishing mental abilities I chronicled in *Rattling the Cage*, as an example of a nonhuman animal for whom it would be reasonable to estimate the probability he's conscious and possesses sophisticated mental abilities as close to 1.0. He concedes, upon present evidence, the probability that some of the million species of animals are simply not conscious, that is, have an autonomy value of 0.0. For many of the millions of intermediate cases, we can only make rough estimates. He thinks that often the best we may be able to do at present is to assign values below 0.50, at 0.50, and above 0.50.[114]

But Griffin actually mentions four categories, below 0.50, at 0.50, above 0.50, and almost 1.0 (Kanzi). I think, however, that the evidence permits us to assign a more precise autonomy value to many nonhuman animals. The more exactly the behavior of any nonhuman resembles ours and the taxonomically closer she is, the more confident we can be that she possesses desires, intentions, and a sense of self resembling ours, and we can fairly assign her an autonomy value closer to ours. Practical autonomy is hard to quantify. In determining whether it exists, and to what degree, we will consider not just those mental abilities that directly speak to it, but mental complexity in general, on the assumption that some rough association between general mental complexity and practical autonomy exists.

When a range of behaviors in an evolutionary cousin closely resembles ours, as Kanzi's does, we can confidently assign him a value of almost 1.0. We'll call Kanzi a 0.98 and place any animal with an autonomy value of 0.90 or greater into Category One. These animals clearly possess practical autonomy sufficient for basic liberty rights. They are probably self-conscious and pass the mirror self-recognition (MSR) test. The standard MSR was developed by psychologist Gordon Gallup, Jr., in the 1970s, working with chimpanzees. Gallup placed red marks on the heads of anesthetized chimpanzees, then watched to see if they touched the marks when peering into a mirror. He assumed if they did, they were self-aware.[115] Gallup's MSR test, and variants adapted for other nonhuman species and human infants, are widely used as a marker for visual self-recognition, though there is disagreement about what it signifies and whether failures mean that self-awareness is lacking. But if one passes, one should automatically be placed into Category One. These animals often have some or all the elements of a theory of mind (they know what others see or know), understand symbols, use a sophisticated language or language-like communication system, and may deceive, pretend, imitate, or solve complex problems.

Into Category Two are animals who fail MSR tests. They may lack self-consciousness and every element of a theory of mind, but possess a simpler consciousness, mentally represent and be able to act insightfully, think, perhaps use a simple communication system, have a primitive, but sufficient, sense of self, and at least be modestly evolutionarily close to humans. Insight is sometimes used as a synonym for thinking, for it allows a being to solve a problem efficiently and safely by mentally "seeing" the solution without having to engage in extensive trial and error.[116] Biologist Bernd Heinrich speculates that consciousness, which he believes implies awareness through mental visualization, developed "for one specific reason only: To make choices."[117] If he is right, insight is strong evidence of practical autonomy.

The strength of each animal's liberty rights will turn upon what mental abilities she has and how certain we are she has them. Category Two covers the immense cognitive ground of every animal with an autonomy value between 0.51 and 0.89. Whether an animal should be placed in the higher (0.80–0.89), middle (0.70–0.79), or lower (0.51–0.69) reaches of Category Two depends upon whether she uses symbols, conceptualizes (mentally represents), or demonstrates other sophisticated mental abilities. Her taxonomic class (mammal, bird, reptile, amphibian, fish, insect) and the nearness of her evolutionary relationship to humans (which are related) may also be important factors.

We can assign taxonomically and evolutionarily remote animals, whose behavior scarcely resembles ours and who may lack all consciousness and be nothing but living stimulus-response machines, an autonomy value below 0.50. The lower the value, the more certain we can be that they utterly lack practical autonomy. They may, or may not, be eligible for equality rights. We'll place them all into Category Four. Finally, we do not know enough about many, perhaps most, nonhuman animals reasonably to assign any value above or below 0.50. Perhaps we have never taken the time to learn about them or our minds are not sufficiently keen to understand them. We assign them to Category Three.

Taking Precautions

Consciousness is the bedrock of practical autonomy. Prominent neuroscientists believe emotions produce consciousness.[118] If true, when did emotions and consciousness arise? Neuroscientist Antonio Damasio writes that the structures responsible for simple consciousness are "of old evolutionary vintage, they are present in numerous nonhuman animals, and they mature early in individual human development."[119] Ethologist Marian Stamp Dawkins argues that mammals and birds are conscious.[120] Nobel Prize–winner Gerald Edelman thinks the brain structures generating simple consciousness can be found in most mammals, some birds, and perhaps in some reptiles; therefore consciousness could be about 300 million years old.[121] Because emotional stress raises the body-core temperature and heart rate of rats, humans, birds, and reptiles, but not amphibians, physiologist Michel Cabanac argues that emotion and consciousness emerged between the evolution of amphibians and reptiles, more than 200 million years ago.[122] A reasonable guess then is that reptiles, mammals, and birds are probably conscious; others probably not.[123]

A Category One animal clearly has practical autonomy and is entitled to the basic liberty rights of bodily integrity and bodily liberty. On the other hand, a Category Four animal probably, perhaps clearly, lacks practical autonomy and is not entitled to any liberty rights. A Category Three animal is there precisely because we know so little about her mental abilities we can't make a rational judgment. The best we can do at present is recognize our ignorance and limitations, determine to learn what we can, be alert to the evolving knowledge that will allow us to place her into another category, and take to heart what philosopher Martha Nussbaum has written: that our choice may be only between being generous and mean-spirited.[124]

How should we assign an autonomy value to an animal about whose mental abilities we know something, but are uncertain? Scientific uncertainty exists whenever data are incomplete or absent, because we can't or don't know how to measure accurately, we sample improperly, our theoretical models are simply wrong, or because we mistake something for cause and effect.[125] Moreover, scientists recognize that absolute scientific truth doesn't exist. Much of what they do is try to gain more certainty.

Uncertainty is no less common in law. But judges lack the scientist's luxury of deferring judgment until the data are more complete. In the face of uncertainty and chance of error, judges must decide and content themselves with deciding on which side they wish to err. In Anglo-American law, a criminal defendant is presumed to be innocent until and unless a jury of twelve unanimously finds him guilty of committing the crime charged beyond a reasonable doubt. Every reasonable doubt is therefore resolved in the defendant's favor. On the other hand, the American Fugitive Slave Act of 1850 did not allow an accused fugitive slave the usual trial by jury nor the ability to testify; a summary hearing, often thirty minutes, sometimes five, was held before a specially appointed commissioner instead of a regular judge, the decision was unappealable, and no court could issue a writ of habeas corpus or delay the trip south.

Tort law normally permits an action unless it can be shown to cause harm.[126] Just as the Fugitive Slave Act assumed an accused slave really was a fugitive, an "assimilation principle" assumes the environment can incorporate vast insults, pollutants, poisons, and toxins—all without serious effect.[127] After scientists found this to be untrue, policy makers began slowly to respond by implementing a "precautionary principle." This constituted a "fundamental shift" in how environmental concerns were faced.[128] The precautionary principle rejects science "as the absolute guide for the environmental policy maker" and instead "embodies the notion that where there is uncertainty regarding the potential impact of a substance or activity, 'rather than await uncertainty, regulators should act in anticipation of environmental harm to ensure that this harm does not occur.' Without such an approach, an activity or substance might have an irreversible impact on the environment while scientists determine its precise effect."[129] At the principle's core is the idea that nonnegligible environmental risks should be prevented, even in the face of scientific uncertainty.

The precautionary principle is finding a home in U.S. and German law, emerging in English, Australian, and European law, even evolving as a customary rule of international environmental law.[130] For example, the U.S. Endangered Species Act requires federal agencies to give a benefit of the doubt to any threatened or endangered species when determining how to act, while the Marine Mammal Protection Act permits takings of marine mammals "only when it is known that the taking would not be to the disadvantage of the species."[131] The World Charter for Nature says, "Activities which are likely to pose a significant risk to nature shall be preceded by an exhaustive examination; their proponents shall demonstrate that expected benefits outweigh potential damage to nature, and where potential adverse effects are not fully understood, the activities should not proceed."[132]

For centuries, law followed an "exploitation principle" in our dealings with nonhuman animals. All were erroneously thought to lack most, perhaps every, sophisticated basic mental ability—desire, intentionality, self, perhaps even consciousness—were categorized as legal things, and mercilessly exploited.[133] But evidence is clear that, for at least some, this is untrue. In light of what we know, it is time to apply a precautionary principle to at least some nonhuman animals. Depriving any being with practical autonomy of basic liberty rights is about the most terrible injustice imaginable. When there is doubt and serious damage is threatened, we should err on the cautious side where evidence of practical autonomy exists. And some evidence is required, for every version of the precautionary principle instructs "how to respond when there is some evidence, but not proof, that a human practice is damaging the environment."[134] Speculation is not enough.[135]

The precautionary principle has at least seven senses.[136] At its weakest, it merely requires a decision maker to think ahead and act cautiously. A stronger version requires a decision maker carefully to regulate her actions, even in the face of insufficient scientific evidence of a threat. Stronger still is the demand that the proponent of a potentially harmful act prove its harmlessness to an unusually stringent degree.[137] This shifting of the normal burden of proof may be tantamount to forbidding the act, for the more uncertain the evidence, the more likely it will be that whoever has the burden of proof will lose.[138]

A kind of precautionary principle has been argued as a reason for not using seriously defective human beings in painful biomedical research. The reason, philosopher Christina Hoff wrote, is not because they are human, for Hoff concedes that is insufficient. It is because we cannot "safely permit anyone to decide which human beings fall short of worthiness. Judgments of this kind and the creation of institutions for making them are fraught with danger and open to grave abuse."[139] When rights for nonhuman animals are involved, there is a compelling reason to apply the precautionary principle, which goes beyond what Hoff says and which doesn't exist in environmental law.

There is another reason, illustrated by John Newton, a former London slaving captain, who wrote at the end of the seventeenth century: "I can't think there is any intrinsic value in one colour more than the other, that white is better than black, only we think it so, because we are so, and are prone to judge favourably in our own case."[140] We should have little confidence in the fairness of a decision reached by a judge with a personal stake in the outcome. This human proneness "to judge favourably in our own case" explains why one of the oldest and most important maxims of the common law is that no one may judge her own case.[141] In the seventeenth century, Lord Coke fixed this into the common law when he voided the right of the Royal College of Physicians to fine medical practitioners, because the college retained half of every fine levied.[142] The U.S. Supreme Court prohibits a judge from having even the "slightest pecuniary interest" in the subject matter of his decision.[143] Whose blood doesn't rise when reading that, in the years before the Civil War, the slaveocracy-dominated Congress of the United States enacted a Fugitive Slave Act that paid the deciding magistrate twice as much for flinging the poor wretch back into bondage than for declaring her free?[144]

If judicial attitudes reflect society's, most judges believe their health or the health of their families and friends may depend, in part, upon the use of nonhuman animals in biomedical research. They probably eat animal flesh, drink animal fluids, wear animal skins and fur, take their children to circuses to enjoy the "performances" of captive nonhuman animals, hunt them, and participate in some of the numerous ways in which society exploits nonhuman animals. They have a personal stake in the outcome of cases that decide whether nonhuman animals have legal rights in much the same way that judges of the antebellum American South had personal stakes in the outcome of slavery cases. They will inevitably be biased and their biases will just as inevitably infect their decisions.[145]

Such conundrums are typically solved by invoking the "rule of necessity," which states that, if all judges are disqualified from deciding a case, none are.[146] But that does not give judges license to indulge their biases. To the contrary. Formal use of the precautionary principle is necessary just to counteract judicial bias. Judges ruling from necessity must exert every ounce of moral strength, every particle of objectivity they possess, to rule as fairly as they can, always keeping in mind they are prone to decide in their own favor and that long-standing inequities have, in Professor Tribe's words, "survived this long because they have become so ingrained in our modes of thought; the U.S. Supreme Court recognized a century ago that 'habitual' discriminations are the hardest to eradicate."[147]

Assigning Autonomy Values

Because it appears likely that at least mammals and birds have emotions, consciousness, desires, intentionality, and selves, the burden of proving at trial that an individual mammal or bird lacks practical autonomy should be shouldered by he who wishes to harm them. When one objects to the proposed harm of an animal neither mammal nor bird, the burden of proving practical autonomy should rest with him.[148]

After reviewing the evidence and taking into account who has the burden of proof, a judge will assign an autonomy value to the nonhuman animal. Unbiased judges may honestly differ, especially as data become less certain. How certain is she an animal has practical autonomy? How strong a scientific argument has been made? How valid are the data? Has the research been replicated? Have data from multiple areas of inquiry begun to converge? How cautious does she want to be? A value of 0.90 or higher will place any animal in Category One; she will be presumed to have practical autonomy sufficient for basic liberty rights. A Category Four animal, scored less than 0.50, will be presumed to lack practical autonomy. Any animal given a score of 0.50 means we haven't a clue.

There may be vast differences among Category Two animals, whose autonomy values range from 0.51 to 0.89. A refusal to apply the precautionary principle would result in every Category Two animal disqualified from liberty rights. An expansive application of the precautionary principle would mean any animal with an autonomy value above 0.50 should be granted some basic liberty rights. I propose an intermediate reading: Any animal with an autonomy value higher than 0.70 is presumed to have practical autonomy sufficient for basic liberty rights. But how should an animal scoring higher than 0.50, but less than 0.70, be treated? By definition, some evidence exists they possess practical autonomy. But it is weak, either because at least one element is missing, or the elements together are feebly supported.

More than a million animal species exist. While Darwinian evolution postulates a natural continuum of mental abilities, the animal kingdom is incredibly diverse. At some taxonomic point, the elements of practical autonomy—self, intentions, desires, sentience, and finally consciousness—begin to evaporate. We don't know precisely where. I have stood on the summit of Cadillac Mountain on Mt. Desert Island in Maine watching the summer sun rise. At four o'clock in the morning, it was indisputably night, at seven o'clock, indisputably day. When did night become day?

We could deal with this problem in one of two ways. Not using the precautionary principle would allow a judge to draw a line. Any animal beneath it would not be entitled to liberty rights. However, there is another way that is consistent with even a moderate reading of the precautionary principle. Personhood and basic liberty rights should be given in proportion to the degree that one has practical autonomy. If you have it, you get rights in full. But if you don't, the degree to which you *approach* it might make you eligible to receive some proportion of liberty rights.[149]

This idea of receiving proportional liberty rights accords with how judges often think. They may give *fewer* legal rights to humans who lack autonomy. But they don't make her a thing. A severely mentally limited human adult or child who lacks the mental wherewithal to participate in the political process may still move freely about. They may give *narrower* legal rights to her. A severely mentally limited human adult or child might not have the right to move in the world at large, but may move freely within her home or within an institution. They may give *parts* of a complex right (remember what we normally think of as a legal right is actually a bundle of them). A profoundly retarded human might have a claim to bodily integrity, but lack the power to waive it, and be unable to consent to a risky medical procedure or the withdrawal of life-saving medical treatment.[150]

Consistent with a moderate use of the precautionary principle, we need not grant basic liberty rights to a nonhuman animal who has just a shadow of practical autonomy, that is, we grant animals with an autonomy value of 0.51 some tiny right. But it would be consistent with such a reading for an animal with an autonomy value of 0.65, perhaps even 0.60, to be given strong consideration for some proportional basic liberty rights.

At some point, autonomy completely winks out and with it any nonarbitrary entitlement to liberty rights on the ground of possessing practical autonomy. Judges and legislators might decide to grant even a completely nonautonomous being basic liberty rights. But it's hard to think of grounds upon which they might do it nonarbitrarily. However, this strengthens the argument that, as a matter of equality, nonautonomous animals of many species should be entitled to basic rights, too.[151]

Human Yardsticks, Nonhuman Animals

Nature writer Henry Beston wrote, "The animal shall not be measured by man. In a world older and more complete than ours they move finished and complete, gifted by extensions of the senses we have lost or never attained, living by voices we shall never hear."[152] However, the liberty rights to bodily integrity and bodily liberty are embedded in law precisely because they are basic to human well-being, and the autonomy values we assign to nonhumans will be based upon human abilities and human values. This argument bridges the present, when the law values only humanlike abilities but must still confront the argument for liberty rights of nonhuman animals who have them, and the future, when the law may value nonhuman abilities as well. For the present, I accept that the law measures nonhuman animals with a human yardstick.

But just because law is so parochial, we must not think human intelligence the only intelligence. Intelligence is a complicated concept that intimately relates to an ability to solve problems.[153] Bernd Heinrich says, "We can't credibly claim that one species is more intelligent than another unless we specify intelligent with respect to what, since each animal lives in a different world of its own sensory inputs and decoding mechanisms of those inputs."[154] Dolphin expert Diana Reiss argues that intelligence cannot properly be conceived solely in human terms and condemns any assumption that "only our kind of intelligence is 'real intelligence.'"[155] We must not think human self the only self or human abilities the only important mental abilities.

In a famous essay, "What Is It Like to Be a Bat?" philosopher Thomas Nagel said he focused on bats, instead of flounders or wasps, because they are mammals, and "if one travels too far down the phylogenetic tree people gradually shed their faith that there is experience at all."[156] Even bats, he wrote, are "a fundamentally *alien* form of life."[157]

How can we know when a nonhuman has practical autonomy? In *Rattling the Cage*, I answered with "de Waal's rule of thumb": In the absence of strong contrary arguments, if closely related species act the same, it is likely, though not certain, they share the same mental processes.[158] Because great apes are evolutionary first cousins with senses identical to ours, we can feel confident that our basic interests are similar. But the likelihood that we will misunderstand or make a mistake increases with evolutionary distance and differences in ecology, information-processing capabilities, or the ways in which we perceive or conceive of the world. Humans, for example, can live happy solitary lives. But a single Atlantic bottle-nosed dolphin is scarcely a dolphin. Humans don't need to swim. But even after seventy generations of being factory farmed in cages, minks expend large amounts of energy just for the opportunity to swim, and when they can't, their bodies produce high levels of cortisol, a stress hormone, similar to that produced when they are denied food.[159]

Elephant researcher Joyce Poole asks us to imagine showing drawings of human and elephant heads to an extraterrestrial. It would be reasonable to assume the creature with the huge ears and nose has terrific hearing and smelling abilities, while the one with the tiny nose and big eyes can see but is unlikely to smell well. This would be correct. Elephants hear sounds below the human threshold.[160] Elephant nasal cavities contain seven of the turbinals specialized for odor detection. Poole concludes that elephants, who also detect hormones with a unique Jacobsen's organ, are so different from us they live in another sensory world.[161] In the 1950s, psychologist Harry Harlow, reviled today by many for his cruel deprivation experiments on baby monkeys, wrote, "It is hazardous to compare learning ability among animals independently of their sensory and motor capacities and limitations."[162] Professor Harry Jerison says, "The nature of self is surely significantly different in different species," but human intuitions about self "are so strong that it is difficult to imagine a creature with information processing capacities comparable to ours, equal to us in intelligence . . . that has a differently constructed self." But they exist, and he gives dolphins as an example.[163]

The animals who fall into Categories Three and Four, and some perhaps in Category Two, may not now be entitled to basic liberty rights simply because we don't value their brand of intelligence, their style of learning, their sense of self. But Category One animals and at least some of those in Category Two measure up even to human standards. These include great apes, Atlantic bottle-nosed dolphins, African elephants, and African grey parrots.[164]

The obstacles to basic legal rights for any nonhuman animal, physical, economic, political, religious, historical, legal, and psychological, that I have set out are major and real. But they have been hurdled before. The most significant example is the abolition of human slavery in the United States. "Considering that slavery had been globally accepted for millennia, it is encouraging that people were able to make such a major shift in their moral view, especially when a cause like abolition conflicted with strong economic interests," David Brion Davis has written. "We can still learn from history the invaluable lesson that an enormously powerful and profitable evil can be overcome."[165] The first, most crucial, step will occur when judges begin recognizing that at least some nonhuman animals are entitled to recognition as legal persons.

NOTES

This chapter is closely adapted from chapters 2 and 3 of *Drawing the Line*.
1. William Lee Miller, *Arguing about Slavery: The Great Battle in the United States Congress* 11 (New York: Knopf, 1996).
2. *See generally,* Hugh Thomas, *The Slave Trade: The Story of the Atlantic Slave Trade 1440–1870* (New York: Simon and Schuster, 1997).

3. David Brion Davis, "The Enduring Legacy of the South's Civil War Victory," *New York Times*, wk1, wk4 (August 26, 2001).

4. Verlyn Klinkenborg, "Cow Parts," 22 *Discover* 52, 53–62 (August 2001).

5. William Lee Miller, *supra* note 1, at 11.

6. Richard A. Epstein, "The Next Rights Revolution," *National Review* 44, 45 (November 8, 1999).

7. Hugh Thomas, *supra* note 2, at 515.

8. Caryl Phillips, *The Atlantic Sound* 33–34 (London: Faber and Faber Limited, 2000).

9. Hugh Thomas, *supra* note 2, at 525, 530, 540.

10. *Id.* at 540.

11. *Id.* at 506, 508, 513, 525, 528, 550, 554.

12. *Id.* at 515, 516.

13. *Id.* at 516, 540.

14. Thomas Roderick Dew, "Abolition of Negro Slavery," 12 *American Quarterly Review* 189 (1832), reprinted in *The Ideology of Slavery: Proslavery Thought in the Antebellum South, 1830–1860* 21, 30 (Drew Gilpin Faust, ed.; Baton Rouge: Louisiana University Press, 1981).

15. William Lee Miller, *supra* note 1, at 13.

16. XV *Oxford English Dictionary* 665 ("slave," def. 1, at 665 [2d ed., 1989]).

17. Slavery Convention, 60 LNTS 253, Article 1 (1926).

18. Isaiah Berlin, "Two Concepts of Liberty," in *The Proper Study of Mankind* 194 (Henry Hardy and Roger Hausheer, eds.; New York: Farrar, Straus and Giroux, 1997).

19. Orlando Patterson, *Slavery and Social Death: A Comparative Study* 7 (Cambridge, Mass.: Harvard University Press, 1982).

20. David Brion Davis, *Slavery and Human Progress* 323 note 14 (New York: Oxford University Press, 1984).

21. *Id.* at 13 (emphasis in the original).

22. Roscoe Pound, IV *Jurisprudence* 192 (St. Paul, Minn.: West Publishing, 1959). (The constitution of the emperor Antonius Pius gave slaves power to bring suits to determine whether they were being cruelly treated, but not to obtain their freedom; *id.* at 192–193.) *See* the introduction to *The Institutes of Justinian* 27 (1876) (Thomas Collett Sanders, trans.; Buffalo, N.Y.: William S. Hein, 1984).

23. Barry Nichols, *An Introduction to Roman Law* 69 (Oxford: Oxford University Press 1962). *See* W. W. Buckland, *A Manual of Roman Private Law* 37 (2d ed.; Cambridge: Cambridge University Press 1939).

24. Barry Nichols, *supra* note 23; *see* John Chipman Gray, *The Nature and Sources of the Law* 43 (2d ed., Macmillan 1931).

25. A. Leon Higginbotham, "Property First, Humanity Second: The Recognition of the Slave's Human Nature in Virginia Slave Law," 50 *Ohio State Law Journal* 511, 512–514 (1989). *See Peter v. Hargrave*, 46 Va. (5 Gratt) 12, 17 (1848).

26. *See George (A Slave) v. The State*, 37 Miss. 316 (1859).

27. Genesis 1:28.

28. I explain this in Steven M. Wise, "The Legal Thinghood of Nonhuman Animals," 23 *Boston College Environmental Affairs Law Review* 471, 480–489 (1996); Steven M. Wise, "How Nonhuman Animals Were Trapped in a Nonexistent Universe," 1 *Animal Law* 15, 30–34 (1995).

29. Robert Speth, "Review of *Rattling the Cage: Toward Legal Rights for Animals*," 6 (2) *Newsletter of the Society for Veterinary Ethics* 6, 7 (May 2000).

30. Louis Henkin, *The Age of Rights* x (New York: Columbia University Press, 1990). *See id.* at 183–188.

31. David Brion Davis, *supra* note 20, at 82–101; Orlando Patterson, *supra* note 19, at 40–41, 117.

32. Ronald Segal, *Islam's Black Slaves: The Other Black Diaspora* (New York: Farrar, Straus and Giroux, 2001); Hugh Thomas, *supra* note 2, at 37, 298; *see id.* at 29–31; Orlando Patterson, *supra* note 19, at 117. *See also* David Brion Davis, *supra* note 20, at 60.

33. Thornton Stringfellow, "A Brief Examination of Scripture Testimony on the Institution of Slavery," reprinted in part in Drew Gilpin Faust, ed., *supra* note 14, at 138; Thornton Stringfellow, *Scriptural and Statistical Views in Favor of Slavery* 105 (J. W. Randolph, 1856). *See* Thornton Stringfellow, "The Bible Argument; or, Slavery in the Light of Divine Revelation," in *Cotton Is King and Pro-slavery Arguments* 459 (Augusta, Ga.: Pritchard, Abbott and Loomis, 1860).

34. David Brion Davis, *supra* note 20, at 112.

35. Dava Sobel, *Galileo's Daughter* 275–276 (New York: Random House, 1999).

36. Ernst Mayr, "Darwin's Influence on Modern Thought," 283 *Scientific American* 79, 83 (July 2000).

37. David Baltimore, "50,000 Genes, and We Know Them All (Almost)," *New York Times*, sec. 4, p. 17 (June 25, 2000).

38. E. g., *Thomas v. Review Board*, 450 U.S. 707, 714 (1981) (interpreting the religious liberty clause of the First Amendment to the U.S. Constitution).

39. Steven M. Wise (*Animal Law*), *supra* note 28, at 18–31.

40. Richard Sorabji, *Animal Minds and Human Morals: The Origin of the Western Debate* 199 (Ithaca, N.Y.: Cornell University Press, 1993); Keith Thomas, *Man and the Natural World* 19–20 (New York: Pantheon, 1983).

41. Richard Sorabji, *supra* note 40, at 195–196. *See* Steven M. Wise (*Animal Law*), *supra* note 28, at 9–22. *See also* a critique, Martha C. Nussbaum, "Book Review: *Animal Rights: The Need for a Theoretical Basis*," 114(5) *Harvard Law Review* 1506, 1513–1526 (2001), and my reply, Steven M. Wise, "Rattling the Cage Defended" 43 *Boston College Law Review* 623, 628–631 (2002), in which I argue that the united voices of Aristotle and the Stoics were among many— including Epicurian, Platonist, Pythagorean, Cynic, and others—competing theories in the ancient world about animal minds and the place of nonhumans in the universe. However, Western Christianity and law listened to just this first theory. With few exceptions, there are no more human slaves. Women and children are not legal things. But each nonhuman animal remains a thing, as she was 2,000 years ago.

42. Steven M. Wise (*Boston College*), *supra* note 28, at 492–538; Steven M. Wise (*Animal Law*), *supra* note 28, at 21–31.

43. Steven M. Wise (*Animal Law*), *supra* note 28, at 34–43.

44. C. S. Lewis, *Vivisection: A Rational Discussion* 7 (New England Anti-Vivisection Society undated).

45. Richard Sorabji, *supra* note 40, 20–21, 42, 58–61.

46. *Id.* at 52, quoting Seneca, *Ep.* 124.16.

47. P. A. Fitzgerald, *Salmond on Jurisprudence* 298 (12th ed.; London: Sweet and

Maxwell, 1966); Roscoe Pound, *supra* note 22, at 194, 529, 530. *See* Carleton Kemp Allen, "Things," 28 *California Law Review* 421, 422 (1940); Thomas Collett Sanders, trans., *supra* note 22, at 26.

48. Roscoe Pound, *supra* note 22, at 192.
49. David Brion Davis, *The Problem of Slavery in Western Culture* 58 (Ithaca, N.Y.: Cornell University Press, 1966); Alan Watson, *Roman Slave Law* 46 (Baltimore, Md.: Johns Hopkins University Press, 1987) (In Rome, a slave "always remained . . . corporeal property whose value could be measured in monetary terms").
50. Daniel Defoe, *The Kentish Petition*, addenda 1.11 (1701).
51. Note, "What We Talk about When We Talk about Persons: The Language of a Legal Fiction," 114 *Harvard Law Review* 1745, 1746 (2001).
52. Barbara W. Tuchman, "Why Policy-Makers Don't Listen," in *Practicing History: Selected Essays* 287 (New York: Knopf, 1981); Stephen R. L. Clark, *The Moral Status of Animals* 7 (Oxford: Oxford University Press, 1984); Thomas S. Kuhn, *The Structure of Scientific Revolutions* 7 (2d ed.; Chicago: University of Chicago Press, 1963); Norwood R. Hanson, *Patterns of Discovery: An Inquiry into the Conceptual Foundations of Science* 4–30 (Cambridge: Cambridge University Press, 1958).
53. Norwood R. Hanson, *supra* note 52, at 4–30.
54. Oliver Wendell Holmes, Jr., "Ideals and Doubts," 19 *Illinois Law Review* 1, 2 (1915).
55. Sandea Blakeslee, "Watching How the Brain Works as It Weighs a Moral Dilemma," *New York Times*, p. D3 (September 25, 2001); Joshua D. Greene et al., "An FMRI Investigation of Emotional Engagement in Moral Judgment," 293 *Science* 2105 (September 15, 2001).
56. *See* Laurence H. Tribe, 1 *American Constitutional Law*, sec. 1.15–17, at 70–89 (3d ed.; Mineola, N.Y.: Foundation Press, 2000); Laurence H. Tribe and Michael C. Dorf, *On Reading the Constitution* 65–80 (Cambridge, Mass.: Harvard University Press, 1991) (values in constitutional decision making). *Cf.* P. S. Atiyah and R. S. Summers, *Form and Substance in Anglo-American Law* 411 (Oxford: Oxford University Press, 1987).
57. Oliver Wendell Holmes, Jr., "Natural Law," 33 *Harvard Law Review* 40, 41 (1918–1919).
58. *Id. See* Cass Sunstein, "Incommensurability and Valuation in Law," 92 *Michigan Law Review* 779, 810–811 (1994); Richard Warner, "Incommensurability as a Jurisprudential Puzzle," 68 *Chicago-Kent Law Review* 147, 168 (1992).
59. David Brion Davis, *supra* note 3, at wk4.
60. William Lee Miller, *supra* note 1, at 15.
61. David Mamet, *Henrietta* 9 (Boston: Houghton Mifflin, 1999).
62. *Id.* at 4.
63. XVI *Oxford English Dictionary* 157 (2d ed. 1989).
64. R. G. Frey, *Rights, Killing, and Suffering* 115 (Oxford: Basil Blackwell, 1983).
65. Wesley Newcomb Hohfeld, *Fundamental Legal Conceptions as Applied in Judicial Reasoning* 64 (Walter Wheeler Cook ed.; New Haven, Conn.: Yale University Press, 1919). *See* W. L. Morison, *John Austin* 164 (London: Edward Arnold, 1982); Joseph William Singer, "The Legal Rights Debate in Analytical Jurisprudence from Bentham to Hohfeld," 1982 *Wisconsin Law Review* 975, 989 note 22; Walter J. Kamba, "Legal Theory and Hohfeld's Analysis of a Legal Right," *Jur. Rev.* 249, 249 (1974).

66. David Lyons, "Correlativity of Rights and Duties," 4 *Nous* 46 (1970).

67. Rex Martin, *A System of Rights* 31 (Oxford: Oxford University Press, 1993).

68. Wesley Newcomb Hohfeld, *supra* note 65, at 38, 39.

69. Steven M. Wise, *Rattling the Cage: Toward Legal Rights for Animals* 57 (Cambridge, Mass.: Perseus, 2000).

70. *Virani v. Jerry M. Lewis Truck Parts and Equipment, Inc.*, 89 F. 3d 574, 577 (9th Cir. 1996), quoting Judith Jarvis Thomson, *The Realm of Rights* 9 (Cambridge, Mass.: Harvard University Press, 1990); P. J. Fitzgerald, *supra* note 47, at 229.

71. Walter J. Kamba, *supra* note 65, at 256.

72. Rex Martin, *supra* note 67, at 3; L. W. Sumner, *The Moral Foundation of Rights* 37–38 (Oxford: Oxford University Press, 1987).

73. Steven M. Wise, *supra* note 69, at 59.

74. *Norway Plains Company v. Boston and Maine Railroad*, 67 Mass. (1 Gray) 263, 267 (1854).

75. Philip Bobbitt, *Constitutional Interpretation* 12 (London: Blackwell, 1991).

76. *Id.* at 12–13. Bobbitt discusses these six modalities of interpretation and their incommensurability in detail at *Constitutional Fate: Theory of the Constitution* 9–119 (Oxford: Oxford University Press, 1982). Professor Laurence Tribe identifies five approaches to constitutional analysis—all of Bobbitt's but "prudential"—but does not agree that each is necessarily true even if applied in an internally consistent way, Laurence H. Tribe, *supra* note 56, at 30–89. *See also* Richard H. Fallon, Jr., "A Constitutional Coherence Theory of Constitutional Interpretation," 100 *Harvard Law Review* 1189 (1987).

77. Prudential because expectations have grown up around what a particular decision may mean; historical because they may seek to divine the intentions of those who laid out such a legal rule as "nonhuman animals are things." Philip Bobbitt, *supra* note 75, at 97–98.

78. Joan Dunayer argues that "companion nonhuman" should be used in preference to "companion animal" or "pet." Joan Dunayer, *Animal Equality: Language and Liberation* 204 note 8 (Durwood, Md.: Ryce, 2001).

79. *Rabideau v. City of Racine*, 238 Wis. 2d 96, 617 N. W. 2d 678 (2001).

80. *Bayliss v. Bishop of London*, 1 Ch. 127, 137 (1913) (Farwell, LJ).

81. *E.g.*, *MacPherson v. Buick Motor Company*, 111 N. E. 1050 (NY 1916).

82. Robert S. Summers, "Form and Substance in Legal Reasoning," in *Legal Reasoning and Statutory Interpretation* 11 (J. van Dunne, ed., Gouda Quint 1989).

83. P. S. Atiyah and R. S. Summers, *supra* note 56, at 5.

84. Melvin Aron Eisenberg, *The Nature of the Common Law* 26–37 (Cambridge, Mass.: Harvard University Press, 1988); Robert S. Summers, "Two Types of Substantive Reasons: The Core of a Theory of Common Law Justification," 63 *Cornell Law Review* 707, 717–718, 722–724 (1978); Harry H. Wellington, "Common Law Rules and Constitutional Double Standards: Some Notes on Adjudication," 83 *Yale Law Journal* 221, 223–225 (1973).

85. Orlando Patterson, *Freedom in the Making of Western Culture* ix (New York: Basic, 1991) (liberty as supreme value); *Legal Consequences for States of the Continued Presence of South Africa in Namibia (South West Africa) Notwithstanding Security Council Resolution 276 (1970)*, 1971 I. C. J. 16, 77 (June 21) (separate opinion of Judge Ammoun, vice president) (equality the most important); Richard A. Posner, "Legal Reasoning from the Top Down and from the

Bottom Up: The Question of Unenumerated Fundamental Rights," 59 *University of Chicago Law Review* 433, 434 (1992).

86. *See* Steven M. Wise, *supra note* 69, at 114–118.

87. Richard A. Posner, "Animal Rights," 110 *Yale Law Journal* 527, 527 (2000).

88. *Id.*

89. *Id.*

90. Steven M. Wise, *supra* note 69, at 194, 196, 197, 198, 199, 203, 232, 236, 237.

91. Carleton Kemp Allen, *supra* note 47, at 424, quoting Baron, *Pandekten*, sec. 37, quoted in Holland, *Jurisprudence* 103 (13th ed. 1924) (emphases in original). *See* Roscoe Pound, *supra* note 22, at 530–531.

92. *See* Roscoe Pound, *supra* note 22, at 194–199.

93. Ellen Langer, *The Power of Mindful Learning* 4 (Boston: Addison Wesley, 1997); Barbara Herman, *The Practice of Moral Judgment* 229 (Cambridge, Mass.: Harvard University Press, 1993), each citing Kant.

94. Immanuel I. Kant, *Groundwork of the Metaphysic of Morals* 114–131 (H. S. Papp, trans., Harper Torchbooks 1964). *See* Barbara Herman, *supra* note 93, at 227–228.

95. Isaiah Berlin, *supra* note 18, at 216. *See* Michael Allen Fox, "Animal Experimentation: A Philosopher's Changing Views," in 3 *Between the Species* 260 (Spring 1987).

96. Carl Wellman, *Real Rights* 113–114 (Oxford: Oxford University Press, 1995). *See* Daniel A. Dombrowski, *Babies and Beasts* 45–140 (Urbana: University of Illinois Press, 1997) (discussing many modern philosophers); H. L. A. Hart, "Are There Any Natural Rights?" in *Theories of Rights* 79, 82 (Jeremy Waldron ed., Oxford University Press 1984); R. G. Frey, *Interests and Rights: The Case against Animals* 30 (Oxford: Clarendon Press, 1980). *See also* A. John Simmons, *The Lockean Theory of Rights* 201 note 93 (Princeton, N.J.: Princeton University Press, 1992) (listing modern philosophers who claim that children cannot have rights because they lack the capacities for agency, rationality, or autonomy); Katherine Hunt Federle, "On the Road to Reconceiving Rights for Children: A Postfeminist Analysis of the Capacity Principle," 42 *DePaul Law Review* 983, 987–999 (1993) (Hobbes, Locke, Rousseau, Bentham, and Mill).

97. Frans de Waal, "We the People (and Other Animals . . .)," *New York Times*, at A23 (August 20, 1999); Frans de Waal, *Good-Natured: The Origins of Right and Wrong in Humans and Other Animals* 215 (Cambridge, Mass.: Harvard University Press, 1995).

98. "Boy, 6, Fatally Shoots Classmate in Mich. School," *Boston Globe* at pp. A1, A16 (March 1, 2000).

99. Isaiah Berlin, *supra* note 18, at 219.

100. *E.g., Airedale NHS Trust v. Bland,* 1 All ER 821 (Family Division 1992), *aff.,* 1 All ER 833, 843, 848 (Ct. of App. 1993) (Butler-Sloss, LJ); *id.* at 852 (Hoffman, LJ) (both of the Court of Appeals); *aff.,* 1 All ER 858, 862 (HL 1993) (Lord Goff of Chieveley); *id.* at 889 (Lord Mustill). *See* Steven M. Wise, *supra* note 69, at 247.

101. *Airedale NHS Trust, supra* note 100, at 851, 852 (Hoffman, LJ); *id.* at 846 (Butler-Sloss, LJ) (both of the Court of Appeals); *id.* at 866 (Lord Goff of Chieveley).

102. *E.g., Winterwerp v. Netherlands,* A. 33, para. 51 (Eur. Ct. Hum. R. 1979); *O'Connor v. Donaldson,* 422 U.S.563 (1975).

103. *E.g., Guardianship of Doe,* 583 N.E. 2d 1263, 1268 (Mass. 1992); *id.* at 1272–1273 (Nolan, J., dissenting); *id.* at 1275 (O'Connor, J., dissenting); *International Shoe Co. v. Washington,* 326 U.S. 310, 316 (1945); *Tauza v. Susquehanna Coal Co.,* 115 N.E. 915, 917 (NY 1917); *Pramatha Nath Nullick v. Pradyumna Kumar Mullick,* 52 Indian L.R. 245, 250 (India 1925). *See* Roscoe Pound, *supra* note 22, at 195, 197, 198.

104. John Chipman Gray, *supra* note 24, at 43.

105. Jeremy Bentham, "Elements of Packing as Applied to Juries," in 5 *The Works of Jeremy Bentham* 92 (J. Bowring ed., 1843) (emphasis in the original).

106. Tom Regan, *The Case for Animal Rights* 84–85 (Philadelphia: Temple University Press, 1983); James Rachels, *Created from Animals* 140, 147 (Oxford: Oxford University Press, 1990); William A. Wright, "Treating Animals as Ends," *J. Value Inquiry* 353, 357, 362 (1993); Christopher Cherniak, *Minimal Rationality* 3–17 (Cambridge, Mass.: MIT Press, 1985).

107. XII *Oxford English Dictionary* 269–270, definitions A.I.1.a and b; A.I.2.a, b, and c; A.I.3; A.I.4 (2d ed.1989).

108. If I were chief justice of the universe, I might make the capacity to suffer, not practical autonomy, sufficient for personhood and dignity rights as well. For why should even a nonautonomous being be forced to suffer? But the capacity to suffer appears irrelevant to common law judges in their consideration of who is entitled to basic rights. At least practical autonomy appears sufficient. This may be anathema to disciples of Bentham and Singer. I may not like it much myself. But philosophers argue moral rights; judges decide legal rights. And so I present a legal, and not a philosophical, argument for the dignity rights of nonhuman animals.

109. Eric Rakowski, *Equal Justice* 359 (Oxford: Oxford University Press, 1991).

110. Joel Feinberg, " Potentiality, Development, and Rights," in *The Problem of Abortion* 145 (2d. ed., Joel Feinberg ed.; Belmont, Calif.: Wadsworth, 1984). *See* H. Tristram Englehardt, Jr., *The Foundations of Bioethics* 143 (2d ed.; Oxford: Oxford University Press, 1996). *See* Stanley I. Benn, "Abortion, Infanticide, and Respect for Persons," in Joel Feinberg, ed., *supra* note 110, at 143.

111. Isaiah Berlin, *supra* note 18, at 208.

112. Steven M. Wise, *supra* note 69, at 243–244.

113. Donald R. Griffin, *Animal Minds: Beyond Cognition to Consciousness* 11 (Chicago: University of Chicago Press, 2001).

114. *Id.* at 12.

115. Gordon G. Gallup, Jr., "Chimpanzees: Self-Recognition," 167 *Science* 86 (1970).

116. Bernd Heinrich, "Testing Insight in Ravens," in *The Evolution of Cognition* 289, 289, 300–301 (Cecelia Heyes and Ludwig Huber eds.; Cambridge, Mass.: MIT Press, 2000); Sandra T. deBlois et al., "Object Permanence in Orangutans (*Pongo pygmaeus*) and Squirrel Monkeys (*Saimiri sciureus*)," 112 *Journal of Comparative Psychology* 137, 148 (1998); Michael Tomasello and Josep Call, *Primate Cognition* 68–69 (Oxford University Press 1997).

117. Bernd Heinrich, *The Mind of the Raven: Investigations and Adventures with Wolf-Birds* 337 (New York: Cliff Street Books, 1999).

118. Steven M. Wise, *Drawing the Line: Science and the Case for Animal Rights* 66–70 (Cambridge, Mass.: Perseus, 2002).

119. Antonio Damasio, *The Feeling of What Happens: Body and Emotion in the Making of Consciousness* 106 (New York: Harcourt Brace, 1999).

120. Donald R. Griffin, *supra* note 113, at 10, discussing Darwin.

121. Gerald M. Edelman and Giulio Tononi, *A Universe of Consciousness: How Matter Becomes Imagination* 107 (New York: Basic, 2000); Gerald M. Edelman, *Bright Air, Brilliant Fire: On the Matter of Mind* 123 (New York: Basic, 1992).

122. Michel Cabanac, "Emotion and Phylogeny," 6 *Journal of Consciousness Studies* 176 (1999).

123. Donald Griffin finds any firm dividing line premature; Donald R. Griffin, *supra* note 113, at 10.

124. Martha C. Nussbaum, *Poetic Justice: The Literary Imagination and Public Life* 38 (Boston: Beacon 1995).

125. Charmian Barton, "The Status of the Precautionary Principle in Australia: Its Emergence in Legislation and as a Common Law Doctrine," 12 *Harvard Environmental Law Review* 509, 510, 547 (1998); James E. Hickey, Jr., and Vern R. Walker, "Refining the Precautionary Principle in International Environmental Law," 14 *Virginia Environmental Law Journal* 423, 448 (1995).

126. W. Page Keeton et al., *Prosser and Keeton on the Law of Torts*, sec. 41, at 263, 269 (5th ed.; St. Paul, Minn.: West Publishing Company, 1984).

127. Naomi Roht-Arriaza, "Precaution, Participation, and the 'Greening' of International Trade Law," 7 *Journal of Environmental Law and Litigation* 57, 60–61 (1992); Ellen Hey, "The Precautionary Concept in Environmental Policy and Law: Institutionalizing Caution," 4 *Georgetown International Environmental Law Review* 303, 307–308 (1992).

128. Naomi Roht-Arriaza, *supra* note 127, at 60.

129. Ellen Hey, *supra* note 127, at 311; Charmian Barton, *supra* note 125, at 513, quoting Daniel Bodansky, "Scientific Uncertainty and the Precautionary Principle," *Environment* 4, 4 (September 1991).

130. Michele Territo, "The Precautionary Principle in Marine Fisheries Conservation and the U.S. Sustainable Fisheries Act of 1996," 24 *Vermont Law Review* 1351, 1352–1358 (1999); Charmian Barton, *supra* note 125, at 514–518; Chris W. Backes and Jonathan M. Verschuren, "The Precautionary Principle in International, European, and Dutch Wildlife Law," 9 *Colorado Journal of International Environmental Law and Policy* 43 (1998); David Bodansky, "The Precautionary Principle in US Environmental Law," in *Interpreting the Precautionary Principle* 203–228 (Tim O'Riordan and James Cameron eds., London: Cameron May, 1996); James E. Hickey, Jr., and Vern R. Walker, *supra* note 125, at 432–436; Sonja Boehmer-Christiansen, "The Precautionary Principle in Germany:
Enabling Government," in *id.* at 31–60; Nigel Haigh, "The Introduction of the Precautionary Principle in the UK," in *id.* at 229–251; Ronnie Harding, "The Precautionary Principle in Australia," in *id.* at 262–283.

131. *Roosevelt Campobello International Park v. Environmental Protection Agency*, 684 F.2d 104, 1049 (D.C. Cir. 1982) (Endangered Species Act); *Committee for Humane Legislation v. Richardson*, 540 F.2d 1141, 1145 (D.C. Cir. 1976) (Marine Mammal Protection Act).

132. World Charter for Nature, A/Res/37/7 art. 11/b (October 28, 1982).

133. *See* Steven M. Wise, *supra* note 69, at 9–22.

134. Barnabas Dickson, "The Precautionary Principle in CITES: A Critical Assessment," 39 *Natural Resources Journal* 211, 213 (1999).

135. James E. Hickey, Jr., and Vern R. Walker, *supra* note 125, at 448–449.

136. Jonas Ebbeson, *Compatibility of International and National Environmental Law* 119 note 73 (The Hague: Kluwer Law International, 1996).

137. Charmian Barton, *supra* note 125, at 520, 550; David Freestone, "The Precautionary Principle," in *International Law and Global Climate Change* 25 (Robin Churchill and David Freestone eds.; London and Boston: Graham & Trotman/M. Nijhoff, 1991); J. Cameron and J. Abouchar, "The Precautionary Principle: A Fundamental Principle of Law and Policy for the Protection of the Global Environment," 14 *Boston College International and Comparative Law Review* 1, 20–23 (1991). *See, e.g.,* David Pearce, "The Precautionary Principle and Economic Analysis," in *id.* at 132, 144.

138. William Rogers, "Benefits, Costs and Risks: Oversight of Health and Environmental Decision-Making," 4 *Harvard Environmental Law Review* 191, 225 (1980).

139. Christina Hoff [Summers], "Immoral and Moral Uses of Animals," 302 *New England Journal of Medicine* 115, 117 (1980).

140. Hugh Thomas, *supra* note 2, at 309, quoting John Newton, "Thoughts on the African Slave Trade," in *Letters and Sermons* 103 (1780).

141. *E.g., Tumey v. Ohio*, 273 U.S. 510, 522 (1927).

142. *Bonham's Case*, 8 Co. 114a, 118a (C. P. 1610). *See* Harold J. Cook, "Against Common Rights and Reason: The College of Physicians versus Dr. Thomas Bonham," 29 *American Journal of Legal History* 301, 315–316 (1985); George P. Smith, "Dr. Bonham's Case and the Modern Significance of Lord Coke's Influence," 41 *Washington Law Review* 297, 301–304 (1966); Theodore F. T. Plucknett, "Bonham's Case and Judicial Review," 40 *Harvard Law Review* 30, 32, 34 (1926).

143. *Tumey, supra* note 141, at 524, 525

144. Fugitive Slave Act of 1850. The text can be read in William Lloyd Garrison's *Liberator* of September 27, 1850.

145. For a detailed argument that this belief is error, *see* Ray Greek and Jean Swingle Greek, *Sacred Cows and Golden Geese* (New York: Continuum International, 2000).

146. *See, e.g., United States v. Will,* 449 U.S. 200, 213–216 (1980).

147. Laurence H. Tribe, *American Constitutional Law* 1518 (2d ed.; Mineola, N.Y.: Foundation Press, 1988), quoting *Strauder v. West Virginia,* 100 U.S. 303, 306 (1880).

148. R. H. Bradshaw advocates treating all animals alike; R. H. Bradshaw, "Consciousness in Non-Human Animals: Adopting the Precautionary Principle," 5 *Journal of Consciousness Studies* 108 (1998).

149. Carl Wellman, *Real Rights* 129 (Oxford: Oxford University Press, 1995); Alan Gewirth, *Reason and Morality* 111, 121 (Chicago: University of Chicago Press, 1978).

150. Carl Wellman, *supra* note 96, at 130–131.

151. For an equality argument, see Steven M. Wise, supra note 69, at 82–87.

152. Henry Beston, *The Outermost House* 25 (Chicago: University of Chicago Press, 1967).

153. Stuart Sutherland, *International Dictionary of Psychology* 211 (New York:

Continuum, 1989).

154. Bernd Heinrich, *supra* note 117, at 327.

155. Diana Reiss, "The Dolphin: An Alien Intelligence," in *First Contact: The Search for Extraterrestrial Intelligence* 31, 39 (Ben Bova and Bryon Press eds.; New York: NAL Books, 1990).

156. Thomas Nagel, "What Is It Like to Be a Bat?" 83(4) *Philosophical Review* 435 (1974), reprinted in *The Nature of Consciousness: Philosophical Debates* 519, 520 (Ned Block et al. eds.; Cambridge, Mass.: MIT Press, 1997).

157. *Id.* (emphasis in the original). *See id.* at 520–521.

158. Frans de Waal, "Foreword," in *Anthropomorphism, Anecdotes, and Animals* viv (Albany: State University of New York Press, 1997) ("if closely related species act the same, the underlying mental processes are probably the same, too"); Frans M. B. de Waal, *Good-Natured: The Origins of Right and Wrong in Humans and Other Animals* 64–65 (Cambridge, Mass.: Harvard University Press 1996); Frans M. B. de Waal, "The Chimpanzee's Sense of Social Regularity and Its Relation to the Human Sense of Justice," 34 *American Behavioral Scientist* 335, 341 (January–February 1991) ("strong arguments would have to be furnished before we would accept that similar behaviors in related species are differently motivated").

159. Georgia J. Mason et al., "Frustrations of Fur-Farmed Mink," 410 *Nature* 35–36 (2001).

160. William R. Langbauer, Jr., et al., "Responses of Captive African Elephants to Playback of Low Frequency Calls," 67 *Canadian Journal of Zoology* 2604 (1989).

161. Joyce Poole, *Coming of Age with Elephants* 114 (London: Hodder and Stoughton, 1996).

162. Harry F. Harlow, "The Evolution of Learning," in *Behavior and Evolution* 269 (Anne Roe and Gaylord Simpson eds.; New Haven, Conn.: Yale University Press, 1958).

163. Harry Jerison, "The Perceptual Worlds of Dolphins," in *Dolphin Cognition and Behavior: A Comparative Approach* 137, 148, 149 (Ronald J. Schusterman et al. eds.; Hillsdale, N.J.: Lawrence Erlbaum, 1986).

164. Steven M. Wise, *supra* note 118, at 87–112, 131–231.

165. David Brion Davis, *supra* note 3.

2

RICHARD A. POSNER

ANIMAL RIGHTS

Legal, Philosophical, and Pragmatic Perspectives

In the work of such philosophers as Peter Singer, it seems merely to be assumed that the virtues of an intellectual theory, such as economy and simplicity, translate into a desirable rationality of social practice. That represents a Platonic rationalism of the most suspect kind.

—BERNARD WILLIAMS, "Auto da Fé: Consequences of Pragmatism"

There is growing debate over whether to recognize "animal rights"—which means whether to create legal duties to treat animals in approximately the same way we treat the human residents of our society, whether, in effect, animals, or some animals, shall be citizens. I shall argue that the best approach to the question of animal rights is a humancentric one that appeals to our developing knowledge and sentiments about animals and that eschews on the one hand philosophical argument and on the other hand a legal-formalist approach to the issue (an approach that turns out, however, to have distinct affinities with philosophical analysis). My stalking horses are a lawyer and a philosopher: Steven Wise, the leading legal advocate of animal rights, and Peter Singer, the leading philosophical advocate of those rights. I start with Wise,[1] who, I shall argue, is also a philosopher of sorts.

LEGAL REASONING ABOUT ANIMAL RIGHTS

Wise urges courts in the exercise of their common law powers of legal rule making to confer legally enforceable rights on animals, beginning with chimpanzees and bonobos (a closely related species), generally believed to be the two most intelligent primate species.[2] Judicial innovation proceeds incrementally; as Oliver Wendell Holmes put it, the courts, in their legislative capacity, are confined from molar to molecular motions. If Wise is to persuade his chosen audience, the common law judges, he must show how courts can proceed incrementally, building on existing cases and legal concepts, toward his goal of dramatically enhanced legal protection for animals. Recall the process by which, starting from the unpromising principle that "separate but equal" was constitutional, the Supreme Court outlawed official segregation. First, certain public facilities were held not to be equal; then segregation of law schools was invalidated as inherently unequal because of the importance to a successful legal practice of the contacts made in law school; then segregation of elementary schools was outlawed on the basis of social scientific evidence that this segregation, too, was inherently unequal; then the separate-but-equal principle itself, having been reduced to a husk, was quietly buried and the no-segregation principle of the education cases was extended to all public facilities, including rest rooms and drinking fountains.

That is the process Wise envisages for the animal rights movement, although the end point is less clear. We have a robust conception of human rights that we apply even to people who by reason of retardation or other mental disability cannot enforce their own rights but need a guardian to do it for them. The evolution of human rights law has involved not only expanding the number of rights but also expanding the number of rights holders, notably by adding women and minorities. We also have a long history of legal protections for animals which recognizes their sentience, their emotional capacity,[3] and their capacity to suffer pain; and these protections have been growing too. Wise wants to merge these legal streams by showing that the apes that are most like us genetically are also very much like us in their mentation, which exceeds that of human infants and profoundly retarded people. They are enough like us, he argues, to be in the direct path of rights expansion. He finds no principled difference, so far as rights deserving is concerned, between the least mentally able people and the most mentally able animals, who overlap them; or at least he finds too little difference to justify interrupting, at the gateway to the animal kingdom, the expansive rights trend that he has discerned. The law's traditional dichotomization of humans and animals is a vestige of bad science and of a hierarchizing tendency, which puts humans over animals just as it put free men over slaves. Wise does not say how many other animal species besides chimpanzees and bonobos he would like to see entitled but makes clear that he regards entitling those two species as a milestone, not the end of the road.

En route to these conclusions, Wise emphasizes the history of bad treatment of animals, treating his readers to such nuggets as that the Old Testament method of punishing a domestic animal who killed a human being reflected a belief that such an act was insurrectional in character, like a slave revolt. But he fails to note the inconsistency between the law's treating animals like slaves and what he takes to be the law's ignorance of the commonality between people and animals. After all, no one ever doubted that slaves were human and had formidable mental capacities, whether or not equal to those of free men. To punish an ox or a rat as if it were a rebelling slave is to accord the animal a considerable dignity.[4] And, as was done in some American states in the eighteenth century, to impose capital punishment on people who have sex with animals on the theory that such couplings may give birth to dangerous monsters is, in modern terminology, to assert that people and animals are one and the same species.[5] When we remember that the Egyptians considered cats sacred[6] and that in Greek mythology Zeus often assumes an animal's form to have sex with women, it becomes apparent that the ancients had a more complex view of animal "humanity" than Wise gives them credit for.[7] It could hardly have been otherwise, given the extraordinary dependence of early societies on wild and domesticated animals as sources of food, clothing, pest control, transportation, power, and even as weapons (Hannibal's elephants, for example).

This point can be put more strongly with considerable support in the scholarly literature on the history of man's relations with animals.[8] For think: Could man successfully have domesticated animals, and successfully hunted animals, and successfully defended himself against animals, without considerable empathy and respect for them? Had early man not felt a kinship with a wide variety of animals, had he not considered it possible to think his way into the animal's mind, would he have undertaken to domesticate animals, known how to do so or how to organize the hunting and trapping of animals, or been able to protect himself from animal predation against crops, livestock, and man himself? Since man's dependence on animals in all these ways was hardly less in the Christian era than previously, it must be reckoned a considerable perversity of Christianity that it was so much less inclined to treat animals with respect than the pagan cultures had been. An ideological explanation offers itself (whether there is some underlying material explanation, I do not know). The pagan religions had tended to sacralize nature, and so in its rivalry with them Christianity tended to view nature, including animals, as the domain of the devil. Christianity was also distinctly hostile to man's "animal" nature, to the sexual and other bodily functions that man shares with animals. Then too, any considerate regard for animals would raise acute issues of theodicy—of how a just and merciful God could have condemned the vast animal kingdom to a brutal, violent, predator-prey existence. The pagan gods had not been considered just and merciful; they reflected rather than surpassed nature, so the issue of theodicy did not arise in the worship of them.

Not until the end of the eighteenth century were laws enacted in the nations of the West forbidding cruelty to animals.[9] The laws were full of loopholes—essentially they just forbade sadistic, gratuitous, blatant cruelty—but still they represented a dramatic change from the law's traditional indifference to animals' welfare. Christianity was losing some of its grip, and the rising urban middle class was both disgusted by the casual cruelty of the lower class and disdainful of hunting as an aristocratic pursuit.[10] Both the lower class and the upper class in eighteenth-century England were primarily rural, and rural people are less squeamish about the shedding of blood than urbanites are.

History, however, is rather to one side of Wise's project. The essential premise of his argument is that animals, or at least some species of them, have consciousness (he means consciousness of self; obviously animals are conscious in the sense that distinguishes being conscious from being unconscious). A scientist, he notes, has speculated that when two gazelles are being chased by a lion, each "gazelle must realize that it was *she* who was being chased, as well as another gazelle who was not her, and . . . she must understand, however dimly, that dire consequences will flow for her if she, and not the other gazelle, is caught."[11] Wise himself is interested in primates rather than gazelles. He points out that while the chimpanzee's cortex is less than a quarter the size of a normal human being's, it still contains an enormous number of neurons, perhaps enough for consciousness, though no one knows.

Wise acknowledges that it is unclear whether chimpanzees can be taught to use language, but he marshals considerable evidence that language is not indispensable to the possession of some, however rudimentary, sense of self, of separateness from other things.[12] Comparisons between chimpanzees and very small children find similar mentation, and, like human beings, chimpanzees develop greater cognitive abilities when raised in a stimulating social environment (either their native habitat or a deliberately "enculturating" laboratory environment) than when they live out their lives in a zoo; so we may tend to underestimate their intelligence. Wise argues that a properly enculturated chimpanzee has the mental ability of a two- or even three-year-old child. One may doubt this,[13] considering that children of those ages have substantial linguistic capabilities, but those capabilities may be separate from, though obviously immensely helpful to, the capacity to reason. Wise is convincing that chimpanzees have formidable mental abilities, including the ability to make mental representations, to make and use tools, to count and perform simple arithmetical operations, to deceive, to imitate, and to empathize; that they are self-aware; and that they have culture, in the sense of know-how transmitted across generations.[14]

If chimpanzees do have consciousness, "minds," perhaps on a level of very small children or severely retarded adults, it becomes pertinent to note that small children and severely retarded adults have legal rights. Wise asks rhetorically whether if a band of Neanderthals suddenly appeared in our midst we would feel free to treat them with the same consideration that we treat, say, calves. The answer is surely no. He draws support for his position from opponents of affirmative action, who argue that group membership, as distinct from one's individual qualities, is an illegitimate basis for claiming rights. We should judge persons, including Neanderthals—and apes—as individuals, rather than basing their legal status on the biological or other ascriptive group to which they happen to belong.

Wise is aware that too much emphasis on cognitive capacity as the basis for rights invites the question: So what about computers? Some computer scientists and philosophers believe that computers will soon achieve consciousness. Wise brushes aside this possibility with the observation that chimpanzees and human beings have traveled a similar evolutionary path, and computers have not—though one might have thought that, since computers are a product of the human mind, they may "think" along somewhat similar lines. Wise makes himself a hostage to future scientific advances by ignoring the possibility that there may some day be computers that have as many "neurons" as chimpanzees, "neurons" that moreover are "wired" similarly. Such computers may well be conscious. This will be a problem for Wise, for whom the essence of equality under law is that individuals with similar cognitive capacities should be treated alike regardless of their species. Nothing in his analysis would permit him to limit this principle to "natural" species—for what if a human being could be created in a laboratory from chemicals, without use of any genetic material? Wise would have to agree that such a human being would have the same rights as any other human being; rights in his view are not based on genes. So why are computers categorically excluded?

From his principle of equality, Wise deduces that chimpanzees should have the same rights that small children and severely retarded adults have: the right to life, to bodily integrity, to subsistence, and to some kind of freedom (how much is unclear), but not the right to vote. He does not discuss whether they should have the right to reproduce. But he is emphatic that since we would not permit invasive or dangerous medical experimentation on small children or severely retarded adults, neither can we permit such experimentation on chimpanzees, no matter how great the benefits for human health.

The framework of Wise's analysis, as we have seen, is the history of extending rights to formerly excluded persons. Working within that conventional, formalistic, lawyerly framework, he seeks to convince his readers that chimpanzees have the essential attribute of persons, which he believes is the level of mentation that we call consciousness, but (to avoid a reductio ad absurdum) that computers do not have it. In short, anyone who has consciousness should have rights; chimpanzees are conscious, therefore they should have rights.

I have called this a conventional legal approach, and it is, but like so much legal reasoning about rights it is also a cousin of deontological moral philosophy. Wise starts with an intuition that he expects his readers to share, having to do with the moral entitlements of children and retarded human adults, and then tries to break down the distinction between them and primates while at the same preserving the distinction between children, retarded adults, and primates, on the one hand, and computers on the other.

Wise wants to show that primates have moral entitlements, trusting his readers to accept that any strong moral entitlement should be given legal standing so that it is enforceable and not merely aspirational.

How convincing is his analysis, if we set to one side the criticisms of it that I have made thus far? The major premise presents the immediate difficulty. Cognitive capacity is certainly *relevant* to rights; it is a precondition of some rights, such as the right to vote. But most people would not think it either a necessary or a sufficient condition of having rights. Wise does not take on their arguments or, more to the point, their intuitions—for his major premise is itself an intuition and so he needs to give a reason for ignoring strongly contrary intuitions. Many people believe, for example, that a one-day-old human fetus, though it has no cognitive capacity, should have a right to life; and the Supreme Court permits the fetus to be accorded a qualified such right after the first trimester of pregnancy, though the cognitive capacity of a second- or even third-trimester fetus is very limited. It is difficult for Wise to resist the fetal analogy, because he thinks that a one-day-old infant has rights, even though the one-day-old infant has little greater cognitive capacity than the infant had as a fetus a few hours earlier. Wise's lack of concern with destroying a "conscious" computer is a further indication that he does not take the idea that rights follow cognitive capacity seriously. Most people would think it distinctly odd to proportion animal rights to animal intelligence, as Wise wishes to do, implying that dolphins, parrots, and ravens are entitled to more legal protection than horses (or most monkeys), and perhaps that the laws forbidding cruelty to animals should be limited to the most intelligent animals, inviting the crack, "They don't have syntax, so we can eat them."[15] And most of us would think it downright offensive to give greater rights to monkeys, let alone to computers, than to retarded people upon a showing that the monkey or the computer has a larger cognitive capacity than a profoundly retarded human being. Cognition and rights deservedness are not interwoven as tightly as Wise believes, though he is not, of course, the first to believe this.[16]

There is a related objection to his approach. He wants judges, in good common law fashion, to move step by step, and for the first step simply to declare that chimpanzees have legal rights. (This corresponds to the casuistic method of doing moral philosophy.) But judges asked to step onto a new path of doctrinal growth want to have some idea of where the path leads even if it would be unreasonable to insist that the destination be clearly seen. Wise gives them no idea. His repeated comparison of animals to slaves and the animal rights cause to the civil rights movement is misleading. When one speaks of freeing slaves and giving them the rights of other people, or giving women the same rights as men, it is pretty clear what is envisioned, although important details may be unclear. When the National Association for the Advancement of Colored People set out on its campaign to persuade the Supreme Court to repudiate separate but equal, it was pretty clear what the end point was: the elimination of official segregation by race. After that was achieved, other race-related legal objectives hove into view, but the campaign's proximate goal was at least clear. But what is meant by liberating animals and giving them the rights of human beings of the same cognitive capacity? Does an animal's right to life place a duty on human beings to protect animals from being killed by other animals? Is capacity to feel pain sufficient cognitive capacity to entitle an animal to at least the most elementary human rights? What kind of habitats must we create and maintain for all the rights-bearing animals in the United States? Should human convenience have *any* weight in deciding what rights an animal has?

What, for example, would Wise make of the bizarre case of the egg-sucking dog?[17] The plaintiff and the defendant lived about a mile apart. For three weeks, the plaintiff's dog came onto the defendant's property and sucked all the eggs that had been laid by the defendant's turkeys and guinea hens. After other remedies failed, the defendant killed the dog, precipitating suit by the dog's owner. The court held that the defendant, having exhausted all other self-help remedies (such as notification to the owner), was entitled to kill the animal. We of course would not permit an egg-sucking human being to be killed. Are dogs to be given an equivalent privilege?

Can common law courts actually work out a satisfactory regime of animal rights without the aid of legislatures? When human rights and animal rights collide, do the former have any priority (as in the egg-sucking case), and if so, why? And what is to be done when animal rights collide with each other, as they do with laws that by protecting wolves endanger sheep? Must entire species of animals be "segregated" from each other and from human beings, and, if so, what does "separate but equal" mean in this context? May we "discriminate" against animals, and if so how much? Do species have "rights," or do just individual animals have rights, and if the latter, does this mean that according special legal protection to endangered species is a denial of equal protection? Is domestication a form of enslavement? Wise does not try to answer any of these questions. He is asking judges to set sail on an uncharted sea without a compass.

Analogy is a treacherous form of argument. Chimpanzees are like human beings, therefore, so far as Wise is concerned, giving animals rights is like giving black people the rights of white people. But chimpanzees are like human beings in some respects but not in others that may be equally or more relevant to the issue of whether to give chimpanzees rights, and legal rights have been designed to serve the needs and interests of human beings, having the usual human capacities, and so make a poor fit with the needs and interests of animals.

Wise has no theory of rights, no notion of why legal rights are created in the first place. It is not in recognition of cognitive capacity. Slaves have cognitive capacity but no rights. Legal rights are instruments for securing the liberties that are necessary if a democratic system of government is to provide a workable framework for social order and prosperity. The conventional rights bearers are with minor exceptions actual and potential voters and economic actors. Animals do not fit this description, and Wise makes no effort to show that extending rights to them would nevertheless serve the purposes for which rights are created. And to the extent that courts are outside the normal political processes, his approach is deeply undemocratic. There are more animals in the United States than people; if the animals are given capacious rights by judges who do not conceive themselves to be representatives of the people—indeed, who use a methodology that owes nothing to popular opinion or democratic preference—the de facto weight of the animal population in the society's political choices will approach or even exceed that of the human population. Judges will become the virtual representatives of the animals, casting in effect millions of votes to override the democratic choices of the human population.

Wise's approach illustrates the severe limitations of legal and cognate moral reasoning, confirming John Dewey's view that we should replace both types of reasoning with the same reasoning methods we use in dealing with practical problems outside of law.[18] Because judges, and therefore the lawyers who argue before them, are reluctant for political and professional reasons to acknowledge that they are expanding or otherwise changing the law rather than just applying it—because, in other words, conventional legal reasoning is backward-looking rather than forward-looking, insisting that decisions be based on, in Dewey's phrase, the "antecedently real"[19]— departures from existing law are disguised as applications of it guided by analogy or deduction. Wise is either playing this old game or has been fooled by it. He pretends that animal rights in the expansive form in which he conceives of them are nothing new—they just plug a hole unaccountably left in the existing case law on rights. Animals just got overlooked, as blacks and women had once been overlooked. But correcting a logical error, removing an inconsistency, in short tidying up doctrine, is not what would be involved in deciding that chimpanzees have the same rights as three-year-old human beings. What Wise's approach really does, rather than supply reasons for changing the law, is supply rationalizations that courts persuaded on other grounds to change the law might use to conceal the novelty of their actions. Judges are not easily fooled by a lawyer who argues for a change in the law on the basis that it would be no change at all but merely the logical entailment of existing law. The value of such an argument is in giving the judges a professionally respectable ground for rationalizing the change, a ground that minimizes the appearance of novelty and so protects rule-of-law values. The judges must have reasons for wanting to make the change, however, and this is where a lawyer's brief, which furnishes the rationalization, the rhetoric, but rarely the reasons, falls down.

ouch

There is a sad poverty of imagination in an approach to animal protection that can think of it only on the model of the civil rights movement. It is a poverty that reflects the blinkered approach of the traditional lawyer, afraid to acknowledge novelty and therefore unable to think clearly about the reasons pro or con for a departure from the legal status quo. It reflects also the extent to which liberal lawyers remain in thrall to the constitutional jurisprudence of the Warren Court and insensitive to the liberating potential of commodification. One way to protect animals is to make them property, because people tend to protect what they own; I shall give an illustration later.

So Wise is another deer frozen in the headlights of *Brown v. Board of Education*. He has overlooked not only the possibilities of animal-protecting commodification but also an approach to the question of animals' welfare that is at once more conservative, methodologically as well as politically, but possibly more efficacious, than rights mongering. That is simply to extend, and more vigorously to enforce, the laws that forbid inflicting gratuitous cruelty on animals. We should be able to agree without help from philosophers and constitutional theorists that gratuitous cruelty is bad—condemnation is built into the word "gratuitous"—and few of us are either so sadistic, or so indifferent to animal suffering, that we are unwilling to incur at least modest costs to prevent gratuitous cruelty to animals; and anyone who supposes that philosophers and constitutional theorists can persuade people to incur huge costs to protect the interests of strangers is surely deluded. Wise gives vivid and disturbing examples of cruel treatment of chimpanzees but is mistaken to think that the best way to prevent such cruelty is to treat chimpanzees like human beings. The best way is to forbid treating chimpanzees, or any other animals with whom we sympathize, cruelly. If that is all that, in the end, "animal rights" are to amount to, we don't need the vocabulary of rights, which is then just an impediment to clear thought as well as a provocation in some legal and philosophical quarters.

PHILOSOPHIZING ABOUT ANIMAL RIGHTS

Where might we go, necessarily outside rather than inside law, for reasons for changing the law to entitle animals? I shall discuss two possible sources, which I shall call the *philosophical* and illustrate primarily with Peter Singer's utilitarian approach,[20] and the *pragmatic* in the everyday sense of the word,[21] the sense that equates it to "practical" and "down-to-earth." Conventional philosophizing over animal rights seeks for first principles to determine how we should treat animals. A utilitarian—someone who believes that our basic moral duty is to maximize happiness or the satisfaction of preferences and thus to minimize pain and disappointment—can readily argue that people should be forbidden to mistreat those animals that have a sufficiently developed nervous system to be able to experience pain, unless that mistreatment (perhaps then misnamed) minimizes pain, or maximizes pleasure, overall. That can easily happen; an example would be a case in which minor animal suffering was a sine qua non for developing a cure for a lethal disease of human beings. Or vice versa—for there is nothing in utilitarian theory to prevent arguing for medical experimentation on human beings that is designed to find cures for fatal animal illnesses, especially painful ones.

The utilitarian cannot, however, establish the validity of his major premise: that maximizing the satisfaction of preferences should be the goal of society. This is the standard problem of moral philosophy in a morally heterogeneous society: finding common ground from which to argue to normative conclusions. But what really undermines the utilitarian's position is the logical implications of his premise. By itself it has a certain appeal; only when one explores its implications does it become unpalatable and even bizarre. Animals experience pain and pleasure, so panspecies utilitarianism seems indeed entailed by the utilitarian premise. But in that case, the life of a healthy pig is likely to be worthier of legal protection than that of a severely retarded human being.[22] Indeed, if pigs are naturally happier than human beings, or if because of their relatively small size the earth can support far more pigs than human beings, a world human population just large enough to support an enormous pig population might be the utilitarian optimum. We might, as I suggested in the last paragraph, have to allow medical experimentation on human beings for the sake of improving animal health.

At the same time, the utilitarian premise implies that killing an animal painlessly and without forewarning can be completely compensated for by creating a new animal[23] to replace it and that carnivorous animals should be killed or sequestered to protect their prey. The first implication undermines the case for vegetarianism. Most people obtain great utility from eating meat. If animals raised for food are treated humanely, have no foreknowledge of death, and are killed painlessly, and if the demand for meat results in a huge population of such animals, then eating meat may well increase rather than reduce overall utility, even when the utility of the animals raised for food is taken into account. Even *animal* utility might be reduced by banning the eating of meat, especially if animal species that are maintained primarily as sources of human food became extinct.

Singer, a strong proponent of vegetarianism, acknowledges that "as a matter of strict logic, perhaps, there is no contradiction in taking an interest in animals on both compassionate and gastronomic grounds. . . . One could consistently eat animals who had lived free of all suffering and been instantly, painlessly slaughtered."[24] But, he adds weakly, "Practically and psychologically it is impossible to be consistent in one's concern for nonhuman animals while continuing to dine on them."[25] He does not consider the gastronomic benefits to human beings who like meat, though nothing in utilitarianism authorizes the exclusion of such a benefit. He is on somewhat firmer ground in disregarding the effect of vegetarianism on the number of animals, for total utilitarianism (maximizing utility without regard to its distribution) is an especially counterintuitive form of utilitarianism. But average utilitarianism is not much more appealing, as it implies that a very small population of exquisitely cosseted, and therefore supremely happy, beings (human or animal) is the goal that we should be striving to attain. If, however, both total and average utilitarianism are rejected, where are we?

At the other end of the spectrum of philosophical analysis of animal rights from the utilitarian is the view of Aquinas and other traditional Catholic thinkers that animals are entitled to no consideration, at least relative to human beings, because animals lack souls. There is no arguing with religious dogmas unless they give hostages to science by incorporating factual claims. And there is even a secular argument for dichotomizing humans and animals, with or without reference to souls. It is that if we fail to maintain a bright line between animals and human beings, we may end up treating human beings as badly as we treat animals, rather than treating animals as well as we treat (or aspire to treat) human beings. Equation is a transitive relation. If chimpanzees equal human infants, human infants equal chimpanzees.

Against this concern it can be argued that Darwinism shows that there is nothing special about human beings; we are an accident of nature's blind processes just like all the other animals and so it is arbitrary for us to put ourselves on a higher plane than the other animals. (This is the negative implication of Darwinism; the positive implication, which seems to me dubious, or at least arbitrary, is that Darwinism establishes our kinship with animals, and we should be kind to our kin.) This may well be true, but it ignores the potential social value of a rhetoric of human specialty—think only of how the Nazis used Darwinian rhetoric to justify a law-of-the-jungle conception of the relations between human groups. And the Nazis, I am about to note, believed passionately in animal rights. What is more, if natural law is understood naturalistically, not as Christianity or any other religion that asserts a deep and wide gulf between animal and human nature but as the law of the jungle, then as denizens of the jungle we have no greater duties to the other animals than the lion, say, has to the gazelle. But all that these points show is that there is no normative significance to our having descended from apes.

Yet are not pragmatists Darwinists?[26] Don't they believe that human beings are just clever animals rather than demiangels? If Christianity, by teaching that people are demiangels, ensouled by and created in the image of God, and that animals are not demiangels, opened up a huge moral gulf between man and the animals (*not* "and the *other* animals"), does not Darwinism, and hence pragmatism, close it? Should not pragmatists therefore be animal liberationists?

There are three misunderstandings here. The first is the conflation of philosophical and everyday pragmatism. The proposition that people are clever animals is part of the philosophical side of pragmatism; it is related to the distinctive pragmatic conception of inquiry and the associated pragmatic rejection of metaphysical realism. Second, it is arbitrary to draw a normative inference from a biological fact (or theory). Why should the percentage of genes that I have in common with other creatures determine how much consideration I owe them? And third, a pragmatist need not be committed to a particular vocabulary, realistic or otherwise, such as "man as animal." A vocabulary of human specialness may have social value despite its descriptive inaccuracy. To call human life "sacred" or to distinguish human beings from animals may be descriptively, which is to say scientifically, inaccurate yet serve a constructive function in political discourse, perhaps nudging people to behave "better" in a sense with which most everyday pragmatists would agree.

A different approach to the issue of animal rights is from the direction of environmentalism. One can hold a religious or Romantic belief in the sacredness or transcendent value of nonhuman nature, of which nonhuman animals are a major component. But this severs the link between animal rights and animal cognition. Nature is not valued by environmentalists for its mental attributes, and so the environmentalist is unlikely to want to give special protection to chimpanzees, dolphins, and other highly intelligent animals.[27] Rather the contrary: Hitler's zoophilia, and Nazi environmentalism more generally,[28] were connected with a hostility to "cosmopolitan" intellect, that is, to intellect not rooted in ethnic or other local particularities. The distinction between humans and nonhumans fell away. The Nazis were constantly blurring the line between the human and animal kingdoms, as when they described Jews as vermin. The other side of this coin was the glorification of animals that had good Nazi virtues, predatory animals like the eagle (the Eagle's Nest was the name of Hitler's summer home in the Bavarian Alps), the tiger, and the panther (both of which animals gave their names to German tanks). Nietzsche's "blond beast," the opposite pole of degenerate modern man, was the lion. These examples show how animal rights thinking can assimilate people to animals as well as assimilating animals to people.

I am not suggesting that the animal rights movement is tainted by Hitler's support, any more than Hitler's enthusiasm for limited-access highways should be an embarrassment to our highway builders. The point is only that animal rights have no particular political valence. They are as compatible with right-wing as with left-wing views.

It is possible, for that matter, here veering back toward utilitarianism, to have a purely sentimental attachment to animals—to like them, or some species at any rate, as much as, or more than, one likes the human species; or if not to "like" them, to sympathize with them sufficiently to feel their pain and want to alleviate it. This solves the utilitarian problem of bounding the community, though not very satisfactorily, by linking animal happiness to the happiness of human beings. The economic definition of *altruism* is positive interdependent utilities: If X's utility is increased by an increase in Y's utility, then increasing Y's utility is a social benefit even if only X, and not Y, belongs to the community whose utility is sought to be maximized. So X might be a human being and Y a sea otter.

Oddly, the sentimental attachment to animals is not well correlated with genetic closeness, as is implicit in my noting that we can like some animals more than we like people. We are more closely related genetically to chimpanzees than to cats or dogs or falcons or leopards, but some of us like chimpanzees less than these other animals, and we might prefer, for example, to have medical experiments conducted on chimpanzees than on these other species, though the relative pain that experiments inflict on different species of animal, as well as differential medical benefits from experiments on different species, would be a relevant factor to most of us. If chimpanzees' greater intelligence increases the suffering that they undergo as subjects of medical experiments, relative to less intelligent animals, the increment in suffering may trump our affection for certain "cuter" animals. To the extent that the happiness of certain animals is bound up with our own happiness, there is, as I have just noted, a utilitarian basis for animal rights (though "rights" is not the best term here) even if the only utility that a utilitarian is obligated to try to maximize is human utility.

The U.S. Department of Agriculture has been collecting data on animal experimentation since 1973. The data show, for example, that between 1973 and 1995 the number of cats and dogs used in experiments fell by more than 50 percent, but the number of primates used in experiments increased. I don't know the reasons (maybe they are scientific), but I would not be surprised if these changes reflected at least in part our greater affection for our pets than for our simian first cousins. In 1999, of some 1.2 million animals used in experiments, 100,000 were reported to have experienced pain or distress not alleviated by drugs, and, of these, 883 were primates, compared to 1,039 dogs and only 191 cats.[29] Wholly excluded from the count of the 1.2 million experimental subjects are the innumerable rats, mice, frogs, lizards, and birds on which experiments are performed; the pain and distress of these animals are apparently not considered worthy of being recorded. Peter Singer claims that 25 million animals are annually subjected to experimentation but does not give a source for this figure.[30]

The philosophical discourse on animal rights is inherently inconclusive because there is no metric that enables utilitarianism, Romanticism, normative Darwinism, and other possible philosophical groundings of animal rights to be commensurated and conflicts among them resolved. Let me nonetheless press on, examining Singer's approach in greater detail because he is the most influential, and also and relatedly the most accessible, philosophical proponent of what I am calling animal rights but that he prefers to call "animal liberation" (utilitarians are not comfortable with "rights"). In his book of that title he make several points with which I agree, such as that human beings are not infinitely superior to nor infinitely more valuable than other animals; indeed, I am prepared to drop "infinitely." I agree that we are animals and not ensouled demiangels, that gratuitous cruelty to and neglect of animals are wrong, and that some costs should be incurred to reduce the suffering of animals raised for food or other human purposes or subjected to medical or other testing and experimentation.

But I do not agree with any of these things under the compulsion of philosophical argument. And I disagree that we have a duty to (the other) animals that arises from their being the equal members of a community composed of all those creatures in the universe that can feel pain, and that it is merely "prejudice" in a disreputable sense akin to racial prejudice or sexism that makes us discriminate in favor of our own species. Singer assumes the existence of the universe-wide community of pain and demands reasons that the boundary of our concern should be drawn any more narrowly: "If a being suffers there can be no moral justification for refusing to take that suffering into consideration."[31] That is sheer assertion, and particularly dubious is his further claim that (the title of the first chapter of his book) "all animals are equal,"[32] a point that he defends by arguing that the case for treating women and blacks equally with white males does not depend on the existence of *factual* equality among these groups. But the history of racial and sexual equality is the history of a growing belief that the factual inequalities among these groups are either a consequence of discrimination or have been exaggerated. Wise wants to argue similarly that the cognitive differences between people and chimpanzees have been exaggerated, but Singer declines to take that route—rightly so, if my criticism of Wise's approach is sound.

Singer wants to seize the commanding heights in the debate over animal rights by using his premises about the moral claims of suffering and the equality of all animals to shift the burden of proof to his opponents. That is just an argumentative gambit and cannot be shown to be superior to proceeding from the bottom up, with the brute fact that we, like other animals, prefer our own—our own family, the "pack" that we happen to run with (because we are a social animal), and the larger sodalities constructed on the model of the smaller ones, of which the largest for most of us is our nation. Americans have less feeling for the pains and pleasures of foreigners than of other Americans and even less for most of the nonhuman animals with which we share the world.

Singer will doubtless reply that these are just facts about human nature, that they have no normative significance. Yet I doubt that he actually believes that in his heart of hearts. Suppose a dog menaced a human infant and the only way to prevent the dog from biting the infant was to inflict severe pain on the dog—more pain, in fact, than the bite would inflict on the infant. Singer would have to say, let the dog bite, for Singer's position is that if an animal feels pain, the pain matters as much as it does when a human being feels pain, provided the pain is as great; and it matters more if it is greater. But any normal person (and not merely the infant's parents), including a philosopher when he is not self-consciously engaged in philosophizing, would say that it would be monstrous to spare the dog, even though to do so would minimize the sum of pain in the world.

I feel no obligation to defend this reaction, any more than I do to prove that my legs remain attached to my body when I am asleep, or for that matter when I am awake. My certitude about my bodily integrity is deeper than any proof that could be offered of it to refute a skeptic. Likewise the superior claim of the human infant than of the dog on our consideration is a moral intuition deeper than any reason that could be given for it and impervious to any reason that anyone could give against it. Membership in the human species is not a morally irrelevant fact, as the race and gender of human beings have come to seem. If the moral irrelevance of humanity is what philosophy teaches, so that we have to choose between philosophy and the intuition that says that membership in the human species *is* morally relevant, philosophy will have to go.

Moral intuitions can change. The difference between science and morality is that while it has never been true, whatever people believed, that the sun revolves around the earth, morality, which as a practical matter is simply a department of public opinion, changes unpredictably; there are no unchanging facts to anchor it. Someday we may think animals as worthy of our solicitude as human beings, or even more worthy. But that will mean that we have a new morality, not that philosophers have shown that we were making an erroneous distinction between animals and humans all along.

I am sure that Singer would react the same way as I do to the dog-child example. He might consider it a weakness in himself if he were unable to act upon his philosophical beliefs. But he would be wrong; it would not be a weakness; it would be a sign of sanity. Just as philosophers who have embraced skepticism about the existence of the external world, or hold that science is just a "narrative" with no defensible claim to yield objective truth, do not put their money where their mouth is by refusing to jump out of the way of a truck bearing down on them, so philosophers who embrace weird ethical theories do not act on those theories even when they could do so without being punished. There are exceptions, but we call them insane.

Singer distinguishes between pain and death and acknowledges that the mental abilities of human beings may make their lives more valuable than those of animals. This is the pleasure side (in a broad sense of the word *pleasure*) of the utilitarian pleasure-pain calculus. People make plans, have intimate relations with other people, who may grieve for their deaths, and for these and other reasons the painless death of a human being causes on average a greater loss of utility than the painless death of a mouse. But even this rather appealing argument turns out to be at war with our deepest intuitions when we consider what it implies. It implies that the life of a chimpanzee is more valuable than the life of a human being who, because he is profoundly retarded (though not comatose), has less ability to make plans or foresee future events than the chimpanzee does. There are undoubtedly such cases. Indeed, there are people in the last stages of Alzheimer's disease who, though conscious, have less mentation than a normal dog. But killing such a person would be murder, while it is no crime at all to have a veterinarian kill one's pet dog because it has become incontinent with age. The logic of Singer's position would require that the law treat these killings alike.

(I assume he would think both permissible.) And if, for example, we could agree that although a normal human being's life is more valuable than a normal chimpanzee's life, it is only a hundred times more valuable, Singer would have to concede that if we had to choose between killing one human being and 101 chimpanzees, we should kill the human being. Against the deep revulsion that such results engender, the concept of a trans-human community of sufferers beats its tinsel wings ineffectually.

For Singer, the ability to see oneself as existing over time, with a past and a future, is an important part of what makes killing some living beings more seriously wrong than killing others. And there is scientific evidence that nonhuman primates have some of that ability. One way to interpret my numerical example is asserting that this ability might be as much as 1 percent of the ability of a *normal* human being—and then it follows from the logic of Singer's position that it is indeed worse to kill 101 of these primates than to kill a single normal human being, let alone a single retarded human being whose ability to see himself as existing over time, with a past and a future, may be little superior to that of the average chimpanzee.

A HUMANCENTRIC APPROACH

What is needed to persuade people to alter their treatment of animals is not philosophy, let alone an atheistic philosophy (for one of the premises of Singer's argument is that we have no souls) in a religious nation. It is to learn to feel animals' pains as our pains and to learn that (if it is a fact, which I do not know) we can alleviate those pains without substantially reducing our standard of living and that of the rest of the world and without sacrificing medical and other scientific progress. Most of us, especially perhaps those of us who have lived with animals, have sufficient empathy for animal suffering to support the laws that forbid cruelty and neglect. We might go further if we knew more about animal feelings and about the existence of low-cost alternatives to pain-inflicting uses of animals.[33] It follows that to expand and invigorate the laws that protect animals will require not philosophical arguments for reducing human beings to the level of the other animals but facts that will stimulate a greater empathic response to animal suffering and alleviate concern about the human costs of further measures to reduce animal suffering.[34] If enough people come to feel the sufferings of these animals as their own, public opinion and consumer preference will induce the business firms and other organizations that inflict such suffering to change their methods. In just the same way, the more altruistic that American people become toward foreigners (for example, the impoverished populations of the Third World), the greater the costs that they will be willing to incur for the benefit of foreigners.

But it does not follow that *ethical* argument either can or should affect how we feel about animals (or foreigners). Indeed I believe that ethical argument is and should be powerless against tenacious moral instincts. Such instincts may, it is true, be based on erroneous factual premises. But then what is needed is to point out the mistakes. The belief to which I referred earlier behind making it a capital offense for a human being to have sexual intercourse with an animal—that such intercourse could produce a monster—was unsound, and showing that it was unsound undermined the case for punishment. To the extent that lack of consideration for animal suffering is rooted in factual errors, pointing out those errors can change our intuitions concerning the consideration that we owe animals. Descartes believed that animals felt no pain, that the outward expressions which we took to reveal pain were deceptive. People who believe this would have no truck with laws forbidding cruelty to animals; they would not think it possible to *be* cruel to an animal, any more than to a stone. We now have good reason to believe that Descartes was mistaken. We likewise have good reason to believe that the Aztecs were mistaken about the efficacy of human sacrifice and that Nazi ideology, like other racist ideologies, rested on misconceptions about evolutionary and racial biology. To accept Cartesian, or Aztec, or Nazi premises and argue merely against the inferences from them would be futile.

The information that Singer's book *Animal Liberation* conveys, partly by means of photographs,[35] about the suffering of animals is a valuable corrective to ignorant thinking. But arguments that do not identify factual errors that underlie or buttress our moral instincts do nothing to undermine those instincts, nor should they. I have said that it is wrong to give as much weight to a dog's pain as to an infant's pain, and wrong to kill one person to save 101 chimpanzees even if a human life is only a hundred times as valuable as a chimpanzee's life. I rest these judgments on intuition. Against this intuition there is no factual reply, as there would be if my intuition were founded on a belief that dogs feel no pain and that chimpanzees have no mentation.

I do not claim that our preferring human beings to other animals is "justified" in some rational sense—only that it is a fact deeply rooted in our current thinking and feeling, a fact based on beliefs that can change but not a fact that can be shaken by philosophy. I particularly do not claim that we are rationally justified in giving preference to the suffering of humans just because it is humans who are suffering. It is because *we* are humans that we put humans first. If we were cats, we would put cats first, regardless of what philosophers might tell us. Reason doesn't enter.

There are more than a few people who would like to be able to sign a contract to be killed if they become demented. Such a contract would be unenforceable, and the physician who honored it by killing the Alzheimer's patient would be a murderer. The moral intuition that powers this result may be vulnerable to factual challenge as we learn more about Alzheimer's, as more people suffer from it, and as people come to accept more than they do today the role of physicians as "angels of mercy." What the moral intuition is not vulnerable to is an ethical argument that makes the issue contingent on a comparison of human and canine mental abilities.

Singer claims that readers of *Animal Liberation* have been persuaded by the ethical arguments in the book and not just by the facts and the pictures. If so, it is probably so only because these readers do not realize the radicalism of the ethical vision that powers Singer's views, an ethical vision that finds greater value in a healthy pig than in a profoundly retarded child, that commands inflicting a lesser pain on a human being to avert a greater pain to a dog, and that implies that, provided only that a chimpanzee has 1 percent of the mental ability of a normal human being, it is right to sacrifice the human being to save the chimpanzees. Had *Animal Liberation* emphasized these implications of Singer's utilitarian philosophy, it would have persuaded many fewer readers—and likewise if it had sought merely to persuade our rational faculty, and not to stir our empathic regard for animals.

Our moral norms regarding race, homosexuality, nonmarital sex, contraception, and suicide have changed in recent times, but not as a result of ethical arguments.[36] Philosophers have not been prominent in any of the movements. (Singer, a philosopher, has been influential in the animal rights movement, but that is a tribute to his rhetorical skills rather than to the cogency of his philosophical reasoning.) Thurgood Marshall, Earl Warren, and Martin Luther King, Jr., had a lot more to do with the development of an antidiscrimination norm than any academic philosopher. The most influential feminists, such as Betty Friedan and Catharine MacKinnon, have not been philosophers either. As far as our changing attitudes toward sex are concerned, the motive forces have again not been philosophical or, even, at root, ideological. They have been material. As the economy shifted from manufacturing (heavy, dirty work) to services (lighter, cleaner), as contraception became safer and more reliable, as desire for large families diminished (the substitution of quality for quantity of children), and as the decline in infant mortality allowed women to reduce the number of their pregnancies yet still hit their target rate of reproduction, both the demand for and the supply of women in the labor market rose. With women working more and having as a consequence greater economic independence, they demanded and obtained greater sexual independence as well. Nonmarital, nonprocreative sex, including therefore homosexual sex, began to seem less "unnatural" than it had. At the same time, myths about homosexual recruitment were exploded; homosexuality was discovered to be genetic or in any event innate rather than a consequence of a "lifestyle" choice; and so hostility to homosexuals diminished. So it is wrong to think that a vow of abstinence from philosophical argument would disempower us to condemn racism and homophobia. It was the lessons of history, and not the thought of Plato or Aristotle or Kant or Heidegger, that caused most philosophers, along with nonphilosophers, eventually to turn against racism and homophobia. Philosophy follows moral change; it does not cause it, or even lead it.

Thrasymachus in Plato's *Republic* teaches that might makes right. Socrates, while rejecting Thrasymachus's definition of justice, advocates censorship, the destruction of the family, and totalitarian rule by—philosophers. So moral philosophy has its hard side (consider also Aristotle's defense of slavery, and Kant's of capital punishment), and it is Singer, the philosopher, who is the tough guy, and I the softy, the sentimentalist, willing to base animal rights on empathy, unwilling to follow the utilitarian logic to the harsh conclusions sketched above.

I am not a moral skeptic in the sense of believing that moral beliefs have no effect on human behavior. I am merely skeptical that such beliefs can be changed by philosophical arguments (especially those of academic philosophers, given the sheltered character of the modern academic career in the United States and other wealthy liberal countries), as distinct from being changed by experience, by changes in material circumstances, by the demonstrated success or failure of particular moral principles as means of coping with the problems of life, and by personal example, charismatic authority, and appeals to emotion.

And although the efficacy and the soundness of moral arguments are *analytically* distinct issues, they are related. One reason that moral arguments are ineffective in changing behavior is their lack of cogency—their radical inconclusiveness—in a morally diverse society such as ours, where people can and do argue from incompatible premises. But there is something deeper. Moral argument often appears plausible when it is not well reasoned or logically complete, but it is almost always implausible when it is carried to its logical extreme. An illogical utilitarian (a "soft" utilitarian, we might call him) is content to say that pain is bad, that animals experience pain, so that, other things being equal, we should try to alleviate animal suffering if we can do so at a modest cost. Singer, a powerfully logical utilitarian, a "hard" utilitarian, is not content with such pabulum. He wants to pursue to its logical extreme the proposition that pain is bad for whoever or whatever experiences it. He does not flinch from the logical implication of his philosophy that if a stuck pig experiences more pain than a stuck human, the pig has the superior claim to our solicitude, or that a chimpanzee is entitled to more consideration than a profoundly retarded human being. (He does not flinch from these implications, but, as I said, in his popular writing, and in particular in *Animal Liberation*, he soft-pedals them so as not to lose his audience.)

The soft-utilitarian position on animal rights is a moral intuition of many Americans. We realize that animals feel pain, and we think that to inflict pain without a reason is bad. Nothing of practical value is added by dressing up this intuition in the language of philosophy; much is lost when the intuition is made a stage in a logical argument. When kindness toward animals is levered into a duty of weighting the pains of animals and of people equally, bizarre vistas of social engineering are opened up. Singer acknowledges that it would be odd for a democratic government to prohibit the eating of meat if the majority of its citizens were strongly and consistently in favor of meat eating, but he does not say that it would be *wrong* to force vegetarianism on the majority (not all democratic legislation is majoritarian). Nor does he indicate any reservations about legislation that would force vegetarianism on a minority of the population that was strongly and consistently in favor of meat eating. If 49 percent of the population very much wanted to eat meat, he apparently would think it right to forbid them to do so, merely because they were a minority in a democratic system.[37]

The approach that I am urging, the humancentric, takes account of such things as worry about leveling down people to animals,[38] people's love of nature and of particular animal species, and people's empathic concern with suffering animals (feeling their pain as our pain). The approach, which draws sustenance from the statistics that I quoted earlier from the Department of Agriculture, assigns no *intrinsic* value to animal welfare. It seeks reasons strictly of human welfare for according or denying rights to animals, and focuses on the consequences *for us* of recognizing animal rights. Those consequences are both good (benefits) and bad (costs—a word I am using broadly without limitation to pecuniary costs) and can be either direct or indirect. A direct humancentric benefit of giving animals rights would be the increase in human happiness brought about by knowledge that the animals we like are being protected. There is nothing surprising about human altruism toward animals. Remember what I said earlier about the dependence of early man on animals. The relationship with animals which that dependence established was not primarily one of kindness, but one of use. As our dependence on animals declined, however, our empathy with animals could stand free from any felt need to kill. If the current regard for animals on the part of members of the animal rights movement seems sentimental, we should remind ourselves that the sentiments are in all likelihood the expression of an adaptive preference that we acquired in the ancestral environment.

An indirect humancentric benefit of animal rights, though only if the welfare of the poor is weighted more heavily than that of the rich, would be the reduction in the price of food if people were vegetarians. That would eliminate the considerable costs involved in having animals process grain into meat. These costs raise nonmeat prices because, in effect, the animals are competing with people for the use of the land on which vegetables and grains are grown. A direct cost of animal rights would be the forgone benefits from medical experimentation,[39] and an indirect cost would be the cost of enforcing animal rights.

These are merely illustrations. A systematic consideration of the benefits and costs of animal rights would require attention to many other factors, such as, on the benefits side, the (unproven) possibility that reducing violence toward animals may make human beings less violent to each other,[40] and, on the costs side, both the reciprocal concern that equating humans to animals will make us less considerate of human rights (remember Hitler's zoophilia) and the concern that attention to animal rights may deflect our attention from human poverty, deprivation, and misery, including the human diseases that medical experimentation on animals may enable to be cured sooner than might otherwise be the case.

The rising interest in animal rights on the part of liberals may be another example (along with the homosexual rights movement, environmentalism generally, and even affirmative action, which tends to benefit the upper tail of the distribution of whatever group is to be helped)[41] of a flight away from the traditional liberal concern with equality in the distribution of wealth, opportunity, and power.[42] It may be a continuation and intensification of the urban-rural conflict that gave rise to animal protection legislation in England at the end of the eighteenth century. Farmers and hunters are an increasingly marginal segment of our population, and the theology of Thomas Aquinas has little hold over the minds of modern Americans, even Catholic ones. On the other hand, liberals may believe that there is a "trickle up" effect from animal rights: If animals deserve protection, a fortiori the weakest human beings do—other than the human fetus, which most modern liberals do not value highly (as highly for example as the convenience factors that motivate many abortions).

On the cost side, the practical impediments to defining and enforcing animal rights require particular emphasis. The questions I raised about Steven Wise's approach were concerned with those costs. For example, what exactly does "freedom" for animals entail, and how do we decide through the case-by-case method of common law rule making which species are to be endowed with what rights? The more we think about these questions, the less apt the vocabulary of "rights" seems. My guess is that, if pressed, Wise would admit that the only right to which most, maybe all, species should be entitled is the right not to be gratuitously tortured, wounded, or killed— and as it happens those were, at least nominally (an important qualification), the rights of Negro slaves in the antebellum South. Yet we think the essence of slavery is to be without rights. To be told now that slaves had important rights shows how the movement for animal rights can depreciate human rights.

Here is an illustration of the paradox of animal "liberation": The Animal Welfare Act to which I referred earlier is a comprehensive federal protection of animals in captivity. In a case argued before my court involving the validity of a regulation issued under the act requiring wild-animal dealers to have higher fences around their animal enclosures,[43] the government's lawyer conceded that the regulation could not be defended by reference to the interest in protecting people from the dangerous animals involved in the case, namely ligers and tigons (crosses between lions and tigers). The reason was that it was not part of the act's purpose to protect people. But, he argued, since dangerous animals that escaped from their enclosures and molested people were likely to be shot, the regulation was in fact an animal protection. Maybe so, but it was protective custody, the antithesis of freedom, that the regulation decreed.

No doubt we should want to do more than merely avoid gratuitous cruelty to animals. One of the horrors in Wise's anecdotes about the treatment of chimpanzees is that the chimps in question had been befriended by humans—had even been used to humans' profit as experimental animals—only to be abandoned to cruel treatment by other humans. Considerations of reliance and gratitude would move most people to share Wise's passionate condemnation of such conduct. More broadly, neglect and cruelty are linked; neglect can be cruel. But neither philosophical reflection nor a vocabulary of rights is likely to add anything to the sympathetic emotions that narratives of the mistreatment of animals can engender in most of us.

In speaking of animals in the large, however, I have yet to consider any distinctions among animals that a humancentric approach might make. People do not have equal regard for all the different animal species. The costs and benefits (humancentrically conceived) of measures for the protection of animals will therefore vary across species. The everyday pragmatist will not try to rank the different species by cognitive capacity or genetic closeness to humans or capacity for pain and pleasure or any other "objective" basis for distinction, the sort of thing attractive to the philosophers who write about animal rights. Yet I admit to being much taken with Richard Rorty's attempt, in a book published just four years after the first edition of Singer's *Animal Liberation*, to offer a philosophical pragmatist's answer to the question of which animal species we are prepared to admit as members of our community (*are* prepared to admit, not *should be* prepared to admit—his is not a normative analysis). He says, "Babies and the more attractive sorts of animal [unlike photoelectric cells and spiders] are credited with 'having feelings' . . . on the basis of that sort of community feeling which unites us with anything humanoid." And to be humanoid, Rorty explains:

> is to have a human face, and the most important part of that face is a mouth which we can imagine uttering sentences in synchrony with appropriate expressions of the face as a whole. . . . To say, with common sense, that babies and bats know what pain and red are like, but not what the motion of molecules or the change of seasons is like, is just to say that we can fairly readily imagine them opening their mouths and remarking on the former, but not on the latter.[44]

And so while "pigs rate much higher than koalas on intelligence tests," "pigs don't writhe in quite the right humanoid way, and the pig's face is the wrong shape for the facial expressions which go with ordinary conversation. So we send pigs to slaughter with equanimity, but form societies for the protection of koalas."[45] Rorty adds that there is nothing irrational about making such a distinction; it is based on sentiment, rather than on some misunderstanding of the "facts" about pigs and koalas.[46]

The humancentric approach establishes continuity between the animal rights movement and the love of pets, both seen as founded on sentiment rather than on philosophical idealism, and by so doing the approach helps explain the movement, parallel to the rise of the animal rights movement, to award damages for emotional suffering to pet owners whose pets are killed or injured by negligence or other (human) misconduct.[47] Animal rights ideologues, in contrast, tend to disparage the keeping of pets and regard the very word *pet* as belittling. How better to end, then, than with a judicial opinion by one of our ablest federal judges, Michael Boudin, in a heartrending pet case.[48] The plaintiff in the case had rescued an orphaned raccoon, whom she named Mia and raised as a pet. Mia lived in a cage attached to the plaintiff's home for seven years until she was seized and destroyed by the state in the episode that provoked the suit. A police officer noticed Mia in her cage and reported her to the local animal control officer, who discovered that the plaintiff did not have a permit for the animal, as required by state law. The police then forcibly seized Mia from her cage, after a struggle with the plaintiff, carried her off, and had her killed and tested for rabies; testing for rabies in a raccoon requires that the animal be killed, and a supposed epidemic of raccoon rabies had led the state (Rhode Island) to require the testing of raccoons to whom humans (namely, the plaintiff) had been exposed. Mia tested negative, but of course it was too late for Mia.

The plaintiff claimed that the state had deprived her of property, namely Mia, without notice or a hearing and thus in violation of the due process clause of the Fourteenth Amendment. Property for these purposes depends on state law, and the court found, undoubtedly correctly, that Rhode Island does not recognize property rights in wild animals unless a permit has been granted; and fear of rabies had deterred the authorities from granting permits to own raccoons. To be owned is the antithesis of being a rights holder. But if Rhode Island had a more generous conception of property in wild animals, the police might have been deterred from what appears to have been the high-handed, indeed arbitrary, treatment of Mia. As the court explained, it does not seem that the plaintiff had been "exposed" to Mia in the relevant statutory sense: There was no indication that the raccoon had bitten the plaintiff nor that her saliva had otherwise entered the plaintiff's bloodstream. And since Mia had been in a cage for seven years, it was highly unlikely that she was infected with rabies. From the standpoint of controlling the spread of rabies, moreover, there was no reason to worry about Mia infecting the plaintiff, since people do not spread rabies. Mia was dangerous, if at all, only to the plaintiff, who was happy to assume the risk. The refusal to allow her to keep the raccoon made no sense at all, but there was no constitutional issue because it was not the plaintiff's "property" within the meaning of the due process clause of the Fourteenth Amendment.

This is just one example, and does not prove that animals are benefited less by having human-type "rights" and thus being "free" than by being "imprisoned" and by being "reduced" to "mere" property. I note in this connection that the average life span of a stray alley cat is only about two years, and of a well-cared-for pet cat at least twelve years, but that is just another example. No doubt the most aggressive implementations of animal rights thinking would benefit animals more than commodification and a more determined program of enforcing existing laws against cruelty to animals. But those implementations are unlikely, and so the modest alternatives are worth serious consideration. We may overlook this simple point if, however much we love animals, we listen too raptly to the siren song of animal rights, whether the singer is a practicing lawyer-deontologist or a distinguished utilitarian philosopher.

NOTES

This chapter is an amalgam with many changes of (1) Posner's book review of Steven Wise's book *Rattling the Cage: Toward Legal Rights for Animals* (2000) ("Animal Rights," 110 *Yale Law Journal* 527 [2000]); (2) a talk he gave at Animal Rights: A Symposium (organized by Martha Nussbaum) at the University of Chicago Law School on April 13, 2001; and (3) a debate that he had with Peter Singer in the online magazine *Slate*, "Dialogue: Animal Rights," *Slate*, June 12–15, 2001, http://slate.msn.com/dialogues/01-06-11/dialogues.asp?iMsg=2D. The author wishes to thank Bryan Dayton and Matthew Powers for research assistance and Michael Boudin, Richard Epstein, Lawrence Lessig, Martha Nussbaum, Charlene Posner, and Cass Sunstein for comments on an early draft of the book review.

1. Steven M. Wise, *Rattling the Cage: Toward Legal Rights for Animals* (2000). Wise's book illustrates a rapidly growing legal literature on the protection of animals. Besides the essays in this book, see, for example, Adam Kolber, "Standing Upright: The Moral and Legal Standing of Humans and Other Apes," 54 *Stanford Law Review* 173 (2001); David Favre, "Equitable Self-Ownership for Animals," 50 *Duke Law Journal* 473 (2000); Cass R. Sunstein, "Standing for Animals (with Notes on Animal Rights)," 47 *UCLA Law Review* 1333 (2000); Gary L. Francione, "Animal Rights and Animal Welfare," 48 *Rutgers Law Review* 397 (1996).

2. These are closely related species, and Wise discusses them more or less interchangeably. For the sake of brevity, I will generally refer only to chimpanzees, but what I say about them applies equally to bonobos.

3. On which, see Martha C. Nussbaum, *Upheavals of Thought: The Intelligence of Emotions*, ch. 2 (2001).

4. See E. P. Evans, *The Criminal Prosecution and Capital Punishment of Animals* (1906), cited in Richard Sorabji, *Animal Minds and Human Morals: The Origins of the Western Debate* 116 n. 54 (1993).

5. Richard A. Posner, *Sex and Reason* 213 (1992).

6. They did not, however, worship cats—a stubborn fallacy. They believed that gods frequently inhabited cats, which made cats sacred animals, meriting exceptional consideration (the killing of a cat was a capital offense), but the cats were not considered gods. See Donald Engels, *Classical Cats: The Rise and Fall of the Sacred Cat*, ch. 1 (1999).

7. Sorabji's book, note 4 above, is an exhaustive examination of this question. See also Martha C. Nussbaum, "Animal Rights: The Need for a Theoretical Basis," 114 *Harvard Law Review* 1506, 1513–1519 (2001).

8. See, for a notable instance, Julian Baldick, *Animal and Shaman: Ancient Religions of Central Asia* 167–170 (2000).

9. On the history of animal protection, see Richard D. Ryder, *Animal Revolution: Changing Attitudes toward Speciesism* (1989).

10. See Hilda Kean, *Animal Rights: Political and Social Change in Britain since 1800* (1998).

11. Wise, note 1 above, at 128 (emphasis in original; footnote omitted).

12. See also Alasdair MacIntyre, *Dependent Rational Animals: Why Human Beings Need the Virtues*, chs. 2–5 (1999).

13. See Michael Tomasello and Josep Call, *Primate Cognition* 393, 400, 426–429 (1997).

14. For scientific support, see, for example, Donald R. Griffin, *Animal Minds: Beyond Cognition to Consciousness* (2d ed. 2001); S. T. Boysen and G. T. Himes, "Current Issues and Emerging Theories in Animal Cognition," 50 *Annual Review of Psychology* 683 (1999); A. Whiten et al., "Cultures in Chimpanzees," 399 *Nature* 682 (1999); Christopher Boesch and Michael Tomasello, "Chimpanzee and Human Cultures," 39 *Current Anthropology* 591 (1998).

15. Sorabji, note 4 above, at 2.

16. See, for example, Bruce Ackerman, *Social Justice in the Liberal State* 80 (1980) ("the rights of the talking ape are more secure than those of the human vegetable").

17. Hull v. Scruggs, 2 So. 2d 543 (Miss. 1941).

18. John Dewey, "Logical Method and Law," 10 *Cornell Law Quarterly* 17 (1924). For amplification of his proposal, see Richard A. Posner, *Law, Pragmatism, and Democracy*, chs. 1–3, 8 (2003).

19. Dewey, note 18 above, at 22.

20. The philosophical literature is extensive. For some illustrative contributions, see Alasdair MacIntyre, note 12 above, at chs. 2–5; Nussbaum, note 7 above, at 1527–1536; Sorabji, note 4 above; James Rachels, *Created from Animals: The Moral Implications of Darwinism* (1990); Tom Regan, *The Case for Animal Rights* (1983); Roger Scruton, *Animal Rights and Wrongs* (3d ed. 2000); Peter Singer, *Animal Liberation* (rev. ed. 1990); Angus Taylor, *Magpies, Monkeys, and Morals: What Philosophers Say about Animal Liberation* (1999); and see generally Ian Hacking, "Our Fellow Animals," *New York Review of Books*, June 29, 2000, p. 20. Scruton's book is a well-written, well-argued, and ingenious attack on the animal liberation movement, but so strange (for example, in its paean to fox hunting, Scruton, above, at 116–122) that it will turn most readers in favor of the movement. The other books that I have cited defend the movement with varying degrees of zeal that will turn some other readers against the movement. Scruton, however, wins the prize for the best chapter title: "Duty and the Beast."

21. The distinction between philosophical and everyday pragmatism is emphasized in Posner, note 18 above.

22. See Gary L. Francione, *Rain without Thunder: The Ideology of the Animal Rights Movement* 10 (1996).

23. See Singer, note 20 above, at 159.

24. Id.

25. Id.

26. "Pragmatists are committed to taking Darwin seriously. They grant that

human beings are unique in the animal kingdom in having language, but they urge that language be understood as a tool rather than as a picture. A species' gradual development of language is as readily explicable in Darwinian terms as its gradual development of spears or pots, but it is harder to explain how a species could have acquired the ability to *represent* the universe—especially the universe as it really is (as opposed to how it is usefully described, relative to the particular needs of that species)." Richard Rorty, "Pragmatism," in *Routledge Encyclopedia of Philosophy* 633, 636 (Edward Craig ed., 1998) (emphasis in original). See also Posner, note 18 above, ch. 1.

27. The tension between environmentalism and animal liberation is emphasized in Taylor, note 20 above, ch. 6.

28. See Luc Ferry, *The New Ecological Order*, ch. 5 (1995); Boria Sax, *Animals in the Third Reich: Pets, Scapegoats, and the Holocaust*, ch. 11 (2000).

29. The sources of the data in this paragraph are the 1996 and 1999 Animal Welfare Reports of the U.S.D.A.

30. Singer, note 20 above, at 220.

31. Id. at 8.

32. Id. at 1.

33. For an illustrative recent study, see Jeffrey Moussaieff Masson, *The Nine Emotional Lives of Cats: A Journey into the Feline Heart* (2002).

34. I do not wish to prejudge the results of these inquiries, which might actually allay some concerns over medical experiments on animals. As Griffin sensibly remarks, note 14 above, at 267, "To test promising new surgical procedures on deeply anesthetized rats that otherwise have lived reasonably optimal lives seems a justifiable trade-off."

35. Singer, note 20 above, following p. 132. Almost half the book (pp. 25–157) is devoted to descriptions of the human infliction of pain and suffering on animals in medical experimentation and in agriculture.

36. See Richard A. Posner, *The Problematics of Moral and Legal Theory*, ch. 1 (1999).

37. For other criticisms of Singer's philosophy of animal liberation, see Kolber, note 1 above, at 182–191.

38. Singer is a "leveler down," arguing that animal liberation provides support for the euthanasia of human beings. Singer, note 20 above, at 20.

39. On the issues involved in minimizing the use of animals, and animal suffering, in medical research, see the comprehensive treatment in *Animal Alternatives: Welfare and Ethics* (L. F. M. Zutphen and M. Balls eds., 1997). Historically, experimentation on animals has been vital to progress in the treatment of human diseases. See discussion and references in Adrian R. Morrison, "Personal Reflections on the 'Animal Rights' Phenomenon," 44 *Perspectives in Biology and Medicine* 62 (2001). But how true that is today I do not know; for a vociferous denial, though without specifics or evidence, see Nedim C. Buyukmihci, "Animal Rights: The Use of Nonhuman Animals in Research," 82 *Law Library Journal* 351 (1990). I have been unable to find estimates of the cost to medical science of doing without any, or with fewer, or with specific species of animals as experimental subjects.

40. Are the Spanish, who watch bullfights in which the bull is killed, more violent toward each other than the Mexicans, who watch bullfights in which the bull is not killed, or than Americans, who do not watch bullfights at all? I don't

think so. But this is not to deny the possibility that children who torture or otherwise abuse animals may be more likely than other children to "graduate" to violent behavior toward human beings. See Frank R. Ascione, "Animal Abuse and Youth Violence," U.S. Dept. of Justice, Office of Juvenile Justice and Delinquency Prevention, *Juvenile Justice Bulletin* (Sept. 2001).

41. When Harvard, for example, bends its admissions standards to increase the representation of blacks or Hispanics in its student body, the blacks or Hispanics benefited are those least in need of a helping hand, since anyone who is just below Harvard's admission standard will be able without affirmative action to win admission to and do well at an excellent college, even if it is not quite Harvard. But recall how Wise uses opposition to affirmative action to reinforce the case for animal rights.

42. Except that Singer derives both a duty to protect animals and a duty to redistribute income from utilitarian premises. See Peter Berkowitz, "Other People's Mothers: The Utilitarian Horrors of Peter Singer," *New Republic*, Jan. 10, 2000, p. 27.

43. Hoctor v. U.S. Dept. of Agriculture, 82 F.3d 165 (7th Cir. 1996).

44. Richard Rorty, *Philosophy and the Mirror of Nature* 189 (1979).

45. Id. at 190.

46. Id. at 190–191.

47. See Miranda Oshige McGowan, "Property's *Portrait of a Lady*," 85 *Minnesota Law Review* 1037, 1103–1106 (2001).

48. Bilida v. McCleod, 211 F.3d 166 (1st Cir. 2000).

3

PETER SINGER

ETHICS BEYOND SPECIES AND BEYOND INSTINCTS

A Response to Richard Posner

I believe that ethical argument is and should be powerless against tenacious moral instincts.

—RICHARD POSNER, "Animal Rights: Legal, Philosophical, and Pragmatic Perspectives"

"Where might we go," Richard Posner asks, "necessarily outside rather than inside law, for reasons for changing the law to entitle animals?" I begin by sketching my answer to that question—briefly, because I have done it at length in other writings.[1] Then I discuss Posner's contrasting views, both on the specific issue of the proper status of animals and on the wider question of the role that ethical argument should play in such questions.

EQUAL CONSIDERATION FOR ANIMALS

Most people draw a sharp moral line between humans and other animals. Humans, they say, are infinitely more valuable than any "lower creatures." If our interests conflict with those of animals, it is always their interests which should be sacrificed. But why should this be so? To say that everyone believes this is not enough to justify it. Until very recently it was the common view that a woman should obey her father, until she is married, and then her husband (and in some countries, this is still the prevailing view). Or, not quite so recently, but still not all that long ago, it was widely held that people of African descent could properly be enslaved. As these examples show, the fact that a view is widespread does not make it right. It may be an indefensible prejudice that survives primarily because it suits the interests of the dominant group.

How should we decide whether a widely held view is justifiable, or a prejudice based on the interests of the dominant group? The obvious answer is that we should consider what reasons are offered for the view. Putting aside religious grounds that would force us to examine the foundations of the particular religions of which they are a consequence, the reason given usually refers to some kind of human superiority over animals. After all, are not human beings more rational, more self-aware, more capable of a sense of justice, and so on, than any nonhuman animals? But while this claim may be true if limited to normal mature human beings, it does not help us to defend the place where we now draw the moral line, which is between *all* members of our species and *all* nonhuman animals. For there are many humans who are not rational, or self-aware, and who have no sense of justice—all humans under one month of age, for a start. And even if infants are excluded on the grounds that they have the potential to become rational, self-aware, and have a sense of justice, not all humans have this potential. Sadly, some are born with brain damage so severe that they will never be rational or self-aware, or capable of a sense of justice. In fact, some of these humans will never possess any intellectual or emotional capacities that are not also possessed by any normal, non-infant chimpanzee, dog, cat, pig, cow, or even laboratory rat.

Hence it seems that no adequate reason can be given for taking species membership, in itself, as the ground for putting some beings inside the boundary of moral protection and others either totally or very largely outside it. That doesn't mean that all animals have the same rights as humans. It would be absurd to give animals the right to vote, but then it would be no less absurd to give that right to infants or to severely retarded human beings. Yet we still give equal consideration to the interests of those humans incapable of voting. We don't raise them for food, nor test cosmetics in their eyes. Nor should we. But we do these things to nonhuman animals who show greater rationality, self-awareness, and a sense of justice than they do.

Once we understand that in respect of any valuable characteristic we can think of, there is no gap between humans and animals, but rather an overlap in the possession of that characteristic by individuals of different species, it is easy to see the belief that all humans are somehow infinitely more valuable than any animal is a prejudice. It is in some respects akin to the prejudice that racists have in favor of their own race, and sexists have in favor of their own gender (although there are also differences, as with any complex social phenomena). Speciesism is logically parallel to racism and sexism, in the sense that speciesists, racists, and sexists all say: The boundary of my own group is also the boundary of my concern. Never mind what you are like, if you are a member of my group, you are superior to all those who are not members of my group. The speciesist favors a larger group than the racist, and so has a larger circle of concern, but all of these prejudices use an

79

arbitrary and morally irrelevant fact—membership in a race, gender, or species—as if it were morally crucial.

The only acceptable limit to our moral concern is the point at which there is no awareness of pain or pleasure and no conscious preferences of any kind. That is why pigs are objects of moral concern, but lettuces are not. Pigs can feel pain and pleasure, they can enjoy their lives, or want to escape from distressing conditions. To the best of our knowledge, lettuces can't. We should give the same weight to the pain and distress of pigs as we would give to a similar amount of pain and distress suffered by a human being. Of course, pigs and humans may have different interests, and there are some human interests that a pig is probably incapable of having—like, for example, our interest in living to see our grandchildren. There may, therefore, sometimes be grounds for giving preference to the human over the pig—but if so, it can only be because in the particular circumstances the human has greater interests at stake, and not simply because the human is a member of our own species.

MORAL AND OTHER INSTINCTS

The argument I have just sketched leads to the conclusion that we should change the moral status of animals in order to give greater consideration to the interests of the animals. We should do this, obviously, for the sake of the animals. In contrast, Posner tells us that he prefers a "pragmatic" to a "philosophical" approach to the question of changing the moral status of animals, and we should do so only insofar as this fits with a "humancentric" perspective. I shall argue that this position is indefensible.

Although Posner contrasts his own pragmatism to a philosophical approach, this rhetorical ploy should not deceive us, any more than we would allow ourselves to be fooled by someone running for Congress on a platform of "let's vote out the politicians." It is no more possible to reject the value of philosophical argument without taking a philosophical position than it is to win public office without being involved in politics. If it were not already obvious that Posner's pragmatism is a philosophical position about the nature of ethics, he would have given the game away by including the words "and should be" in the sentence I have quoted at the head of this essay—words which, as we shall see, cry out for justification. So the only question is which philosophical position we should accept.

The foundation of Posner's position is summed up in that quoted sentence, which also appeared in an earlier exchange I had with Posner in the online magazine *Slate*. On that occasion I criticized the inclusion of the words "and should be," and charitably—as I thought—suggested that perhaps they had been slipped in without too much thought. But now here they are again, with exactly the same words, in a scholarly essay. We have to assume that Posner means what he says, at least when he says it twice.

The meaning of the sentence is not as clear as it first appears. What are "moral instincts"? If the word *moral* is doing any work here, Posner must have a way of distinguishing moral instincts from nonmoral instincts. Drawing lines between what is moral and what is nonmoral is a much-debated issue in moral philosophy. I am willing to save Posner the work of investigating it by offering him a criterion for drawing the distinction. Here it is:

> We can distinguish the moral from the nonmoral by appeal to the idea that when we think, judge, or act within the realm of the moral, we do so in a manner that we are prepared to apply to all others who are similarly placed.

Thus, if I am making moral judgments about thefts of loaves of bread from a bakery, I may make different judgments in cases in which the thief was well-fed from cases in which the thief was starving, but I may not do so in cases in which I am the thief and other cases in which I am the baker. "It makes *me* better off" is not an acceptable ground for differentiating two otherwise relevantly similar moral situations. Thus to make a moral judgment is to accept constraints on the extent to which you can give preference to your own interests or to those of your own group.

If the criterion I offer lacks originality, at least it comes with the endorsement of a long line of philosophers going back through Kant to Stoics like Marcus Aurelius. Following R. M. Hare, I shall use the term *universalizable* to refer to this distinguishing feature of moral judgments.[2] Universalizability does not mean that it is never justifiable to give preference to one's own family, or nation. Giving preference to one's own group may itself be justifiable from a universal point of view, for example, in accordance with the principle "all parents should put the welfare of their own children above the welfare of other children." But this principle must itself be justifiable from a universal point of view.

Suppose that Posner accepts this solution to the problem of distinguishing the moral from the nonmoral, and uses it to explain his claim that ethical argument is and should be powerless against tenacious moral instincts. He would then be saying that ethical argument is and should be powerless against those instincts which are both tenacious and universalizable. But note that this way of distinguishing moral instincts from nonmoral instincts already provides scope for a certain amount of ethical argument. Whenever Posner claims that an instinct is a moral one, we can inquire whether those who act on this instinct, or make judgments based on it, are acting or judging in a way that they are prepared to apply universalizably. Hence the sentence I quoted must be rewritten as: "I believe that ethical argument is and should be powerless against those tenacious instincts that survive the universalizability test." But now the sentence has become much less significant than it first appeared, because the whole issue will come down to: Which instincts survive the test of universalizability? One cannot know whether one

81

is prepared to hold a judgment universalizably unless one is prepared to put oneself in the position of all those affected by it. That requires both information—about what it is like to be one of those affected by the act being judged—and sincerity in taking on, and not discounting, the perspectives of others affected.

Indeed, to return to the specific topic with which this volume is concerned, I would argue that many of our instincts regarding animals *cannot* survive the test of universalizability. We humans instinctively do things to animals that are for our benefit, without in any way putting ourselves in their situation. The humancentric view that Posner endorses is prima facie based on just such an instinct and will not, without more argument, survive the universalizability test.

By this time the reader will have realized that in offering Posner a solution to his problem of distinguishing moral and nonmoral instincts, I was not being entirely altruistic. But if Posner rejects my offer, what else might do the job of distinguishing moral and nonmoral interests?

Since the word *instincts* suggests something fairly deeply rooted in human nature, and Posner accepts that human nature is best understood as the outcome of Darwinian evolution (on this, we are in agreement) the most obvious candidate is that by "moral instincts" we mean those instincts that evolved in the social mammals to make it easier for them to survive together in the small groups in which we and our ancestors lived for most of our evolutionary history. This is very vague, however, and fails to provide any clear line between moral instincts and other instincts. Presumably a sense of reciprocity counts as a moral instinct, since it helps primates to bond with unrelated members of the group and can be seen as the basis for ethical precepts that are universal, or virtually so, among humans, such as the precept of gratitude, or doing good to those who do good to us, and the precept of retribution, or doing harm to those who harm us. Some sense of group loyalty, leading us to respond more favorably to members of our own group than we do to strangers, might be another moral instinct. But what else?

Consider two more examples of instincts that are very typical of humans and other primates: parent-child bonds and competition for leadership among males. Is care for one's own children, in preference to the children of others, a moral instinct? Is the male drive to get to the top a moral instinct? Both offer some benefit to the wider group—without the former, the group would have no future, and the latter serves to ensure that the group is led by aggressive males—but both also benefit the parent and the successful males and can lead to conflict within the group, sometimes with fatal results. Without a criterion like universalizability by which to screen such instincts, the decision to include or reject them within the sphere of moral instincts seems arbitrary.

Nevertheless, suppose that Posner were to agree, as many people might, that to care for one's own children is a moral instinct, whereas ambition to get to the top is a nonmoral instinct. Then the sentence under discussion would mean that ethical argument is and should be powerless against the instinct to care for one's own children in preference to those of others but is not, or should not be, powerless against the instinct to get to the top. In factual terms, ethical argument seems as effective (or not) against the latter as it is against the former. Can Posner defend the conclusion that it *should* be powerless against the former, but not against the latter? It is hard to see how Posner could produce an argument for this conclusion that would not violate his own (sound) warning that we should not "draw a normative inference arbitrarily from a biological fact." An evolutionary account of the formation of some of our instincts does not allow us to deduce what ought to be the case.

Even at a commonsense level, Posner's position is implausible. Whatever the moral instincts may turn out to be, why exempt just those ones from the power of ethical argument? Our instincts, moral and nonmoral, developed during the eons of time in which we and our ancestors lived in circumstances very different from those in which we live today. For most of our evolutionary history, we lived in small groups in which everyone knew everyone else in the group, and interactions with members of our species who were not also members of our group were rare. The planet was sparsely populated, which was just as well, since we had no way of consciously regulating our reproductive capacities. There were ample uncleared forests, no ill effects from our emissions of greenhouse gases, and our weapons killed one at a time, and only in close proximity. Isn't it highly probable that moral instincts formed under those circumstances *should* be changed by ethical argument based on our current, very different circumstances?

The only way in which Posner is prepared to allow argument to have an impact on our moral instincts is by demonstrating a factual error in the assumptions on which our instincts are based. (For example, correcting factual errors about the capacities of animals to suffer, or that sexual intercourse with an animal leads to the birth of a monster, is in his view an acceptable way of arguing against an instinct.) Sometimes, however, we need to change moral instincts that do not rest on factual errors. Although it is always controversial what is really an instinct, and what is acquired by culture and education, we can take, as an example, preference for my "own kind" over someone who talks, looks, or smells differently. This preference, which is plausibly instinctive, does not require any false factual beliefs. Rather, people add factual beliefs about the negative characteristics of the outsiders in order to strengthen the hold of the instinct that they already have.

So far I have been arguing that Posner's inclusion of the word *moral* in the sentence we are discussing creates a dilemma for him. Either he uses something like the universalizability criterion to separate the moral instincts from the nonmoral ones, in which case he has to admit that there is scope for ethical argument, or he is left with a distinction between different kinds of instincts that is irrelevant to which of them should, and which should not, be immune from the power of ethical argument. Faced with this dilemma, Posner might contemplate dropping the word *moral* from the sentence. But Posner would still have to explain why he thinks ethical argument (based, for example, on the requirement that we hold our judgments universalizably) not only is, but *should be* powerless to change *any* tenacious instinct, no matter how aggressive, murderous, or xenophobic that instinct may be.

IS ETHICAL ARGUMENT POWERLESS AGAINST INSTINCTS?

Perhaps, in seeking to understand why Posner might want to defend this view, we should return to his original sentence. I have focused on the claim that ethical argument *should be* powerless against instincts, and so far have not considered the claim that ethical argument *is* powerless against instincts. Logically, these are separate claims, and Posner himself phrased the question he wished to pursue, in the second half of his essay, as an inquiry into "reasons for changing the law to entitle animals." What actually leads people to change their votes about laws relating to animals or to change their diets or other aspects of their behavior toward animals is one thing; what reasons there are for changing the law about animals is another thing. It would be perfectly possible to hold that ethical argument *is* powerless against instincts, but that it *should not* be. Nevertheless, the way in which Posner amalgamates the two claims in the sentence we are examining suggests that he may believe that the two claims go together. This much can, at least, be said for that amalgamation: If the factual claim were true, the normative claim would become much less interesting. "Ought implies can" is a widely accepted principle in moral philosophy (although its correct use requires careful attention to the different varieties of impossibility in action), and if ethical argument simply cannot have any power over tenacious instincts, then there isn't a lot of point in discussing whether it ought to have such power. Hence it is worth examining the truth of the factual claim.

Is ethical argument powerless against tenacious instincts? If so, it would be hard to explain the moral progress that has been made in areas in which, previously, some of our most tenacious moral instincts have held sway. Consider areas like race relations, crimes of genocide and crimes against humanity, gender issues, attitudes to homosexuality, and the area here under discussion, the treatment of animals. In discussing such changes, Posner provides us with a textbook example of *ignoratio elenchi*, or the fallacy of the irrelevant conclusion:

> Our moral norms regarding race, homosexuality, nonmarital sex, contraception, and suicide have changed in recent times, but not as a result of ethical arguments. Philosophers have not been prominent in

any of the movements. . . . Thurgood Marshall, Earl Warren, and Martin Luther King, Jr., had a lot more to do with the development of an antidiscrimination norm than any academic philosopher.

Note how the initial claim that "ethical arguments" did not bring about these changes is suddenly turned into the entirely separate claim that "philosophers" were not prominent in these movements, and then at the end, this becomes a claim about "academic philosopher[s]." But that is not what was to be shown. Can anyone read the judgments of Thurgood Marshall or Earl Warren, or the speeches of Martin Luther King, Jr., and not believe that they were putting forward ethical arguments?

Elsewhere Posner says, "There were strong arguments, vigorously advanced, against Negro slavery before 1861, but it took a Civil War to end the practice." But that is a parochial view. Neither in France nor in Britain, both of which had extensive colonial slave-owning interests, did it take a civil war to abolish slavery. In the French case, it took a revolution, and the influence of the eighteenth-century *philosophes* on the revolutionaries was, prima facie, strong. In the British case, William Wilberforce and his friends consistently put their case in ethical terms and were successful on that basis. Perhaps Posner might like to restrict his claims about the powerlessness of ethical arguments, acknowledging that such arguments can be effective in other countries, but maintaining that they are powerless in the United States? Currently, the differences between the United States and most other governments in the developed world on issues like global warming and the International Criminal Court, as well as the very low level of foreign aid that the United States gives to the world's poorest countries, would lend some support to such a claim.

As another example, take the tenacious instinct that leads humans to show unprovoked hostility, sometimes to the point of murder, against those who belong to different tribes or nations. Those who believe that this is not an instinct, but the product of relatively recent economic, social, or cultural circumstances, should read the Bible, and see how often the Israelites massacred their neighbors, often without serious provocation.[3] But in ancient times, there was nothing unusual about this. War, as Lawrence Keeley has shown, has been a regular part of the existence of the overwhelming majority of human cultures. Massacres of entire groups seem not to have been unusual.[4] Additional evidence that this killing has its roots deep in our biological nature is provided by observations of similar intraspecies killing among our close relatives, the chimpanzees.[5] Yet, tenacious as this instinct is, we are making progress in confronting it. It is a sobering thought that in many tribal societies, despite the absence of machine guns and high explosives, the percentage of the population killed annually in warfare far exceeds that of any modern society, including Germany and Russia in the twentieth century.[6] Though the conflict between Israel and Palestine is tragic and depressing, there is widespread agreement that it should not be solved by the methods used by the ancient Israelites. Since the mass genocides of the twentieth century, we have developed principles of humanitarian intervention to stop such occurrences, and even instituted an International Criminal Court to bring to justice those who commit crimes against humanity. Needless to say, these positive developments have been accompanied by plenty of ethical argument, from the Universal Declaration of Human Rights—a document drafted, incidentally, by a commission on which two men who had been "academic philosophers" played a significant role[7]—to the statements of countless prominent secular and religious figures. While one could certainly wish that these ethical arguments had been more effective, to claim that they are *all* completely without effect is, to use one of Posner's phrases, sheer assertion, and not particularly plausible assertion at that.

Posner's claim, even in its narrow application to academic philosophers, is directly contradicted by the two most authoritative studies of the history of the modern animal movement. In *The Animal Rights Crusade: The Growth of a Moral Protest*, the American sociologists James Jasper and Dorothy Nelkin write, "As 'professionals' of moral discourse, philosophers who deal with ethical questions have a natural—and central—role to play in moral crusades, and they were crucial to the birth of the animal rights movement. . . . Philosophers served as midwives of the animal rights movement in the late 1970s."[8]

In a study that focuses more on the British animal movement, politics professor Robert Garner takes a similar view:

> Central to this explosion of concern [about the need to alleviate harms done to animals] has been the philosophical input. For the first time, those concerned about the treatment of animals have had the benefit of a sustained attempt by academic philosophers to change radically the status afforded to animals in moral thinking. The result has been the development of a "new" ideology (or, to be more precise, ideologies) which has had profound implications both for the movement which seeks to protect animals and for the way in which the debate about their treatment has been conducted.[9]

In the animal movement, at least, the truth is diametrically the opposite of Posner's assertion that "philosophy follows moral change; it does not cause it, or even lead it."

How is it possible that ethical argument can be effective given that, as Posner and many others have pointed out, there is great difficulty in establishing the first premises of any ethical position? The answer is that ethical argument does not always proceed from first premises. It may, for example, show that a widely held view is inconsistent, or leads to conflicts with other views that its supporters hold. (Look again at the ethical argument about the moral status of animals with which this essay opened, and you will see that it takes this form.) Ethical argument can also show that particular views have been held unreflectively. Once they are subjected to critique, and applied to a wider range of situations than had previously been considered, the view may become less attractive. Though ethical argument would be easier if we could establish first premises, it is a mistake to assume that without it, it must be ineffective.

Universalizability also plays a role, as we have already seen. We are reasoning beings, capable of seeking broader justifications. There may be some who are ruthless enough to say that they care only for their own interests or for the interests of those of their own group, and if anyone else gets in the way, too bad for them; but many of us seek to justify our conduct in broader, more widely acceptable terms. That is how ethical argument gets going, and why it can examine, criticize, and, in the long run, overturn tenacious moral instincts.

THE USEFULNESS OF AVOIDING PRAGMATISM IN ETHICS

Shorn of the pretension of being something other than a philosophical position and of its belief in the total inefficacy of ethical reasoning, Posner's pragmatism turns out to be an undefended and indefensible form of selective moral conservatism. It is also, ironically, a potentially dangerous position, which makes it self-refuting, or at least self-effacing (i.e., those who hold it will, if they follow their own principles, pretend that they don't). Consider the way in which Posner takes the "brute fact that we, like other animals, prefer our own" as a starting point for moral argument. If this supports our current treatment of animals, why should it not also be used to support other preferences for "our own," which appear to be just as much a brute fact about human beings as a preference for our own species? Here is one example: "We must be honest, decent, loyal, and friendly to members of our blood and to no one else. What happens to the Russians, what happens to the Czechs, is a matter of utter indifference to me." The speaker is Heinrich Himmler. He goes on to say, "Whether the other races live in comfort or perish of hunger interests me only insofar as we need them as slaves for our culture; apart from that it does not interest me."[10]

I am, of course, far from suggesting that Posner would support such sentiments. But how, consistently with what he says about one instinctive preference, can he reject the other? Posner's difficulty is made totally intractable by his refusal to defend his preference for humans over animals: "I do not claim that our preferring human beings to other animals is 'justified' in some rational sense—only that it is a fact deeply rooted in our current thinking and feeling." Why should Himmler not say the same, with the substitution of "Germans" for "human beings" and "human beings" for "animals"? The Nazis were, in fact, strong defenders of moral "feeling," elevating "the healthy sensibility of the people" (*gesundes Volksempfinden*) to a supreme legal precept and using it as the basis for outlawing homosexuality.[11] Moreover, looking coolly at human history, an instinctive preference for "our own" in a racial or ethnic sense seems scarcely less firm and enduring than the preference for our own species. So Himmler could have been quite at home with a Posner-style, pragmatic defense of his position.[12]

Posner comments on the possible application of his argument for a preference for "our own" to race and gender, but what he says raises more questions than it answers: "Membership in the human species is not a morally irrelevant fact, as the race and gender of human beings have come to seem." Note the curious choice of the words "have come to seem," in respect of the relevance of race and gender. This suggests that, for Posner, there is no fact of the matter here. If race and gender had not "come to seem" morally irrelevant, they would not be morally irrelevant. Posner has to say that, given what he has said about ethical argument. For the rest of us, however, it is precisely because there is and should be such a thing as ethical argument that we do not have to accept racism and sexism, whether they *seem* morally relevant to people or not.

Unfortunately, Posner's statement that race and gender have come to seem irrelevant is still not globally true. Even in the United States, there are many people who believe that race and gender are morally relevant, and no doubt would like to return to earlier, more traditional ways of separating both whites and nonwhites, and males and females. If it comes to be widely believed that there is no ethical argument that should count against such views, it is entirely possible that many more people would feel free openly to state that they are happier mixing only with "their own" racial or ethnic group in schools, colleges, restaurants, bars, and holiday resorts, and many men may come out into the open about their desire to push women back into a more traditional subordinate status.

REBUTTALS

Now that we have disposed of the foundations of Posner's view that ethical argument should be powerless against tenacious moral instincts, let us turn briefly to some of the arguments and counterarguments that he, in dubious consistency with his own premise, assembles in his essay.

First, Posner's critical remarks against my own position are often astray: "[Singer] does not consider the gastronomic benefits to human beings who like meat, though nothing in utilitarianism authorizes the exclusion of such a benefit." On the contrary, I am sufficiently concerned with "gastronomic benefits" to argue, in *Animal Liberation*, that those who switch to a vegetarian diet will, over time, enjoy their food at least as much as they did before, and that they are likely to be healthier and fitter as well.[13] In the first edition of the book, I even provided my readers with recipes, to ensure no loss of gastronomic benefits.[14] Elsewhere, I argue that these are minor human interests that we should not allow to outweigh the more major interests of nonhuman animals.[15]

Another piece of sloppy scholarship gives a misleading impression of my own scholarly standards. Posner writes: "Peter Singer claims that 25 million animals are annually subjected to experimentation, but does not give a source for this figure." The footnote to this sentence refers to *Animal Liberation*. That puzzled me, because the third chapter of that book contains a long, fully documented account of research on animals that includes a discussion of five separate official and unofficial estimates of the numbers of animals used in the United States. The source of each estimate is given.[16] So I checked the page number that Posner gives. It is to a passing reference in a much later chapter, where I am not discussing research on animals, but simply reminding the reader of the scale of the suffering that humans inflict on animals in various ways, including experimentation. I thought I could assume that a reader wanting more detailed information on animals used in research would look at the chapter devoted exclusively to that subject.

One final example before I come to more serious issues:

> [Singer] is on somewhat firmer ground in disregarding the effect of vegetarianism on the number of animals, for total utilitarianism (maximizing utility without regard to its distribution) is an especially counterintuitive form of utilitarianism. But average utilitarianism is not much more appealing, as it implies that a very small population of exquisitely cosseted, and therefore supremely happy, beings (human or animal) is the goal that we should be striving to attain.

Since I am sure that Posner would not deliberately mislead his readers, his suggestion that the choice between forms of utilitarianism is limited to total and average utilitarianism can only be the result of complete ignorance of the extensive literature discussing alternatives to total utilitarianism other than average utilitarianism. No philosopher familiar with the field would pose the choice in those terms, because average utilitarianism has long been refuted and abandoned. In the 1980s, in *Practical Ethics*, I suggested that the choice is between total utilitarianism and what I called the "prior existence" view, namely, that we should be concerned only with the welfare of those beings who already exist, or whose existence is not at issue in the decision under consideration. There have been many other suggestions as well, but the issue is too complex and difficult to discuss in a paragraph or two.[17]

Finally I come to the issue of the treatment of animals. Posner seems to be a kind person, and significantly kinder than his philosophy requires. He writes: "I agree that . . . gratuitous cruelty to and neglect of animals are wrong, and that some costs should be incurred to reduce the suffering of animals raised for food or other human purposes or subjected to medical or other testing and experimentation." But one has to wonder why, on his own terms, he believes this. He favors a humancentric approach, which "assigns no *intrinsic* value to animal welfare" and "seeks reasons strictly of human welfare for according or denying rights to animals." Why then should humans incur any costs in order to reduce the suffering of farm animals? If we are unhappy knowing that animals are suffering in factory farms, we have a choice between changing the conditions that cause this suffering, or instigating a campaign of public education to persuade people not to worry about animal suffering. If we opt for the latter, perhaps we could combine with the public education an offer of free psychotherapy for those who are still unable to get rid of their unhappiness about animal suffering. If there is no intrinsic value to animal welfare, the "pragmatic" approach to this choice would be to work out which option will most benefit us. That will depend on the costs of public education and psychotherapy, as compared with the costs of changing our ways of raising farm animals. Is that really the basis on which Posner thinks we should make such a choice? I do him the honor of believing that if he had the power to make such a decision, he would not be consistent with his own pragmatist philosophy.

Posner concludes his essay with a lengthy account of a case in which there was no constitutional remedy for the senseless killing of a raccoon, because the raccoon was not recognized as the plaintiff's property in the relevant sense. He uses this case to support an earlier remark about "the liberating potential of commodification." He believes that animals may be better off as property than they would be if they had "human-type 'rights.'" It is significant that the case he uses to illustrate this thesis deals with a raccoon. I wonder how many raccoons die or suffer each year because they are not clearly someone's property? In contrast, we don't have to wonder how many animals suffer and die because they *are* someone's property. Or rather, we know that the minimum number is several *billion* animals, because there are 10 billion animals raised for food in the United States each year.[18] The overwhelming majority of those animals endure miserable factory-farm conditions and are slaughtered by workers trying to kill the largest possible number of animals per hour, conditions that allow them to give little or no care or attention to the welfare of the individual animals. All of those animals are fully "commodities," and their property status is indisputable. It does them no good at all. We need to look elsewhere for an ethic that will provide a basis for improving their position. That ethic is the principle of equal consideration of interests, which was the outcome of the ethical argument that I defended at the beginning of this essay. Posner has not refuted this argument. Nor has he given any sound reasons for believing that it should not prevail over whatever "tenacious moral instincts" to the contrary that we may have.

NOTES

1. See Peter Singer, *Animal Liberation*, New York Review/Random House, New York, 1975, ch. 1, or Peter Singer, *Practical Ethics*, Cambridge University Press, New York, 2d ed., 1993, ch. 3.

2. See R. M. Hare, *Freedom and Reason*, Oxford University Press, New York, 1963, chs. 2 and 6, or *Moral Thinking*, Clarendon Press, Oxford, 1981, ch. 3; for further discussion, see Peter Singer, *Practical Ethics*, ch. 1.

3. See, for example, Numbers 31:1–18; Deuteronomy 3:1–7, 7:1–26, 20:13–17; 1 Samuel 15:3; Joshua 8:26–28; Ezekiel 9:5.

4. Lawrence Keeley, *War before Civilization*, Oxford University Press, New York, 1996. See especially ch. 6.

5. Richard Wrangham and Dale Peterson, *Demonic Males: Apes and the Origins of Human Violence*, Houghton Mifflin, Boston, 1996, pp. 5–21; see also Jane Goodall, *The Chimpanzees of Gombe*, Belknap Press of Harvard University Press, Cambridge, Mass., 1986, pp. 530–534.

6. Keeley, *op. cit.*

7. Of the five-member commission, Charles Malik and P. C. Chang were both philosophers who had held university teaching positions in philosophy. For a detailed account, see Mary Ann Glendon, *A World Made New: Eleanor Roosevelt and the Universal Declaration of Human Rights*, Random House, New York, 2001.

8. James Jasper and Dorothy Nelkin, *The Animal Rights Crusade: The Growth of a Moral Protest*, Free Press, New York, 1992, p. 90.

9. Robert Garner, *Animals, Politics and Morality*, Manchester University Press, Manchester, England, 1993, pp. 1–2.

10. Heinrich Himmler, Speech to SS leaders in Poznan, Poland, October 4, 1943; cited from http://www.historyplace.com/worldwar2/timeline/Poznan.htm. Last visited October 2, 2003.

11. James D. Steakley, *The Homosexual Emancipation Movement in Germany*, Arno Press, New York, 1975, p. 110.

12. Readers may suspect that my introduction of Himmler into this essay is repayment for what Posner says about the Nazis and animal rights. Perhaps, but Posner still needs to show why his position would not have lent itself easily to a defense of a position like Himmler's, perhaps without its factually erroneous racial theories. In contrast, Posner's assertion that the Nazis "believed passionately in animal rights" is a ludicrous exaggeration. Under an authoritarian regime that imposed its ideology on most aspects of German life, meat eating went on undisturbed (unless you were an observant Jew and required kosher meat), and painful experiments on animals also continued. Boria Sax, the more thorough of the two sources Posner cites for his claim, reports that "the [Nazi] army ordered . . . extensive tests on monkeys and baboons which vomited, excreted uncontrollably, lost control of their bodily movements, and went into convulsions as they died" (Boria Sax, *Animals in the Third Reich: Pets, Scapegoats, and the Holocaust*, Continuum, New York, 2000, p. 113). That hardly sounds like the army of a regime of passionate believers in animal rights. Hitler was not even a consistent vegetarian: He was keen on Bavarian sausage, liver dumplings, and stuffed squab. See Robert Payne, *The Life and Death of Adolf Hitler*, Praeger, New York, 1973, pp. 346–347; John Toland, *Adolf Hitler*, Doubleday, Garden City, N.Y., 1976, p. 256; Dione Lucas with Darlene Geis, *The Gourmet Cooking School Cookbook*, Bernard Geis Associates, New York, 1964, p. 89. I am indebted to Rynn Berry for this information. Further details are available at http://www.peta.org/liv/c/hitler.html. Last visited October 3, 2003.

13. Peter Singer, *Animal Liberation*, pp. 177–179.
14. *Id.*, appendix I.
15. See Peter Singer, *Practical Ethics*, p. 63.
16. Peter Singer, *Animal Liberation*, pp. 36–37.
17. See Peter Singer, *Practical Ethics*, pp. 101–105. The now-classic discussion is Derek Parfit, *Reasons and Persons*, Clarendon Press, Oxford, 1984; to sample the debate, see also B. Barry and R. I. Sikora, eds., *Obligations to Future Generations*, Temple University Press, Philadelphia, 1984, pp. 111–124; Stuart Rachels, "Is It Good to Make Happy People?" *Bioethics* 12 (1998), pp. 93–110; Melinda Roberts, *Child versus Childmaker: Future Persons and Present Duties in Ethics and the Law*, Rowman and Littlefield, Lanham, Md., 1998.
18. This figure is taken from Farm Animal Reform Movement, *The Farm Report*, Winter–Spring 2002, p. 7. The original sources are reports covering meat and poultry issued by the U.S. Department of Agriculture's National Agricultural Statistics Service in 2001 and 2002.

4

CORA DIAMOND

EATING MEAT AND
EATING PEOPLE

This essay is a response to a certain sort of argument defending the rights of animals. Part I is a brief explanation of the background and of the sort of argument I want to reject; part II is an attempt to characterize those arguments: They contain fundamental confusions about moral relations between people and people *and* between people and animals. And part III is an indication of what I think can still be said on—as it were—the animals' side.

I

The background to this chapter is the discussions of animals' rights by Peter Singer and Tom Regan and a number of other philosophers.[1] The basic type of argument in many of these discussions is encapsulated in the word *speciesism*. The word, I think, is originally Richard Ryder's, but Peter Singer is responsible for making it popular in connection with an obvious sort of argument: that in our attitude to members of other species we have prejudices which are completely analogous to the prejudices people may have with regard to members of other races, and these prejudices will be connected with the ways we are blind to our own exploitation and oppression of the other group. We are blind to the fact that what we do to them deprives them of their rights; we do not want to see this because we profit from it, and so we make use of what are really morally irrelevant differences between them and ourselves to justify the difference in treatment. Putting it fairly crudely; if we say, "You cannot live here because you are black," this would be supposed to be parallel to saying, "You can be used for our experiments, because you are only an animal and cannot talk." If the first is unjustifiable prejudice, so equally is the second. In fact, both Singer and Regan argue, if we, as a justification for differential treatment, point to things like the incapacity of animals to use speech, we should be committed to treating in the same way as animals those members of our own species who (let us say) have brain damage sufficient to prevent the development of speech—committed to allowing them to be used as laboratory animals or as food or whatever. If we say, "These *animals* are not rational, so we have a right to kill them for food," but we do not say the same of *people* whose rationality cannot develop or whose capacities have been destroyed, we are plainly not treating cases alike. The fundamental principle here is one we could put this way (the formulation is based on Peter Singer's statements): We must give equal consideration to the interests of any being which is capable of having interests; and the capacity to have interests is essentially dependent only on the capacity for suffering and enjoyment. This we evidently share with animals.

Here I want to mention a point only to get it out of the way. I disagree with a great deal of what Singer and Regan and other defenders of animals' rights say, but I do not wish to raise the issue how we can be certain that animals feel pain. I think Singer and Regan are right that doubt about that is, in most ordinary cases, as much out of place as it is in many cases in connection with human beings.

It will be evident that the form of argument I have described is very close to what we find in Bentham and Mill; and Mill, in arguing for the rights of women, attacks Chartists who fight for the rights of all men and drop the subject when the rights of women come up, with an argument of exactly the form that Singer uses. The confinement of your concern for rights to the rights of *men* shows that you are not really concerned with equality, as you profess to be. You are only a Chartist because you are not a lord.[2] And so too we are told more than a century later that the confinement of moral concern to human animals is equally a denial of equality. Indeed the description of human beings as "human animals" is a characteristic part of the argument. The point being made there is that just as our language may embody prejudices against blacks or against women, so may it against nonhuman animals. It supposedly embodies our prejudice, then, when we use the word *animal* to set them apart form us, just as if we were not animals ourselves.

It is on the basis of this sort of claim, that the rights of all animals should be given equal consideration, that Singer and Regan and Ryder and the others have argued that we must give up killing animals for food, and most drastically cut back—at least—the use of animals in scientific research. And so on.

That argument seems to me to be confused. I do not dispute that there are analogies between the case of our relations to animals and the case of a dominant group's relation to some other group of human beings which it exploits or treats unjustly in other ways. But the analogies are not simple and straightforward, and it is not clear how far they go. The Singer-Regan approach makes it hard to see what is important *either* in our relationship with other human beings *or* in our relationship with animals. And that is what I shall try to explain in part II. My discussion will be limited to eating animals, but much of what I say is intended to apply to other uses of animals as well.

II

Discussions of vegetarianism and animals' rights often start with discussions of human rights. We may then be asked what it is that grounds the claims that people have such rights, and whether similar grounds may not after all be found in the case of animals.

All such discussions are beside the point. For they ask why we do not kill people (very irrational ones, let us say) for food, or why we do not treat people in ways which would cause them distress or anxiety and so on, when for the sake of meat we are willing enough to kill animals or treat them in ways which cause them distress. This is a totally wrong way of beginning the discussion, because it ignores certain quite central facts—facts which, if attended to, would make it clear that *rights* are not what is crucial. *We do not eat our dead,* even when they have died in automobile accidents or been struck by lightning, and their flesh might be first class. We do not eat them; or if we do, it is a matter of extreme need, or of some special ritual—and even in cases of obvious extreme need, there is very great reluctance. We also do not eat our amputated limbs. (Or if we did, it would be in the same kinds of special circumstances in which we eat our dead.) Now the fact that we do not eat our dead is not a consequence—not a direct one in any event—of our unwillingness to kill people for food or other purposes. It is not a direct consequence of our unwillingness to cause distress to people. Of course it *would* cause distress to people to think that they might be eaten when they were dead, but it causes distress because of what it is to eat a dead person. Hence we cannot elucidate what (if anything) is wrong—if that is the word—with eating people by appealing to the distress it would cause, in the way we can point to the distress caused by stamping on someone's toe as a reason why we regard it as a wrong to him. Now if we do not eat people who are already dead and also do not kill people for food, it is at least prima facie plausible that our reasons in the two cases might be related, and hence must be looked into by anyone who wants to claim that we have no good reasons for not eating people which are not also good reasons for not eating animals. Anyone who, in discussing this issue, focuses on our reasons for not killing people or our reasons for not causing them suffering quite evidently runs the risk of leaving altogether out of his discussion those fundamental features of our relationship to other human beings which are involved in our not eating them.

It is in fact part of the way this point is usually missed that arguments are given for not eating animals, for respecting their rights to life and not making them suffer, which imply that there is absolutely nothing queer, nothing at all odd, in the vegetarian eating the cow that has obligingly been struck by lightning. That is to say, there is nothing in the discussion which suggests that a cow is *not* something to eat; it is only that one must not help the process along. One must not, that is, interfere with those rights with which we should usually have to interfere if we are to eat animals at all conveniently. But if the point of the Singer-Regan vegetarian's argument is to show that the eating of meat is, morally, in the same position as the eating of human flesh, he is not consistent unless he says that it is just squeamishness, or something like that, which stops us eating our dead. If he admitted that what underlies our attitude to dining on ourselves is the view that *a person is not something to eat,* he could not focus on the cow's right not to be killed or maltreated, as if that were the heart of it.

I write this as a vegetarian, but one distressed by the obtuseness of the normal arguments, in particular, I should say, the arguments of Singer and Regan. For if vegetarians give arguments which do not begin to get near the considerations which are involved in our not eating people, those to whom their arguments are addressed may not be certain how to reply, but they will not be convinced either, and really are quite right. They themselves may not be able to make explicit what it is they object to in the way the vegetarian presents our attitude to not eating people, but they will be left feeling that beyond all the natter about "speciesism" and equality and the rest, there is a difference between human beings and animals which is being ignored. This is not just connected with the difference between what it is to eat the one and what it is to eat the other. It is connected with the difference between giving people a funeral and giving a dog one, with the difference between miscegenation and *chacun à son goût* with consenting adult gorillas. (Singer and Regan give arguments which certainly appear to imply that a distaste for the latter is merely that, and would no more stand up to scrutiny than a taboo on miscegenation.) And so on. It is a mark of the shallowness of these discussions of vegetarianism that the only tool used in them to explain what differences in treatment are justified is the appeal to the capacities of the beings in question. That is to say, such-and-such a being—a dog, say—might be said to have, like us, a right to have its interests taken into account, but its interests will be different because its capacities are. Such an appeal may then be used by the vegetarian to explain why he need not in consistency demand votes for dogs (though even there it is not really adequate), but as an explanation for the appropriateness of a funeral for a child two days old and not for a puppy it will not do; and the vegetarian is forced to explain that—if he tries at all—in terms of what it is *to us*, a form of explanation which for him is evidently dangerous. Indeed, it is normally the case that vegetarians do not touch the issue of our attitude to the dead. They accuse philosophers of ignoring the problems created by animals in their discussions of *human* rights, but they equally may be accused of ignoring the hard cases for their own view. (The hardness of the case for them, though, is a matter of its hardness for any approach to morality deriving much from utilitarianism—deriving much, that is, from a utilitarian conception of what makes something a possible object of moral concern.)

I do not think it an accident that the arguments of vegetarians have a nagging moralistic tone. They are an attempt to show something to be morally wrong, on the assumption that *we all agree* that it is morally wrong to raise people for meat, and so on. Now the objection to saying that *that* is morally wrong is not, or not merely, that it is too weak. What we should be going against in adopting Swift's "Modest Proposal" is something we should be going against in salvaging the dead more generally: useful organs for transplantation, and the rest for supper or the compost heap. And "morally wrong" is not too weak for that, but in the wrong dimension. One could say that it would be impious to treat the dead so, but the word "impious" does not make for clarity; it only asks for explanation. We can most naturally speak of a kind of action as morally wrong when we have some firm grasp of what *kind* of beings are involved. But there are some actions, like giving people names, that are part of the way we come to understand and indicate our recognition of *what* kind it is with which we are concerned. And "morally wrong" will often not fit our refusals to act in such a way, or our acting in an opposed sort of way, as when Gradgrind calls a child "Girl number twenty." Doing her out of a name is not like doing her out of an inheritance to which she has a right and in which she has an interest. Rather, Gradgrind lives in a world, or would like to, in which it makes no difference whether she has a name, a number being more efficient, and in which a human being is not *something to be named, not numbered.* Again, it is not "morally wrong" to eat our pets; people who ate their pets would not have pets in the same sense of that term. (If we call an animal that we are fattening for the table a pet, we are making a crude joke of a familiar sort.) A pet is not something to eat; it is given a name, is let into our houses, and may be spoken to in ways in which we do not normally speak to cows or squirrels. That is to say, it is given some part of the character of a person. (This may be more or less sentimental; it need not be sentimental at all.) Treating pets in these ways is not at all a matter of recognizing some *interest* which pets have in being so treated. There is not a class of beings, pets, whose nature, whose capacities, are such that we owe it to them to treat them in these ways. Similarly, it is not out of respect for the interests of beings of the class to which we belong that we give names to each other, or that we treat human sexuality or birth or death as we do, marking them—in their various ways—as significant or serious. And again, it is not respect for our interests which is involved in our not eating each other. These are all things that go to determine what sort of concept "human being" is. Similarly with having duties to human beings. This is not a consequence of what human beings are; it is not justified by what human beings are. It is itself one of the things which go to build our notion of human beings. And so too—very much so—with the idea of the difference between human beings and animals. We learn what a human being is in—among other ways—sitting at a table where *we* eat *them*. We are around the table and they are on it. The difference between human beings and animals is not to be discovered by studies of Washoe or the activities of dolphins. It is not that sort of study or ethology or evolutionary theory that is going to tell us the difference between us and animals: The difference is, as I have suggested, a central concept for human life and is more an object of contemplation than observation (though that might be misunderstood; I am not suggesting it is a matter of intuition). One source of confusion here is that we fail to distinguish between "the difference between animals and people" and "the differences between animals and people"; the same sort of confusion occurs in discussions of the relationship of men and women. In both cases people appeal to scientific evidence to show that "the difference" is not as deep as we think; but all that such evidence can show, or show directly, is that the differences are less sharp than we think. In the case of the difference between animals and people, it is clear that we form the idea of this difference, create the concept of the difference, knowing perfectly well the overwhelmingly obvious similarities.

It may seem that by the sort of line I have been suggesting, I should find myself having to justify slavery. For do we not learn—if we live in a slave society—what slaves are and what masters are through the structure of a life in which we are here and do this, and they are there and do that? Do we not learn *the difference between a master and a slave* that way? In fact I do not think it works quite that way, but at this point I am not trying to justify anything, only to indicate that our starting point in thinking about the relationships among human beings is not *a moral agent* as an item on one side, and on the other *a being capable of suffering, thought, speech,* etc; and similarly (*mutatis mutandis*) in the case of our thought about the relationship between human beings and animals. We cannot point and say, "This *thing* (whatever concepts it may fall under) is at any rate capable of suffering, so we ought not to make it suffer." (That sentence, Jonathan Bennett said, struck him as so clearly false that he thought I could not have meant it literally; I shall come back to it.) That "this" is a being which I ought not to make suffer, or whose suffering I should try to prevent, constitutes a *special* relationship to it, or rather, any of a number of such relationships—for example, what its suffering is in relation to me might depend on its being my mother. That I ought to attend to a being's sufferings and enjoyments is not *the* fundamental moral relation to it, determining how I ought to act toward it—no more fundamental than that this man, being my brother, is a being about whom I should not entertain sexual fantasies. What a life is like in which I recognize such relationships as the former with at any rate some animals, how it is different from those in which no such relationships are recognized, or different ones, and how far it is possible to say that some such lives are less hypocritical or richer or better than those in which animals are for us mere things would then remain to be described. But a starting point in any such description must be understanding what is involved in such things as our not eating people: No more than our not eating pets does *that* rest on recognition of the claims of a being simply as one capable of suffering and enjoyment. To argue otherwise, to argue as Singer and Regan do, is not to give a defense of animals; it is to attack significance in human life. The Singer-Regan arguments amount to this: Knee-jerk liberals on racism and sexism ought to go knee-jerk about cows and guinea pigs; and they certainly show how that can be done, not that it ought to be. They might reply: If you are right, then we are, or should be willing to let animals suffer for the sake of significance in *our* life—for the sake, as it were, of the concept of the human. And what is that but speciesism again—more highfalutin perhaps than the familiar kind but no less morally disreputable for that? Significance, though, is not an end, is not something I am proposing as an alternative to the prevention of unnecessary suffering, to which the latter might be sacrificed. The ways in which we mark what human life is belong to the source of moral life, and no appeal to the prevention of suffering which is blind to this can in the end be anything but self-destructive.

III

Have I not then, by attacking such arguments, completely sawn off the branch I am sitting on? Is there any other way of showing anyone that he does have reason to treat animals better than he is treating them?

I shall take eating them as an example, but want to point out that eating animals, even among us, is not just one thing. To put it at its simplest by an example, a friend of mine raises his own pigs; they have quite a good life, and he shoots and butchers them with help from a neighbor. His children are involved in the operations in various ways, and the whole business is very much a subject of conversation and thought. This is obviously in some ways very different from picking up out of the supermarket freezer one of the several billion chicken breasts we Americans eat every year. So when I speak of eating animals I mean a lot of different cases, and what I say will apply to some more than others.

What then is involved in trying to show someone that he ought not to eat meat? I have drawn attention to one curious feature of the Peter Singer sort of argument, which is that your Peter Singer vegetarian should be perfectly happy to eat the unfortunate lamb that has just been hit by a car. I want to connect this with a more general characteristic of the utilitarian vegetarians' approach. They are not, they say, especially fond of, or interested in, animals. They may point that out they do not "love them." They do not want to anthropomorphize them, and are concerned to put their position as distinct from one which they see as sentimental anthropomorphizing. Just as you do not have to prove that underneath his black skin the black man has a white man inside in order to recognize his rights, you do not have to see animals in terms of your emotional responses to people to recognize their rights. So the direction of their argument is: *We* are only one kind of *animal*; if what is fair for us is concern for our interests, that depends only on our being living animals *with* interests—and if that *is* fair, it is fair for *any* animal. They do not, that is, want to move from concern for people to concern for four-legged people or feathered people—to beings who deserve that concern only because we think of them as having a little person inside.

To make a contrast, I want to take a piece of vegetarian propaganda of a very different sort:

> *Learning to be a Dutiful Carnivore*
> Dogs and cats and goats and cows,
> Ducks and chickens, sheep and sows
> Woven into tales for tots,
> Pictured on their walls and pots.
> Time for dinner! Come and eat
> All your lovely, juicy meat.
> One day ham from Percy Porker
> (In the comics he's a corker),
> Then the breast from Mrs. Cluck
> Or the wing from Donald Duck.
> Liver next from Clara Cow
> (No, it doesn't hurt her now).
> Yes, that leg's from Peter Rabbit
> Chew it well; make that a habit.
> Eat the creatures killed for sale,
> But never pull the pussy's tail.
> Eat the flesh from "filthy hogs"
> But never be unkind to dogs.
> Grow up into double-think—
> Kiss the hamster; skin the mink.
> Never think of slaughter, dear,
> That's why animals are here.
> They only come on earth to die,
> So eat your meat, and don't ask why.
> —Jane Legge[3]

What that is trying to bring out is a kind of inconsistency, or confusion mixed with hypocrisy—what it sees as that—in our ordinary ways of thinking about animals, confusions that come out, not only but strikingly, in what children are taught about them. That is to say, the poem does not ask you to feel in this or the other way about animals. Rather, it takes a certain range of feelings for granted. There *are* certain ways of feeling reflected in our telling children classical animal stories, in our feeding birds and squirrels in the winter, say—in our interfering with what children do to animals as we interfere when they maltreat smaller children: "Never pull the pussy's tail." The poem does not try to get us to behave like that, or to get us to feel a "transport of cordiality" toward animals. Rather, it is addressed to people whose response to animals already includes a variety of such kinds of behavior, and taking that for granted it suggests that other features of our relationship to animals show confusion or hypocrisy. It is very important, I think, that it does not attempt any justification for the range of responses against the background of which certain other kinds of behavior are supposed to look hypocritical. There is a real question whether justification would be in place for these background responses. I want to bring that out by another poem, not a bit of vegetarian or any other propaganda. This is a poem of Walter de la Mare's:

Titmouse
If you would happy company win,
Dangle a palm-nut from a tree,
Idly in green to sway and spin,
Its snow-pulped kernel for bait; and see
    A nimble titmouse enter in.

Out of earth's vast unknown of air,
Out of all summer, from wave to wave,
He'll perch, and prank his feathers fair,
Jangle a glass-clear wildering stave,
    And take his commons there—

This tiny son of life; this spright,
By momentary Human sought,
Plume will his wing in the dappling light,
Clash timbrel shrill and gay—
And into Time's enormous Nought,
    Sweet-fed will flit away.[4]

What interests me here is the phrase "This tiny son of life." It is important that this is connected in the poem with the bird's appearing out of earth's vast unknown of air, and flitting off into Time's enormous Nought. He is shown as fellow creature, with this very striking phrase "son of life." I want to say some things about the idea of a fellow creature.

First, it indicates a direction of thought very unlike that of the Singer argument. There we start supposedly from the biological fact that we and dogs and rats and titmice and monkeys are all species of animal, differentiated indeed in terms of this or the other capacity, but what is appropriate treatment for members of our species would be appropriate to members of any whose capacities gave them similar interests. We are all equally animals, though, for a start—with, therefore, an equal right to have whatever our interests are taken into account. The starting point for our thought is what is general and in common and biologically given. Implicitly in the Jane Legge poem, and explicitly in the de la Mare, we have a different notion, that of living creature, or fellow creature—which is *not* a biological concept. It does not mean, biologically an animal, something with *biological life*—it means a being in a certain boat, as it were, of whom it makes sense to say, among other things, that it goes off into Time's enormous Nought, and which may be sought as *company*. The response to animals as our fellows in mortality, in life on this earth (think here of Burns's description of himself to the mouse as "thy poor earthborn companion, / An' fellow mortal"), depends on a conception of *human* life. It is an extension of a nonbiological notion of what human life is. You can call it anthropomorphic, but only if you want to create confusion. The confusion, though, is created only because we do not have a clear idea of what phenomena the word *anthropomorphic* might cover, and tend to use it for cases which are sentimental in certain characteristic ways, which the de la Mare poem avoids, however narrowly.

The extension to animals of modes of thinking characteristic of our responses to human beings is extremely complex, and includes a great variety of things. The idea of an animal as company is a striking kind of case; it brings it out that the notion of a fellow creature does not involve just the extension of moral concepts like charity or justice. Those are, indeed, among the most familiar of such extensions; thus the idea of a fellow creature may go with feeding birds in winter, thought of as something akin to charity, or again with giving a hunted animal a sporting chance, where that is thought of as something akin to justice or fairness. I should say that the notion of a fellow creature is extremely *labile*, and that is partly because it is not something over and above the extensions of such concepts as justice, charity, and friendship-or-companionship-or-cordiality. (I had thought that the extension of the "friendship" range of concepts was obviously possible only in some cases, titmice and not hippopotamuses, e.g.; but films of the relation between whales and their Greenpeace rescuers show that I was probably taking an excessively narrow view.) Independence is another of the important extended concepts, or rather, the idea of an independent life, subject, as any is, to contingencies, and this is closely connected with the idea of something like a *respect* for the animal's independent life. We see such a notion in, for example, many people's objections to the performance of circus tricks by animals, as an *indignity*. The conception of a hunted animal as a "respected enemy" is also closely related. *Pity* is another central concept here, as expressed, for example, in Burns's "To a Mouse"; and I should note that the connection between pity and sparing someone's life is wholly excluded from vegetarian arguments of the sort attacked in part I—it has no place in the rhetoric of a "liberation movement."

It does normally, or very often, go with the idea of a fellow creature that we do eat them. But it then characteristically goes with the idea that they must be hunted fairly or raised without bad usage. The treatment of an animal as simply a stage (the self-moving stage) in the production of a meat product is not part of this mode of thinking; and I should suggest also that the concept of "vermin" is at least sometimes used in excluding an animal from the class of fellow creatures. However, it makes an importantly different kind of contrast with "fellow creature" from the contrast you have when animals are taken as stages in the production of a meat product, or as "very delicate pieces of machinery" (as in a recent BBC program on the use of animals in research). I shall have more to say about these contrasts later; the point I wish to make now is that it is not a *fact* that a titmouse *has a life*; if one speaks that way it expresses a particular relation within a broadly specifiable range to titmice. It is no more biological than it would be a biological point should you call another person a "traveler between life and death": that is not a biological point dressed up in poetical language.

The fellow-creature response sits in us alongside others. This is brought out by another poem of de la Mare's, "Dry August Burned," which begins with a child weeping her heart out on seeing a dead hare lying limp on the kitchen table. But hearing a team of field artillery going by, she runs out and watches it all in the bright sun. After they have passed, she turns and runs back into the house, but the hare has vanished—"Mother," she asks, "please may I go and see it skinned?" In a classic study of intellectual growth in children, Susan Isaacs describes at some length what she calls the extraordinarily confused and conflicting ways in which we adults actually behave toward animals in the sight of children, and in connection with which children have to try to understand our horror at the cruelty they may display toward animals, our insistence that they be "kind" to them.[5] She mentions the enormously varied ways in which animal death and the killing of animals are a matter-of-course feature of the life children see and are told about. They quite early grasp the relation between meat and the killing of animals, see insect pests killed, or spiders or snakes merely because they are distasteful; they hear about the killing of dangerous animals or of superfluous puppies and kittens, and are encouraged early to fish or collect butterflies—and so on.

I am not concerned here to ask whether we should or should not do these things to animals, but rather to bring out that what is meant by doing something *to an animal*, what is meant by something's being an animal, is shaped by such things as Mrs. Isaacs describes. Animals—these objects we are acting upon—are not given for our thought independently of such a mass of ways of thinking about and responding to them. This is part of what I meant earlier when I dismissed the idea of saying of something that whatever concepts it fell under, it was capable of suffering and so ought not to be made to suffer—the claim Bennett found so clearly false that he thought I must not have meant it. I shall return to it shortly.

This mass of responses, and more, Mrs. Isaacs called confused and contradictory. But there are significant patterns in it; it is no more just a lot of confused and contradictory modes of response than is the mass which enables us to think of our fellow human beings as such. For example, the notion of vermin makes sense against the background of the idea of animals in general as not mere things. Certain groups of animals are then singled out as *not* to be treated fully as the rest are, where the idea might be that the rest are to be hunted only fairly and not meanly poisoned. Again, the killing of dangerous animals in self-defense forms part of a pattern in which circumstances of immediate danger make a difference, assuming as a background the independent life of the lion (say), perceived in terms not limited to the way it might serve our ends. What I am suggesting here is that certain modes of response may be seen as withdrawals from *some* animals (vermin), or from animals in *some* circumstances (danger), what would otherwise belong to recognizing them as animals, just as the notion of an enemy or of a slave may involve the withdrawing from the person involved of some of what would belong to recognition of him as a human being. Thus, for example, in the case of slaves, there may be no formal social institution of the slave's name in the same full sense as there is for others, or there may be a denial of socially significant ancestry, and so on. Or a man who is outlawed may be killed like an animal. Here then the idea would be that the notion of a slave or an enemy or an outlaw assumes a background of response to persons, and recognition that what happens in *these* cases is that we have something which we are *not* treating as what it—in a way—is. Of course, even in these cases, a great deal of the response to "human being" may remain intact, as for example what may be done with the dead body. Or again, if the enemyhood is so deep as to remove even these restraints, and men dance on the corpses of their enemies, as for example in the 1970s in Lebanon, the point of this can only be understood in terms of the violation of what is taken to be how you treat the corpse of a human being. It is because you know it *is* that, that you are treating it with some point as that is *not* to be treated. And no one who does it could have the slightest difficulty—whatever contempt he might feel—in understanding why someone had gone off and been sick instead.

Now suppose I am a practical-minded, hardheaded slaveholder whose neighbor has, on his deathbed, freed his slaves. I might regard such a man as foolish, but not as batty, not batty in the way I should think of someone if he had, let us say, freed his cows on his deathbed. Compare the case Orwell describes, from his experience in the Spanish Civil War, of being unable to shoot at a half-dressed man who was running along the top of the trench parapet, holding up his trousers with both hands as he ran. "I had come here to shoot at 'Fascists,' but a man who is holding up his trousers is not a 'Fascist,' he is visibly a fellow-creature, similar to yourself, and you do not feel like shooting at him."[6] The notion of enemy (Fascist) and fellow creature are there in a kind of tension, and even a man who could shoot at a man running holding his trousers up might recognize perfectly well why Orwell could not. The tension there is in such cases (between "slave" or "enemy" and "fellow human being") may be reflected not merely in recognition of the point of someone else's actions, but also in defensiveness of various sorts, as when you ask someone where he is from and the answer is "South Africa and you do not treat them very well here either." And that is like telling someone I am a vegetarian and getting the response "And what are your shoes made of?"

What you have then with an image or a sight like that of the man running holding his trousers up is something which may check or alter one's actions, but something which is not compelling, or not compelling for everyone who can understand its force, and the possibility, even where it is not compelling for someone, of making for discomfort or of bringing discomfort to awareness. I should suggest that the Jane Legge poem is an attempt to bring a similar sort of discomfort closer to the surface—but that images of fellow creatures are naturally much less compelling ones than images of "fellow human beings" can be.

I introduced the notion of a fellow creature in answer to the question: How might I go about showing someone that he had reason not to eat animals? I do not think I have answered that so much as shown the direction in which I should look for an answer. And clearly the approach I have suggested is not usable with someone in whom there is no fellow-creature response, nothing at all in that range. I am not therefore in a weaker position than those who would defend animals' rights on the basis of an abstract principle of equality. For although they purport to be providing reasons which are reasons for anyone, Martian or human being or whatnot, to respect the rights of animals, Martians, and whatnot, in fact what they are providing, I should say, is images of a vastly more uncompelling sort. Comically uncompelling, as we can see when similar arguments are used in *Tristram Shandy* to defend the rights of homunculi. But that takes me back to the claim I made earlier, that we cannot start thinking about the relations between human beings and animals by saying, "Well, here we have me, the moral agent, and there we have it, the thing capable of suffering," and pulling out of that "Well, then, so far as possible I ought to prevent its suffering." When we say that sort of thing, whatever force our words have comes from our reading in such notions as human being and animal. I am not now going to try to reply to Bennett's claim that my view is clearly false. I shall instead simply connect it with another clearly false view of mine. At the end of part II I said that the ways in which we mark what human life is belong to the source of moral life, and no appeal to the prevention of suffering which is blind to this can in the end be anything but self-destructive. Did I mean that? Bennett asked, and he said that he could see no reason why it should be thought to be so. I meant that if we appeal to people to prevent suffering, and we, in our appeal, try to obliterate the distinction between human beings and animals and just get people to speak or think of "different species of animals," there is no footing left from which to tell us what we ought to do, because it is not members of one among species of animals that have moral obligations to anything. The moral expectations of other human beings demand something of me as other than an animal; and we do something like imaginatively read into animals something like such expectations when we think of vegetarianism as enabling us to meet a cow's eyes. There is nothing wrong with that; there *is* something wrong with trying to keep that response and destroy its foundation.

More tentatively, I think something similar could be said about imaginatively reading into animals something like an appeal to our pity. Pity, beyond its more primitive manifestations, depends upon a sense of human life and loss and a grasp of the situations in which one human being can appeal for pity to another, ask that he relent. When we are unrelenting in what we do—to other people or to animals—what we need is not telling that their interests are as worthy of concern as ours. And the trouble—or a trouble—with the abstract appeal to the prevention of suffering as a principle of action is that it encourages us to ignore pity, to forget what it contributes to our conception of suffering and death, and how it is connected with the possibility of relenting.

My nonreply to Bennett then comes to an expansion of what he would still take as false, namely, that our *hearing* the moral appeal of an animal is our hearing it speak—as it were—the language of our fellow human beings. A fuller discussion of this would involve asking what force the analogy with racism and sexism has. It is not totally mistaken by any means. What might be called the dark side of human solidarity has analogies with the dark side of sexual solidarity or the solidarity of a human group, and the pain of seeing this is, I think, strongly present in the writings I have been attacking. It is their arguments I have been attacking, though, and not their perceptions, not the sense that comes through their writings of the awful and unshakable callousness and unrelentingness with which we most often confront the nonhuman world. The mistake is to think that the callousness cannot be condemned without reasons which are reasons for anyone, no matter how devoid of all human imagination or sympathy. Hence their emphasis on rights, on capacities, on interests, on the biologically given; hence the distortion of their perceptions by their arguments.[7]

NOTES

This chapter was originally published in *Philosophy* 53 (1978): 465–479. Permission to quote the poems was kindly given by the Vegetarian Society and by the Society of Authors as representative of the Literary Trustees of Walter de la Mare.

1. See especially Peter Singer, *Animal Liberation* (New York: New York Review, 1975); Tom Regan and Peter Singer, eds., *Animal Rights and Human Obligations* (Englewood Cliffs, N.J.: Prentice-Hall, 1976); Stanley Godlovitch, Roslind Godlovitch, and John Harris, eds., *Animals, Men and Morals* (New York: Grove, 1972); and Richard Ryder, *Speciesism: The Ethics of Vivisection* (Edinburgh: Scottish Society for the Prevention of Vivisection, 1974).

2. "The Enfranchisement of Women," *Dissertations and Discussions* (Boston: Spencer, 1864), vol. III, pp. 99–100. Mill's share in writing the essay is disputed, but his hand is evident in the remarks about Chartism. For the origin of the remark, see also John Stuart Mill, *Collected Works*, ed. J. M. Robson (Toronto: University of Toronto Press, 1963–1989), vol. VI, p. 353n.

3. *British Vegetarian*, Jan./Feb. 1969, p. 59.

4. *The Collected Poems of Walter de la Mare* (London: Faber and Faber, 1979), p. 129.

5. *Intellectual Growth in Young Children* (London: Routledge, 1930), pp. 160–162.

6. *Collected Essays, Journalism and Letters* (London: Secker and Warburg, 1968), vol. II, p. 254.

7. For much in this essay I am indebted to discussions with Michael Feldman. I have also been much helped by Jonathan Bennett's comments on an earlier version of part II.

5

GARY L. FRANCIONE

ANIMALS—PROPERTY
OR PERSONS?

When it comes to other animals, we humans exhibit what can best be described as moral schizophrenia. Although we claim to take animals seriously and to regard them as having morally significant interests, we routinely ignore those interests for trival reasons. In this essay, I argue that our moral schizophrenia is related to the status of animals as property, which means that animals are nothing more than *things* despite the many laws that supposedly protect them. If we are going to make good on our claim to take animal interests seriously, then we have no choice but to accord animals one right: the right not to be treated as our property.

Our acceptance that animals have this one right would require that we abolish and not merely better regulate our institutionalized exploitation of animals. Although this is an ostensibly radical conclusion, it necessarily follows from certain moral notions that we have professed to accept for the better part of 200 years. Moreover, recognition of this right would not preclude our choosing humans over animals in situations of genuine conflict.

ANIMALS: OUR MORAL SCHIZOPHRENIA

There is a profound disparity between what we say we believe about animals, and how we actually treat them. On one hand, we claim to take animals seriously. Two-thirds of Americans polled by the Associated Press agree with the following statement: "An animal's right to live free of suffering should be just as important as a person's right to live free of suffering," and more than 50 percent of Americans believe that it is wrong to kill animals to make fur coats or to hunt them for sport.[1] Almost 50 percent regard animals to be "just like humans in all important ways."[2] These attitudes are reflected in other nations as well. For example, 94 percent of Britons[3] and 88 percent of Spaniards[4] think that animals should be protected from acts of cruelty, and only 14 percent of Europeans support the use of genetic engineering that results in animal suffering, even if the purpose is to create drugs that would save human lives.[5]

On the other hand, our actual treatment of animals stands in stark contrast to our proclamations about our regard for their moral status.[6] Consider the suffering of animals at our hands. In the United States alone, according to the U.S. Department of Agriculture, we kill more than 8 billion animals a year for food; every day, we slaughter approximately 23 million animals, or more than 950,000 per hour, or almost 16,000 per minute, or more than 260 every second. This is to say nothing of the billions more killed worldwide. These animals are raised under horrendous intensive conditions known as "factory farming," mutilated in various ways without pain relief, transported long distances in cramped, filthy containers, and finally slaughtered amid the stench, noise, and squalor of the abattoir. We kill billions of fish and other sea animals annually. We catch them with hooks and allow them to suffocate in nets. We buy lobsters at the supermarket, where they are kept for weeks in crowded tanks with their claws closed by rubber bands and without receiving any food, and we cook them alive in boiling water.

Wild animals fare no better. We hunt and kill approximately 200 million animals in the United States annually, not including animals killed on commercial game ranches or at events such as pigeon shoots. Moreover, hunters often cripple animals without killing or retrieving them. It is estimated, for example, that bow hunters do not retrieve 50 percent of the animals hit with their arrows. This increases the true death toll from hunting by at least tens of millions of uncounted animals. Wounded animals often die slowly, over a period of hours or even days, from blood loss, punctured intestines and stomachs, and severe infections.

In the United States alone, we use millions of animals annually for biomedical experiments, product testing, and education. Animals are used to measure the effects of toxins, diseases, drugs, radiation, bullets, and all forms of physical and psychological deprivations. We burn, poison, irradiate, blind, starve, and electrocute them. They are purposely riddled with diseases such as cancer and infections such as pneumonia. We deprive them of sleep, keep them in solitary confinement, remove their limbs and eyes, addict them to drugs, force them to withdraw from drug addiction, and cage them for the duration of their lives. If they do not die during experimental procedures, we almost always kill them immediately afterward, or we recycle them for other experiments or tests and then kill them.

We use millions of animals for the sole purpose of providing entertainment. Animals are used in film and television. There are thousands of zoos, circuses, carnivals, race tracks, dolphin exhibits, and rodeos in the United States, and these and similar activities, such as bullfighting, also take place in other countries. Animals used in entertainment are often forced to endure lifelong incarceration and confinement, poor living conditions, extreme physical danger and hardship, and brutal treatment. Most animals used for entertainment purposes are killed when no longer useful, or sold into research or as targets for shooting on commercial hunting preserves.

And we kill millions of animals annually simply for fashion. Approximately 40 million animals worldwide are trapped, snared, or raised in intensive confinement on fur farms, where they are electrocuted or gassed or have their necks broken. In the United States, 8–10 million animals are killed every year for fur.

For all of these reasons, we may be said to suffer from a sort of moral schizophrenia when it comes to our thinking about animals. We claim to regard animals as having morally significant interests, but our behavior is to the contrary.

ANIMALS AS THINGS

Before the nineteenth century, the foregoing litany of animal uses would not have raised any concern. Western culture did not recognize that humans had any moral obligations to animals because animals did not matter morally at all. We could have moral obligations that concerned animals, but these obligations were really owed to other humans and not to animals. Animals were regarded as things, as having a moral status no different from that of inanimate objects.

As late as the seventeenth century, the view was advanced that animals are nothing more than machines. René Descartes (1596–1650), considered the founder of modern philosophy, argued that animals are not conscious—they have no mind whatsoever—because they do not possess a soul, which God invested only in humans. In support of the idea that animals lack consciousness, Descartes maintained that they do not use verbal or sign language—something that every human being does but that no animal does. Descartes certainly recognized that animals act in what appear to be purposive and intelligent ways and that they seem to be conscious, but he claimed that they are really no different from machines made by God. Indeed, he likened animals to "automatons, or moving machines."[7] Moreover, just as a clock can tell time better than humans can, so some animal machines can perform some tasks better than humans can.

An obvious implication of Descartes's position was that animals are not sentient; they are not conscious of pain, pleasure, or anything else. Descartes and his followers performed experiments in which they nailed animals by their paws to boards and cut them open to reveal their beating hearts. They burned, scalded, and mutilated animals in every conceivable manner. When the animals reacted as though they were suffering pain, Descartes dismissed the reaction as no different from the sound of a machine that is functioning improperly. A crying dog, Descartes maintained, is no different from a whining gear that needs oil.

In Descartes's view, it is as senseless to talk about our moral obligations to animals, machines created by God, as it is to talk about our moral obligations to clocks, machines created by humans. We can have moral obligations that concern the clock, but any such obligations are really owed to other humans and not to the clock. If I smash the clock with a hammer, you may object because the clock belongs to you, or because I injure you when a piece of the clock accidentally strikes you, or because it is wasteful to destroy a perfectly good clock that could be used by someone else. I may be similarly obliged not to damage your dog, but the obligation is owed to you, not to the dog. The dog, like the clock, according to Descartes, is nothing more than a machine and possesses no interests in the first place.

There were others who did not share Descartes's view that animals are merely machines but who still denied that we can have any moral obligations to animals. For example, the German philosopher Immanuel Kant (1724–1804) recognized that animals are sentient and can suffer, but denied that we can have any direct moral obligations to them because, according to Kant, they are neither rational nor self-aware. According to Kant, animals are merely a means to human ends; they are "man's instruments." They exist only for our use and have no value in themselves. To the extent that our treatment of animals matters at all for Kant, it does so only because of its impact on other humans: "[H]e who is cruel to animals becomes hard also in his dealings with men."[8] Kant argued that if we shoot and kill a faithful and obedient dog because the dog has grown old and is no longer capable of serving us, our act violates no obligation that we owe to the dog. The act is wrong only because of our moral obligation to reward the faithful service of other humans; killing the dog tends to make us less inclined to fulfill these human obligations. "[S]o far as animals are concerned, we have no direct duties." Animals exist "merely as a means to an end. That end is man."[9]

The view that we have no direct moral obligations to animals was also reflected in Anglo-American law. Before the nineteenth century, it is difficult to find any statutory recognition of legal obligations owed directly to animals.[10] To the extent that the law provided animals any protection, it was, for the most part, couched solely in terms of human concerns, primarily property interests. If Simon injured Jane's cow, Simon's act might violate a malicious mischief statute if it could be proved that the act manifested malice toward Jane. If Simon had malice toward the cow but not toward Jane, then he could not be prosecuted. It was irrelevant whether Simon's malice was directed toward Jane's cow or toward her inanimate property. Any judicial condemnation of animal cruelty was, with rare exceptions, expressed only as concern that such conduct would translate into cruelty to other humans, or that acts of cruelty to animals might offend public decency and cause a breach of the peace. That is, the law reflected the notion expressed by Kant and others that if there were any reason for us to be kind to animals, it had nothing to do with any obligation that we owed to animals, but only with our obligations to other humans.

THE HUMANE TREATMENT PRINCIPLE: A REJECTION OF ANIMALS AS THINGS

Consider the following example. Simon proposes to torture a dog by burning the dog with a blowtorch. Simon's only reason for torturing the dog is that he derives pleasure from this sort of activity. Does Simon's proposal raise any moral concern? Is Simon violating some moral obligation not to use the animal in this way for his amusement? Or is Simon's action morally no different from crushing and eating a walnut?

I think that most of us would not hesitate to maintain that blowtorching the dog simply for pleasure is not a morally justifiable act under any circumstances. What is the basis of our moral judgment? Is it merely that we are concerned about the effect of Simon's action on other humans? Do we object to the torture of the dog merely because it might upset other humans who like dogs? Do we object because by torturing the dog Simon may become a more callous or unkind person in his dealings with other humans? We may very well rest our moral objection to Simon's action in part on our concern for the effect of his action on other humans, but that is not our primary reason for objecting. After all, we would condemn the act even if Simon tortures the animal in secret, or even if, apart from his appetite for torturing dogs, Simon is a charming fellow who shows only kindness to other humans.

Suppose that the dog is the companion animal of Simon's neighbor, Jane. Do we object to the torture because the dog is Jane's property? We may very well object to Simon's action because the dog belongs to Jane, but again, that is not our first concern. We would find Simon's action objectionable even if the dog were a stray.

The primary reason that we find Simon's action morally objectionable is its effect on the dog. The dog is sentient; like us, the dog is the sort of being who has the capacity to suffer and has an interest in not being blowtorched.[11] The dog prefers, or wants, or desires not to be blowtorched. We have an obligation—one owed directly to the dog and not merely one that concerns the dog—not to torture the dog. The sole ground for this obligation is that the dog is sentient; no other characteristic, such as humanlike rationality, reflective self-consciousness, or the ability to communicate in a human language, is necessary. Simply because the dog can experience pain and suffering, we regard it as morally necessary to justify our infliction of harm on the dog. We may disagree about whether a particular justification suffices, but we all agree that some justification is required, and Simon's pleasure simply cannot constitute such a justification. An integral part of our moral thinking is the idea that, other things being equal, the fact that an action causes pain counts as a reason against that action, not merely because imposing harm on another sentient being somehow diminishes us, but because imposing harm on another sentient being is wrong in itself. And it does not matter whether Simon proposes to blowtorch for pleasure the dog or another animal, such as a cow. We would object to his conduct in either case.

In short, most of us claim to reject the characterization of animals as things that has dominated Western thinking for many centuries. For the better part of 200 years, Anglo-American moral and legal culture has made a distinction between sentient creatures and inanimate objects. Although we believe that we ought to prefer humans over animals when interests conflict, most of us accept as completely uncontroversial that our use and treatment of animals are guided by what we might call the *humane treatment principle*, or the view that because animals can suffer, we have a moral obligation that we owe directly to animals not to impose unnecessary suffering on them.

The humane treatment principle finds its origins in the theories of English lawyer and utilitarian philosopher Jeremy Bentham (1748–1832). Bentham argued that despite any differences, humans and animals are similar in that they both can suffer, and it is only the capacity to suffer and not the capacity for speech or reason or anything else that is required for animals to matter morally and to have legal protection. Bentham maintained that animals had been "degraded into the class of *things*," with the result that their interest in not suffering had been ignored.[12] In a statement as profound as it was simple, Bentham illuminated the irrelevance of characteristics other than sentience: "[A] full-grown horse or dog, is beyond comparison a more rational, as well as a more conversable animal, than an infant of a day, or a week, or even a month, old. But suppose the case were otherwise, what would it avail? the question is not, Can they *reason*? nor, Can they *talk*? but, Can they *suffer*?"[13]

Bentham's position marked a sharp departure from a cultural tradition that had never before regarded animals as other than things devoid of morally significant interests. He rejected the views of those, like Descartes, who maintained that animals are not sentient and have no interests. He also rejected the views of those, like Kant, who maintained that animals have interests but that those interests are not morally significant because animals lack characteristics other than sentience, and that our treatment of animals matters only to the extent that it affects our treatment of other humans. For Bentham, our treatment of animals matters because of its effect on beings that can suffer, and our duties are owed directly to them. Bentham urged the enactment of laws to protect animals from suffering.

Bentham's views had a profound effect on various legal reformers, and the result was that the legal systems of the United States and Britain (as well as other nations) purported to incorporate the humane treatment principle in animal welfare laws. These laws are of two kinds: general and specific. General animal welfare laws, such as anticruelty laws, prohibit cruelty or the infliction of unnecessary suffering on animals without distinguishing between various uses of animals. For example, New York law imposes a criminal sanction on any person who "overdrives, overloads, tortures or cruelly beats or unjustifiably injures, maims, mutilates or kills any animal."[14] Delaware law prohibits cruelty and defines as cruel "every act or omission to act whereby unnecessary or unjustifiable physical pain or suffering is caused or permitted," and includes "mistreatment of any animal or neglect of any animal under the care and control of the neglector, whereby unnecessary or unjustifiable physical pain or suffering is caused."[15] In Britain, the Protection of Animals Act of 1911 makes it a criminal offense to "cruelly beat, kick, ill-treat, over-ride, over-drive, over-load, torture, infuriate, or terrify any animal" or to impose "unnecessary suffering" on animals.[16] Specific animal welfare laws purport to apply the humane treatment principle to a particular animal use. For example, the American Animal Welfare Act, enacted in 1966 and amended on numerous occasions,[17] the British Cruelty to Animals Act, enacted in 1876,[18] and the British Animals (Scientific Procedures) Act of 1986[19] concern the treatment of animals used in experiments. The American Humane Slaughter Act, originally enacted in 1958, regulates the killing of animals used for food.[20]

As we saw earlier, if Simon injured Jane's cow, malicious mischief statutes required a showing that Simon bore malice toward Jane. To the extent that courts had any concern about cruelty to animals, this concern was limited to the effect that cruelty might have on public sensibilities or on the tendency of cruelty to animals to encourage cruelty to other humans. The passage of anticruelty laws allowed for Simon's prosecution even if he bore Jane no ill will and instead intended malice only to her cow. Moreover, these laws reflect concern about the moral significance of animal suffering, in addition to the detrimental repercussions of cruelty to animals for humans. Anticruelty laws are often explicit in applying to all animals, whether owned or unowned. Thus, whereas malicious mischief statutes were "intended to protect the beasts as property instead of as creatures susceptible of suffering," anticruelty statutes are "designed for the protection of animals."[21] They are intended "for the benefit of animals, as creatures capable of feeling and suffering, and [are] intended to protect them from cruelty, without reference to their being property."[22] The purpose of these laws is, in part, to instill in humans "a humane regard for the rights and feelings of the brute creation by reproving the evil and indifferent tendencies in human nature in its intercourse with animals."[23] They are said to "recognize and attempt to protect some abstract rights in all that animate creation, made subject to man by the creation, from the largest and noblest to the smallest and most insignificant."[24] Anticruelty laws acknowledge that because animals are sentient, we have legal obligations that we owe directly to animals to refrain from imposing unnecessary pain and suffering on them: "Pain is an evil," and "[i]t is impossible for a right minded man . . . to say that unjustifiable cruelty [to animals] is not a wrong."[25] Other animal welfare laws similarly focus on the suffering of animals as intrinsically undesirable.[26]

Many animal welfare laws, such as anticruelty statutes, are criminal laws. For the most part, only those moral rules that are widely accepted, such as prohibitions against killing other humans, inflicting physical harm on them, or taking or destroying their property, are enshrined in criminal laws. That many animal welfare laws are criminal laws suggests that we take animal interests seriously enough to punish violations of the humane treatment principle with the social stigma of a criminal penalty.

The humane treatment principle and the operation of the animal welfare laws that reflect it purport to require that we balance the interests of animals against our interests as humans in order to determine whether animal suffering is necessary. To balance interests means to assess the relative strengths of conflicting interests. If our suffering in not using animals outweighs the animal interest in not suffering, then our interests prevail, and the animal suffering is regarded as necessary. If no justifiable human interests are at stake, then the infliction of suffering on animals must be regarded as unnecessary. For example, the British law regulating the use of animals in experiments requires, before any experiment is approved, a balancing of "the likely adverse effects on the animals concerned against the benefit likely to accrue."[27]

In sum, the principle assumes that we may use animals when it is necessary to do so—when we are faced with a conflict between animal and human interests—and that we should impose only the minimum amount of pain and suffering necessary to achieve our purpose. If a prohibition against unnecessary suffering of animals is to have any meaningful content, it must preclude the infliction of suffering on animals merely for our pleasure, amusement, or convenience. If there is a feasible alternative to our use of animals in a particular situation, then the principle would seem to proscribe such use.

THE PROBLEM: UNNECESSARY SUFFERING

Although we express disapproval of the unnecessary suffering of animals, nearly all of our animal use can be justified *only* by habit, convention, amusement, convenience, or pleasure.[28] To put the matter another way, most of the suffering that we impose on animals is completely unnecessary, and we are not substantially different from Simon, who proposes to blowtorch the dog for pleasure. For example, the uses of animals for sport hunting and entertainment purposes cannot, by definition, be considered necessary. Nevertheless, these activities are protected by laws that supposedly prohibit the infliction of unnecessary suffering on animals. It is certainly not necessary for us to wear fur coats, or to use animals to test duplicative household products, or to have yet another brand of lipstick or aftershave lotion.

More important in terms of numbers of animals used, however, is the animal agriculture industry, in which billions of animals are killed for food annually. It is not necessary in any sense to eat meat or animal products; indeed, an increasing number of health care professionals maintain that these foods may be detrimental to human health. Moreover, respected environmental scientists have pointed out the tremendous inefficiencies and resulting costs to our planet of animal agriculture. For example, animals consume more protein than they produce. For every kilogram (2.2 pounds) of animal protein produced, animals consume an average of almost 6 kilograms, or more than 13 pounds, of plant protein from grains and forage. It takes more than 100,000 liters of water to produce one kilogram of beef, and approximately 900 liters to produce one kilogram of wheat. In any event, our only justification for the pain, suffering, and death inflicted on these billions of farm animals is that we enjoy the taste of their flesh.

Although many regard the use of animals in experiments as involving a genuine conflict of human and animal interests, the necessity of animal use for this purpose is open to serious question as well. Considerable empirical evidence challenges the notion that animal experiments are necessary to ensure human health and indicates that, in many instances, reliance on animal models has actually been counterproductive.

ANIMALS AS PROPERTY: AN UNBALANCED BALANCE

The profound inconsistency between what we say about animals and how we actually treat them is related to the status of animals as our property.[29] Animals are commodities that we own and that have no value other than that which we, as property owners, choose to give them. Although Bentham changed moral thinking and legal doctrine by introducing the idea that sentience is the only characteristic required for animals to matter, neither he nor the reformers interested in incorporating his views into law ever questioned the property status of animals.[30] Under the law, "animals are owned in the same way as inanimate objects such as cars and furniture."[31] They "are by law treated as any other form of movable property and may be the subject of absolute, *i.e.*, complete ownership . . . [and] the owner has at his command all the protection that the law provides in respect of absolute ownership."[32] The owner is entitled to exclusive physical possession of the animal, the use of the animal for economic and other gain, and the right to make contracts with respect to the animal or to use the animal as collateral for a loan. The owner is under a duty to ensure that her animal property does not harm other humans or their property, but she can sell or bequeath the animal, give the animal away, or have the animal taken from her as part of the execution of a legal judgment against her. She can also kill the animal. Wild animals are generally regarded as owned by the state and held in trust for the benefit of the people, but they can be made the property of particular humans through hunting or by taming and confining them.

The property status of animals renders meaningless any balancing that is supposedly required under the humane treatment principle or animal welfare laws, because what we really balance are the interests of property owners against the interests of their animal property. It is, of course, absurd to suggest that we can balance human interests, which are protected by claims of right in general and of a right to own property in particular, against the interests of property, which exists only as a means to the ends of humans. Although we claim to recognize that we may prefer animal interests over human interests only when there is a conflict of interests, there is always a conflict between the interests of property owners who want to use their property and the interests of their animal property. The human property interest will almost always prevail. The animal in question is always a "pet" or a "laboratory animal," or a "game animal," or a "food animal," or a "rodeo animal," or some other form of animal property that exists solely for our use and has no value except that which we give it. There is really no choice to be made between the human and the animal interest because the choice has already been predetermined by the property status of the animal; the "suffering" of property owners who cannot use their property as they wish counts more than animal suffering. We are allowed to impose any suffering required to use our animal property for a particular purpose even if that purpose is our mere amusement or pleasure. As long as we use our animal property to generate an economic benefit, there is no effective limit on our use or treatment of animals.[33]

There are several specific ways in which animal welfare laws ensure that there will never be a meaningful balance of human and animal interests. First, many of these laws explicitly exempt most forms of institutionalized property use, which account for the largest number of animals that we use. The most frequent exemptions from state anticruelty statutes involve scientific experiments, agricultural practices, and hunting.[34] The Animal Welfare Act, the primary federal law that regulates the use of animals in biomedical experiments, does not even apply to most of the animals used in experiments—rats and mice—and imposes no meaningful limits on the amount of pain and suffering that may be inflicted on animals in the conduct of experiments.[35]

Second, even if anticruelty statutes do not do so explicitly, courts have effectively exempted our common uses of animals from scrutiny by interpreting these statutes as not prohibiting the infliction of even extreme suffering if it is incidental to an accepted use of animals and a customary practice on the part of animal owners.[36] An act "which inflicts pain, even the great pain of mutilation, and which is cruel in the ordinary sense of the word" is not prohibited "[w]henever the purpose for which the act is done is to make the animal more serviceable for the use of man."[37] For example, courts have held consistently that animals used for food may be mutilated in ways that unquestionably cause severe pain and suffering and that would normally be regarded as cruel or even as torture. These practices are permitted, however, because animal agriculture is an accepted institutionalized animal use, and those in the meat industry regard the practices as normal and necessary to facilitate that use. Courts often presume that animal owners will act in their best economic interests and will not intentionally inflict more suffering than is necessary on an animal because to do so would diminish the monetary value of the animal.[38] For example, in *Callaghan v. Society for the Prevention of Cruelty to Animals*, the court held that the painful act of dehorning cattle did not constitute unnecessary abuse because farmers would not perform this procedure if it were not necessary. The self-interest of the farmer would prevent the infliction of "useless pain or torture," which "would necessarily reduce the condition of the animal; and, unless they very soon recovered, the farmer would lose in the sale."[39]

Third, anticruelty laws are generally criminal laws, and the state must prove beyond a reasonable doubt that a defendant engaged in an unlawful act with a culpable state of mind. The problem is that if a defendant is inflicting pain or suffering on an animal as part of an accepted institutionalized use of animals, it is difficult to prove that she acted with the requisite mental state to justify criminal liability.[40] For example, in *Regalado v. United States*,[41] Regalado was convicted of violating the anticruelty statute of the District of Columbia for beating a puppy. Regalado appealed, claiming that he did not intend to harm the puppy and inflicted the beating only for disciplinary purposes. The court held that anticruelty statutes were "not intended to place unreasonable restrictions on the infliction of such pain as may be necessary for the training or discipline of an animal" and that the statute only prohibited acts done with malice or a cruel disposition.[42] Although the court affirmed Regalado's conviction, it recognized that "proof of malice will usually be circumstantial, and the line between discipline and cruelty will often be difficult to draw."[43]

Fourth, many animal welfare laws have wholly inadequate penalty provisions, and we are reluctant, in any event, to impose the stigma of criminal liability on animal owners for what they do with their property.[44] Moreover, those without an ownership interest generally do not have standing to bring legal challenges to the use or treatment of animals by their owners.[45]

As the foregoing makes clear, because animals are property, we do not balance interests to determine whether it is necessary to use animals at all for particular purposes. We simply assume that it is appropriate to use animals for food, recreation, entertainment, clothing, or experiments—the primary ways in which we use animals as commodities to generate social wealth and most of which cannot be described plausibly as involving any genuine conflict of human and animal interests. Animal welfare laws do not even apply to many of these uses. To the extent that we do ask whether the imposition of pain and suffering is necessary, the inquiry is limited to whether particular treatment is in compliance with the customs and practices of property owners who, we assume, will not inflict more pain and suffering on their animal property than is required for the purpose. The only way to characterize this process is as a "balancing" of the property owner's interest in using animal property against the interest of an animal in not being used in ways that fail to comply with those customs and practices. Although animal welfare laws are intended to protect the interests of animals without reference to their being property, animal interests are generally protected only insofar as it serves the goal of rational property use.[46]

Our infliction of suffering on animals raises a legal question only when it does not conform to the customs and practices of those institutions— when we intentionally inflict suffering in ways that do not maximize social wealth, or when the only explanation for the behavior can be characterized as "the gratification of a malignant or vindictive temper."[47] For example, in *State v. Tweedie*,[48] the defendant was found to have violated the anticruelty law by killing a cat in a microwave oven. *In re William G.*[49] upheld a cruelty conviction where a minor kicked a dog and set her on fire because she would not mate with his dog. In *Motes v. State*,[50] the defendant was found guilty of violating the anticruelty statute when he set fire to a dog merely because the dog was barking. In *Tuck v. United States*,[51] a pet shop owner was convicted of cruelty when he placed animals in an unventilated display window and refused to remove a rabbit whose body temperature registered as high as the thermometer was calibrated—110 degrees Fahrenheit. In *People v. Voelker*,[52] the court held that cutting off the heads of three live, conscious iguanas "without justification" could constitute a violation of the anticruelty law. In *LaRue v. State*,[53] a cruelty conviction was upheld because the defendant collected a large number of stray dogs and failed to provide them with veterinary care; the dogs suffered from mange, blindness, dehydration, pneumonia, and distemper and had to be killed. In *State v. Schott*,[54] Schott was convicted of cruelty to animals when police found dozens of cows and pigs dead or dying from malnutrition and dehydration on Schott's farm. Schott's defense was that bad weather prevented him from caring for his livestock. The jury found Schott guilty of cruelty and neglect, and the appellate court affirmed. These are, however, unusual cases and constitute a minuscule fraction of the instances in which we inflict suffering on animals.

Moreover, the very same act may be either protected or prohibited depending only on whether it is part of an accepted institution of animal exploitation. If someone kills a cat in a microwave, sets a dog on fire, allows the body temperature of a rabbit to rise to the point of heat stroke, severs the heads of conscious animals, or allows animals to suffer untreated serious illnesses, the conduct may violate the anticruelty laws. But if a researcher engages in the exact same conduct as part of an experiment (and a number of researchers have killed animals or inflicted pain on them in the same and similar ways) the conduct is protected by the law because the researcher is supposedly using the animal to generate a benefit. A farmer may run afoul of the anticruelty law if she neglects her animals and allows them to suffer from malnutrition or dehydration for no reason, but she may mutilate her animals and raise them in conditions of severe confinement and depriva- tion, if she intends to sell them for food. The permitted actions cause as much if not more distress to animals as does neglecting them, but they are considered part of normal animal husbandry and are, therefore, protected under the law.

Thus, because animals are our property, the law will require their inter- ests to be observed only to the extent that it facilitates the exploitation of the animal. This observation holds true even in countries where there is ar- guably a greater moral concern about animals. Britain, for instance, has more restrictions on animal use than does the United States, but the differ- ences in permitted animal treatment are more formal than substantive. In discussing British animal welfare laws, one commentator has noted that "much of the animal welfare agenda has been obstructed and it is difficult to think of legislation improving the welfare of animals that has seriously dam- aged the interests of the animal users."[55] The law may in theory impose regulations that go beyond the minimum level of care required to exploit animals, yet it has rarely done so, for there are significant economic and other obstacles involved.[56] Voluntary changes in industry standards of ani- mal welfare generally occur only when animal users regard these changes as cost-effective.[57]

The status of animals as property renders meaningless our claim that we reject the status of animals as things. We treat animals as the moral equiva- lent of inanimate objects with no morally significant interests. We bring bil- lions of animals into existence annually simply for the purpose of killing them. Animals have market prices. Dogs and cats are sold in pet stores like compact discs; financial markets trade in futures for pork bellies and cattle. Any interest that an animal has represents an economic cost that may be ignored to maximize overall social wealth and has no intrinsic value in our assessments. That is what it means to be property.

TAKING ANIMAL INTERESTS SERIOUSLY: THE PRINCIPLE OF EQUAL CONSIDERATION

We claim to accept that animals are not merely things. We may use animals when there is a conflict between human and animal interests that requires us to make a choice, but we have a moral obligation that we owe directly to animals not to inflict unnecessary suffering on them. Despite what we say, most of our animal use cannot be described as involving any conflict of interests, and we inflict extreme pain and suffering on animals in the process. Even if we treated animals better, that would still leave open the question of our moral justification for imposing any suffering at all if animal use is not necessary. We may, of course, decide to discard the humane treatment principle and acknowledge that we regard animals as nothing more than things without any morally significant interests. This option would at least spare us the need for thinking about our moral obligations to animals. We would not have any.

Alternatively, if we are to make good on our claim to take animal interests seriously, then we can do so in only one way: by applying the *principle of equal consideration*—the rule that we ought to treat like cases alike unless there is a good reason not to do so—to animals.[58] The principle of equal consideration is a necessary component of every moral theory. Any theory that maintains that it is permissible to treat similar cases in a dissimilar way would fail to qualify as an acceptable moral theory for that reason alone. Although there may be many differences between humans and animals, there is at least one important similarity that we all already recognize: our shared capacity to suffer. In this sense, humans and animals are similar to each other and different from everything else in the universe that is not sentient. If our supposed prohibition on the infliction of unnecessary suffering on animals is to have any meaning at all, then we must give equal consideration to animal interests in not suffering.

The suggestion that animal interests should receive equal consideration is not as radical as it may appear at first if we consider that the humane treatment principle incorporates the principle of equal consideration. We are to weigh our suffering in not using animals against animal interests in avoiding suffering. If there is a conflict between human and animal interests and the human interest weighs more, then the animal suffering is justifiable. If there is no conflict, or if there is a conflict of interests but the animal interest weighs more, then we are not justified in using the animal. And if there is a conflict of interests but the interests at stake are similar, then we should presumably treat those interests in the same way and impose suffering on neither or both unless there is some nonarbitrary reason that justifies differential treatment. Moreover, the humane treatment principle as it developed historically explicitly included the principle of equal consideration. Bentham recognized that the only way to ensure that animal interests in not suffering were taken seriously was to apply the principle of equal consideration to animals, and Bentham's position therefore "incorporated the essential basis of moral equality . . . by means of the formula: 'Each to count for one and none for more than one.'"[59] Animal suffering cannot be discounted or ignored based on the supposed lack of some characteristic other than sentience if animals are not to be "degraded into the class of *things*." But Bentham never questioned the property status of animals because he mistakenly believed that the principle of equal consideration could be applied to animals even if they are property.[60] Bentham's error was perpetuated through laws that purported to balance the interest of property owners and their property.

The problem is that, as we have seen, there can be no meaningful balancing of interests if animals are property. The property status of animals is a two-edged sword wielded against their interests. First, it acts as blinders that effectively block even our perception of their interests as similar to ours because human "suffering" is understood as any detriment to property owners. Second, in those instances in which human and animal interests are recognized as similar, animal interests will fail in the balancing because the property status of animals is always a good reason not to accord similar treatment unless to do so would benefit property owners. Animal interests will almost always count for less than one; animals remain as they were before the nineteenth century—things without morally significant interests.

The application of the principle of equal consideration similarly failed in the context of North American slavery, which allowed some humans to treat others as property.[61] The institution of human slavery was structurally identical to the institution of animal ownership. Because a human slave was regarded as property, the slave owner was able to disregard all of the slave's interests if it was economically beneficial to do so, and the law generally deferred to the slave owner's judgment as to the value of the slave. As chattel property, slaves could be sold, willed, insured, mortgaged, and seized in payment of the owner's debts. Slave owners could inflict severe punishments on slaves for virtually any reason. Those who intentionally or negligently injured another's slave were liable to the owner in an action for damage to property. Slaves could not enter into contracts, own property, sue or be sued, or live as free persons with basic rights and duties.

It was generally acknowledged that slaves had an interest in not suffering: Slaves "are not rational beings. No, but they are the creatures of God, sentient beings, capable of suffering and enjoyment, and entitled to enjoy according to the measure of their capacities. Does not the voice of nature inform everyone, that he is guilty of wrong when he inflicts on them pain without necessity or object?"[62] Although there were laws that ostensibly regulated the use and treatment of slaves, they failed completely to protect slave interests. The law often contained exceptions that eviscerated any protection for the slaves. For example, North Carolina law provided that the punishment for the murder of a slave should be the same as for the murder of a free person, but this law "did not apply to an outlawed slave, nor to a slave 'in the act of resistance to his lawful owner,' nor to a slave 'dying under moderate correction.'"[63] A law that prohibits the murder of slaves but permits three general and easily satisfied exceptions, combined with a general prohibition against the testimony of slaves against free persons, cannot effectively deter the murder of slaves. That the law refused to protect the interests of slaves against slave owners is underscored in *State v. Mann*, in which the court held that even the "cruel and unreasonable battery" of one's own slave is not indictable: Courts cannot "allow the right of the master to be brought into discussion in the courts of justice. The slave, to remain a slave, must be made sensible that there is no appeal from his master."[64] To the extent that the law regulated the conduct of slave owners, it had nothing to do with concern for the interests of the slaves. For example, in *Commonwealth v. Turner*, the court determined that it had no jurisdiction to try the defendant slave owner, who beat his slave with "rods, whips and sticks," and held that even if the beating was administered "wilfully and maliciously, violently, cruelly, immoderately, and excessively," the court was not empowered to act as long as the slave did not die.[65] The court distinguished private beatings from public chastisement; the latter might subject the master to liability "not because it was a slave who was beaten, nor because the act was unprovoked or cruel; but, because ipso facto it disturbed the harmony of society; was offensive to public decency, and directly tended to a breach of the peace. The same would be the law, if a horse had been so beaten."[66]

Slave welfare laws failed for precisely the same reason that animal welfare laws fail to establish any meaningful limit on our use of animal property. The owner's property interest in the slave always trumped any interest of the slave who was ostensibly protected under the law. The interests of slaves were observed only when it provided an economic benefit for the owners or served their whim. Alan Watson has noted that "[a]t most places at most times a reasonably economic owner would be conscious of the chattel value of slaves and thus would ensure some care in their treatment."[67] Any legal limitations on the cruelty of slave owners reflected the concern that they should not use their property in unproductive ways; as expressed by the Roman jurist Justinian, "'it is to the advantage of the state that no one use his property badly.'"[68] Although some slave owners were more "humane" than others and some even treated slaves as family members, any kind treatment was a matter of the master's charity and not of the slave's right, and slavery as a legal institution had the inevitable effect of treating humans as nothing more than commodities. The principle of equal consideration had no meaningful application to the interests of a human whose only value was as a resource belonging to others. Slaves were rarely considered to have any interests similar to slave owners or other free persons; in those instances in which interests were recognized as similar, the property status of the slave was always a good reason not to accord similar treatment unless to do so would benefit the owner.

We eventually recognized that if humans were to have any morally significant interests, they could not be the resources of others and that race was not a sufficient reason to treat certain humans as property.[69] Although we tolerate varying degrees of exploitation, and we may disagree about what constitutes equal treatment, we no longer regard it as legitimate to treat any humans, irrespective of their particular characteristics, as the property of others. Indeed, in a world deeply divided on many moral issues, one of the few norms steadfastly endorsed by the international community is the prohibition of human slavery. It matters not whether the particular form of slavery is "humane" or not; we condemn all human slavery. More brutal forms of slavery are worse than less brutal forms, but we prohibit human slavery in general because all forms of slavery more or less allow the interests of slaves to be ignored if it provides a benefit to slave owners, and humans have an interest in not suffering the deprivation of their fundamental interests merely because it benefits someone else, however "humanely" they are treated. It would, of course, be incorrect to say that human slavery has been eliminated from the planet. But the peremptory norms in international law—those few, select rules regarded as of such significance that they admit of no derogation by any nation—include the prohibition of slavery, which humanity deems so odious that no civilized nation can bear its existence.

The interest of a human in not being the property of others is protected by a right. When an interest is protected by a right, the interest may not be ignored or violated simply because it will benefit others. Rights are "moral notions that grow out of respect for the individual. They build protective fences around the individual. They establish areas where the individual is entitled to be protected against the state and the majority *even where a price is paid by the general welfare*."[70] If we are going to recognize and protect the interest of humans in not being treated as property, then we must use a right to do so; if we do not, then those humans who do not have this protection will be treated merely as commodities whenever it will benefit others. Therefore, the interest in not being treated as property must be protected against being traded away even if a price is paid by the general welfare.

The right not to be treated as the property of others is basic and different from any other rights we might have because it is the grounding for those other rights; it is a prelegal right that serves as the precondition for the possession of morally significant interests. The basic right is the right to the equal consideration of one's fundamental interests; it recognizes that if some humans have value only as resources, then the principle of equal consideration will have no meaningful application to their interests. Therefore, the basic right must be understood as prohibiting human slavery, or any other institutional arrangement that treats humans *exclusively* as means to the ends of others and not as ends in themselves.[71]

The protection afforded by the basic right not to be treated as property is limited. The basic right does not guarantee equal treatment in all respects nor protect humans from all suffering, but it protects all humans, irrespective of their particular characteristics, from suffering any deprivation of interests as the result of being used exclusively as the resources of others and thereby provides essential protections. We may not enslave humans nor, for that matter, may we exert total control over their bodies by using them as we do laboratory animals, or as forced organ donors, or as raw materials for shoes, or as objects to be hunted for sport or tortured—irrespective of whether we claim to treat them "humanely" in the process.[72] An employer may treat her employees instrumentally and disregard their interest in a midmorning coffee break, or even their interest in health care, in the name of profit. But there are limits. She cannot force her employees to work without compensation. Pharmaceutical companies cannot test new drugs on employees who have not consented. Food-processing plants cannot make hot dogs or luncheon meats out of workers. To possess the basic right not to be treated as property is a minimal prerequisite to being a moral and legal *person*; it does not specify what other rights the person may have. Indeed, the rejection of slavery is required by any moral theory that purports to accord moral significance to the interests of all humans even if the particular theory otherwise rejects rights.[73]

Animals, like humans, have an interest in not suffering, but, as we have seen, the principle of equal consideration has no meaningful application to animal interests if they are the property of others just as it had no meaningful application to the interests of slaves. The interests of animals as property will almost always count for less than do the interests of their owners. Some owners may choose to treat their animals well, or even as members of their families as some do with their pets, but the law generally will not protect animals against their owners. Animal ownership as a legal institution inevitably has the effect of treating animals as commodities. Moreover, animals, like humans, have an interest in not suffering at all from the ways in which we use them, however "humane" that use may be. To the extent that we protect humans from being used in these ways and we do not extend the same protection to animals, we fail to accord equal consideration to animal interests in not suffering.

If we are going to take animal interests seriously, we must extend to animals the one right that we extend to all humans irrespective of their particular characteristics. To do so would not mean that animals would be protected from all suffering. Animals in the wild may be injured, or become diseased, or may be attacked by other animals. But it would mean that animals could no longer be used as the resources of humans and would, therefore, be protected from suffering at all from such uses. Is there a morally sound reason not to extend to animals the right not to be treated as property, and thereby recognize that our obligation not to impose unnecessary suffering on them is really an obligation not to treat them as property? Or, to ask the question in another way, why do we deem it acceptable to eat animals, hunt them, confine and display them in circuses and zoos, use them in experiments or rodeos, or otherwise to treat them in ways in which we would never think it appropriate to treat any human irrespective of how "humanely" we were to do so?

The usual response claims that some empirical difference between humans and animals constitutes a good reason for not according to animals the one right we accord to all humans. According to this view, there is some qualitative distinction between humans and animals (all species considered as a single group) that purportedly justifies our treating animals as our property. This distinction almost always concerns some difference between human and animal minds; we have some mental characteristic that animals lack, or are capable of certain actions of which animals are incapable as a result of our purportedly superior cognitive abilities. The list of characteristics that are posited as possessed only by humans includes self-consciousness, reason, abstract thought, emotion, the ability to communicate, and the capacity for moral action.[74] We claimed to reject the relevance of these characteristics 200 years ago when we supposedly embraced the idea that the capacity to suffer was the only attribute needed to ground our moral obligation to animals not to impose unnecessary suffering on them. Yet, the absence of these same characteristics continues to serve as our justification for treating animals as our resources and has been used to keep animals "degraded into the class of *things*" despite our claim to take animal interests seriously.

The problem started with Bentham himself.[75] Although Bentham's analysis of slavery is not entirely clear, he arguably opposed human slavery at least in part because the principle of equal consideration would not apply to humans who are slaves. He acknowledged that a particular slave owner might treat a slave well and that some forms of slavery were better than others, but "slavery once established, was always likely to be the lot of large numbers. 'If the evil of slavery were not great its extent alone would make it considerable.'"[76] Slavery as an institution would inevitably result in humans being treated as things and "abandoned without redress to the caprice of a tormentor."[77] Slaves would necessarily count for less than did those who were not slaves. Bentham regarded the concept of moral rights as metaphysical nonsense, but he did, in effect, recognize that humans had a right not to be treated as property.[78] He noted that just as the color of skin was an insufficient reason to abandon humans to the caprice of a tormentor, "the number of the legs, the villosity of the skin, or the termination of the *os sacrum*, are reasons equally insufficient for abandoning a sensitive being to the same fate."[79] Why, then, did Bentham not reject the treatment of animals as property as he had rejected the treatment of humans as property?

The answer is related to Bentham's view that animals, like humans, have interests in not suffering but, unlike humans, have no interest in their continued existence. That is, Bentham believed that animals do not have a sense of self; they live moment to moment and have no continuous mental existence. Their minds consist of collections of unconnected sensations of pain and pleasure. On this view, death is not a harm for animals; animals do not care about whether we eat them, or use and kill them for other purposes, as long as we do not make them suffer in the process: "If the being eaten were all, there is very good reason why we should be suffered to eat such of them as we like to eat: we are the better for it, and they are never the worse. They have none of those long-protracted anticipations of future misery which we have."[80] Although Bentham explicitly rejected the position that, because animals lack characteristics beyond sentience, such as self-awareness, we could treat them as things, he maintained that because ani-

mals lack self-awareness, we do not violate the principle of equal consideration by using animals as our resources as long as we give equal consideration
to their interests in not suffering.

Bentham's position is problematic for several reasons. Bentham failed to
recognize that although particular animal owners might treat their animal
property kindly, institutionalized animal exploitation would, like slavery,
become "the lot of large numbers," and animals would necessarily be treated
as economic commodities that were, like slaves, "abandoned without redress
to the caprice of a tormentor." Moreover, Bentham never explained how to
apply the principle of equal consideration to animals who were the property
of humans.[81] But most important, Bentham was simply wrong to claim
that animals are not self-aware and have no interest in their lives.

Sentience is not an end in itself. It is a means to the end of staying alive.
Sentient beings use sensations of pain and suffering to escape situations that
threaten their lives and sensations of pleasure to pursue situations that en-
hance their lives. Just as humans will often endure excruciating pain in order
to remain alive, animals will often not only endure but inflict on themselves
excruciating pain—as when gnawing off a paw caught in a trap—in order to
live. Sentience is what evolution has produced in order to ensure the survival of certain complex organisms. To claim that a being who has evolved
to develop a consciousness of pain and pleasure has no interest in remaining
alive is to say that conscious beings have no interest in remaining conscious,
a most peculiar position to take.

Moreover, the proposition that humans have mental characteristics
wholly absent in animals is inconsistent with the theory of evolution. Darwin maintained that there are no uniquely human characteristics: "[T]he
difference in mind between man and the higher animals, great as it is, is certainly one of degree and not of kind."[82] Animals are able to think, and possess many of the same emotional responses as do humans: "[T]he senses and
intuitions, the various emotions and faculties, such as love, memory, attention, curiosity, imitation, reason, &c., of which man boasts, may be found
in an incipient, or even sometimes in a well-developed condition, in the
lower animals."[83] Darwin noted that "associated animals have a feeling of
love for each other" and that animals "certainly sympathise with each other's
distress or danger."[84]

Even if we cannot know the precise nature of animal self-awareness, it
appears that *any* being that is aware on a perceptual level must be self-aware
and have a continuous mental existence. Biologist Donald Griffin has observed that if animals are conscious of anything, "the animal's own body and
its own actions must fall within the scope of its perceptual consciousness."[85]
Yet we deny animals self-awareness because we maintain that they cannot
"think such thoughts as 'It is *I* who am running, or climbing this tree, or
chasing that moth.'"[86] Griffin maintains that "when an animal consciously
perceives the running, climbing, or moth-chasing of another animal, it
must also be aware of who is doing these things. And if the animal is per-

ceptually conscious of its own body, it is difficult to rule out similar recognition that it, itself, is doing the running, climbing, or chasing."[87] Griffin concludes that "[i]f animals are capable of perceptual awareness, denying them some level of self-awareness would seem to be an arbitrary and unjustified restriction."[88] Griffin's reasoning can be applied in the context of sentience. Any sentient being must have some level of self-awareness. To be sentient means to be the sort of being who recognizes that it is *that* being, and not some other, who is experiencing pain or distress. When a dog experiences pain, the dog necessarily has a mental experience that tells her "this pain is happening to me." In order for pain to exist, some consciousness—some*one*—must perceive it as happening to her and must prefer not to experience it.

Antonio Damasio, a neurologist who works with humans who have suffered strokes, seizures, and conditions that cause brain damage, maintains that such humans have what he calls "core consciousness." Core consciousness, which does not depend on memory, language, or reasoning, "provides the organism with a sense of self about one moment—now—and about one place—here."[89] Humans who experience transient global amnesia, for example, have no sense of the past or the future but do have a sense of self with respect to present events and objects, and such humans would most certainly regard death as a harm. Damasio maintains that many animal species possess core consciousness. He distinguishes core consciousness from what he calls "extended consciousness," which requires reasoning and memory, but not language, and involves enriching one's sense of self with autobiographical details and what we might consider a representational sense of consciousness. Extended consciousness, of which there are "many levels and grades," involves a self with memories of the past, anticipations of the future, and awareness of the present.[90] Although Damasio argues that extended consciousness reaches its most complex level in humans, who have language and sophisticated reasoning abilities, he maintains that chimpanzees, bonobos, baboons, and even dogs may have an autobiographical sense of self.[91] Even if most animals do not have extended consciousness, most of the animals we routinely exploit undoubtedly have at least core consciousness, which means that they are self-conscious. In short, the fact that animals may not have an autobiographical sense of their lives (or one that they can communicate to us) does not mean that they do not have a continuous mental existence, or that they do not have an interest in their lives, or that killing them makes no difference to them.

Cognitive ethologists and others have confirmed that animals, including mammals, birds, and even fish, have many of the cognitive characteristics once thought to be uniquely human.[92] Animals possess considerable intelligence and are able to process information in sophisticated and complex ways. They are able to communicate with other members of their own species as well as with humans; indeed, there is considerable evidence that nonhuman great apes can communicate using symbolic language. The similarities between humans and animals are not limited to cognitive or emotional attributes alone. Some argue that animals exhibit what is clearly moral behavior as well. For example, Frans de Waal states that "honesty, guilt, and the weighing of ethical dilemmas are traceable to specific areas of the brain. It should not surprise us, therefore, to find animal parallels. The human brain is a product of evolution. Despite its larger volume and greater complexity, it is fundamentally similar to the central nervous system of other mammals."[93] There are numerous instances in which animals have acted in altruistic ways toward unrelated members of their own species and toward other species, including humans.

Although it is clear that animals other than humans possess characteristics purported to be unique to humans, it is also clear that there are differences between humans and other animals. For example, even if animals are self-aware on some level, that does not mean that animals can recognize themselves in mirrors (although some nonhuman primates do) or keep diaries or anticipate the future by looking at clocks and calendars; even if animals have the ability to reason or think abstractly, that does not mean that they can do calculus or compose symphonies. Yet for at least two related reasons, the humanlike varieties of these characteristics cannot serve to provide a morally sound, nonarbitrary basis for denying the right not to be treated as property to animals who may lack these characteristics.[94]

First, any attempt to justify treating animals as resources based on their lack of supposed uniquely human characteristics begs the question from the outset by assuming that certain human characteristics are special and justify differential treatment. Even if, for instance, no animals other than humans can recognize themselves in mirrors or can communicate through symbolic language, no human is capable of flying, or breathing underwater, without assistance. What makes the ability to recognize oneself in a mirror or use symbolic language better in a moral sense than the ability to fly or breathe underwater? The answer, of course, is that *we* say so. But apart from our proclamation, there is simply no reason to conclude that characteristics thought to be uniquely human have any value that allows us to use them as a nonarbitrary justification for treating animals as property. These characteristics can serve this role only after we have assumed their moral relevance.

Second, even if all animals other than humans lack a particular characteristic beyond sentience, or possess it to a different degree than do humans, there is no logically defensible relationship between the lack or lesser degree of that characteristic and our treatment of animals as resources. Differences between humans and other animals may be relevant for other purposes—no sensible person argues that we ought to enable nonhuman animals to drive cars or vote or attend universities—but the differences have no bearing on whether animals should have the status of property. We recognize this inescapable conclusion where humans are involved. Whatever characteristic we identify as uniquely human will be seen to a lesser degree in some humans and not at all in others.[95] Some humans will have the exact same deficiency that we attribute to animals, and although the deficiency may be relevant for some purposes, most of us would reject enslaving such humans, or otherwise treating such humans exclusively as means to the ends of others.

Consider, for instance, self-consciousness. Peter Carruthers defines self-consciousness as the ability to have a "conscious experience . . . whose existence and content are available to be consciously thought about (that is, available for description in acts of thinking that are themselves made available to further acts of thinking)."[96] According to Carruthers, humans must have what Damasio refers to as the most complex level of extended consciousness, or a language-enriched autobiographical sense of self, in order to be self-conscious. But many humans, such as the severely mentally disabled, do not have self-consciousness in that sense; we do not, however, regard it as permissible to use them as we do laboratory animals, or to enslave them to labor for those without their particular disability. Nor should we. We recognize that a mentally disabled human has an interest in her life and in not being treated exclusively as a means to the ends of others even if she does not have the same level of self-consciousness that is possessed by normal adults; in this sense, she is similarly situated to all other sentient humans, who have an interest in being treated as ends in themselves irrespective of their particular characteristics. Indeed, to say that a mentally disabled person is not similarly situated to all others for purposes of being treated exclusively as a resource is to say that a less intelligent person is not similarly situated to a more intelligent person for purposes of being used, for instance, as a forced organ donor. The fact that the mentally disabled human may not have a particular sort of self-consciousness may serve as a nonarbitrary reason for treating her differently in some respects—it may be relevant to whether we make her the host of a talk show, or give her a job teaching in a university, or allow her to drive a car—but it has no relevance to whether we treat her exclusively as a resource and disregard her fundamental interests, including her interest in not suffering and in her continued existence, if it benefits us to do so.

The same analysis applies to every human characteristic beyond sentience that is offered to justify treating animals as resources. There will be some humans who also lack this characteristic, or possess it to a lesser degree than do normal humans. This "defect" may be relevant for some purposes, but not for whether we treat humans exclusively as resources. We do not treat as things those humans who lack characteristics beyond sentience simply out of some sense of charity. We realize that to do so would violate the principle of equal consideration by using an arbitrary reason to deny similar treatment to similar interests in not being treated exclusively as a means to the ends of others.[97] "[T]he question is not, Can they *reason*? nor, Can they *talk*? but, Can they *suffer*?"

In sum, there is no characteristic that serves to distinguish humans from all other animals for purposes of denying to animals the one right that we extend to all humans. Whatever attribute we may think makes all humans special and thereby deserving of the right not to be the property of others is shared by nonhumans. More important, even if there are uniquely human characteristics, some humans will not possess those characteristics, but we would never think of using such humans as resources. In the end, the only difference between humans and animals is species, and species is not a justification for treating animals as property any more than is race a justification for human slavery.

ANIMALS AS PERSONS

If we extend the right not to be property to animals, then animals will become moral persons. To say that a being is a person is merely to say that the being has morally significant interests, that the principle of equal consideration applies to that being, that the being is not a thing. In a sense, we already accept that animals are persons; we claim to reject the view that animals are things and to recognize that, at the very least, animals have a morally significant interest in not suffering. Their status as property, however, has prevented their personhood from being realized.

The same was true of human slavery. Slaves were regarded as chattel property. Laws that provided for the "humane" treatment of slaves did not make slaves persons because, as we have seen, the principle of equal consideration could not apply to slaves. We tried, through slave welfare laws, to have a three-tiered system: things, or inanimate property; persons, who were free; and in the middle, depending on your choice of locution, "quasi-persons" or "things plus"—the slaves. That system could not work. We eventually recognized that if slaves were going to have morally significant interests, they could not be slaves any more, for the moral universe is limited to only two kinds of beings: persons and things. "Quasi-persons" or "things plus" will necessarily risk being treated as things because the principle of equal consideration cannot apply to them.

Nor can we use animal welfare laws to render animals "quasi-persons" or "things plus." They are either persons, beings to whom the principle of equal consideration applies and who possess morally significant interests in not suffering, or things, beings to whom the principle of equal consideration does not apply and whose interests may be ignored if it benefits us. There is no third choice. We could, of course, treat animals better than we do; there are, however, powerful economic forces that militate against better treatment in light of the status of animals as property. But simply according better treatment to animals would not mean that they were no longer things. It may have been better to beat slaves three rather than five times a week, but this better treatment would not have removed slaves from the category of things. The similar interests of slave owners and slaves were not accorded similar treatment because the former had a right not to suffer at all from being used exclusively as a resource, and the latter did not possess such a right. Animals, like humans, have an interest in not suffering at all from the ways in which we use them, however "humane" that use may be. To the extent that we protect humans from suffering from these uses and we do not extend the same protection to animals, we fail to accord equal consideration to animal interests in not suffering.

If animals are persons, that does not mean that they are human persons; it does not mean that we must treat animals in the same way that we treat humans or that we must extend to animals any of the legal rights that we reserve to competent humans. Nor does this mean that animals have any sort of guarantee of a life free from suffering, or that we must protect animals from harm from other animals in the wild or from accidental injury by humans. As I argue below, it does not necessarily preclude our choosing human interests over animal interests in situations of genuine conflict. But it does require that we accept that we have a moral obligation to stop using animals for food, biomedical experiments, entertainment, or clothing, or any other uses that assume that animals are merely resources, and that we prohibit the ownership of animals. The abolition of animal slavery is required by any moral theory that purports to treat animal interests as morally significant, even if the particular theory otherwise rejects rights, just as the abolition of human slavery is required by any theory that purports to treat human interests as morally significant.[98]

FALSE CONFLICTS

The question of the moral status of animals addresses the matter of how we ought to treat animals in situations of conflict between human and animal interests. For the most part, our conflicts with animals are those that we create. We bring billions of sentient animals into existence for the sole purpose of killing them. We then seek to understand the nature of our moral obligations to these animals. Yet by bringing animals into existence for uses that we would never consider appropriate for any humans, we have already placed nonhuman animals outside the scope of our moral community altogether. Despite what we say about taking animals seriously, we have already decided that the principle of equal consideration does not apply to animals and that animals are things that have no morally significant interests.

Because animals are property, we treat every issue concerning their use or treatment as though it presented a genuine conflict of interests, and invariably we choose the human interest over the animal interest even when animal suffering can be justified only by human convenience, amusement, or pleasure. In the overwhelming number of instances in which we evaluate our moral obligations to animals, however, there is no true conflict. When we contemplate whether to eat a hamburger, buy a fur coat, or attend a rodeo, we do not confront any sort of conflict worthy of serious moral consideration. If we take animal interests seriously, we must desist from manufacturing such conflicts, which can only be constructed in the first place by ignoring the principle of equal consideration and by making an arbitrary decision to use animals in ways in which we rightly decline to use any human.

Does the use of animals in experiments involve a genuine conflict between human and animal interests? Even if a need for animals in research exists, the conflict between humans and animals in this context is no more genuine than a conflict between humans suffering from a disease and other humans we might use in experiments to find a cure for that disease. Data gained from experiments with animals require extrapolation to humans in order to be useful at all, and extrapolation is an inexact science under the best of circumstances. If we want data that will be useful in finding cures for human diseases, we would be better advised to use humans. We do not allow humans to be used as we do laboratory animals, and we do not think that there is any sort of conflict between those who are afflicted or who may become afflicted with a disease and those humans whose use might help find a cure for that disease. We regard all humans as part of the moral community, and although we may not treat all humans in the same way, we recognize that membership in the moral community precludes such use of humans. Animals have no characteristic that justifies our use of them in experiments that is not shared by some group of humans; because we regard some animals as laboratory tools yet think it inappropriate to treat any humans in this way, we manufacture a conflict, ignoring the principle of equal consideration and treating similar cases in a dissimilar way.

There may, of course, be situations in which we are confronted with a true emergency, such as the burning house that contains an animal and a human, where we have time to save only one. Such emergency situations require what are, in the end, decisions that are arbitrary and not amenable to satisfying general principles of conduct. Yet even if we would always choose to save the human over the animal in such situations, it does not follow that animals are merely resources that we may use for our purposes.[99] We would draw no such conclusion when making a choice between two humans. Imagine that two humans are in the burning house. One is a young child; the other is an old adult, who, barring the present conflagration, will soon die of natural causes anyway. If we decide to save the child for the simple reason that she has not yet lived her life, we would not conclude that it is morally acceptable to enslave old people, or to use them for target practice. Similarly, assume that a wild animal is just about to attack a friend. Our choice to kill the animal in order to save the friend's life does not mean that it is morally acceptable to kill animals for food, any more than our moral justification in killing a deranged human about to kill our friend would serve to justify our using deranged humans as forced organ donors.

In sum, if we take animal interests seriously, we are not obliged to regard animals as the same as humans for all purposes any more than we regard all humans as being the same for all purposes; nor do we have to accord to animals all or most of the rights that we accord to humans. We may still choose the human over the animal in cases of genuine conflict—when it is truly necessary to do so—but that does not mean that we are justified in treating animals as resources for human use.[100] And if the treatment of animals as resources cannot be justified, then we should abolish the institutionalized exploitation of animals. We should care for domestic animals presently alive, but we should bring no more into existence. The abolition of animal exploitation could not, as a realistic matter, be imposed legally unless and until a significant portion of us took animal interests seriously. Our moral compass will not find animals while they are lying on our plates. In other words, we have to put our vegetables where our mouths are and start acting on the moral principles that we profess to accept.

If we stopped treating animals as resources, the only remaining human-animal conflicts would involve animals in the wild. Deer may nibble our ornamental shrubs; rabbits may eat the vegetables we grow. The occasional wild animal may attack us. In such situations, we should, despite the difficulty inherent in making interspecies comparisons, try our best to apply the principle of equal consideration and to treat similar interests in a similar way. This will generally require at the very least a good-faith effort to avoid the intentional killing of animals to resolve these conflicts, where lethal means would be prohibited if the conflicts involved only humans. I am, however, not suggesting that the recognition that animal interests have moral significance requires that a motorist who unintentionally strikes an animal be prosecuted for an animal equivalent of manslaughter. Nor do I suggest that we should recognize a cause of action allowing a cow to sue the farmer. The interesting question is why we have the cow here in the first instance.

NOTES

Copyright © 2003 by Gary L. Francione. Many thanks to Anna Charlton, Cora Diamond, Lee Hall, and Alan Watson for their helpful comments. The ideas and arguments discussed in this essay were developed and are expanded in Gary L. Francione, *Animals, Property, and the Law* (1995), *Introduction to Animal Rights: Your Child or the Dog?* (2000), and *Rain Without Thunder: The Ideology of the Animal Rights Movement* (1996). The notes will direct the reader to further discussion in these books. This essay is dedicated to my seven rescued canine companions, who are undoubtedly persons.

1. David Foster, "Animal Rights Activists Getting Message Across: New Poll Findings Show Americans More in Tune with 'Radical' Views," *Chicago Tribune*, Jan. 25, 1996, at C8.
2. John Balzer, "Creatures Great and—Equal," *L.A. Times*, Dec. 25, 1993, at A1.
3. Julie Kirkbride, "Peers Use Delays to Foil Hedgehog Cruelty Measure," *Daily Telegraph*, Nov. 3, 1995, at 12.
4. Edward Gorman, "Woman's Goring Fails to Halt Death in the Afternoon," *Times* (London), June 30, 1995, Home News Section.
5. Malcolm Eames, "Four Legs Very Good," *Guardian*, Aug. 25, 1995, at 17.
6. For sources discussing the numbers of animals used for various purposes, see

Gary L. Francione, *Introduction to Animal Rights: Your Child or the Dog?*, at xx–xxi (2000).

7. René Descartes, "Discourse on the Method," pt. V, *in* 1 *The Philosophical Writings of Descartes* 111, 139 (John Cottingham, Robert Stoothoff, & Dugald Murdoch trans., Cambridge Univ. Press 1985) (1637). Some scholars have argued that Descartes did recognize animal consciousness in certain respects, and that traditional interpretations of Descartes are incorrect. *See, e.g.*, Daisie Radnor & Michael Radnor, *Animal Consciousness* (1989). There is, however, no doubt that Descartes regarded animals as morally indistinguishable from inanimate objects and, to the extent that he viewed animals as conscious and as having interests in not suffering, he ignored those interests.

8. Immanuel Kant, *Lectures on Ethics* 240 (Louis Infield trans., Harper Torchbooks, 1963).

9. *Id.* at 239. There were others, such as Aristotle, St. Thomas Aquinas, and John Locke, who recognized that animals are sentient but who claimed that they lack characteristics, such as rationality or abstract thought, and we could, therefore, treat them as things. *See* Francione, *supra* note 6, at 103–29. *See also* notes 74–97 and accompanying text.

10. A possible exception is the 1641 legal code of the Massachusetts Bay Colony, which prohibited cruelty to domestic animals. *See* Gary L. Francione, *Animals, Property, and the Law* 121 (1995). It is not clear whether this provision prohibited cruelty at least in part out of concern for the animals themselves, or only because cruelty to animals might adversely affect humans.

11. The neurological and physiological similarities between humans and nonhumans render the fact of animal sentience noncontroversial. Even mainstream science accepts that animals are sentient. For example, the U.S. Public Health Service states that "[u]nless the contrary is established, investigators should consider that procedures that cause pain or distress in human beings may cause pain or distress in other animals." U.S. Department of Health and Human Services, National Institutes of Health, "Public Health Service Policy and Government Principles Regarding the Care and Use of Animals," *in Institute of Laboratory Animal Resources, Guide for the Care and Use of Laboratory Animals* 117 (1996).

12. Jeremy Bentham, *An Introduction to the Principles of Morals and Legislation,* ch. XVII, para. 4, at 282 (footnote omitted) (J.H. Burns & H.L.A. Hart eds., Athlone Press 1970) (1781). I do not mean to suggest that Bentham was the first person ever to express a concern about animal suffering distinct from its effect on human character, nor that he was the only or the first to argue that humans and animals have morally significant interests in not suffering. Several years before Bentham, Rev. Humphry Primatt expressed the view that suffering was an evil irrespective of species. *See* Humphry Primatt, *A Dissertation on the Duty of Mercy and Sin of Cruelty to Brute Animals* (London, T. Cadell 1776). Bentham clearly had a greater impact on both moral and legal thinking concerning the issue.

13. Bentham, *supra* note 12, at 282–83 n.b.

14. N.Y. Agric. & Mkts. Law § 353 (Consol. 2002). The first known anticruelty statute in the United States was passed in Maine in 1821. New York passed a statute in 1829, but New York courts held as early as 1822 that cruelty was an offense at common law.

15. Del. Code. Ann. tit. 11, §§ 1325(a)(1) & (4) (2002).
16. Protection of Animals Act, 1911, c. 27 § 1(1)(a) (Eng.). British legislation prohibiting cruelty to animals was passed as early as 1822.
17. 7 U.S.C. §§ 2131–2159 (2003).
18. Cruelty to Animals Act, 1876 (Eng.).
19. Animals (Scientific Procedures) Act, 1986 (Eng.).
20. 7 U.S.C. §§ 1901–1907 (2003).
21. State v. Prater, 109 S.W. 1047, 1049 (Mo. Ct. App. 1908).
22. Stephens v. State, 65 Miss. 329, 331 (1887).
23. Hunt v. State, 29 N.E. 933, 933 (Ind. Ct. App. 1892).
24. Grise v. State, 37 Ark. 456, 458 (1881).
25. People v. Brunell, 48 How. Pr. 435, 437 (N.Y. City Ct. 1874).
26. *See, e.g.*, Francione, *supra* note 10, at 193 (discussing the federal Animal Welfare Act).
27. Animals (Scientific Procedures) Act, 1986, c. 14, § 5(4) (Eng.).
28. For a discussion about the necessity of various animal uses, see Francione, *supra* note 6, at 9–49. *See also* Stephen R.L. Clark, *The Moral Status of Animals* (1977) (arguing that much animal use cannot be regarded as necessary).
29. *See generally* Francione, *supra* note 10 (discussing the status of animals as property as a general matter, and in the context of anticruelty laws and the federal Animal Welfare Act). The status of animals as property has existed for thousands of years. Indeed, historical evidence indicates that the domestication of animals is closely related to the development of the concepts of property and money. The property status of animals is particularly important in Western culture for two reasons. First, property rights are accorded a special status and are considered to be among the most important rights we have. Second, the modern Western concept of property, whereby resources are regarded as separate objects that are assigned and belong to particular individuals who are allowed to use the property to the exclusion of everyone else, has its origin in God's grant to humans of dominion over animals. *See id.* at 24–49; Francione, *supra* note 6, at 50–54.
30. *See infra* notes 75–81 and accompanying text.
31. Godfrey Sandys-Winsch, *Animal Law* 1 (1978).
32. T.G. Field-Fisher, *Animals and the Law* 19 (1964).
33. To the extent that animal uses, such as certain types of animal fighting, have been prohibited, this may be understood more in terms of class hierarchy and cultural prejudice than in terms of moral concern about animals. *See* Francione, *supra* note 10, at 18.
34. *See id.* at 139–42.
35. *See id.* at 224. For a discussion of the Animal Welfare Act, see *id.* at 185–249.
36. *See id.* at 142–56; Francione, *supra* note 6, at 58–63.
37. Murphy v. Manning, 2 Ex. D. 307, 313, 314 (1877) (Cleasby, B.).
38. *See* Francione, *supra* note 10, at 127–28; Francione, *supra* note 6, at 66–67. This presumption not only insulates customary practices from being found to violate anticruelty laws, but also militates against finding the necessary criminal intent in cases involving noncustomary uses. *See, e.g.*, Commonwealth v. Barr, 44 Pa. C. 284 (Lancaster County Ct. 1916). *See infra* notes 40–43 and accompanying text.
39. 16 L.R. Ir. 325, 335 (C.P.D. 1885) (Murphy, J.). In Britain, the dehorning of

older cattle was found to violate the anticruelty statute but only because dehorning had been discontinued and was no longer an accepted agriculture practice. *See* Ford v. Wiley, 23 Q.B. 203 (1889). In his opinion, Hawkins, J., noted that the fact that the practice had been abandoned by farmers who were acting in their economic self-interest was proof that the practice was unnecessary. *See id.* at 221–22.

40. *See* Francione, *supra* note 10, at 135–39; Francione, *supra* note 6, at 63–66.
41. 572 A.2d 416 (D.C. 1990).
42. *Id.* at 420.
43. *Id.* at 421.
44. *See* Francione, *supra* note 10, at 156; Francione, *supra* note 6, at 67–68. In recent years, many states have amended their anticruelty laws and have increased penalties for at least certain violations. It remains to be seen whether this will make any real difference because most animal uses will remain exempt and there will still be problems with proof of criminal intent.
45. *See* Francione, *supra* note 10, at 65–90, 156–58; Francione, *supra* note 6, at 69–70.
46. *See* Francione, *supra* note 10, at 27–32.
47. Commonwealth v. Lufkin, 89 Mass. (7 Allen) 579, 581 (1863). *See* Francione, *supra* note 10, at 137–38, 153–56; Francione, *supra* note 6, at 70–73.
48. 444 A.2d 855 (R.I. 1982).
49. 447 A.2d 493 (Md. Ct. Spec. App. 1982).
50. 375 S.E.2d 893 (Ga. Ct. App. 1988).
51. 477 A.2d 1115 (D.C. 1984).
52. 172 Misc.2d 564 (N.Y. Crim. Ct. 1997).
53. 478 S.2d 13 (Ala. Crim. App. 1985).
54. 384 N.W.2d 620 (Neb. 1986).
55. Robert Garner, *Animals, Politics and Morality* 234 (1993).
56. *See* Francione, *supra* note 6, at 13, 73–76, 181–82. *See generally* Gary L. Francione, *Rain Without Thunder: The Ideology of the Animal Rights Movement* (1996) [hereinafter, Francione, *Rain Without Thunder*] (discussing unsuccessful efforts by the animal protection movement to obtain animal welfare laws that exceed the minimal standards required to exploit animals). Cass R. Sunstein argues that the property status of animals does not necessarily mean that they will be treated as means to human ends. *See* Cass R. Sunstein, "Slaughterhouse Jive," *The New Republic,* Jan. 29, 2001, at 40, 44. It is unrealistic to think that animal interests will be accorded significant weight when those interests are balanced against the interests of humans in exploiting their animal property. The fact that animal interests have become increasingly commodified despite 200 years of animal welfare law and philosophy is striking proof of the failure of animal welfare. Moreover, Sunstein ignores that animals have an interest in not suffering at all from our instrumental use of them. *See infra* notes 69–74 and accompanying text.
57. For example, McDonald's, the fast-food chain, announced that it would require its suppliers to observe standards of animal welfare that went beyond current standards: "Animal welfare is also an important part of quality assurance. For high-quality food products at the counter, you need high quality coming from the farm. Animals that are well cared for are less prone to illness, injury, and stress, which all have the same negative impact on the condition of

livestock as they do on people. Proper animal welfare practices also benefit producers. Complying with our animal welfare guidelines helps ensure efficient production and reduces waste and loss. This enables our suppliers to be highly competitive." Bruce Feinberg & Terry Williams, "McDonald's Corporate Social Responsibility, Animal Welfare Update: North America," *at* http://www.mcdonalds.com/corporate/social/marketplace/welfare/update/northamerica/index.html (last visited Dec. 1, 2003). The principal expert advisor to McDonald's states: "Healthy animals, properly handled, keep the meat industry running safely, efficiently and profitably." Temple Grandin, *Recommended Animal Handling Guidelines for Meat Packers* 1 (1991).

58. *See* Francione, *supra* note 6, at 81–102. A reason not to treat similar cases in a similar way must not be arbitrary and thereby itself violate the principle of equal consideration.

59. Peter Singer, *Animal Liberation* 5 (2d ed. 1990) (quoting Bentham).

60. *See infra* note 81 and accompanying text.

61. The principle of equal consideration also failed in other systems of slavery, but because of differences among these systems, I confine my description to North American slavery. For a discussion of various systems of slavery and slave law, see Alan Watson, *Slave Law in the Americas* (1989); Alan Watson, *Roman Slave Law* (1989); Alan Watson, "Roman Slave Law and Romanist Ideology," 37 *Phoenix* 53 (1983).

62. Chancellor Harper, "Slavery in the Light of Social Ethics," *in Cotton Is King, and Pro-Slavery Arguments* 549, 559 (E.N. Elliott ed., 1860).

63. Stanley Elkins and Eric McKitrick, "Institutions and the Law of Slavery: Slavery in Capitalist and Non-Capitalist Cultures," *in The Law of American Slavery* 111, 115 (Kermit L. Hall ed., 1987) (quoting William Goodell, *The American Slave Code in Theory and Practice* 180 (1853)). For a discussion of slave law in the context of animal welfare law, see Francione, *supra* note 6, at 86–90; Francione, *supra* note 10, at 100–12.

64. 13 N.C. (2 Dev.) 263, 267 (1829).

65. 26 Va. (5 Rand.) 678, 678 (1827).

66. *Id.* at 680.

67. Watson, *Slave Law in the Americas, supra* note 61, at xiv.

68. *Id.* at 31 (quoting Justinian).

69. Even after the abolition of slavery, race continued to serve as a reason to justify differential treatment, often on the ground that whites and people of color did not have similar interests and, therefore, did not have to be treated equally in certain respects, and often on the ground that race was a reason to deny similar treatment to admittedly similar interests. But abolition recognized that, irrespective of race, all humans had a similar interest in not being treated as the property of others.

70. Bernard E. Rollin, "The Legal and Moral Bases of Animal Rights," *in Ethics and Animals* 103, 106 (Harlan B. Miller & William H. Williams eds., 1983). *See* Francione, *supra* note 6, at xxvi–xxx. For a general discussion of the concept of rights and rights theory in the context of laws concerning animals, see Francione, *supra* note 10, at 91–114.

71. Similar concepts have been recognized by philosophers and political theorists. Kant, for example, maintained that there is one "innate" right—the right of "innate *equality*," or the "independence from being bound by others to more

than one can in turn bind them; hence a human being's quality of being *his own master.*" Immanuel Kant, *The Metaphysics of Morals*, §§ 6:237–38, at 30 (Mary Gregor trans. & ed., Cambridge Univ. Press 1996). This innate right "grounds our right to *have* rights." Roger J. Sullivan, *Immanuel Kant's Moral Theory* 248 (1989). The basic right not to be treated as property is different from what are referred to as natural rights insofar as these are understood to be rights that exist apart from their recognition by any particular legal system because they are granted by God. For example, John Locke regarded property rights as natural rights that were grounded in God's grant to humans of dominion over the earth and animals. The basic right not to be treated as property expresses a proposition of logic. If human interests are to have moral significance (i.e., if human interests are to be treated in accordance with the principle of equal consideration), then humans cannot be resources; the interests of humans who are property will not be treated the same as the interests of property owners. For a further discussion of this basic right and the related concept of inherent value, see Francione, *supra* note 6, at 92–100. *See also* Henry Shue, *Basic Rights* (2d ed. 1996).

72. Human experimentation is prohibited by the Nuremberg Code and the Helsinki Declaration. Torture is prohibited by the International Convention against Torture and Other Cruel, Inhuman or Degrading Treatment or Punishment. The notable exception to the protection provided by the basic right is compulsory military service, which is controversial precisely because it does treat humans exclusively as means to the ends of others in ways that other acts required by the government, such as the payment of taxes, do not.

73. *See* Francione, *supra* note 6, at 94, 131–33. *See also supra* note 71; *infra* note 78 and accompanying text.

74. Some claim that the relevant difference between humans and nonhumans is that the former possess souls and the latter do not. For a discussion of this and other purported differences, see Francione, *supra* note 6, at 103–29. *See also supra* note 9 and accompanying text. I do not mean to suggest that everyone after 1800 who has relied on these differences to justify our treatment of animals as resources acknowledges that animals have any morally significant interests; indeed, some accept and defend the status of animals as things morally indistinguishable from inanimate objects. *See, e.g.,* Peter Carruthers, *The Animals Issue: Moral Theory in Practice* (1992).

75. For a discussion of the views of Bentham and his modern proponent, Peter Singer, see Francione, *supra* 6, at 130–50.

76. H.L.A. Hart, *Essays on Bentham* 97 (1982) (quoting Bentham).

77. Bentham, *supra* note 12, at 282–83 n.b. (further note omitted).

78. I recognize that most Bentham scholars regard Bentham's objections to slavery to be based exclusively on the consequences of slavery and claim that Bentham did not think that slavery violated any moral right. It appears, however, that Bentham, who is generally regarded as an act utilitarian, was at the very least a rule utilitarian when it came to slavery; that is, he thought that the consequences of the institution of slavery were necessarily undesirable and, in effect, he recognized that the human interest in not being treated as a resource should be accorded rights-type protection. Moreover, Bentham did talk in terms of moral rights when he discussed human slavery and the treatment of animals, *see id.,* although he was probably referring to the right to equal con-

sideration in that passage. Bentham may well have recognized on some level that a right to equal consideration is inconsistent with the status of being a slave. *See* Francione, *supra* note 6, at 132–33.

79. Bentham, *supra* note 12, at 282–83 n.b.

80. *Id.* Bentham also claimed that "[t]he death [that animals] suffer in our hands commonly is, and always may be, a speedier, and by that means a less painful one, than that which would await them in the inevitable course of nature." *Id.* Bentham ignored the fact that the domestic animals that we raise for food would not have a death "in the inevitable course of nature," because they are only brought into existence as our resources in the first place. It is, therefore, problematic to defend the killing of domestic animals by comparing their deaths with those of wild animals, saying that the infliction of unnecessary pain on domestic animals that we do not need to eat is less than the pain that may necessarily be suffered by wild animals.

81. Peter Singer, who, like Bentham, is a utilitarian and eschews moral rights, adopts Bentham's position and argues that most animals do not have an interest in their lives, but that the principle of equal consideration can nevertheless be applied to their interests in not suffering even if animals are the property of humans. Singer's argument fails in a number of respects. First, Singer requires that we make interspecies comparisons of pain and suffering in order to apply the principle of equal consideration to animal interests. *See* Singer, *supra* note 59, at 15. Such comparisons would, of course, be inherently difficult if not impossible to make. Second, because most humans are self-aware and most animals are not (in Singer's view), it is difficult to understand how animals and humans will ever be considered as similarly situated for purposes of equal consideration. Singer recognizes that because we are unlikely to regard human and animal interests as similar in the first place, we are also unlikely to find any guidance in the principle of equal consideration. *Id.* at 16. That is, however, tantamount to admitting that animal interests are not morally significant because the principle of equal consideration will never have any meaningful application to animal interests. Singer avoids this conclusion by claiming that even if the principle of equal consideration is inapplicable, it is still clear that much animal suffering is not morally justifiable. He states, for example, that we need not apply the principle of equal consideration in order to conclude that the positive consequences for animals of abolishing intensive agriculture would be greater than any detrimental consequences for humans. It remains unclear how Singer can arrive at this conclusion other than through mere stipulation. The abolition of intensive agriculture would have a profound impact on the international economy and would cause an enormous rise in the price of meat and animal products. If the issue hinges only on consequences, it is not at all clear that the consequences for self-aware humans would not be weightier than the consequences for non-self-aware animals. Fourth, even if Singer's theory would lead to more "humane" animal treatment, it would still permit us to use animals as resources in ways that we do not use any humans. Singer's response to this would be that he would be willing to use similarly situated humans, such as the mentally or physically disabled, as replaceable resources. *Id.*; *see also* Peter Singer, *Practical Ethics* 186 (2d ed. 1993). For the reasons discussed below, most of us would reject Singer's views on the use of vulnerable humans. *See infra* notes 95–97 and accompanying text. For a dis-

cussion of Singer's views, see Francione, *supra* note 6, at 135–48; Francione, *Rain Without Thunder, supra* note 56, at 156–60, 173–76.

82. Charles Darwin, *The Descent of Man* 105 (Princeton Univ. Press 1981). *See* James Rachels, *Created From Animals: The Moral Implications of Darwinism* (1990).

83. Darwin, *supra* note 82, at 105.

84. *Id.* at 76, 77.

85. Donald R. Griffin, *Animal Minds: Beyond Cognition to Consciousness* 274 (2001).

86. *Id.*

87. *Id.*

88. *Id.*

89. Antonio R. Damasio, *The Feeling of What Happens: Body and Emotion in the Making of Consciousness* 16 (1999).

90. *Id.*

91. *See id.* at 198, 201.

92. *See, e.g.,* Griffin, *supra* note 85; Marc D. Hauser, *The Evolution of Communication* (1996); Marc D. Hauser, *Wild Minds: What Animals Really Think* (2000); *Readings in Animal Cognition* (Marc Bekoff & Dale Jamieson eds., 1996); Sue Savage-Rumbaugh & Roger Lewin, *Kanzi: The Ape at the Brink of the Human Mind* (1994).

93. Frans de Waal, *Good-Natured: The Origins of Right and Wrong in Humans and Other Animals* 218 (1996).

94. There are problems in relying on similarities between humans and animals beyond sentience to justify the moral significance of animals. *See* Francione, *supra* note 6, at 116–19. For example, a focus on similarities beyond sentience threatens to create new hierarchies in which we move some animals, such as the great apes or dolphins, into a preferred group, and continue to treat other animals as our resources. There has for some years been an international effort to secure certain rights for the nonhuman great apes. This project was started by the publication of a book entitled *The Great Ape Project* (Paola Cavalieri & Peter Singer eds., 1993), which seeks "the extension of the community of equals to include all great apes: human beings, chimpanzees, gorillas, and orangutans." *Id.* at 4. I was a contributor to *The Great Ape Project. See* Gary L. Francione, "Personhood, Property, and Legal Competence," *in id.* at 248–57. The danger of *The Great Ape Project* is that it reinforces the notion that characteristics beyond sentience are necessary and not merely sufficient for equal treatment. In my essay in *The Great Ape Project,* I tried to avoid this problem by arguing that although the considerable cognitive and other similarities between the human and nonhuman great apes are sufficient to accord the latter equal protection under the law, these similarities are not necessary for animals to have a right not to be treated as resources. *See id.* at 253. *See also* Lee Hall & Anthony Jon Waters, "From Property to Person: The Case of Evelyn Hart," 11 *Seton Hall Const. L.J.* 1 (2000). For an approach that argues that characteristics beyond sentience are necessary and not merely sufficient for preferred animals to have a right not to be treated as resources in at least some respects, see Steven M. Wise, *Drawing the Line: Science and the Case for Animal Rights* (2002), and Steven M. Wise, *Rattling the Cage: Toward Legal Rights for Animals* (2000).

95. Some argue that although certain humans may lack a particular characteristic, the fact that all humans have the potential to possess the characteristic means that a human who actually lacks it is for purposes of equal consideration distinguishable from an animal who may also lack it. *See, e.g.,* Carl Cohen, "The Case for the Use of Animals in Biomedical Research," 315 *New Eng. J. Med.* 865 (1986). This argument begs the question because it assumes that some humans have a characteristic that they lack and thereby ignores the factual similarity between animals and humans who lack the characteristic. Moreover, in some instances, animals may possess the characteristic to a greater degree than do some humans.

96. Carruthers, *supra* note 74, at 181. Peter Singer also requires this sort of self-consciousness before animals or humans can be considered to have an interest in their lives. *See* Singer, *supra* note 59, at 228–29. *See also supra* note 81.

97. In this sense, the equality of all humans is predicated on factual similarities shared by all humans irrespective of their particular characteristics beyond sentience. All humans have an interest in not being treated exclusively as means to the ends of others. All humans value themselves even if no one else values them. *See* Francione, *supra* note 6, at 128, 135 n.18. Moreover, justice (not charity) may require that we be especially conscientious about protecting humans who lack certain characteristics precisely because of their vulnerability.

98. *See supra* notes 73, 78 and accompanying text; Francione, *supra* note 6, at 148. The theory presented in this essay is different in significant respects from that of Tom Regan. *See* Tom Regan, *The Case for Animal Rights* (1983). Regan argues that animals have rights and that animal exploitation ought to be abolished and not merely regulated, but he limits protection to those animals who have preference autonomy, and he thereby omits from the class of rights holders those animals who are sentient but who do not have preference autonomy. The theory discussed in this essay applies to any sentient being. Regan uses the concept of basic rights and although he does not discuss the status of animals as property or the basic right not to be property, he maintains that some animals should be accorded the right not to treated exclusively as means to human ends. Moreover, Regan does not acknowledge that this basic right can be derived solely from applying the principle of equal consideration to animal interests in not suffering, nor that the right must be part of any theory that purports to accord moral significance to animal interests even if that theory otherwise rejects rights. For a further discussion of the differences between my theory and that of Regan, see Francione, *supra* note 6, at xxxii–xxxiv, 94 n.25, 127–28 n.61, 148 n.36, 174 n.1.

99. A common argument made against the animal rights position is that it is acceptable to treat animals as things because we are justified in choosing humans over animals in situations of conflict. *See, e.g.,* Richard A. Posner, "Animal Rights," Slate Dialogues, *at* http://slate.msn.com/id/110101/entry/110129/ (last visited Dec. 1, 2003).

100. The choice of humans over animals in situations of genuine emergency or conflict does not necessarily represent speciesism because there are many reasons other than species bias that can account for the choice. *See* Francione, *supra* note 6, at 159–62.

6

RICHARD A. EPSTEIN

ANIMALS AS OBJECTS,
OR SUBJECTS, OF RIGHTS

INTRODUCTION: TWO CONCEPTIONS OF ANIMALS

One of the more persistent and impassioned struggles of our time is now being waged over the legal status of animals. Should they be treated as objects of human ownership, or as bearers of independent rights? Many modern writers, most notably Steven Wise and Gary Francione, have championed the latter position. In this essay, I shall offer a tempered version of the original position that in the eyes of many will convict me of the new offense of speciesism. In order to evaluate this choice, it is necessary to examine first the historical rules that comprised the law of animals and that set the backdrop for the modern reforms. Part I of this chapter will set these out in brief compass. Its mission is to show that the historical accounts of animals did not rest on any fundamental misconception as to their capacities, but on the simple but powerful proposition that the survival and advancement of human civilization depended on the domestication and use of animals. Part II of this chapter then explores the moral status of animals, and their relationship to women, children, and slaves, under the traditional synthesis of legal rights. Part III then notes the benefits to animals that arise from the system of human ownership. Part IV relates this history to the modern debates over the legal status of animals, and rejects the proposition that the creation of rights for animals is a logical extension of the creation of full rights for women and slaves. Part V discusses efforts to create animal rights based on their cognitive or sentient capacity, and concludes that these help justify many past initiatives for the protection of animals, but not the more aggressive claims for animal rights.

ANIMALS AS OBJECTS

Under traditional conceptions of law, animals were typically regarded as objects of rights vested in their human owners but not as the holders of rights against human beings. Even as objects, animals historically occupied a large place in the overall system of legal rights and social relations. Animals in a bygone age represented a larger fraction of social wealth than they do today. As Jared Diamond reminds us, there were "many ways in which big domestic animals were crucial to those human societies possessing them. Most notably, they provided meat, milk products, fertilizer, land transport, leather, military assault vehicles, plow traction, and wool, as well as germs that killed previously unexposed people."[1] Smaller animals, such as birds, were likewise domesticated for their "meat, egg[s] and feathers."[2]

In order to frame the modern debate, it is useful to give some brief outline of the basic legal rights and duties of people toward animals. These rules are subject to small but unimportant local variations over both time and place, largely on matters of detail and formality. The classical biblical and Roman law, however, applies in its original form today in both civil and common law countries, except where specific protective legislation intrudes.[3] As with other objects of ownership, these rules are conveniently divided into three areas: acquisition, transfer, and liability.[4]

Acquisition

Animals count as assets with positive economic value, and as such are important objects of a system of property law. In the state of nature, every animal was a *res nullius*, that is, a thing owned by no person. In contrast to a *res commune* (such as air or water), a *res nullius* could be reduced to private ownership by capture.[5] The rule was followed under Roman and English law, subject to one fine difference, which went not to the question of *whether* animals could be owned, but only to the question of *who* owned a particular animal. Under Roman law, if A captured a wild animal on the land of B, he could keep it;[6] under English law, the animal became the property of the owner of the locus in quo.[7] Once captured, an animal remained the property of its owner until it was abandoned. An owner did not abandon possession even by sending out animals, unsupervised, to graze in the hills or fields,[8] so long as the animals had the "intention to return" (the so-called *animus revertendi*) to their original owner, which in turn was evidenced by their "habitual" return.[9] But if that pattern were broken, then the animals were regarded as abandoned and subject to capture by another.

Universally, the owner of the female animal also owned its offspring.[10] That practice follows from the manifest inconvenience of the alternatives. To treat the offspring as a *res nullius* raised the specter that some interloper could snatch the newborn from its mother, which could not happen under the dominant rule, which eliminated any dangerous gaps in ownership. Nor did it make any sense to give the newborn animal to the owner of the land on which the birth took place, for that rule would only induce the owner of an animal to keep in an animal against its natural inclination, perhaps reducing its chances of reproductive success. Nor did it make sense to allocate ownership of the offspring jointly to the owners of both the male and female parents, assuming that the former was in captivity. It is never easy to identify the father, and even if he is known with certainty, a rule of joint ownership forces neighbors into an unwanted partnership between relative strangers. Anyone who wants joint ownership can contract for it voluntarily. The rule that assigned offspring to the mother was treated as a universal proposition of natural law.

Transfer

Next, the law had to provide some mechanism to transfer the ownership of animals. In the absence of exchange, the value of any animal is limited to its use (or consumption) value to its owner. Once exchange is allowed, both sides could profit, when animals were sold, given away, or used as security for loans. Transfers were common once young animals were weaned.

In the grand scheme of things, the methods of transfer have at most instrumental virtues. The customary mode of transfer is by way of delivery either by gift or by sale. In an economy that lacked mechanical or electrical sources of power, draft animals were regarded not solely as sources of food, but often as capital items on a par with land and slaves.[11] While a simple delivery might transfer ownership of small or newborn animals, higher levels of formality (such as the ritual of *mancipatio* in Roman law) were routinely used to make effective the transfer of more valuable animals.[12]

Liability

All legal systems develop elaborate liability rules that set out both an owner's *responsibility* for the wrongs committed by his animals, and likewise the owner's *rights* to recover for injuries to his animals.[13] Theories of liability have spanned the gamut: One possibility was to hold owners vicariously liable for animals that they owned, much as ancient owners were liable for the torts of their slaves, or modern employers are liable for the wrongs of their employees committed within the scope of their employment. Alternatively, owners could be held liable not for the animal's act as such, but for their own antecedent failure to keep their animals confined. In both cases, an extensive debate could arise over whether any liability, whether for act or omission, was governed by negligence or strict liability principles. Under the so-called principles of noxal liability, an owner in some instances could escape further liability by surrendering the animal in question—a strategy that made sense when the value of the animal was less than the harms so caused. Special rules were developed in connection with cattle trespass. On that subject there were immense debates (known as range wars) in arid countries over whether to switch from the common law rule that required cattle owners to fence their cattle *in* to the alternative rule that requires landowners, often at enormous expense, to fence these animals *out*.[14] Special rules were introduced to allow, without liability, minor harm to property beside public roads on which animals traveled.

Often, the mental states both of animal and owner were key to deciding liability. It could matter whether an animal committed a deliberate or accidental harm. It could also matter whether the animal was provoked or whether it acted in self-defense against, say, the attack of other animals. Sometimes the decisive mental state was that of the owner, not of the animal. Thus, in Exodus, if an ox gored, then it could be put to death, but the owner was spared—a variation on the theme of noxal liability. But if the owner had been aware of the propensity of the animal to gore, then he could be held liable if he did not keep the animal under his control.[15] Even when animals could no longer be put to death, the *damages feasant* allowed the victim of the wrong to hold the trespassing animals as security for the damages they caused—no questions asked.[16] In this context, liability remained stubbornly strict not because farmers were oblivious to the mental states of animals, but because they understood that this entire self-help regime would collapse if a landowner could only hold for amends a stray that had escaped through its owner's negligence, which they could not infer simply from the presence of the animal.[17] The principle of no liability without fault made few inroads into this area, even though it received spirited philosophical defense.[18] The farmers, whose interests were intensely practical, much preferred to retain the more administrable strict liability laws.[19]

THE MORAL STATUS OF ANIMALS UNDER THE CLASSICAL SYNTHESIS

In shaping these theories of tort liability, neither the ancients nor their modern successors committed any obvious blunder in treating animals "just like" land or inanimate objects. Nonetheless, that claim has often been advanced. As Steven Wise puts the point: "Although blinded by teleological anthropocentrism, the Greeks were not blind. They could see that nonhuman animals (and slaves) were not literally 'lifeless tools.' They were alive.

They had senses and could perceive. But Aristotle compared them to 'automatic puppets.'"[20]

Wise's use of the term "nonhuman animals" is a nice, but transparent, rhetorical ploy to undercut the traditional firm line between human beings (not human animals) and (some other kind of) animals. But even if we put that point aside, his position is overdrawn. Surely the early legal systems outlined above did not make this mistake, given the importance that they attached to the mental states of animals as well as people. Nor does it appear that Aristotle made that error either. Even a quick peek at his *History of Animals* shows a subtlety and appreciation on this point:

> In a number of animals we observe gentleness or fierceness, mildness or cross temper, courage or timidity, fear or confidence, high spirit or low cunning, and, with regard to intelligence, something equivalent to sagacity. Some of these qualities in man, as compared with the corresponding qualities in animals, differ only quantitatively: that is to say, a man has more or less of this quality, and an animal more or less of some other; other qualities in men are represented by analogous and not identical qualities; for instance, just as in man we find knowledge, wisdom, and sagacity, so in certain animals there exists some other natural potentiality akin to these.[21]

None of this sounds remotely like a flattening of animals' intellectual or emotional states in the manner portrayed by Wise. Of course Aristotle's treatment of animals is marred by his unavoidable ignorance of the rudiments of reproduction: He had no microscope, and thus no clue, that sperm differs from semen (which in its primary sense still refers to the "fluid" that carries the seed), or that the females of the species produce eggs.[22] But it does not take a microscope to observe *and exploit* the rudiments of animal behavior for human survival. It is well known, for example, that the domestication of all major groups of large animals was completed at least two millennia before Aristotle wrote, that is, between 8000 and 2500 B.C.[23] The ancients, no matter how ignorant they were of the mechanics of reproduction, knew how to use artificial selection—breeding—in order to modify animal and plant species for their own benefit. "Darwin, in the *Origin of the Species* didn't start with an account of natural selection. His first chapter is instead a lengthy account of how our domesticated plants and animals arose through artificial selection by humans."[24]

On the issues that matter, then, nothing seems further from the truth than Wise's highly stilted account of how ancient peoples viewed animals. A contemporary case for animal rights cannot be premised on the dubious assumption that our *new* understanding of animals justifies a revision of our old legal understandings. The ancients may not have known much about the fine points of animal behavior and reproduction. Still, their understanding of animal personality, their understanding of dispositions and mental states, their skills in domestication belie the belief that either farmer or jurist, ancient or modern, had some difficulty in distinguishing animals from inanimate objects, or for that matter from slaves. The key differences could never have been overlooked by any person in daily contact with those animals on which their survival depended.

"Survival" is the right word, for nothing less is at stake in primitive societies that labor under conditions of scarcity when every calorie counts. Animals were a source of work in the fields, of food, of protection, and of companionship. They received the extensive protection of the law because they were valuable to the human beings who owned them. To imagine an ancient society in which animals had rights against human beings solely because they were sentient creatures is to envision a society in which human beings would be prepared to put themselves and their families at risk for the sake of brute, if sentient, creatures. The ancients devoted considerable ingenuity in determining the proper status of animals, but, as far as I can tell, their speculations never denied the agency of animals. Yet at no time did they talk themselves into thinking that animals should be holders of legal rights. Those altruistic sentiments are the indulgence of the rich and secure. They play no part whatsoever in the formative thinking of any individual or society whose bodily or collective security is at risk. Such intellectual developments had to wait until, at the earliest, the nineteenth century.

THE BENEFITS TO ANIMALS
OF THEIR OWNERSHIP BY HUMANS

The historical backdrop invites a further inquiry: Why is it that anyone assumes the human ownership of animals necessarily leads to their suffering, let alone their destruction? Often, quite the opposite is true. Animals that are left to their own devices may have no masters; nor do they have any peace. Life in the wild leaves them exposed to the elements, to attacks by other animals, to the inability to find food or shelter, to accidental injury, and to disease. The expected life of animals in the wild need not be solitary, poor, nasty, brutish, and short. But it is often rugged, and rarely placid and untroubled.

Human ownership changes this natural state of animals for the better as well as for the worse. Because they use and value animals, owners will spend resources for their protection. Veterinary medicine may not be at the level of human medicine, but it is only a generation or so behind. When it comes to medical care, it's better to be a sick cat in a middle-class U.S. household than a sick peasant in a Third World country. Private ownership of many pets (or, if one must, "companions") gives them access to food and shelter (and sometimes clothing) which creates long lives of ease and comfort. Even death can be done in more humane ways than in nature, for any slaughter that spares cattle, for example, unnecessary anxiety, tends to improve the amount and quality of the meat that is left behind. No one should claim a perfect concurrence between the interests of humans and animals: Ownership is not tantamount to partnership. But by the same token there is no necessary conflict between owners and their animals. Over broad areas of human endeavor, the ownership of animals has worked to their advantage, and not to their detriment.

ANIMALS AS HOLDERS OF RIGHTS

The modern debates over animals go beyond the earlier historical arguments by asking whether animals are, or should be treated as, the holders of rights against their would-be human masters. In dealing with this debate one common move is to exploit the close connection, already noted, between slaves and animals in the ancient world. The injustice of owning slaves is said to be paralleled by the injustices done to animals. Thus in *Rattling the Cage*, Steven Wise starts with the observation that Aristotle lumped animals with slaves and women as beings that were lower than (Greek) males in the explicit hierarchy found in Arthur Lovejoy's *Great Chain of Being*.[25] He notes that Aristotle observed that "the ox is the poor man's slave."[26] The Romans in his view did no better by lumping animals with slaves, women, and insane persons. Now that we have repented our errors with slaves and women, let us, Wise urges, redress human injustices to animals.

I have several responses to this line of argument. The first rejects the asserted, if elusive, historical equation among women, slaves, and animals. Of course animals were lumped with (some) human beings for limited purposes. If only some human beings had full legal rights, then others had either fewer or none, and to that extent were "like" animals. But this gross oversimplification does not capture, for example, the full subtleties of the law of "persons" in Roman law or any other ancient legal system. Given the divisions among human beings, the law of persons was always more complex in ancient legal systems than in modern ones. The Roman rules for men within the power of their fathers and for women and for insane persons all differed from each other in important particulars. Men within the power of their father could become heads of their own families at the death of their father; they had full rights to participate in political life even while consigned to a subordinate position within the family.[27] That subordinate status in turn was softened by the social recognition of the separate property—the so-called *peculium*—with which the paterfamilias would not interfere.[28] In addition, the emancipation of sons during the life of their father was commonplace. Marriage for its part was a consensual union, in which formalities were evidentiary and thus not strictly required.[29] Animals did not marry. With a nod toward modernity, the woman, as well as the man, was free to renounce the marriage at any time.[30] Women, slaves (not to mention sons), and animals were each subject to distinct rules tailored to their own distinct status.

More to the point, it is critical to note *why* the older classification of persons slowly broke down over time. From Justinian forward, the basic philosophical position held that all men (by which they meant people) by nature were born free.[31] The use of the words "by nature" carried vital intellectual freight about the presocial status of human beings. Even before Locke, the clear implication was that social arrangements should be organized to preserve, not undermine, the natural freedom of human beings. Therefore any limitation on human freedom within civil society was an evident embarrassment to this normative view. But Roman jurists were not reformers. Rather, they were mainly chroniclers of their own system, often in the pay of the leaders of a slave society. They confined their philosophical reflections to a few grand introductory observations. But they never entered into open warfare with the operative rules of their own legal system.

Others of course could appeal to natural law principles to advance reformist as well as conservative causes. Faced with sharp rebuke, the defense of the status quo ante on slaves and women slowly crumbled precisely because they were human beings and not animals. Any defender of full legal capacity for some but not all humans had to find some independent reason to justify the differential legal status. It is hard to do this with slaves, many of whom were acquired by conquest. Is there anyone who could deny with a straight face that an ingenious slave was smarter than his or her indolent master?

It is, in a sense, easier to maintain the line against women because of the prominence of sex differences. But in the end this has to fail as well. Aristotle, for example, imputed to women a set of inferior characteristics to justify their second-class legal status. But it rings hollow in face of the obvious objection that every man is not better than every woman on every (male) dimension that matters. Some women are taller than men, stronger than men, smarter than men. Depending on your fondness for stereotypes, a majority of women may be more empathic and cooperative than men. Indeed with the passage of time and the progress of civilization, warlike skills and brute strength diminish in relative importance, so the balance of social advantage shifts to traits which women have in relative abundance. (After all, the grand social contract whereby everyone renounces force against everyone else works more to the advantage of women than men.) In this environment, no one could defend the strict rank order judgments needed to prop up the sharp differences in legal status between men and women.

None of these categorical differences then work. But there is another approach that does make sense, and which in the end prevailed. One great task of any legal system is to set out the basic relationships between strangers. Such is the function of the "keep off" rules generated by the recognition of universal rights to individual autonomy and private property. One does not have to endorse either property or autonomy in their entirety to understand their basic logic. Coordinating the rights and duties of countless pairs of unrelated individuals cannot rest on subtle sliding scales with uncertain substantive content. It depends on clear classifications known and observable by all—which helps explain why the clear, if unprincipled, classifications based on sex, race, and slavery were able to function as long as they did. But once the dichotomous view of the world—all Xs are better under some metric than all Ys—is rejected, then only one social approach makes sense. We adopt the central proposition of modern liberalism, namely, that *all natural persons, that is, all human beings, should be treated as legal persons,* with the full rights to own property, to make and enforce contracts, to give legal evidence, to participate in political life, to marry and raise families, to engage in common occupations, to worship God, and to enjoy the protection of the state when they participate in any of these activities.[32]

On this view, the great impetus of the reform movement lay in the simple fact that the individuals who were consigned to subordinate status had roughly the same natural, that is human, capacities as those individuals in a privileged legal position. We still think in categories, but now all human beings are in one category; animals fall into another. The use of the single word *capacities* carries two different meanings and in so doing reflects a profound empirical truth. With time, most of the personal limitations on individual capacity disappeared, but not without epic struggles over the abolition of slavery, and the extension of civil capacity and suffrage to women. But even before the change in formal legal status, it would be a mistake to assume that slaves were treated like women, or that animals were treated like either. The variations in social status were just too great.

The defenders of animal rights place a slightly different twist on this history, which seizes on the fact that equal legal capacities are conferred on individuals with known differences in talents and abilities. The point requires a response. The movement for equal rights of all human beings must take into account the fact that all people do not have anything remotely like the same cognitive abilities. The phrase *ordinary intelligence* itself conceals a multitude of differences. But even that range does not capture the full extent of the problem, even if we put aside the case of children: What fate lies for adult human beings whose mental disabilities *in fact* preclude them from taking advantage of many of the rights they are afforded? Our standard position is to give them extra protection, not to exterminate them, and to do so because they are human beings, entitled to protection as such.

It follows therefore that we should resist any effort to extrapolate legal rights for animals from the change in legal rights of women and slaves. There is no next logical step to restore parity between animals on the one hand and women and slaves on the other. Historically, the elimination, first of slavery and then of civil disabilities to women, occurred long before the current agitation for animal rights. What is more, the natural cognitive and emotional limitations of animals, even the higher animals, preclude any creation of full parity. What animal can be given the right to contract? To testify in court? To vote? To participate in political deliberation? To worship?

None of these make any sense owing to the lack of intrinsic animal abilities. The claim for animal rights thus tends to boil down to a singular claim: protection against physical attack or, perhaps, as Gary Francione has urged, a somewhat broader right whereby animals cannot be used as resources subject to the control of human beings, or, more generally, "the right not to be treated as things" or resources, owned by human beings, even, it appears, when it is to their benefit.[33] The most that can be offered is protection against physical attack by human beings, and perhaps by other animals, and perhaps some recognition of the limited ownership that animals can acquire over certain external things from territories to acorns. A change in legal position, yes, but a restoration of some imagined parity, no.

PARTIAL PARITY FOR ANIMALS: SENSATION OR COGNITION?

So the question now arises: On what grounds ought animals be accorded these limited, but real, legal protections against human beings? In essence, there are two ways to go. The first emphasizes sensation, and the second cognition. Both in my view fail to sustain the claim for the new wave of animal rights.

Start with sensation. Animals experience pleasure and pain and should not be made to suffer as the instruments of human satisfaction. The nature of this claim exposes at the very least one of the fundamental soft spots in any kind of libertarian or utilitarian theory. It is therefore no accident that Robert Nozick, for example, devotes much thought to the question of animals. His mode of argument runs as follows. He first develops the theme that the "moral side constraints" that reflect our "separate existences" make it wholly appropriate to conclude that "there is no justified sacrifice of some of us for others."[34] This insight leads quickly to the libertarian side constraint against aggression. To probe just how powerful that constraint is, Nozick then turns to the moral side constraints that should be established in virtue that animals are sentient creatures.[35] As befits his darting intelligence, Nozick never quite comes down in favor of the proposition that animals should be treated with the same respect as people, but he is quite emphatic in concluding that they should not be treated as mere things either. He thinks that a total ban on hunting for pleasure is in order, and is doubtful that the case can be made for eating meat given that "*eating* animals is not necessary for *health.*"[36] But this statement over the concern for animal welfare is not a plea for moral parity. The side constraints may exist, but they are not the same side constraints that apply to human beings.

The exact same issues arise within the utilitarian framework. Once again, start with the view that what ultimately matters are gains and losses, such that rights are just a means to secure those social arrangements that maximize social gains (or pleasures) over social losses (or pains). One obvious question is how to measure these pleasures and pains. A number of different approaches can be taken. The easy way to avoid a comparison across persons is to insist that everyone has to be better off in one state of the world than in another. But that test for social welfare is so restrictive that it has little use in evaluating ordinary arrangements. Alternatively, one could argue that one state of the world is better than another if the winners in that state could (in principle, but not in fact) compensate the losers for their pain and still come out ahead of where they would otherwise be. There are enormous administrative difficulties in sorting all this out in human arrangements. But when the dust settles, the ultimate challenge to the utilitarian is the same as it is to the libertarian. In determining the excess of pleasure over pain, who or what deserves a place in the overall social utility function? The great challenge for utilitarian theory is *whom* ought to be counted in the felicific calculus.

Do animals then deserve a place in the social utility function, whether it is constructed on an aggregate or individual basis? The test for this right is the capacity to suffer and enjoy. Such is the point of Jeremy Bentham's blunt assertion: "The question is not, Can they *reason?* nor, Can they *talk?* but, Can they *suffer?*"[37] Our intervention to prevent suffering is, however, usually confined to questions of how human beings ought to interact with animals, and there the problems are difficult enough. Does one increase or reduce the suffering of animals by domestication? How would we know, and what would we do with that information if we had it? And if there are any increases in longevity, do those justify or excuse putting animals to death, after a happy life, for food or medical experimentation? As Nozick observes, one common justification for eating animals is that human ingenuity brought them into the world in the first place. But think of how that argument plays out with human beings. Surely, parents are not allowed to kill their children at three hours, days, months, or years just because they gave them the initial gift of life. "Once a person exists, not everything compatible with his overall existence being a net plus can be done, even by those who created him."[38] Stated otherwise, we think of parents as guardians, not owners of their children. The parity argument would insist that animals, once brought into this same world, receive this same protection.

Even if we could answer these conundrums, we still face a greater challenge: Do we have it within our power to arbitrate the differences among animals? Do we train the lion to lie down with the lamb, or do we let the lion consume the lamb in order to maintain his traditional folkways? Do we ask chimpanzees to forgo eating monkeys? It is odd to intervene in nature to forestall some deadly encounters, especially if our enforced nonaggression could lead to the extermination of predator species. But, if animals have rights, then how do we avoid making these second-tier judgments? We could argue that animals should not be restrained because they are not moral agents because they do not have the deliberative capacity to tell right from wrong, and therefore cannot be bound by rules that they can neither articulate nor criticize nor defend. But at this point we must ask whether we could use force in self-defense against such wayward creatures, or must we let them have their way with us, just as they do with other animals? In answer to this question, it could be said that animals cannot be held responsible by human standards because of their evident lack of capacity to conform.

Yet, there's the rub. Once that concession is made, then the next question is: Do we really think that suffering is the only criterion by which rights are awarded after all? It does seem troublesome—nothing is fatal in this counterintuitive metaphysics—to assume that animals are entitled to limited rights on a par with humans while denying that they are moral agents because they are incapable of following any universal dictates. And do we attach any weight to the unhappy fact that these animals are themselves imprinted "speciesists," in that they have instinctively different relationships with members of their own kind than they do with members of prey or predator populations? The test of sensation cannot generate a clean account of legal rights for animals.

So what about cognition? In his book *Drawing the Line*,[39] Steven Wise advances the claim that limited cognitive capacity supports the claims for negative rights, that is, for rights not be used as objects for human advantage. The preconditions run as follows. The animal

1. can desire;
2. can intentionally try to fulfill her desires; and
3. possesses a sense of self-sufficiency to allow her to understand, even dimly, that it is she who wants something and it is she who wants to get it.[40]

He then shows how to greater or lesser extents these criteria are satisfied by young children, chimps, bonobos, gorillas, orangutans, dogs, and even honeybees. It is no surprise that by these tests, all these animals do fairly well, as of course would rats, hyenas, and raccoons. Unless an animal has some sense of self, it cannot hunt, and it cannot either defend himself or flee when subject to attack. Unless it has a desire to live, it will surely die. And unless it has some awareness of means and connections, it will fail in all it does. We do not need experts to make judgments under these standards. It is quite enough that the mother senses danger when a stranger comes between her and her young. That happens all the time and meets, with room to spare, each of the ostensible criteria that Wise sets out in his campaign for animal rights.

But why follow these tests on the questions of entitlements? At one level, the entire discussion gets creepy when we make these comparisons organism by organism: How do we compare an intelligent chimp with a profoundly retarded child? It seems clear that even Wise has to engage in species-like comparisons to frame his general inquiry, and to proceed in that matter means that we do not draw any real distinctions within any particular animal or human grouping however defined. Indeed, to move in the other direction invites scorn from all quarters: Are dumb chimps entitled to no protection? May retarded children be killed at will because they will always flunk Wise's three tests? May infants be killed with impunity because they do not yet have higher cognitive powers? These variations have little to do with the rights of species. The question is how matters fare when we look at humans and chimps of ordinary intelligence: Show me the chimp that can learn her multiplication tables or do crossword puzzles at any age. The actual differences in the higher capacities are enormous on a species-to-species comparison. After all, no chimp could ever utter a word in defense of its own rights. The individual variations do not matter. So long as retarded children have human parents and siblings, they will never be regarded as appropriate fodder for indiscriminate slaughter. So with the rules and regulations that humans develop to protect chimps, where variations in cognitive abilities among chimps would in the end play little role in deciding the care and treatment that they receive.

The subject provokes still deeper ironies. In part, Steven Wise undertook his newer venture because in his earlier work, *Rattling the Cage: Toward Legal Rights for Animals*, he sought to establish limited legal rights for chimpanzees, only to face the same boundary question among species as everyone else. What about lions, tigers, alley cats, and jellyfish? None of these can be excluded if the capacity for suffering is decisive. Nor ironically can any be excluded on grounds of a (more) limited cognitive capacity under Wise's new tests. In the end, even the proponents of animal rights must adopt an explicit speciesist approach, complete with arbitrary distinctions. The line between humans and chimps is no longer decisive, but then some other line has to be. Perhaps it is the line between chimps and great apes, or between both and horses and cows, or between horses and cows and snails and fish. Which of these lines are decisive and why? The continuum problem continues to plague any response to the universalistic claim that the suffering of (some) animals counts as much as the suffering as a human being—at least to the human beings who are calling the shots. It turns out that Lovejoy's idea of a great chain of being influences not only the traditional attitude toward animals but also the revisionist beliefs of Steven Wise.

There is still another easy way to test the asserted parity between human beings and animals, even the chimps. Instead of looking at the duties of noninterference (by force) with animals, consider the opposite side of the coin: the affirmative duties that the state owes to animals. It is fashionable today to argue that all human beings are entitled to some minimal level of support in order to flourish as human beings and to develop their varied capacities. That desire for certain minimal rights is intended to impose on some individuals the correlative duties to support other people, so as to build a profound and enduring set of economic cross-subsidies into the system.

My simple question is this: Do we as human beings owe the same level of minimal support to chimps, or other animals, that we do to other people?

If we give Medicare to persons, do we have to supply it to chimps in the wild, at least if they are in our territory? Or suppose that we manufacture limited supplies of a new pill that is a cure for some disease that is ravaging both human and chimpanzee populations. There is not enough to go around for both man and beast. Is there some kind of affirmative duty to assist chimps to the same extent that we assist other human beings? I should be stunned if any real world scenario would ever produce any result other than humans first, chimps second. The blunt point is that we have had and will continue to have different moral obligations to members of our own species than we do to chimps or members of any other species.

This point is in some degree challenged by Gary Francione, who asks whether "we cannot prefer humans over animals in situations of true emergencies or conflicts."[41] As the subtitle of his recent book, "Your Child or the Dog?" indicates, the moment of truth comes when an individual needs to choose to save a child or a dog if both are trapped inside a burning house. The child, darn it, even if the child is unrelated and the dog is one's own. Francione waffles about this point, by noting that rescuers have to make similar choices among human beings. Should the rescuer save the infant who has yet to live his life over the very old adult who is near death? But this does not preclude a judgment that saves any human being over any animal. Nor would the reluctance to prefer the old and infirm over the young and healthy make it proper to treat old people as slaves, or as unwilling objects of medical experimentation. The same of course can be said of animals. It seems preferable to rescue a trapped animal than to remove a chair or a bush. But a priceless painting? All these comparisons only show that rankings are possible, with more or less precision. Animals are not treated just as though they were inanimate objects. Yet that hardly establishes that they are entitled to (limited) treatment as human beings.

WHERE NOW?

At this point, the question does arise: What ought to be the correct legal regimes with respect to animals? Here it would be simply insane to insist that animals should be treated like inanimate objects. The level of human concern for animals, in the abstract, makes this position morally abhorrent to most people, even those who have no truck whatsoever with the animal rights movement. That concern, moreover, can manifest itself in perfectly sensible ways short of the animal rights position even if it doesn't go quite as far as Nozick's anxious concern. It is of course pretty straightforward to pass and enforce a general statute that forbids cruelty to animals. Even if cruelty is narrowly defined so as to exclude, as it routinely does, the killing of animals for human consumption, at least it blocks some truly egregious practices without any real human gain, gory lust to one side. We can also engage in humane (note the choice of word) practices for the killing of animals so as to reduce their anxiety and fear. There are doubtless many ways to reduce animal suffering without compromising human satisfactions—ways that might even improve the human condition—and adopting those should count as important priorities. Who can oppose measures that benefit humans and animals alike?

The harder question arises when there is a trade-off between human gain and animal suffering. But actions that fit that description are, and have long been, staples of human society. Taking the first easy steps to protect animals still allows for the domestication and ownership of animals, and their use as human food. Nor do these address what is perhaps the hottest topic of controversy: the use of animals for medical experimentation. But that practice, with some important caveats, continues. It goes without saying that the use of animals for medical experimentation counts as a prima facie bad. We should not choose to inflict it lightly on any animals for some ephemeral gain. But that is a far cry from saying that no human benefit will *ever* justify in human terms the killing of animals, given their right to bodily integrity. That per se approach will not succeed, nor should it.

Examples are easy to state. Let it be shown that the only way to develop an AIDS vaccine that would save thousands of lives is through painful or lethal tests on chimpanzees. People will clamor for those tests (if they had the certainty announced here). Other cases are even easier. Suppose that the shortage of human kidneys could be at long last eliminated by the genetic engineering of pig kidneys so as to overcome the risk of human rejection? Does anyone think that we would impose a per se ban on the use of those organs in human beings because of the devotion to animal rights? Right now we have enormous safeguards, excessive in my view, on the use of human organs for transplantation.[42] Even after death, the practice is hard to implement. Efforts to persuade a reluctant nation to allow for voluntary transfers of human organs for cash have fallen largely on deaf ears. Systems of voluntary donations have not picked up the slack. The use of animal organs represents the hope of thousands of individuals for future salvation. An animal right to bodily integrity would stop that movement in its tracks. It will not happen, and it should not happen.

So what then should be done once we, as humans, decide not to extend something akin to Mill's categorical harm principle to animals, so as to leave them outside the orbit of any and all human uses. Lots, I suspect. For a start, we can recognize that in dealing with animals, there are two dimensions in which it is necessary to strive for the appropriate balance. The first of these is with the hierarchy of animals. The blunt truth, as Wise's own work shows, is that the more animals look and act like human beings, the greater the level of protection that we as humans are willing to afford them. Rights of bodily integrity do not have much of a future for mosquitoes. Yet, even if it was cheap to do, it would be wholly inappropriate to capture or breed chimpanzees for food, whatever our views on their use for medical experimentation. Conversely, it would be wholly inappropriate to think that we could only justify the sacrifice of cattle for medical experimentation, given their common use as food.

All that said, human beings have to think hard about the proper treatment of animals and to regulate, as we have long done, our interactions with animals. In sensing our way to the proper balance, we should take into account improvements in technology that lessen our dependence on particular uses of animals, and we should be alert for ways in which we could improve their lot without damaging our own (at least very much). It is all to the good if we could check the irritations that shampoo causes to the eye without animal experimentation. But here we have to fight and refight a thousand small skirmishes without the benefit of any categorical rules for guidance. Yet notwithstanding the mushiness of the method, we will probably do better with this approach as a human society than we would by invoking any categorical rule that says that animals, or some animals, rank so high that we can do nothing to compromise their bodily integrity for human ends. I am tempted to call this a Kantian-like absolutism, but such would be false to Kant, whose own views on animals (or *Vieh*, i.e., dumb animals) were wholly dismissive of their position in the legal firmament given their inability to act as rational agents capable of acting in accordance with some universal law. Nonetheless, the animal rights advocates show the same stubborn insistence about the inviolable position of animals that Kant defended in dealing with human beings. I do not think that the Kantian counsel of perfection is capable of being consistently followed in human affairs, however lofty the ideal. But for animals, my judgment is that this borrowed, if Kantian-like, absolute cannot be maintained against the objections to it. Yet mounting this heroic campaign is likely to divert our attention from the smaller improvements that can and should be made in our dealing with animals: Just how do we deal with foot-and-mouth disease? With exponential growth in alligator or deer populations? With hunting and the common pool?

No matter what adjustments we make, this enterprise will always touch a raw nerve. The root of our discontent is that in the end we have to separate ourselves from (the rest of) nature from which we evolved. Unhappily but insistently, the collective *we* is prepared to do just that. Such is our lot, and perhaps our desire, as human beings.

NOTES

1. Jared Diamond, *Guns, Germs, and Steel: The Fates of Human Societies 158* (New York & London, W. W. Norton & Co. 1997). The entire book offers a rich and powerful explanation of the patterns of domestication and should be required reading for anyone interested in this subject.
2. Id.
3. Barry Nicholas, *An Introduction to Roman Law* 131 (Oxford, Clarendon Press 1962).

4. For a general discussion of these principles, see Richard A. Epstein, *Simple Rules for a Complex World* 59–111 (Cambridge & London, Harvard University Press 1995); for an earlier philosophical version of the same theme, see Robert Nozick, *Anarchy, State, and Utopia* 150–153 (New York, Basic Books 1974).

5. Gaius, *Institutes*, II, 66 (Oxford, Clarendon Press, F. De Zulueta ed. 1946).

6. *The Digest of Justinian*, Gaius, 41.3 (T. Mommsen & P. Krueger eds., Eng. Translation, A. Watson), 41.

7. See, *Blade v. Higgs*, 11 H.L. Cases 521, 11 Eng. Rep. 1474 (1865) (adopting the rule of ownership *ratione soli*, or by reason of the land).

8. See, e.g., Digest, Ulpian 41.2.12.1: "Property has nothing in common with possession." For discussion, Nicholas, supra note 3 at 110–115. The rule in question has been the source of much philosophical discussion, see, e.g., Immanuel Kant, *Metaphysical Elements of Justice* 56–73 (ed. John Ladd 1999); and the editorial explication, id. xxxiii.

9. Gaius, *Institutes*, II, 67.

10. See, e.g., 4 *Am. Jur., 2d., Animals*, Sec. 10 at, p. 257: "The general rule, in the absence of an agreement to the contrary, is that the offspring or increase of tame or domestic animals belongs to the owner of the dam or mother. . . . In this respect the common law follows the civil and is founded on the maxim, 'partus sequitur ventrem.' . . . Furthermore, the increase of the increase, ad infinitum, of domestic animals comes within the rule and belongs to the owner of the original stock." For application, see *Carruth v. Easterling*, 150 So. 2d 852, 854–855 (Miss. 1963)

11. See, e.g., F. H. Lawson, *Negligence in Civil Law* (Oxford, Clarendon Press 1950), at 23, 24, which discusses death or injury to "slave or animal" in the same breath.

12. For a description of the formalities, see, Gaius, *Institutes*, I, 119; for discussion see Nicholas, supra note 3, 103–105.

13. For a general discussion, see Richard A. Epstein, *Torts* §13.3 (Gaithersburg, New York, Aspen 1999).

14. On which see, e.g., *Garcia v. Sumrall*, 121 P.2d 640 (Ariz. 1942), noting that the switch tends to take place on large tracts of barren land suitable only for grazing, where there is no arable land worthy of protection. Yet the presumption generally stays in favor of the common law rule of fencing. See Kenneth Vogel, "The Coase Theorem and California Animal Trespass Law," 16 *J. Legal Stud.* 149 (1987). Vogel notes that in a regime in which the landowner is required to fence out intruders he can make agricultural use of his property only by contracting with *all* potential interlopers; but when animals must be fenced in, a given owner can allow his land to be used for grazing by dealing with only a single individual; for a study of the evolution of these norms in Shasta County California, see Robert Ellickson, *Order without Law: How Neighbors Settle Disputes*, chs. 2 & 3 (Cambridge, Mass., Harvard University Press 1991).

15. The relevant passages are in Exodus: "If an ox gores a man or woman to death, the ox shall be stoned to death, its flesh may not be eaten, but the owner of the ox is innocent" (21.28); "But if the ox was previously reputed to have had the propensity to gore, its owner having been so warned, yet he did not keep it under control, so that it then killed a man or a woman, the ox shall be stoned to death, and its owner shall be put to death as well" (21.29); "Should a ran-

som be imposed upon him, however, he shall pay as the redemption of his life as much as is assessed upon him" (21.30).

The evident sophistication of these passages can not be ignored. Exodus 21.28 speaks in terms of a strict liability, which leaves open the possibility of defenses based, for example, on provocation, but probably not the defense that the owner used all due care to keep the animal in. But once there was warning of a dangerous propensity—itself a sophisticated dispositional concept—then if the owner did not keep the animal under control, he could be held liable, unless of course he was able to redeem his own life by paying some assessment. One could argue with the wisdom of the rules, but cannot impute to those who authored them a lack of the permutations of legal analysis.

16. See, e.g., *Marshall v. Welwood*, 38 N.J. L. 339(1876)

17. Id. at 341.

18. See Glanville Williams, *Liability for Animals* (Cambridge, Cambridge University Press 1939).

19. Report of the Committee on the Law of Civil Liability for Damage Done by Animals, CMD 8746 ¶3 (1953). The explanation was: "This class of liability is of interest only to farmers and landowners and the general public are not affected thereby." The impulse was that any deviation from the standard rules of tort law were justified by the reciprocal nature of the interactions between the parties in a closed community. See, on reciprocity in tort law generally, George Fletcher, "Fairness and Utility in Tort Theory," 85 *Harv. L. Rev.* 537, 547–548 (1972), with explicit reference to the rules of liability for wild animals.

20. Steven Wise, *Rattling the Cage: Toward Legal Rights for Animals* 14 (Cambridge, Mass., Perseus Books 2000)

21. Aristotle, *The History of Animals*, Book VIII, 588a (D'Arcy Wentworth Thompson, trans. in R. McKeon, *The Basic Works of Aristotle*, New York, Random House 1942).

22. See Aristotle, *On the Generation of Animals* 721l–730 (Arthur Platt trans., id).

23. See, Diamond, supra note 1, at 165. Similar strenuous efforts were made for the domestication of plants. Id. at 114–125.

24. Id. at 130.

25. Steven Wise, *Rattling the Cage* 9. The reference here is to Arthur Lovejoy, *The Great Chain of Being: A Study of the History of an Idea* (New York, Harper 1960).

26. Aristotle *Politics*, Bk. I, Ch. 2, 1252b 10 Id.

27. See, Nicholas, supra note 3, at 65, 66 (1962).

28. Id. at 66.

29. Id. 80–82.

30. Id. at 81.

31. See Justinian's *Institute*, Book I, ch. 2, 2 (Oxford, Clarendon Press, J.B. Moyle, ed., 5th ed 1913).

32. For that list, see, e.g., *Meyer v. Nebraska*, 262 U.S. 390, 399 (1923) (speaking of liberty as used in the context of substantive due process analysis).

33. Gary L. Francione, *Introduction to Animal Rights: Your Child or the Dog?* xxix (Philadelphia, Temple University Press 2000), and at 50–80.

34. Nozick, supra note at 33.

35. Id. at 35-42.

36. Id. at 36.

37. Jeremy Bentham, *The Principles of Morals and Legislation*, ch. XVII, note 1, at 311 (Oxford, Clarandon Press 1781), quoted in Francione, *Animal Rights*, at 5.
38. Nozick, at 38
39. Steven M. Wise, *Drawing the Line: Science and the Case for Animal Rights* (Cambridge, Mass., Perseus Books, 2002).
40. Id. at 32.
41. Francione, supra note 32, at xxx.
42. See Richard A. Epstein, *Mortal Peril: Our Inalienable Right to Health Care?* (Reading, Mass., Addison-Wesley 1997).

7

JAMES RACHELS

DRAWING LINES

When people are skeptical of the idea that we have moral responsibilities with respect to animals or that we should have laws protecting them, they will ask, "But where do we draw the line?" They may have two things in mind: (1) Where do we draw the line with respect to the *kinds of animals* to whom we have duties, or on whom we should confer legal protection? Do we have duties to fish? Snails? Insects? Viruses? (2) Where do we draw the line with respect to the *kinds of duties* we should acknowledge? Do we have a duty not to harm them? To protect them from harm? To feed them? I will begin by discussing the first question. But as we shall see, the two are related. If we understand the right way to answer one, we will know how to answer the other.

Here is an example of line drawing in the law. The U.S. Animal Welfare Act, enacted in 1966 and amended several times since then, instructs the secretary of agriculture to take steps to protect animals used in various ways, including research. Originally, the act defined *animal* as follows:

> The term "animal" means any live or dead dog, cat, monkey (nonhuman primate mammal), guinea pig, hamster, rabbit, or such other warm-blooded animal, as the Secretary may determine is being used, or is intended for use, for research, testing, experimentation, or exhibi-

tion purposes or as a pet; but such term excludes horses not used for research purposes and other farm animals, such as, but not limited to livestock or poultry, used or intended for use as food or fiber, or livestock or poultry used or intended for improving animal nutrition, breeding, management or production efficiency, or for improving the quality of food or fiber. With respect to a dog the term means all dogs including those used for hunting, security, or breeding purposes. (Animal Welfare Act as Amended [7 U.S.C. 2132(g)])

Of course this is not intended as a proper definition of *animal*, but only a specification of which animals are included within the scope of the act.

Mice, rats, and birds are not specifically mentioned, but they seem to be included because they are "warm-blooded animals." However, soon after the act was passed, the secretary of agriculture issued a regulation that excluded them from its scope. There the matter stood until the 1990s, when the Humane Society of the United States and some other pro-animal groups challenged the regulation in court, arguing that there is no legal basis for exempting these species. The court agreed, and the Department of Agriculture began to draft new regulations which would have brought the mice, rats, and birds back under the act's somewhat feeble protections. At this point, Senator Jesse Helms of North Carolina stepped in and proposed an amendment to the act that would make the new regulations unnecessary. He proposed to change the definition of *animal* so that "birds, rats of the genus Rattus, and mice of the genus Mus" would be specifically excluded.[1] The Helms amendment was adopted without debate and was signed into law by President George W. Bush in May 2002.

Why shouldn't mice, rats, and birds have the same status as guinea pigs, hamsters, and rabbits? On what grounds could such distinctions be made? For the American Association of Universities, and others who supported Senator Helms's proposal, the issue appears to have been entirely practical. More than 90 percent of laboratory animals are mice, rats, or birds, so if they don't count, there will be enormously less paperwork needed to comply with federal regulations.[2] On the Senate floor, Mr. Helms also mentioned the "paperwork burden."[3] Of course there is nothing wrong with modifying a policy for the sake of efficiency, especially if the administrative burden would be great and there is no important matter of principle involved.

The problem is that, for those on the other side, there are important matters of principle involved. The principles are ethical. Central among them is the idea that the interests of animals are important for their own sakes, and that it is indecent of humans not to respect those interests. It is problematic whether ethical principles should be enforced by law, especially when they are not shared by everyone, and I will say nothing about that. But I will assume that at least part of the motivation behind the Animal Welfare Act is a concern for the animals' own interests. This is consistent with the language of the act, which lists as its first purpose "to insure that animals intended for use in research facilities or for exhibition purposes or for use as pets are provided humane care and treatment" (7 U.S.C. 2131[1]).

The fact that the Animal Welfare Act does not treat all animals as equals will not offend most people. Most people—and by this I mean people who are at least moderately thoughtful about such matters—think of some animals as more worthy of protection than others. They seem to think in terms of a hierarchy in which the animal's rank depends, more or less, on its perceived degree of similarity to humans. Thus the mistreatment of primates is seen as a serious matter, and dogs and cats also rate high, but snakes and fish count for little. The act's original definition of *animal* reflects this: "Cold-blooded" animals were never included.

THEORIES OF MORAL STANDING

Theories of moral standing try to answer the question: To whom do we have direct duties? A *direct duty* is a duty to an individual as contrasted with a duty that merely involves the individual. If I promise you that I will feed your cat while you are away, the duty created by the promise is not a duty to your cat, even though it involves the cat; it is a duty to you. No one doubts that there can be duties involving animals. The question is whether we have duties *to* them, and if so, why.

The concept of moral standing was introduced by philosophers in the 1970s to deal with a number of issues that had arisen, such as the treatment of animals, but also abortion, euthanasia, and the environment. Philosophers thought they could make progress in these areas by establishing the moral standing of animals, fetuses, comatose persons, trees, and so on. The notion of "standing" was, of course, borrowed from the law.[4] Just as legal standing means that you have the right to bring your claims before a court, moral standing means that, from a moral point of view, you have claims that must be heard—that your interests constitute morally good reasons why you may, or may not, be treated in this or that way. So a key question became: What qualifies one for moral standing? Here is a quick summary of four main kinds of theories that have been proposed:

1. The first thought that occurred to many philosophers was that simply being human confers moral standing. This had the advantage of being nondiscriminatory, at least as far as humans were concerned. It echoed the rhetoric of the civil rights movement, which proclaimed that people of all races have equal rights "simply in virtue of being human," with no other qualification necessary. But only a little reflection was needed to see that this can't be taken literally. Even if it were true that all and only humans have full moral standing, we should be able to say *what it is* about being human that gives us this special status. Simply being human cannot be what does the job.

2. A more substantial type of theory connects moral standing with such qualities as self-consciousness, autonomy, and rationality. Humans, it was said, have full moral standing because they have such characteristics. These theories have a long history from Aristotle, who believed that human rationality gives us a supremely important place in the scheme of things, to Kant, who held that only self-conscious beings can be direct beneficiaries of obligations. Recently Kantians such as Christine Korsgaard have argued that exercising one's capacity for rational choice necessarily involves acknowledging the special moral status of human beings.[5]

3. Still another idea is that *having moral standing* and *being a moral agent* go together—the same characteristics that make for one make for the other. Thus, you have moral standing if you have the capacity for moral judgment and action. This type of theory is especially attractive to contractarians, who see moral obligations as arising from agreements between people, who are then expected to keep their bargains. John Rawls asks to whom the duties of justice are owed, and he replies: "The natural answer seems to be that it is precisely the moral persons who are entitled to equal justice. . . . they are capable of having (and are assumed to acquire) a sense of justice, a normally effective desire to apply and to act upon the principles of justice, at least to a certain minimum degree. . . . Those who can give justice are owed justice."[6]

   However, there is a problem with theories that emphasize qualities like self-consciousness, autonomy, and moral agency: They set the bar too high. Although the proponents of these theories emphasize that moral standing is not limited by definition to normal adult humans—it is at least possible for some nonhuman animals (as well as hypothetical extraterrestrials) to be self-conscious, autonomous persons, or to be moral agents—it turns out that in fact only normal adult humans uncontroversially satisfy such demanding criteria. This means, for one thing, that these theories make unwelcome discriminations among human beings. They leave us with a problem about what to say about babies and mentally handicapped people, who may not be self-conscious, autonomous moral agents. Moreover, animals, as is frequently noted, can feel pain, even if they do not possess the fancier qualities. So it seems wrong to torture them, and it seems wrong because of what is being done to them.

4. For this reason, many philosophers, especially utilitarians, were attracted to a more modest theory which says that, to have moral standing, it is only necessary that one be able to feel pain. Thus Mark Bernstein writes: "The realm of the morally considerable is constituted by those individuals with the capacity for modifiable, hedonic conscious experience. If we use 'phenomenology' or 'sentience' as abbreviations for this capacity, we can say that experientialism dictates that all and

only those with moral standing are phenomenological or sentient individuals."[7]

Finally, we may note that, in working their way toward a conception of moral standing, many writers take a detour through the concept of personhood. They take "What qualifies one for moral standing?" and "What is a person?" to be essentially the same question. I believe that Joseph Fletcher was the first to produce a list of "conditions for personhood" with an eye to addressing ethical issues,[8] but others soon followed. Mary Anne Warren's list of person-making qualities in her much-anthologized 1973 paper on abortion is perhaps the most famous.[9] Warren produced an account of what it means to be a person—where *person* is not just a biological category but denotes individuals with the psychological and "personal" dimensions of human beings—in order to argue that, because fetuses lack the characteristics of persons, they do not have the full moral rights of persons. This became a familiar strategy. In 1988 some of the literature that had been generated was gathered into an anthology called *What Is a Person?* and the editor wrote:

> The problems of personhood . . . are central to issues in ethics ranging from the treatment or termination of infants with birth defects to the question whether there can be rational suicide. But before questions on such issues as the morality of abortion, genetic engineering, infanticide, and so on, can be settled, the problems of personhood must be clarified and analyzed. . . . What qualities/attributes must a being have to be considered a person? Why are those qualities, and not others, significant?[10]

Connecting moral standing with personhood provides an intuitively plausible way of identifying the characteristics that are important for moral standing. We are confident that persons have moral standing, and so, if certain qualities are central to personhood, it is reasonable to conjecture that those qualities are also central to moral standing. If those qualities happen to be the grand, impressive features of human nature that have always led humans to regard themselves as special, so much the better. In this way the appeal to such qualities as rationality, autonomy, self-consciousness, and moral agency were made to seem less arbitrary.

CHARACTERISTICS AND TYPES OF TREATMENT

The theories I have mentioned will be familiar to anyone who is acquainted with the literature produced by moral philosophers since the 1970s. I have summarized these theories, without going into any detail about them, because I want to make a general point about their structure. Despite differences in detail, the theories have this in common: They all assume that the answer to the question of how an individual may be treated depends on whether the individual qualifies for a general sort of status, which in turn depends on whether the individual possesses a few general characteristics. But no answer of this form can be correct. In what follows, I will explain why this is so and why it is important.

Each of the theories offers an account of the relation between (i) how individuals may be treated and (ii) facts about them—facts about their capacities, abilities, and other characteristics, such as whether they are rational, self-conscious, or sentient. But what, exactly, is the relation between the facts about an individual and how the individual may be treated? Let us consider how this works, first for normal adult humans, where our intuitions are firmest.

Facts about people often figure into the reasons why they may or may not be treated in this or that way. Adam may be ejected from the choir because he can't sing. Betty may be given Prozac because she is depressed. Charles may be congratulated because he has just gotten engaged. Doris may be promoted because she is a hard worker. Notice, however, that a fact that justifies one type of treatment may not justify a different type of treatment: Unless something unusual is going on, we could not justify giving Betty Prozac on the grounds that she can't sing or throwing Adam out of the choir because he has become engaged.

The same is true of the more impressive characteristics that are mentioned in the theories of moral standing. Autonomy and self-consciousness are not ethical superqualities that entitle the bearer to every possible kind of favorable treatment. Like musical ability and betrothal, they are relevant to some types of treatment but not to others.

Autonomy

Humans are rational, autonomous agents who can guide their own conduct according to their desires and their conceptions of how they ought to live. Does this fact make a difference in how they may be treated? Of course it does. Suppose someone wants to live her life in a way that involves risks we think are foolish. We may try to change her mind; we may point out the risks and argue that they are not worth it. But may we compel her to follow our advice? We may not, for she is, after all, a rational, autonomous agent.

It is different for someone who is not fully rational—a small child, for example. Then we may prevent her from harming herself. The fact that the child is not yet a fully rational agent justifies us in treating her differently than we would treat someone who is a fully rational agent.

Once we understand why autonomy makes a difference in how someone may be treated, in the cases in which it does make a difference, it becomes clear that possession of this quality is not relevant in other sorts of cases. Suppose the treatment at issue is not paternalistic interference, but torture: Why would it be wrong to poke you with a stick? The answer is not that you are autonomous; the answer is that it would cause you pain.

Self-Consciousness

To be self-conscious is to be able to make oneself the object of one's thoughts, to have beliefs about oneself, and to be able to reflect on one's own character and conduct. As the term is used by most philosophers, self-consciousness also includes the capacity for conceiving of oneself as extended through time—for understanding that one has a past and a future.

There are, therefore, a number of goods that self-consciousness makes possible: self-confidence, hope for the future, satisfaction with one's life, the belief that you are someone of value, and the knowledge that you are loved and appreciated by other people. Without self-consciousness, there could be no sense of pride or self-worth. Considered in this light, it is no wonder that some philosophers have singled out self-consciousness as a supremely important human quality.

At the same time, a person who has this capacity is thereby vulnerable to a special range of harms. Because you are capable of reflecting on your own conduct and your own place in the world, you may feel embarrassed, humiliated, guilty, and worthless. Because you can think about your own future, you may despair and lose hope. Your capacity for self-referential beliefs and attitudes makes it possible for you to feel that your life and activities have no meaning, and you can believe, rightly or wrongly, that other people have no regard for you.

This being so, there are ways of treating people that are objectionable on grounds that involve their capacity for self-consciousness. I should not do things that would embarrass or humiliate you. I should not unjustly curse you or hold you in contempt. I should not question or criticize you in ways that would cause you debilitating self-doubt or self-loathing. I should not belittle you in ways that would injure your self-respect. I should not treat you in such a way as to take away your hope for the future.

Moral Agency

Humans have the capacity for moral judgment and action, and this, it is often said, gives them an especially noble nature that sets them apart from other animals. But, self-congratulation aside, how is the possession of this capacity relevant to how an individual may be treated? There are three ways of treating people that are appropriate if they are moral agents.

First, and most obviously, moral agents may merit praise or blame for what they do. Beings who lack a sense of right and wrong are not eligible for such responses.

Second, the fact that someone has moral capacities may be important when we need to influence their conduct. When we are dealing with moral agents, we can reason with them—we can influence their behavior by appealing to their sense of right. This may be better than bribes, threats, or other cajolery not only in that it respects their autonomy, but because such influence might be more stable and longer lasting. Demands for social justice, for example, are more effective in the long run if they address people's consciences than if they are merely exercises of power.

Third, moral agency includes the capacity for cooperating with others, and so moral agents are individuals with whom we can make agreements. This is the critical capacity for rational-choice contractarians, who believe that moral obligations exist only as a result of such agreements. But general views aside, it is important in everyday life to discern whom one can trust and with whom one can profitably cooperate. So this is another respect in which someone's being a moral agent makes a difference in our dealings with them.

The Ability to Feel Pain

The ability to feel pain is perhaps the most obviously relevant characteristic anyone possesses. The fact that it would cause you pain is a complete and sufficient reason why I should not jab you with a stick. This reason does not need to be supplemented or reinforced by considerations having to do with your dignity as a rational being, your autonomy, or anything like that. It is enough that being jabbed hurts.

Of course, your interests as an autonomous agent may be affected by debilitating pain. Chronic pain may prevent you from leading the kind of life you want to lead, and even a short experience of intense pain may have lasting psychological effects. But this only means that, in the case of autonomous beings, there is an additional reason why torture is wrong. The additional reason does not replace the original one, nor is one a mere shorthand for the other.

But regardless of how important the ability to feel pain may be, when other types of treatment are involved it may be irrelevant: What entitles you to remain in the choir is not the same as what makes it objectionable to poke you with the stick.

We may draw the following conclusions from all this: There is no characteristic, or reasonably small set of characteristics, that sets some creatures apart from others as meriting respectful treatment. That is the wrong way to think about the relation between an individual's characteristics and how he or she may be treated. Instead we have an array of characteristics and an array of treatments, with each characteristic relevant to justifying some types of treatment but not others. If an individual possesses a particular characteristic (such as the ability to feel pain), then we may have a duty to treat it in a certain way (not to torture it), even if that same individual does not possess other characteristics (such as autonomy) that would mandate other sorts of treatment (refraining from coercion).

We could spin these observations into a theory of moral standing that would compete with the other theories. Our theory would start like this: There is no such thing as moral standing *simpliciter*. Rather, moral standing is always moral standing with respect to some particular mode of treatment. A sentient being has moral standing with respect to not being tortured. A self-conscious being has moral standing with respect to not being humiliated. An autonomous being has moral standing with respect to not being coerced. And so on. If asked, toward whom is it appropriate to direct fundamental moral consideration?[11] we could reply: It is appropriate to direct moral consideration toward any individual who has any of the indefinitely long list of characteristics that constitute morally good reasons why he or she should or should not be treated in any of the various ways in which individuals may be treated.

You may think this isn't a very appealing theory. It is tedious; it lacks the crispness of the other theories; it doesn't yield quick and easy answers to practical questions; and worse, it isn't exciting. But it is the truth about moral standing. (I believe it was Bertrand Russell who once said it wasn't his fault if the truth wasn't exciting.)

It would do no harm, however, and it might be helpful for clarity's sake, to drop the notion of "standing" altogether and replace it with a simpler conception. We could just say that the fact that doing so-and-so would cause pain to someone (to any individual) is a reason not to do it. The fact that doing so-and-so would humiliate someone (any individual) is a reason not to do it. And so on. Sentience and self-consciousness fit into the picture like this: Someone's sentience and someone's self-consciousness are facts about them that explain why they are susceptible to the evils of pain and humiliation.

We would then see our subject as part of the theory of reasons for action. We would distinguish three elements: what is done to the individual; the reason for doing it or not doing it, which connects the action to some benefit or harm to the individual; and the pertinent facts about the individual that help to explain why he or she is susceptible to that particular benefit or harm:

Action: Poking you with a sharp stick
Reason for not doing that: It would cause you pain.
Facts about you that explain why you are capable of feeling pain: You have conscious experiences and a nervous system of a certain kind: You are sentient.

Action: Telling your husband's friends that he is impotent
Reason for not doing that: It would humiliate him.
Facts about him that explain why he is capable of being humiliated: He has attitudes and beliefs about himself and about how others regard him: He is self-conscious.

So, part of our theory of reasons for action would go like this: We always have reason not to do harm. If treating an individual in a certain way harms him or her, that is a reason not to do it. The fact that he or she is autonomous, or self-conscious, or sentient simply helps to explain why he or she is susceptible to particular kinds of harms.

KINDS OF ANIMALS AND THE ANIMAL WELFARE ACT

How will a morally decent human treat nonhuman animals? The answer will depend, in part, on what we think nonhumans are like, and most of us are willing to attribute a fairly broad range of morally important characteristics to them. Ever since Darwin taught us to see ourselves as kin to the other animals, we have increasingly come to think of them as like us in morally significant ways.[12] We believe that monkeys have cognitive and social abilities similar to our own, that all sorts of animals are self-conscious, and that dogs have qualities such as courage and loyalty. And even if the "lower animals" do not have these impressive qualities, we think it is undeniable that they can at least feel pain.

There are, of course, those who are skeptical about this consensus. Daniel Dennett chides animal rights advocates for assuming too much and for trusting their intuitions too easily. Even the consciousness of animals, he says, can be doubted:

> Cog, a delightfully humanoid robot being built at MIT, has eyes, hands, and arms that move the way yours do—swiftly, relaxedly, compliantly. Even those of us working on the project, knowing full well that we haven't even begun to program the high level processes that might arguably endow Cog with consciousness, get an almost overwhelming sense of being in the presence of another conscious observer when Cog's eyes still quite blindly and stupidly follow one's hand gestures. Once again, I plead for symmetry: when you acknowledge the power of such elegant, lifelike motions to charm you into an illusion, note that it ought to be an open question, still, whether you are also being charmed by your beloved dog or cat, or the noble elephant. Feelings are too easy to provoke for them to count for much here.[13]

It is a stretch to doubt the consciousness of "your beloved dog or cat," and there is no evidence that would compel such a major change in how we think of those animals. Indeed, Dennett does not say there is any such evidence: He only pleads for us not to preclude the possibility. The plea for open-mindedness is hard to fault. Nonetheless, I believe the most reasonable approach, when formulating ethical and social policies, is to assume that the prevailing consensus is correct except where we have good evidence to the contrary.

On the fundamental question of whether animals can feel pain, scientific investigations tend to confirm the commonly held belief that most animals, especially the "higher" animals, do feel pain. The mechanisms that enable us to feel pain are not fully understood, but we do know a good bit about them. In humans, nocioceptors—neurons specialized for sensing noxious stimuli—are connected to a central nervous system, and the resulting signals are processed in the brain. Until recently it was believed that the brain's work was divided into two distinct parts: a sensory system operating in the somatosensory cortex, resulting in our conscious experiences of pain, and an affective-motivational system associated with the frontal lobes, responsible for our behavioral reactions. Now, however, this picture has been called into question, and it may be that the best we can say is that the brain's system for processing the information from the nocioceptors seems to be spread over multiple regions. At any rate, the human nocioceptive system also includes endogenous opiods, or endorphins, which provide the brain with its natural "pain-killing" ability.

The question of which other animals feel pain is a real and important issue, not to be settled by appeals to "common sense," as Dennett insists. Only a complete scientific understanding of pain, which we do not yet have, could tell us all that we need to know. In the meantime, however, we do have a rough idea of what to look for. If we want to know whether it is reasonable to believe that a particular kind of animal is capable of feeling pain, we may ask: Are there nocioceptors present? Are they connected to a central nervous system? What happens in that nervous system to the signals from the nocioceptors? And are there endogenous opiods? In our present state of understanding, this sort of information, together with the obvious behavioral signs of distress, is the best evidence we can have that an animal is capable of feeling pain.[14]

It is harder to devise experimental tests for the presence of other, more sophisticated capacities. Yet there is some evidence even for such capacities as self-consciousness. One idea is to see whether animals can recognize themselves in mirrors (after it has been established that they know how mirrors work and can recognize other objects in mirrors). In 1970, the psychologist Gordon Gallup devised a clever experiment to test this: While chimpanzees were unconscious, he placed a red mark on one of their eyebrows and ears. Then, he showed each chimp a full-length mirror. The chimps would immediately rub the marked spots and examine their fingers. We are apt to agree with Gallup that this provides strong evidence that the chimps are self-aware. However, Gallup's experiment was subsequently tried on other species, with very different results. Surprisingly, gorillas and monkeys failed the test. But more recently, using a modified form of the Gallup test, Marc Hauser has shown that cotton-top tamarins do show mirror self-recognition.[15]

It is clear, then, that we should proceed cautiously. But bearing all this in mind, let us return to our question: How will a morally decent human treat nonhuman animals? No general answer is possible, because animals are different from one another—a chimpanzee has little in common with a mockingbird. So how, for example, may a chimpanzee be treated? Once again, it depends on what sort of treatment we have in mind. There are lots of ways of treating chimps, just as there are lots of ways of treating people. This means that, if we seriously want to know how chimps may be treated, we will have to consider a long list of treatments and relevant characteristics.

Is there anything about a chimp that makes it objectionable to poke it with a stick? Yes, the chimp can feel pain. Is there anything about a chimp that makes it objectionable to confine it to a barren cage? Yes, chimps are active, intelligent creatures that cannot thrive without a stimulating environment. Is there anything about a female chimp that makes it objectionable to separate her from her babies? Yes, chimpanzee mothers and babies are emotionally bonded in much the same way as are human mothers and babies.

Is there anything about a chimp that makes it objectionable to exclude them from college classrooms? No, they lack the intellectual capacities necessary to participate in college classes. Is there anything about a chimp that makes it objectionable to exclude them from the choir? No, they can't sing. Is there anything about a chimp that makes it impermissible to forcibly vaccinate it against a disease? No, the chimp lacks the cognitive capacities that would enable it to choose for itself in the relevant sense.

Obviously, we could continue in this way indefinitely. The point, though, is that there is no general answer to the question of how chimps may be treated. There are only the various ways of treating them and the various considerations that count for and against those treatments. Among other things, this means that the question "Where do we draw the line?" is misguided. As we noted at the outset, the question may be taken in two ways: (1) Where do we draw the line with respect to the kinds of animals to whom we have duties? and (2) Where do we draw the line with respect to which duties we have? But in neither instance is there one place to draw the line. There is only an indefinitely long series of lines: Where causing pain is concerned, we draw the line between individuals who can feel pain and individuals who cannot; where separating mothers and babies is concerned, we draw the line between mothers who are bonded with their babies (and babies who need their mothers), and those who are not; and so on.

For purposes of public policy, however, we may need to draw rough lines, and we can do this by attending to the characteristics that are typical of the members of various species and the kinds of treatment that they are likely to receive in relevant contexts. For example, if the relevant context is laboratory research, in which the animals are liable to be separated from their own kind, kept for long periods in sterile cages, and caused a lot of pain, and we are seeking to ensure "humane care and treatment," then it is reasonable to draw the line between species whose members are social, intelligent, and can feel pain, and species whose members lack those qualities.

The Animal Welfare Act's list of included and excluded species is a jerry-rigged affair which looks like the result of compromise and political bargaining. But in some respects it isn't bad. When the context is "research, testing, [and] experimentation," the secretary of agriculture is authorized to ensure "humane care and treatment" for "dog[s], cat[s], monkey[s] (nonhu-man primate mammal[s]), guinea pig[s], hamster[s], rabbit[s], or such other warm-blooded animal[s]." The six kinds of animals mentioned by name appear to be no more than examples of the kinds intended; the language of the act includes all warm-blooded animals, *such as* guinea pigs, hamsters, or rabbits. This category seems to capture the social, intelligent, and sensitive animals about whom we should be concerned when they are taken into the laboratory. At the same time, the act's protections do not extend to snakes, snails, or fish, where the presence of the relevant qualities seems less certain. And what of the Helms amendment? In this context, if a mouse or a rat isn't relevantly similar to a guinea pig or a hamster, what is? The Helms amend-ment is contrary not only to good sense but to the intent of the original legislation. Its adoption was a lamentable step backward.

NOTES

1. The amendment replaced the words "excludes horses not used for research purposes" with "excludes birds, rats of the genus Rattus, and mice of the genus Mus bred for use in research, horses not used for research purposes."
2. Letter from AAU president Nils Hasselmo to Senator Helms, February 21, 2002.
3. *Congressional Record,* February 12, 2002, S624.
4. I believe that Christopher Stone's book *Should Trees Have Standing?* (Los Altos, CA: William Kaufmann, 1972) prompted the borrowing.
5. Christine Korsgaard, *The Sources of Normativity* (Cambridge: Cambridge University Press, 1996).
6. John Rawls, *A Theory of Justice* (Cambridge, MA: Harvard University Press, 1971), 505, 510.
7. Mark Bernstein, *On Moral Considerability: An Essay on Who Morally Matters* (New York: Oxford University Press, 1998), 24.
8. Joseph Fletcher, "Indicators of Humanhood: A Tentative Profile of Man," *Hastings Center Report* 2 (November 1972): 1–4.
9. Mary Anne Warren, "On the Moral and Legal Status of Abortion," *Monist* 57 (1973): 43–61. Warren's more recent views are presented in her book *Moral Status: Obligations to Persons and Other Living Things* (Oxford: Clarendon, 1997).
10. Michael F. Goodman, ed., *What Is a Person?* (Clifton, NJ: Humana, 1988), vii.
11. Arthur Kuflick, "Moral Standing," *Routledge Encyclopedia of Philosophy*, vol. 6 (London and New York: Routledge, 1998), 550.
12. See James Rachels, *Created from Animals* (Oxford: Oxford University Press, 1990).
13. Daniel Dennett, *Brainchildren* (Cambridge, MA: Bradford, 1998), 340.
14. The best treatment of these issues of which I am aware is an (as yet) unpub-lished paper by Colin Allen, "Animal Pain," from which I have learned a great deal.
15. Marc Hauser, *Wild Minds: What Animals Really Think* (New York: Henry Holt, 2000), 100–109.

8

LESLEY J. ROGERS AND GISELA KAPLAN

ALL ANIMALS ARE *NOT* EQUAL

The Interface between Scientific Knowledge
and Legislation for Animal Rights

INTRODUCTION

Any current legislation or code of practice for animal welfare must take into account current scientific knowledge on the biology and behavior of different species. We have guidelines for rodents, dogs, cats, apes, and any number of animals to ensure that research and other practices meet the needs of specific orders, families, or even species. The call for animal rights, it seems, functions on a different intellectual trajectory, namely, the notion of "sameness" and perhaps even of "universality"—as indeed do human rights. At least, in human rights, the conferment of rights on a global scale is for one species, although cultural differences and different legal traditions may also decisively impinge on ideas of universality. How much more difficult is it to decide rights for animals!

One of the hallmarks of animal existence is its diversity and difference, the specificity of their requirements, skills, and needs in very concrete ecological settings. If we attempt to find as a measuring stick a common denominator, we inevitably encounter the problem of deciding which species will be included in, and which excluded from, the new legislative practices. In other words, where does one draw the line between those to be given the privilege of protection from abuse and those to be not so treated? As we will show, this important decision cannot be made lightly, and the deeper we look at it, the more we realize that drawing the line accurately is bedeviled by gaps in the relevant scientific knowledge about most species and the inaccuracies of attempting to rate species according to a single criterion, or even a small set of criteria.

It has been proposed that animal rights should be awarded according to a set of criteria related to higher cognition. The greater an animal's sense of self-awareness and the more advanced its higher cognition, the better the case to include its species as the recipient of a set of new privileges.

The Mirror Test

To illustrate our point, let us consider the well-known mirror test of self-recognition, proposed by Steven Wise as a criterion on which species might be categorized and accordingly assigned liberty rights (Wise, 2002). If an individual recognizes that the image it sees in the mirror is indeed itself and not merely another member of its species, it can be said to be self-aware and, being self-aware, it should be afforded rights. Then, if that individual is representative of its species (i.e., conspecifics also recognize themselves in mirrors), we can safely extend rights to the entire species.

We have no objection to the extension of rights to self-aware living organisms, but is performance on the mirror test an appropriate criterion on which to base this decision? While this might seem to be a simple test, it is not without problems of method and interpretation, particularly in comparisons between species (for details see Rogers, 1997).

There are two ways of assessing an animal's response to seeing its image in the mirror; one is to see whether it uses the mirror to examine parts of its body that it cannot see otherwise (it may pick its teeth or clean its eyes), and the other is to see how it reacts to seeing a red spot of paint on its forehead or some other part of its body concealed from direct vision. In the latter case, the animal is meant to touch the red spot on its own forehead (or elsewhere on its body) rather than touch the image of the spot. This indicates that it is aware that the image is of itself. Chimpanzees perform both of these variants of the test in ways that indicate that they are self-aware (Gallup, 1970; Gallup et al., 1995). Despite the poorly controlled experiments using the mirror test, especially the earlier ones, the overall results confirm that apes are self-aware.

However, the awareness of chimpanzees measured in this mirror task is limited to the visual modality and does not take into account that the representation of self includes auditory, tactile, and olfactory information, any of which may be more important than the visual image in different species. Dogs, for example, pay relatively little attention to how other dogs look but are extraordinarily attentive to how they smell. A dog, therefore, may not be expected to recognize its visual image, and so would fail the test, even though it is likely to recognize its own smell and even the smell of different parts of its body, as we know it can do so in recognizing humans (Rogers and Kaplan, 2003). The test is simply not applicable to dogs, and this illustrates the problem in using it to rank species against each other.

A mirror test has also been conducted with an avian species, a European magpie (*Pica pica*), and the results suggest that this bird is indeed able to recognize the image in the mirror as its own (Prior, Pollok, and Güntürkün, 2000). However, the test had to be modified for testing a bird. Most birds have laterally placed eyes, and each eye is controlled by the opposite brain hemisphere with different functions (discussed later). Would it fail by looking on one side rather than the other? Second, birds have no hands and can therefore not easily wipe off a red dot from their foreheads, as used when the test is applied to primates. Hence, even if the cognitive abilities of a certain species of bird and primates are exactly the same, the anatomical differences can make the observable responses qualitatively and operationally very different from one another indeed. The same problems arise when other species are compared, although they are usually less extreme than in this example.

Furthermore, the mirror test tells us little, if anything, of the mental aspects of self, although researchers who have used the mirror technique have often led us to believe that they are studying self in a general sense. We believe that the research on self-recognition in mirrors has assumed too central a place in attempts to measure self-recognition in animals. Another notable drawback of the test is the fact that it can be used only on captive animals, which may not be representative of their species. This is but one example of the problems of using a single test to compare species.

Intelligence

Other attempts have been made to measure "intelligence" in a similar way. These stumble against the nebulous and ephemeral concept of intelligence. Intelligence is not an entity that can be measured by performance on just one task, nor can it be inferred from brain size, as we discuss below. Here it is worth noting that pigeons, tested on a task based on one problem taken from a standard IQ test for humans, which required them to recognize symbols rotated at different angles, surpassed humans in performance of the same task (Delius, 1987). Would we therefore rank them above us in intelligence? Obviously, the single criterion of assessment is an inadequate measure for intelligence in a broad sense. Although IQ tests have some degree of limited validity in terms of predictability of academic success in a given culture and class in humans (Sternberg, Grigorenko, and Bundy, 2001), there is in fact no scientifically acceptable way of measuring intelligence as a broad set of characteristics in humans, let alone in animals. Add to this the ambition of making comparisons of intelligence *across* species and it is easy to see how flawed such attempts would have to be. Pigeons, and for that matter machines too, may be clever at solving certain problems but intelligence, no matter how we attempt to define it, means much more than this. In other words, not all behavior that *appears* to be intelligent actually depends on higher cognitive processes. Furthermore, there is no evidence that different species use the same cognitive processes to carry out similar types of behavior.

It would be pointless to attempt to devise a battery of tests that might attempt to measure the equivalent of IQ in humans and to apply the same test, even with slight modifications, to different species because species vary so much in their senses, their ways of processing information, and so on. As a general rule, we consider animals that are more like us to be more intelligent, but it is important to recognize that each species is adapted to its particular environmental habitat, or niche, and each one performs intelligently, or "cleverly," in its own niche. One could say that there are many different intelligences, rather than ranking all species on the same scale of intelligence. Some species that may appear to be less intelligent than others when they are all tested on the same, rather arbitrarily chosen task (e.g., going around a barrier to reach something on the other side) may perform strikingly well on tasks better suited to their own specialized abilities.

As a general statement we do recognize that a species with greater cognitive capacity is more likely to display intelligent behavior and more likely to be self-aware than one with smaller cognitive capacity. In fact, flexibility of behavior might be the best marker of intelligence.

Unfortunately, we have as yet little information about the breadth of the potential behavioral repertoire of many species and little basis on which to compare species and so make a well-founded decision on which species should be given rights. There are about 5,000 extant mammalian species and about 9,000 avian species alive today, and a greater number of reptiles and amphibians than both avian and mammalian species put together, a still greater number of fishes, millions of insects and spiders, and so on. We don't even know them all, let alone can claim to have studied in depth more than a fraction of them, and only the smallest fraction of those have been investigated for cognitive abilities, among them dolphins and whales (Rendell and Whitehead, 2001), the great apes, some avian species, canids, and elephants—just a handful, in fact, out of the thousands more that await further research.

One set of legal proposals would require that we single out some species for special treatment. Can current knowledge in neuroscience and animal behavior assist in the decisions that have to be made? Can we find a relevant discontinuity between one group of animals and the rest? To put it bluntly: Does biology match the needs of legislating for animal rights?

SELECTING SPECIES FOR ANIMAL RIGHTS

The Evolutionary Argument

The Great Ape Project makes a perfectly acceptable argument to include all apes in the same genus, thus for "including all great apes within the community of equals" (Cavalieri and Singer, 1993, p. 6). The great apes are our closest relatives; the chimpanzees separated from our line of evolution 5–6 million years ago; the gorilla separated 8 million years ago; and the line that leads to the present-day orangutan separated from our line between 8 and 12 million years ago. The genetic material of the great apes is very similar to our own: Even the orangutan has 98 percent of the same genetic material as humans, and the match is even closer for the other apes (Gribbin and Gribbin, 1988; Kaplan and Rogers, 2000). It is, therefore, logically expected that the great apes will be the most similar to us of all animals in both their physiology and behavior. There are, however, two issues that arise from this line of thinking.

The first concerns finding proof that the great apes do show unique capacities resembling our own, that is, in self-awareness and other cognitive abilities. Despite the concentrated effort to find cognitive abilities in great apes that surpass those of monkeys and other species, no single characteristic has yet been found to uphold this position, as we will discuss later. More specifically, it is unclear why the lesser apes, the gibbons, should be left out of this exclusive group. Certainly, the gibbons branched off from the line of evolution to humans 17 million years ago and their genetic material is slightly less of a match to ours, but we see no major discontinuity between the gibbons and the great apes that would allow us to place them among the "have-nots." Of course, proof might come from comparing the cognitive abilities of the gibbons with those of the great apes but, so far, very little investigation has been made of this. We know only that gibbons have very complex vocalizations and clearly that they engage in complex communication. This suggests that it might be a convenient yet arbitrary step to separate them from the great apes.

The second point of relevance to this argument is that similarity of genetic material is determined by mixing together two DNA samples in a test tube (hybridizing them) and then measuring how much the strands of DNA match. This tells us about the code and the potential of the genetic material, but it does not tell us exactly which genes are expressed (i.e., are functional). Not all genes are expressed at any one time or, indeed, ever expressed during a lifetime (explained by Marks, 2002). When we speak of intelligence or any other aspect of brain function, we are referring to the aspects of the individual that result from those genes that are actually expressed. Two factors influence which genes are expressed: the course of evolution and the influence of the environment. Thus, to put it simply, two species may have the same gene but it may be expressed in only one of those species. The net effect is two very different functional states. Hence, genetic similarity may be an indicator of functional similarity but it cannot stand alone as the criterion on which we should base arguments for fundamental division between species.

Awareness of Self

We have mentioned above that apes can recognize themselves in mirrors. Some researchers have claimed that monkeys are unable to do this, but this negative result may have been merely due to the experiment being an inappropriate method for testing them. Hauser et al. (1995) tested cotton-top tamarin monkeys with mirrors and to make sure that they would attend to the spot marked with dye they applied differently colored dyes to the tuft of hair on the top of the head. This is a visually distinctive feature of the species and one likely to be used in social situations. The tamarins with dyed hair looked in the mirror longer than control tamarins with only white dye painted on their tuft of hair. By including this control group, the experimenters eliminated the possibility that the aftereffect of anesthesia could explain the results. Looking for longer in the mirror could have had something to do with being attracted by the color of the dyed hair rather than recognition of self. However, only the individuals with dyed hair, and prior experience with mirrors, touched their heads while looking in the mirror, and some of them used the mirror to examine inaccessible parts of their own bodies, as the chimpanzees had done. By improving the test and modifying it to suit the species under examination, the researchers had shown that the tamarins were able to recognize their images. Such approaches need to be made for other species.

The need for considering species differences in mirror-recognition tests is also highlighted by a study testing elephants on the mirror test (Povinelli, 1989). Two Asian elephants failed the test, but we are not convinced that the method used was valid. The elephants were tested by using a large mirror, but it was not large enough compared to an elephant. Given that elephants have their eyes on the sides of their heads, they mainly look sideways. Therefore, they probably recognize each other from the side and attend to the whole side of the body, not just the head. The entire side of an elephant was not always visible in the mirror, and this may explain why they did not show recognition. Added to this, elephants rely on vocalizations, odors, and tactile sensations and may use these cues to recognize self, as well as other elephants. They would receive none of these cues from their images in the mirror. They may fail to recognize themselves on visual cues alone, but this experiment tells us nothing more than that.

Before leaving the topic of mirror recognition, we note that both pigeons and dolphins have "passed the test" in ways that have been interpreted as showing self-awareness in primates (pigeons, Epstein, Lanza, and Skinner, 1981; dolphins, Marten and Psarakos, 1995). In the case of dolphins, self-view television was used instead of a mirror and, in fact, this has certain advantages because the image is not left-right inverted and movement can be interpreted more easily.

Based on these tests alone, an avian species, a nonprimate mammal, and at least one primate in addition to the great apes should be afforded the same rights. As more species are tested in appropriate ways, the list is likely to become longer. It is worth noting here that the age at which human infants can recognize themselves in mirrors is eighteen to twenty-four months.

Theory of Mind

Knowing what another individual might be thinking or what another individual believes is an important aspect of awareness in humans. In fact, simply knowing that another person can be thinking about something different than we are is an important aspect of higher cognition. This ability to attribute mental states to others is referred to as having a *theory of mind.* Empirical studies have shown that human children are unable to attribute mental states to others until they are two or three years old. What then can animals do in this regard?

Not surprisingly, our close relative, the chimpanzee, was tested first to see whether it had such ability, but eventually all great apes were investigated (Tomasello and Call, 1997). The test was designed to determine whether chimpanzees could attribute the mental states of "knower" and "guesser" to each of two humans (Povinelli, Nelson, and Boysen, 1990). The chimpanzees were presented with four cups, only one of which was baited with food. The knower was the person who had baited the cup in the presence of the chimpanzee but without the animal being able to see exactly which cup was baited. The guesser either waited outside the room while the cups were being baited or stood in the room with a bag over his head. At testing, the knower pointed to the baited cup and the guesser pointed to any cup at random. The chimpanzees were able to learn to act on the advice of the knower and ignore the guesser. This result was interpreted as showing that chimpanzees are capable of interpreting the mind state of others.

Rhesus macaque monkeys tested in a situation similar to that of the chimpanzees were unable to learn who was the knower and who was the guesser (Povinelli, Parks, and Novak, 1991). This could mean that the monkeys lack a theory of mind, but we have to recognize that the result could have been due to species differences in attention, the social behavior of some, or the past experiences of the particular animals tested. All of these factors, which may influence performance on the task, should be considered before making any general statement about the ability of a species. The task is a highly artificial one and the animals were in captivity. The results might well depend on how the individuals tested relate to humans and specifically to the humans who tested them.

Another test of whether an animal has theory of mind is following the direction of another's eye gaze. By attending to the direction in which another is looking, the individual must have first realized that the other is attending to something different and at a distance. At around twelve months of age, the human infant will look to where another person is looking or pointing and therefore look at the same thing, or at least in the same vicinity, as that person. This behavior is said to be a prerequisite for being aware of the mind state of others. Some researchers claim that autistic children do not follow the direction of eye gaze, which is consistent with their less-developed awareness of the mental states of others, but autistic children can recognize themselves in mirrors. Here, however, we are interested in whether animals follow the direction of eye gazing of another.

So far, the experimental results show that apes follow the direction of eye gaze of humans, whereas monkeys do not. However, it would be more important to know whether monkeys follow the eye gaze of other members of their own species, and some such work has been done (Tomasello, Call, and Hare, 1998). Perhaps, the monkeys tested had not formed as strong a bond as the apes with their human caregivers and that is why they did not follow the direction of their eye gaze.

Mutual looking in the same direction is often observed in the wild in a wide range of species, but this may simply occur because all members of the group have spotted the same visual stimulus or heard a sound coming from that direction. To be gaze following, one individual must follow the gaze of another simply because that individual is looking there and not in response to any other cue. Researchers working on wild primates have reported examples that might meet this requirement, but it is difficult to prove that there has been no other signal to cue the same behavior (Kaplan and Rogers, 2002). Following the direction of eye gaze would, of course, be most usefully applied to detecting predators, and this would be a strong reason for the evolution of the behavior in many species.

Recent research has shown that eye gaze following occurs in domestic dogs. In fact, in following the direction of a human's gaze, they perform better than great apes (Call, 2003). Hare et al. (2002) have shown that dogs are more skillful than great apes in a number of tasks that demand that they interpret signals given by humans. These signals indicated the location of hidden food and included looking at the place where the food had been hidden, pointing at it, or looking at it and then placing a marker on it. Most primates need many trials before they learn to follow these signals, whereas dogs are able to follow them almost immediately, and some individual dogs can follow them even in the first trial.

This finding that domestic dogs are superior to chimpanzees in using social cues to find the hidden food is extremely relevant to the debate on extending rights to animals, largely because it counters the reasoning behind *The Great Ape Project*. In fact, Hare et al. (2002) showed that domestic dogs performed this task better than wolves, from which they are derived (Vila,

Maldonado, and Wayne, 1999; Wayne and Ostrander, 1999; also see Rogers and Kaplan, 2003), and that it may not be a learned behavior because domestic dog puppies performed the task very well. It seems, therefore, that dogs may have acquired these special skills during the process of domestication, which occurred over more than 100,000 years (Ruvinsky and Sampson, 2001).

Remembering and Planning

Humans are able to remember and contemplate the past and to plan for the future, referred to by some as "mental time travel" (Suddendorf and Corballis, 1997) and said by some to be a uniquely human characteristic (e.g., Bischof, 1978), but some recent evidence suggests that this is not the case. There is ample evidence that all animals can form memories and that these memories are essential to their development and survival. The point under question here is not if they are able to form memories but whether they can recall and reflect on them.

EPISODIC MEMORY

We will consider the memory aspect first. Recollection and re-experiencing of past events require the use of a specific form of memory, known as *episodic memory*. It is possible to find out what an animal is thinking if we can communicate directly with it, and the gorilla Koko communicates using sign language how she felt in past situations. She signs that she was sad when her pet cat died and also expresses sadness when asked to recall her feeling about that loss (Patterson and Linden, 1982). This indicates that she has episodic memory, but the examples are few and regrettably little emphasis has been placed on examining this aspect of cognition in any of the apes that have been taught sign language.

Episodic memories encode information about *when* some event happened, *what* it was, and *where* it happened. Since we cannot ask animals, apart from those taught sign or symbolic language, questions that might tell us that they can re-experience when, what, and where an event occurred, we are limited in our ability to test the claim that episodic memory is a special characteristic of humans. Nevertheless, some experimental evidence indicates that animals may have episodic-like memory (Griffiths, Dickinson, and Clayton, 1999).

Most tasks testing memory in animals require them to respond in a way that indicates whether they recall seeing the same stimulus that they are looking at now (e.g., press the key displaying the stimulus that has been seen before) but not where and when they saw the stimulus before. Although it would seem that, for example, members of a monkey troop must be able to remember which animals did what to whom and where it took place in order to maintain a functioning social group, it is not easy to see how this could be tested accurately. However, birds that cache their food for later retrieval (in winter) have provided researchers with an opportunity to reveal their ability for episodic-like memory (Emery and Clayton, 2003). Birds that store their food have remarkable memories: European marsh-tits can retrieve their stored caches accurately from a large number of sites days after they have stored them (Krebs, 1990). Some species (e.g., the Clark's nutcracker) in very cold climates even remember where their many caches are located from autumn until the following spring, and they store several thousands of seeds over a period of just a few weeks. Some species (e.g., the scrub jay) cache different types of food, and they remember not only where they have cached each item but also what type of food it is. In particular, they retrieve perishable food items sooner than nonperishable ones, which shows that they remember what, when, and where (Clayton and Dickinson, 1998; Clayton, Yu, and Dickinson, 2001; Clayton et al., 2001). Even young domestic chicks are able to remember what as well as where characteristics of food (Cozzutti and Vallortigara, 2001), although they cannot be tested easily for the when aspect since they do not cache their food.

It is likely that primates also remember what, when, and where. For example, orangutans remember where their favorite fruiting trees are located and when the fruit ripens since they return to particular trees at just the right time at each fruiting season (Kaplan and Rogers, 2000). However, there has been little research investigating episodic memory in primates so far. Menzel (1999) demonstrated that chimpanzees are able to remember both what and where aspects of food sources but not when they were placed in the location.

INTENTIONALITY

Now we will consider the ability to plan for the future, known as *intentionality*. The idea that humans are unique possessors of this ability infers that animals are bound to their present and their current motivation state, unable to anticipate the future and so unable to adjust their behavior with a conscious plan in mind.

Animals appear to make plans for the future (e.g., storing food for the winter, building a nest in preparation for raising their young), but do they perform these patterns of behavior according to an automatic program in response to immediate demands, or do they think ahead? The main obstacle in answering this question is our inability to determine what they might be thinking.

Only in the case of the few animals that have been taught to communicate with humans using sign language or symbols (see below) can we inquire what thought patterns are taking place, and some examples of thinking ahead have been found. The "language"-trained subjects have been reported to express wishes to go places and show pleasure when they are taken to the desired location, but this is not conclusive evidence.

There are notably few reliable studies testing whether animals plan for the future, but some recent work on the jays that cache food suggests that planning for the future is possible (summarized in Emery and Clayton, 2003). The jays were allowed to cache either peanuts or worms in the morning and retrieve them in the afternoon, by which time the worms would have become unpalatable. Compared to other jays that were given the opportunity to retrieve the worms before they became unpalatable, these jays cached more peanuts and fewer worms. This might suggest that they were able to plan ahead, but other explanations for the result are possible, such as retrospective association of a negative reward (degraded worms) with the earlier caching event followed by a simple and immediate stimulus-response association not requiring forward planning.

All that we can say about planning ahead is that it has not yet been tested in any more than a preliminary way, and so it is premature to claim that animals other than humans lack this ability.

HUNTING: A CASE STUDY OF PLANNED ACTION?

Countless studies show that those species hunting in groups do not simply run along with each other. As far as we know from any species with characteristics of cooperation, hunting is a well-coordinated activity. There was considerable excitement (and shock) when it was discovered that chimpanzees went on hunts and captured and consumed live prey in the manner of carnivores. Theories were then developed that their hunts showed higher cognitive abilities and that these abilities were unique among animals (Stanford, 1995). However, hunting group expeditions carried out by chimpanzees to kill and then eat a favorite monkey species (white or red colobus monkeys) function very much like those of wolf packs. Wolves, being much closer to apes in their social characteristics than perhaps any other species in this regard, live in close-knit groups. Even among some birds of prey that hunt socially, group cohesion is strong (Bednarz, 1988). Insurmountable evidence confirms that the behavior of a pack of wild dogs is intentional and tactical (Fox, 1984). Group members have different tasks and often have to take up different positions during the hunt. Chimpanzee hunts use the same range of strategies that wild dogs use. The argument to promote cooperative hunting as evidence for "intelligence" in chimpanzees is largely based on the assumption that hunting in chimpanzees alone is regarded as a deliberate, planned, and coordinated act (Wrangham and Peterson, 1997). However, Tomasello and Call (1997), for instance, are not convinced that each individual in the hunting party actually knows what its role is (as do dogs and socially hunting birds of prey) and it is possible that the tactics being used derive from trial and error, not from insight. On the other hand, if hunting is intelligent, other species, in addition to chimpanzees, also show intelligence. At the very least, coordination requires excellent communication, and this is something that only close-knit group living usually achieves (for more elaboration, see Kaplan, 2003c). Efficient hunting in packs (e.g., by African wild dogs, wolves, and chimpanzees) requires group cooperation and it may require mind reading (or a theory of mind) of the group members and the prey (Rogers and Kaplan, 2003). This is an extremely complex process. When chimpanzees set out to hunt down another primate to kill it for food, they appear to be doing so with intent. They use integrated strategies to corner their prey that cannot be completely preprogrammed and that are certainly clever, if not conscious. The same appears to be the case with wild dogs that stalk and kill their prey in groups. This highly social behavior *appears* to be planned ahead (i.e., is intentional), and we would definitely say that this were so, were we observing the same behavior in humans.

Mental Images of Objects That Cannot Be Seen

Humans can form internal images, known as *representations*, in their minds. These may be of objects or events. They take on a kind of presence in the mind, but they are elusive, invisible, and without objective existence. We use them as a basis for communication by language and to make symbolic art forms, also used in communication (Deacon, 1997). A sculpture or a painting may be the physical manifestation of the artist's internal representation. We also form mental images of sounds, smells, and the feel of objects. Such representations are an aspect of consciousness and the basis on which symbolism and art developed.

Without doubt, higher cognitive processes are used to form mental representations. Of course, humans may be unique in the way that they use mental images in communication, but it is unlikely that we are alone in our ability to form representations of objects. To take an example, we will consider the use of a *searching image*. When we are searching for something that we have lost, we are able to visualize the object in our minds. The mental representation of the lost object becomes foremost in our mind, and we are said to have formed a searching image. Human infants of less than eight months of age will not search for objects hidden from them but, quite remarkably, young domestic chicks will do so (Regolin, Vallortigara, and Zanforlin, 1995; Vallortigara et al., 1998).

First, the chick is imprinted on a red ball so that it is highly motivated to stay near that ball and will follow after it and go around barriers to get to it. The chick is then placed inside a small cage with transparent walls and that is placed inside a large circular arena. From its cage, the chick can see two screens placed at equal distances from its position and the red ball on which it has imprinted. While the chick watches, the red ball is moved behind one of the screens. The chick is held in the cage for two or three minutes while the ball is out of its sight, and then it is released into the arena. Now it approaches the screen behind which the red ball disappeared, thus showing that it has formed and stored a mental representation of the red ball while that ball was no longer present. When the delay between the disappearance of the ball and the chick's release into the arena is longer than three minutes, the chick approaches either screen at random. Therefore, while they can form mental representations, perhaps they are unable to retain them for long periods. This may be a consequence of their young age (adult fowl have not been tested for this ability) or because the species lacks the ability to make long-term representations. Regardless, this three minutes is quite a long time, and it compares with findings for primates (as discussed by Vallortigara, 2003). Primates can also form mental representations, and it is known that, in the primate prefrontal cortex, there are neurons that sustain elevated firing while an internal representation of an absent stimulus is maintained "in thought" (Funahashi, Bruce, and Goldman-Rakic, 1989).

Mental representations are also used to recognize objects that are partly hidden behind an obstacle. Humans have no problem in recognizing the whole object when only parts of it can be seen and can do this at just four months of age provided that the parts seen move in consistent ways. We have to be somewhat older before we can recognize a partly hidden stationary object. Some have argued that this ability is unique to humans, but it would seem to be critical for all species because prey, predators, and other members of the species are often only partly visible, being obscured by bushes or other barriers. In fact, Regolin, Vallortigara, and Zanforlin (1995) have shown that young chicks can recognize their imprinting object from its parts and they can do so when it is stationary.

However, there are inexplicable differences between species in the results obtained so far. Whereas mice have been found to be able to recognize occluded objects from their parts (Kanizsa et al., 1993), pigeons are not able to do so (Sekuler, Lee, and Shettleworth, 1996; Fujita, 2001), at least during the laboratory tests using unnatural stimuli. It seems inconceivable that pigeons could navigate in their natural habitat or recognize conspecifics without having this ability. In fact, when pigeons were tested on more natural stimuli, such as images of the heads of other pigeons, they did show recognition of the occluded images (Watanabe and Ito, 1991). The experimental results with primates have been variable, one study of a chimpanzee showing that it could recognize an object from its parts (Sato, Kanazawa, and Fujita, 1997), another showing that a species of baboon (*Papio papio*) can do it too (Deruelle et al., 2000), and one finding that Japanese macaques cannot complete the image to see it as a whole (Sugita, 1999). Despite these contradictions, it seems probable that the ability to recognize objects and other stimuli from their parts is widespread among animals and certainly not a feature by which humans can be separated from the rest of the animal kingdom. Nor does it separate apes from other primates or, indeed, primates from birds (for further discussion, see Vallortigara, 2003).

Communicating with Animals

By teaching apes to communicate with us using sign language or by pointing to symbols, we have opened up one channel by which we might determine whether they are conscious and how similar they are to us, but the emphasis on this research has, so far, been on whether or not they can use language. It is to be hoped that the interest will expand to controlled experiments using these special subjects to assess some of the issues of higher cognition raised above.

Here we can ask: Are animals capable of communicating by using anything at all similar to language? We might ask exactly what is meant by language and enter into the controversy that has surrounded the teaching of sign language to apes (Terrace, 1979). This exceptionally heated controversy began in the wake of the research with the chimpanzee Washoe (Gardner and Gardner, 1969). Skeptics argued that certain controls were missing from these studies and that Washoe did not use language like humans. From his work with a sign-language-trained chimpanzee called Nim, Terrace (1979) deduced that what had at first appeared to be self-generated conversation in the chimpanzees was only mimicry of subtle signs that the humans were not conscious of sending, as in the case of Clever Hans, the horse that was said to be able to count but was really relying on subtle cues from his trainer (Boakes, 1984). We believe that Terrace went out of his way to find reasons to criticize and that he did not understand the bond that must develop between animal and human teacher for communication to occur, even though he trained a chimpanzee himself. Also, subsequent to their original research with Washoe, the Gardners trained several more chimpanzees and tested their abilities to sign in response to seeing images on a television screen placed in a room without the presence of human observers (Gardner and Gardner, 1989). Without any nonverbal cues that might be provided by a human, the chimpanzees were able to sign accurately, which goes a long way to showing that Terrace was incorrect (discussed also by Nissani, 2003).

The language-in-apes controversy is still with us today, but now we have the impressive example of a bonobo (pygmy chimpanzee) using symbols to communicate and being able to understand spoken English (Savage-Rumbaugh, 1994). Kanzi's ability to understand requests improves when they are made in syntactically complete sentences, compared to truncated pidgin English. This indicates that his mental processes are similar to ours. It also suggests that the ability to comprehend at least some aspects of language preceded the ability to actually speak. In fact, it is entirely possible that some of the mental processes that are used for language in humans are present in animals although they may be used for other functions. They may be used as part of the animal's own communication system or for complex perception, as in forming mental representations of the visual world and for problem solving.

It is also possible that the vocalizations of animals have some aspects in common with human language. The complexity of song in birds might be suggestive of this. In some species, forms of communication other than vocalizations are used to communicate, and these might serve as a "language," even though they may not have all of the same characteristics as human language. For example, facial expressions, body posture, and even odors may be used to transmit information from one individual to another (Rogers and

Kaplan, 2000). The question is: Do any of the many and varied forms of communication that animals use have anything in common with human language, and do they use it to communicate about events that have occurred in the past or in another place or to make plans for the future? Until we can decipher the meanings of their various forms of communication, we will not be able to answer these questions. But some of the recent research showing that a number of species have referential communication is laying the basis for such understanding.

Many animals use vocal signals to refer to specific predators, and when their conspecifics hear such a call, they make the appropriate evasive response. It could once be argued that alarm calls were simply an automatic, unintentional signal of emotional state, because predators induce a state of fear (summarized in Rogers and Kaplan, 2000). An aerial predator might elicit more fear than a ground predator (or vice versa), and different calls for each one might thus reflect the amount of fear elicited. In fact, even to switch from producing one call to producing another, completely different call may be an indication of increased fear, and this does appear to occur in some species.

However, since the renewed interest in cognition in animals and the work on vervet monkeys by Seyfarth and colleagues (1980), studies of ground-dwelling mammals, including squirrels (Greene and Meagher, 1998), suricats (meerkats) (Manser, 2001), marmots (Blumstein and Armitage, 1997), and Diana monkeys (Zuberbühler, 2000), have confirmed that the ability to discriminate between different alarm calls that signal the presence of different predators exists in a variety of species and that such signals lead to predictable behavioral responses by the receivers. Hence many other mammals, not in the primate order, possess referent signals in their vocal repertoires and may thus show at least rudiments of higher cognitive abilities (Hoage and Goldman, 1986; Rogers, 1997; Hauser, 2000; Baron-Cohen, Tager-Flusberg, and Cohen, 2000). Research on an avian species has also established that domestic chickens have distinctly different alarm calls reserved for ground predators and aerial predators, respectively (Marler and Evans, 1996; Evans, 1997). Recent research on the Australian magpie (*Gymnorhina tibicen*), one of Australia's foremost songbirds, also indicates that a complex system of communication has developed in this species, including referential signaling (Kaplan, 2003a, 2003b). Thus, alarm calls may be intentional and convey meaning beyond a simple "read-out" of the sender's emotional state (Kaplan and Rogers, 2001).

Discontinuity in the Increase in Brain Size and Capacity

Interest in brain size, as an indicator of its cognitive capacity, has a long history, beginning with attempts to find discontinuities between humans and other animals and including subdivisions within *Homo sapiens* to demark differences between races, between men and women, and even between the social classes (Kaplan and Rogers, 1994). At the present time, there is revived interest in ranking species according to brain size.

WHOLE BRAIN SIZE

Within a taxonomic category, those species with bigger bodies have proportionately larger brains, and there is a direct relationship between brain and body weight across all of the species: The log of brain weight plotted against the log of body weight for the different species within a class (or order) generates a straight-line relationship (Jerison, 1973, 1976). The plotted points for fish and reptiles fall on close to the same line; those of lower mammals and birds are on lines slightly above this, meaning that they have consistently larger brains relative to their body weights. The line for anthropoid primates is a little above that of birds and lower mammals. In other words, when adjusted for body size, the brain weight of primates is greater than for the other groups, although there is still variation within the groups. Separate regression lines can also be drawn for lower primates (prosimians) and anthropoid primates, and these too shift stepwise up the y-axis.

These steps from fish and reptiles to birds and lower mammals and then to lower primates and on to anthropoid primates reflect the order of evolution. There is a further step from the anthropoid primates and cetaceans to the apes, and humans are set apart and presented at the highest point on the y-axis. The steps are said to represent increasing encephalization, which in turn is said to indicate increasing brain capacity for processing information (Jerison, 1994). The human brain is the largest in proportion to body weight compared to all other species. The volume of the human cranium, and hence the brain, relative to body weight increased over 2 or 3 million years ago and may have done so somewhat more rapidly around 1.5 million years ago (Noble and Davidson, 1996; discussed also by Rogers, 1997).

It is interesting to note, and relevant to our discussion here, that, on the measure of encephalization, some cetaceans (dolphins, porpoises, and whales) are closer to humans than even the chimpanzee (Marino, 1998). Does this way of measuring brain size indicate superior intelligence in higher primates and cetaceans compared to all other species? Although this question is often answered in the affirmative, and it is a valid starting point for investigations (e.g., Marino, 2002), to find any answer at all requires glossing over the complexities and making an enormous leap from brain size to a general assessment of behavior. Brain size is a very crude measure of capacity: A likely better measure might be number of neurons versus glial cells, number of dendrites per neuron, or the number of synaptic connections per neuron, all of which are known to vary across mammals (Braitenberg and Schüz, 1998), or some other measure reflecting neural mechanisms. Different methods of scaling behavior produce different results when they are correlated with the size of the brain (Deaner, Nunn, and Van Schaik, 2000), although some earlier studies have found positive correlations between indices of brain size and behavioral ability provided that they have been confined to one class of animals (usually mammals) and specific behavioral measures (always made in the laboratory). For example, Riddell and Corl (1977) found a number of positive correlations between indices of brain size in mammals and measurements of behavior on operant learning tasks. Whether this would translate into behavior in the natural habitats of the species is anyone's guess.

COMPARATIVE COGNITION AND BRAIN SIZE

Some researchers have conducted comparative studies of primate cognition to see whether there might be a discontinuity between apes and other primates and to relate this to brain size. Rumbaugh (1997) looked at the ability of different species of primates to transfer learning from one task to another, by testing them on a series of two-choice discrimination problems (see also Rumbaugh, Beran, and Hillix, 2000). He looked at how flexible they were in transferring learning to tasks on which they had to reverse the associations that they had made previously. When lower primates (also the smaller ones) were well trained on one task, they showed a decrease in ability to transfer this learning to another task. In other words, their reversal learning was impeded. By contrast, the larger monkeys (macaques) and the apes tested in the same way showed an increase in learning transfer. This result suggested that there might be a qualitative shift in transfer ability, despite the quantitative and systematic change in brain size relative to body size across these species (Rilling and Insel, 1999). In other words, increasing encephalization in primates may have led to flexibility in learning and so learning became relational and rule based rather than being bound simply to a stimulus-response paradigm. However, although this general trend may be valid, there are some notable exceptions to the rule: Macaque monkeys show facilitation of reversal learning, but the more highly evolved gibbons, which are apes, show no such facilitation. More attention to these exceptions may shed as much light on the evolutionary processes as does generalizing to see the overall trends. In any case, the exceptions to the rule should not simply be ignored, as so far seems to be the case.

The avian brain provides the most important evidence against using brain size as an indicator of cognitive capacity and, therefore, as a criterion for deciding where to draw the line. The avian brain is much smaller than the primate brain, even when considered relative to body weight, but the cognitive abilities of some avian species equal those of higher primates. We have mentioned the study showing that pigeons perform rotation tasks better than humans. Pigeons are also able to form abstract concepts, such as those allowing them to categorize objects according to sphericity and symmetry, or to follow abstract rules, such as detecting the odd stimulus in a group. Added to this, a Grey parrot, Alex, has acquired the ability to use English words with meaning just as well as have the great apes (Pepperberg, 1999). Finally, the complex behavior of manufacturing and using tools has been shown in the crows of New Caledonia, and in this they rival the tool-using chimpanzees (Hunt, 1996, 2000).

Given their highly developed cognitive abilities, despite their smaller brain size, it would seem that birds process information differently and more efficiently than do mammals, including the great apes. In their case especially, brain size is not an accurate indicator of intelligence. Moreover, birds do not have a neocortex, the part of the brain that evolved only in mammals. The neocortex has been considered to be essential for higher cognitive function. In mammals with large brains, the neocortex is expanded relative to the rest of the brain and this expansion has occurred mainly along its surface rather than thickness, causing fissures or crevices. In fact, over the period of evolution from the earliest mammals to higher primates, the surface area of the neocortex increased more than a thousandfold with no comparable increase in thickness. It is argued frequently that the neocortex is associated with higher cognition or intelligence and, in humans, with consciousness (Bayer and Altman, 1991; Eccles, 1989; Innocenti and Kaas, 1995; Kaas, 1995; Krubitzer, 1995). Comparison of the behavior and cognitive abilities of birds and mammals now makes it clear that the neocortex is not essential for higher cognition, even though it serves these functions in mammals and, within the mammals, the size of the neocortex correlates with certain ecologically important behavior patterns.

NEOCORTEX

Within primates, the size of the neocortex relative to the rest of the brain correlates positively with social group size (Dunbar, 1992, 2001; Sawaguchi, 1992). Kudo and Dunbar (2001) examined neocortex size and the size of social networks in primates and found that the size of grooming cliques correlated with troop or group size and also with the relative size of the neocortex. This approach controlled for the number of other animals that interact regularly within the larger group/troop. Social group size and size of the neocortex also correlate positively in carnivores and some insectivores (Dunbar and Bever, 1998) and cetaceans (Marino, 1996). It should be noted, however, that these studies do not explain all of the variations in size of the neocortex since other factors are also associated with size of the neocortex. Sawaguchi (1992) also found that the neocortex is larger in species that feed primarily on fruit than in species that feed predominantly on leaves. This may depend on the need to remember where, when, and what fruit is ripening (see previous discussion on memory).

As a final point on this topic, we should mention that brain lateralization, which refers to the specialization of each hemisphere of the brain to process different types of information and to control different patterns of behavior, has been considered to be a unique characteristic of humans, manifested in our right-handedness and underlying our ability to make and use tools and language (e.g., Corballis, 1991). However, there now exists a body of evidence showing that brain lateralization is ubiquitous among the

ALL ANIMALS ARE *NOT* EQUAL

vertebrates (summarized in Rogers, 2002; Rogers and Andrew, 2002). Yet there are those who remain unconvinced by the evidence of lateralization in animals and still cling to the unique association between lateralization, right-handedness, and language in *Homo sapiens* and even suggest that a single gene event might have caused it (Crow, 2002). Although the appearance of language in humans might have depended on the existence of brain lateralization and that aspect might have been different from the other forms of lateralization present in nonhuman vertebrates, it seems most likely that these characteristics had precursors in primates, and those in turn in mammals, and so on (e.g., great apes have lateralization in the area of the cortex used for speech in humans, Broca's area; Cantalupo and Hopkins, 2001). Although primates are not noted for their handedness (McGrew and Marchant, 1997; Palmer, 2002), they are lateralized for other brain functions (Weiss et al., 2002; Hopkins and Carriba, 2002), and limb preferences are present in other vertebrates (Rogers and Andrew, 2002). Therefore, we feel no need to dwell further on this point here but merely mention that lateralization (also referred to as hemispheric specialization) has been incorrectly used as a demarcation between humans and other vertebrates.

CAN WE DRAW A LINE?

We have presented evidence that current research into higher cognition of animals, and hence their degree of awareness, is in its infancy. A handful of species have been researched in depth, and current findings would suggest that many more species might be found to have exceptional cognitive abilities, if we only looked. Drawing a line and giving animal rights to a select few on the grounds of higher cognition, for instance, cannot, at this moment in time, be based in scientific facts because too few are at hand, that is, decisions at the policy level are undersupplied by scientific information.

The thought of drawing such a line needs very careful consideration for reasons of our specific Western heritage in the history of ideas. One very powerful and long-standing idea comes from Descartes. It is all too well known that it was at the heart of the Cartesian notion to presume that all animals are genetically hard-wired, unaware of their actions, and act purely mechanistically. This view has been one of the most enduring standpoints in science and popular culture, and it might as well be spelled out here again because of the enormous influence such thinking has had on the way science is conducted.

Kleiner (2002), reviewing the book by Steven Wise, *Drawing the Line*, begins by saying that his high school biology classes still taught that animals are mere instinct-driven automatons, and that notions of intelligence, reasoning, and even emotions were a mark of poor science and of anthropomorphizing. It is thus in living memory that Descartes's views have found a continued reflection in everyday attitudes.

Recent anti-Cartesian thought has attempted to show experimentally and in field observations that animals have capabilities far beyond those that had been credited to them. The discovery of the 1960s that chimpanzees were capable of tool use, for example, was greeted with great excitement because, until then, it was thought that tool use was unique to humans (Goodall, 1986). However, the evidence that Koko, the gorilla, was capable of mourning for her lost kitten, an event in the past, and able to communicate this to her human researchers was an overwhelming finding and raised the stakes in the debates about animal consciousness considerably (Patterson and Linden, 1982). What if the great apes are self-aware? What if they do not just share so much of their DNA with us but also their thoughts, feelings, memories, and insights? Many studies since have suggested that great apes are indeed cognitively complex and may think and act deliberately.

In the meantime, of course, as we have tried to show, a number of species, not on the same evolutionary trajectory, have also been found to have characteristics associated with higher cognitive abilities. Recent experimental work shows that crows have considerable tool-related cognitive abilities (Hunt 1996; Chappell and Kacelnik, 2002). There is also positive circumstantial evidence that transmission of tool use in crows involves social learning (Tebbich et al., 2001). Ravens are known to be capable of insight learning (Heinrich, 1999, 2000); parrots may have conceptual abilities comparable to apes (Pepperberg, 1990); nutcrackers have phenomenal spatial memory (Emery and Clayton, 2003); and birds use referential signals (Evans, 1997; Kaplan, 2003b).

Pitted against this, although not always in an obvious manner, are two streams of neo-Cartesian thought that emerged in the 1990s. No matter how different in intent, both are based on the same notion of believing in a divide between "thinking" (intelligence), including self-awareness, and being "unthinking," that is, automatons. One stream of thought arises in the theory of mind writing. For instance, Povinelli and colleagues argue that great apes have higher cognition but an "empty mind" (Povinelli and Eddy, 1996), that they may be competent in their cognitive abilities but, ultimately, they cannot reason (see also Wynne, 1999).

At the heart of the reluctance to grant even great apes, let alone monkeys or other vertebrates, a modicum of mind is a persistent view that evolution proceeded in a unidirectional way from "lower" to "higher" complexity, and regardless of how complex animal behavior may be, it is ultimately seen to be limited to preconscious stages. Much research has focused on exposing the limits of animal (especially primate) comprehension and on setting up experiments which could not but lead to self-fulfilling prophecies involving, for instance, contrived laboratory tasks of a kind that the primate in question would never encounter in its natural habitat.

The other stream of neo-Cartesians comes from within subschools of animal liberation. This, to an extent, includes *The Great Ape Project* and writers like Wise (2002). They propose to give animals, such as the great apes and even parrots, elephants, dolphins, and whales, human legal rights. It may come as a surprise to some that we claim this to be neo-Cartesian as well. We do so because proponents of selective animal rights either base their claims on the Descartian principle *cogito, ergo sum* (I think, therefore I am), or at least they cannot break away from the Cartesian bind. Wise (2002) wants to assign a score for cognitive abilities to each animal and then make a cut-off point for either awarding or not awarding legal rights. By implication, those that are deemed incapable of thinking (are not intelligent or self-aware), according to criteria set by human society, are also not of moral interest (a point that also Immanuel Kant made). Moral obligation may end completely or, in some more favorable scenario, moral obligation may exist but according to a set of substantially reduced or different standards than applied to humans. Animals lacking in the qualifying criteria could once again be cast adrift as "things."

This idea ultimately falls victim to the perception of an ordered world by gradation of achievement (Hodos and Campbell, 1969). Gradation of achievement, incidentally, is also typically linked to DNA correspondences. The closer the connection to humans, the more likely the species is to make the grade (see Marks, 2002). Tantalizingly promising, as the rights-by-consciousness idea may be, it is dangerously laissez-faire. In this view, rights seem to be tied to a binding precondition. Organisms need to show the irrefutable existence of thought and complexity, and rights are then concerned with these conditions, not with life itself. Animal rights are not implausible and represent a very important new debate in our use of animals, as long as such debates do not surreptitiously resurrect *scala naturae* and make intelligence the linchpin for worthiness.

Considerations of animal welfare and animal rights aside, such views block our ability to look for examples of behavioral complexity wherever they may occur. There has been a tendency to focus far too exclusively on the primate line (Rogers and Kaplan, 2003), and this primatecentric view is ultimately part of the gradation-of-achievement syndrome.

OVERCOMING THE PROBLEMS ENCOUNTERED WHEN BIOLOGY MEETS THE LAW

It is not surprising that the more enlightened supporters of animal welfare and animal rights come from a philosophical and legal tradition. That tradition, particularly the latter, has been based on a biological capacity that is said to unite all humans. Marcus T. Cicero, the Roman statesman and famous orator under Caesar, in his *De Legibus*, wrote: "No single thing is so like another, so exactly its counterpart, as all of us are to one another. . . .

And so, however, we define man, a single definition will apply to all. . . . For those creatures who have received the gift of reason from Nature have also received right reason, and therefore they have also received the gift of Law" (Cicero, *De Legibus*, vol. I, x, 29; xii, 33).

The gift of reason is thus the unifying sense of humanity, and whosoever possesses reason may therefore receive the law as an equal. Equality before the law on the grounds of the faculty of reason alone has been one of the oldest and strongest pillars of legal practice for no less than 2,000 years (Kaplan and Rogers, 2003). It would be one of the greatest advances in thinking about the living world if we, by a similar stroke of genius, could find a single unifying characteristic for all animals. The only one that has so far been found that might account for most species is Jeremy Bentham's concept of pain. It has had major impact on the welfare of all animals that are held captive or are domesticated. However, this may not be enough. The ultimate aim must surely be that we do not just want animals to survive but want them to have a quality of life commensurate with their needs and dignity: physical, psychological, social, and cultural (Kaplan, 1999).

Animal welfare has dealt largely with negative freedoms, as freedoms from something (such as stress or pain), and while such negative freedoms may have achieved a very important reduction in the undesirable treatment of animals, they have often not challenged the basic tenet that animals merely exist for our use and gain. Associated with this, there are thorny issues of considering animals in different contexts—as wildlife, in captivity, in human companionship, or for human "use"—and the price tags that come with perceived value. We may well reasonably think that any interference with wildlife (for food/product harvesting, for fun, as in hunting, or for human expansion) could be regarded as reprehensible altogether and that laws, rather than giving rights, should be ultimately dealing with negative freedoms (forbidding hunting; reducing or stopping fishing in the open seas, lakes, and rivers; forbidding dangerous pollution or willful or economically intentional habitat destruction). We could embark on this course of action purely on ethical grounds (i.e., without knowing much of their individual biology). Ethical grounds and the question of an ethics of care can come into play in every category. For companion animals, it would be feasible to include animals under the legislation of minors, hence giving current "owners" a position of guardianship and responsibilities in law equivalent or identical with those in place for the protection of the child.

However, rights deal with positive freedoms, and such freedoms may well be enjoyed if they are context and species specific. However, given our present state of knowledge of the needs and capabilities of classes of animals, let alone individual species, we feel, as biologists, that we first and foremost ought to guard against, or at least be very cautious about, the temptation of creating a scale of lesser or greater value of one species over another.

REFERENCES

Baron-Cohen, Simon, Helen Tager-Flusberg, and Donald J. Cohen, eds. 2000. *Understanding Other Minds: Perspectives from Developmental Cognitive Neuroscience* (Oxford: Oxford University Press, 2d ed.).
Bayer, Shirley A., and Joseph Altman. 1991. *Neocortical Development* (New York: Raven Press).
Bednarz, James C. 1988. *Cooperative Hunting in the Harris Hawks* (*Parabuteo Unicinctus*), 239 Science 1525–1527.
Bischof, Norbert. 1978. *On the Phylogeny of Human Morality,* in Morality as a Biological Phenomenon 53–74 (Gunther S. Stent ed., Berlin: Abakon).
Blumstein, Daniel T., and Kenneth B. Armitage. 1997. *Alarm Calling in Yellow-Bellied Marmots: The Meaning of Situationally Variable Alarm Calls,* 53 Animal Behavior 143–171.
Boakes, Robert A. 1984. *From Darwinism to Behaviorism: Psychology and the Minds of Animals* (Cambridge: Cambridge University Press).
Braitenberg, Valentino, and A. Schuz. 1998. *Cortex: Statistics and Geometry of Neuronal Connectivity* (Berlin: Springer-Verlag).
Call, Josep. 2003. *The Use of Social Information in Chimpanzees and Dogs,* in Comparative Vertebrate Cognition: Are Primates Superior to Non-Primates? (L. J. Rogers and G. Kaplan eds., New York: Kluwer Academic).
Cantalupo, Claudio. 2001. *Asymmetric Broca's Area in Great Apes,* 414 Nature 505.
Cavalieri, Paola, and Peter Singer, eds. 1993. *The Great Ape Project: Equality beyond Humanity* 6 (London: Fourth Estate).
Chappell, Jackie, and Alex Kacelnik. 2002. *Tool Selectivity in a Non-Primate: The New Caledonian Crow (Corvus moneduloides),* in 5 Animal Cognition 71–78.
Clayton, Nicola, and Anthony Dickinson. 1998. *Episodic-like Memory during Cache Recovery by Scrub Jays,* 395 Nature 272–274.
Clayton, Nicola, K. Yu, and Anthony Dickinson. 2001. *Scrub Jays (Aphelocoma Coerulescens) Can Form an Integrated Memory for Multiple Features of Caching Episodes,* 27 Journal of Experimental Psychology: Animal Behavior Proceedings 17–29.
Clayton, Nicola, et al. 2001. *Elements of Episodic-like Memory in Animals,* 356 Philosophical Transactions of the Royal Society London, B:1483–1491.
Corballis, Michael C. 1991. *The Lopsided Ape: Evolution of the Generative Mind* (New York: Oxford University Press).
Cozzutti, Claudio, and Giorgio Vallortigara. 2001. *Hemispheric Memories for the Content and Position of Food Caches in the Domestic Chick,* 115 Behavioral Neuroscience 305–313.
Crow, T. J., ed. 2002. *The Speciation of Modern Homo Sapiens* (Oxford: Oxford University Press).
Deacon, Terrence William. 1997. *The Symbolic Species: The Co-Evolution of Language and the Brain* (New York: Norton).
Deaner, Robert O., Charles L. Nunn, and Carel P. Van Schaik. 2000. *Comparative Tests of Primate Cognition: Different Scaling Methods Produce Different Results,* 55 Brain Behavior and Evolution 44–52.
Delius, Juan D. 1985. *Cognitive Processes in Pigeons,* in Cognition: Information Processing and Motivation 3–18 (G. D'Ydelvalle ed., Amsterdam: Elsevier).

Deruelle, Christine, et al. 2000. *Perception of Partly Occluded Figures by Baboons (Papio Papio)*, 29 Perception 1483–1497.

Dunbar, Robin I. M. 2001. *Brains on Two Legs: Group Size and the Evolution of Intelligence, in* Tree of Origin: What Primate Behavior Can Tell Us about Human Social Evolution 174–191 (Frans B. M. de Waal ed., Cambridge, MA: Harvard University Press).

Dunbar, Robin I. M. 2000. *Neocortex Size as a Constraint on Group Size in Primates, in* The Evolution of Cognition 205–219 (Cecilia Heyes and Ludwig Huber eds., Cambridge, MA: MIT Press).

Dunbar, Robin I. M., and J. Bever. 1998. *Neocortex Size Predicts Group Size in Carnivores and Some Insectivores*, 104 Ethology 695–708.

Eccles, John C. 1989. *Evolution of the Brain: Creation of the Self* (London: Routledge).

Emery, Nathan, and Nicola Clayton. 2003. *Comparing the Complex Cognition of Birds and Primates, in* Comparative Vertebrate Cognition: Are Primates Superior to Non-Primates? (L. J. Rogers and G. Kaplan eds., New York: Kluwer Academic).

Epstein, Robert, Robert P. Lanza, and B. F. Skinner. 1981. *"Self-Awareness" in the Pigeon*, 212 Science 695–696.

Evans, Christopher S. 1997. *Referential Signals*, 12 Perspectives in Ethology 99–143.

Fox, Michael W. 1984. *The Whistling Hunters* (Albany: State University of New York Press).

Fujita, Kazuo. 2001. *Perceptual Completion in Rhesus Monkeys (Macaca Mulatta) and Pigeons (Columba Livia)*, 63 Perception and Psychophysics 115–125.

Funahashi, Shintaro, Charles Bruce, and Patricia S. Goldman-Rakic. 1989. *Mnemonic Coding of Visual Space in the Monkey's Dorsolateral Prefrontal Cortex*, 61 Journal of Neurophysiology 331–349.

Gallup, Gordon G., Jr. 1970. *Chimpanzees: Self-Recognition*, 167 Science 86–87.

Gallup, Gordon G., Jr., et al. 1995. *Further Reflections on Self-Recognition in Primates*, 50 Animal Behavior 1525–1532.

Gardner, Beatrix T., and R. Allen Gardner. 1969. *Teaching Language to a Chimpanzee*, 165 Science 664–672.

Gardner, R. Allen, Beatrix T. Gardner, and Thomas E. Van Cantfort. 1989. *Teaching Sign Language to Chimpanzees* (Albany: State University of New York Press).

Goodall, Jane. 1986. *The Chimpanzees of Gombe: Patterns of Behavior* (Cambridge, MA: Harvard University Press).

Greene, Erick, and Thomas Meagher. 1998. *Red Squirrels (Tamiasciurius Hudsonicus) Produce Predator-Class Specific Alarm Calls*, 55 Animal Behavior 511–518.

Gribbin, John, and Mary Gribbin. 1988. *The One Percent Advantage: The Sociobiology of Being Human* (Oxford: Blackwell).

Griffiths, D. P., Anthony Dickinson, and Nicola S. Clayton. 1999. *Episodic and Declarative Memory: What Can Animals Remember about Their Past?* 3 Trends in Cognitive Sciences 74–80.

Hare, Brian, et al. 2002. *The Domestication of Social Cognition in Dogs*, 2298 Science 1634–1636.

Hauser, Marc D. 2000. *Wild Minds: What Animals Really Think* (New York: Holt).

Hauser, Marc, et al. 1995. *Self-Recognition in Primates: Phylogeny and Salience of Species-Typical Features*, 92 Proceedings of the National Academy of Sciences

10811–10814.

Heinrich, Bernd. 2000. *Testing Insight in Ravens, in* The Evolution of Cognition (Celia Heyes and Ludwig Huber eds., Cambridge, MA: MIT Press).

———. 1999. *Mind of the Raven: Investigations and Adventures with Wolf-Birds* (New York: Cliff Street Books).

Hoage, R. J., and Larry Goldman, eds. 1986. *Animal Intelligence: Insights into the Animal Mind* (Washington, DC: Smithsonian Institution Press).

Hodos, William, and C. B. G. Campbell. 1969. *Scala naturae: Why There Is No Theory in Comparative Psychology*, 76 Psychology Review 337–350.

Hopkins, William D., and Samuel Fernandez-Carriba. 2002. *Laterality of Communicative Behaviors in Non-Human Primates: A Critical Analysis, in* Comparative Vertebrate Lateralization 445–479 (Lesley J. Rogers and Richard J. Andrew eds., Cambridge: Cambridge University Press).

Hunt, Gavin R. 2000. *Human-Like, Population-Level Specialization in the Manufacture of Pandanus Tools by the New Caledonian Crows (Corvus Moneduloides)*, 267 Proceedings of the Royal Society of London, B:403–413.

———. 1996. *Manufacture and Use of Hook-Tools by New Caledonian Crows*, 379 Nature 249–251.

Innocenti, Giorgio M., and Jon H. Kaas. 1995. *The Cortex*, 18 Trends in Neuroscience 371–372.

Jerison, Harry J. 1994. *Evolution of the Brain, in* Neuropsychology 53–104 (Dahlia W. Zaidel ed., San Diego, CA: Academic).

———. 1976. *Principles of the Evolution of the Brain and Behavior, in* The Evolution of Brain and Behavior in Vertebrates 23–45 (R. B. Masterton et al. eds., Hillsdale, NJ: Erlbaum).

———. 1973. *Evolution of Brain and Intelligence* (New York: Academic).

Kaas, Jon H. 1995. *The Evolution of the Isocortex*, 46 Brain, Behavior and Evolution 187–196.

Kanizsa, Gaetano, et al. 1993. *Amodal Completion in Mouse Vision*, 22 Perception 713–722.

Kaplan, Gisela. 2003a. *The Australian Magpie (Gymnorhina Tibicen)* (Sydney, Australia: University of New South Wales Press).

———. 2003b. *Alarm Calls, Communication and Cognition in Australian Magpies (Gymnorhina Tibicen), in* Acta Zoologica Sinica (IOC symposium paper, Beijing 2002).

———. 2003c. *Meaningful Communication in Birds, Primates, and Other Animals, in* Comparative Vertebrate Cognition: Are Primates Superior to Non-Primates? (Lesley J. Rogers and Gisela Kaplan eds., New York: Kluwer Academic).

———. 1999. *Animal Rehabilitation: An Exercise in the Practice of Bio-Diversity and a Tool for Conservation*, 3 Animal Issues 1–25.

Kaplan, Gisela, and Lesley J. Rogers. 2003. *Gene Worship: Moving beyond the Nature/Nurture Debate over Genes, Brain, and Gender* (New York: Other Press LLC).

———. 2002. *Patterns of Eye Gazing in Orangutans*, 23(3) International Journal of Primatology 501–526.

———. 2001. *Birds: Their Habits and Skills* (Sydney, Australia: Allen and Unwin).

———. 2000. *The Orangutans: Their Evolution, Behavior, and Future* (Cambridge: Perseus).

————. 1994. *Race and Gender Fallacies: The Paucity of Biological Determinist Explanations of Difference, in* Challenging Racism and Sexism (Ethel Tobach and Betty Rosoff eds., New York: Feminist Press), *reprinted in* The Gender and Science Reader 323–342 (Muriel Lederman and Ingrid Bartsch eds., New York: Routledge, 2001).

Kleiner, Kurt. 2002. *Review: Steven Wise's "Drawing the Line": Science and the Cases for Animal Rights,* http://www.salon.com/books/review/2002/09/04/wise/print.html, downloaded May 11, 2003.

Krebs, John R. 1990. *Food-Storing Birds: Adaptive Specialisation in Brain and Behavior?* 329 Philosophical Transactions of the Royal Society of London B:153–160.

Krubitzer, Leah. 1995. *The Organization of the Neocortex in Mammals: Are Species Differences Really So Different?* 18 Trends in Neuroscience 408–417.

McGrew, William C., and Linda F. Marchant. 1997. *On the Other Hand: Current Issues in and Meta-Analysis of the Behavioral Laterality of Hand Function in Nonhuman Primates,* 40 Yearbook of Physical Anthropology 210–232.

Manser, Marta. 2001. *The Acoustic Structure of Suricates' Alarm Calls Varies Depending on Predator Type and the Level of Urgency,* 268 Proceedings of the Royal Society of London B:2315–2324.

Marino, Lori. 2002. *Convergence of Complex Cognitive Abilities in Cetaceans and Primates,* 59 Brain Behavior and Evolution 21–32.

————. 1998. *A Comparison of Encephalization between Odontocete Cetaceans and Anthropoid Primates,* 51 Brain Behavior and Evolution 230–238.

————. 1996. *What Dolphins Can Tell Us about Primate Evolution,* 5 Evolutionary Anthropology 81–86.

Marks, Jonathan. 2002. *What It Means to Be 98 Percent Chimpanzee: Apes, People, and Their Genes* (Berkeley: University of California Press).

Marler, Peter, and Christopher Evans. 1996. *Bird Calls: Just Emotional Displays or Something More?* 138 Ibis 26–33.

Marten, Ken, and Suchi Psarakos. 1995. *Using Self-View Television to Distinguish between Self-Examination and Social Behavior in the Bottle-nose Dolphin (Tursiops Truncatus),* 4 Consciousness and Cognition 205–224.

Menzel, Charles R. 1999. *Unprompted Recall and Reporting of Hidden Objects by a Chimpanzee (Pan Troglodytes) after Extended Delays,* 113 Journal of Comparative Psychology 1–9.

Nissani, Moti. 2003. *Theory of Mind and Insight in Chimpanzees, Elephants and Other Animals in* Comparative Vertebrate Cognition: Are Primates Superior to Non-Primates? (Lesley J. Rogers and Gisela Kaplan eds., New York: Kluwer Academic).

Noble, William, and Iain Davidson. 1996. *Human Evolution, Language and Mind* (Cambridge: Cambridge University Press).

Palmer, A. R. 2002. *Chimpanzee Right-Handedness Reconsidered: Evaluating the Evidence with Funnel Plots,* 118 American Journal of Physical Anthropology 191–199.

Patterson, Francine, and Eugene Linden. 1982. *The Education of Koko* (London: Andre Deutsch).

Pepperberg, Irene. 1999. *The Alex Studies: Communication and Cognitive Capacities of an African Grey Parrot* (Cambridge, MA: Harvard University Press).

Povinelli, Daniel J. 1989. *Failure to Find Self-Recognition in Asian Elephants (Elephas Maximus) in Contrast to Their Use of Mirror Cues to Discover Hidden Food,* 103 Journal of Comparative Psychology 122–131.

Povinelli, Daniel J., and Timothy J. Eddy. 1996. *What Young Chimpanzees Know about Seeing,* 61 Monogr. Soc. Res. Child Dev. no. 2, serial no. 247.

Povinelli, Daniel J., Kurt E. Nelson, and Sarah T. Boysen. 1990. *Inferences about Guessing and Knowing by Chimpanzees (Pan troglodytes),* 1104 Journal of Comparative Psychology 203–210.

Povinelli, Daniel J., K. A. Parks, and M. A. Novak. 1991. *Do Rhesus Monkeys (Macaca Mulatta) Attribute Knowledge and Ignorance to Others?* 105 Journal of Comparative Psychology 318–325.

Prior, H., B. Pollok, and O. Güntürkün. 2000. *Sich Selbst Vis-à-Vis: Was Elstern Wahrnehmen,* 2 Rubin 26–30.

Regolin, Lucia, Giorgio Vallortigara, and Mario Zanforlin. 1995. *Detour Behavior in the Domestic Chick: Searching for a Disappearing Prey or a Disappearing Social Partner,* 50 Animal Behavior 203–211.

Rendell, Luke, and Hal Whitehead. 2001. *Culture in Whales and Dolphins,* 24 Behavioral Brain Sciences 309–382.

Riddell, W. I., and K. G. Corl. 1977. *Comparative Investigation of the Relationship between Cerebral Indices and Learning Abilities,* 14 Brain Behavior and Evolution 385–398.

Rilling, James K., and Thomas R. Insel. 1999. *The Primate Neocortex in Comparative Perspective Using Magnetic Resonance Imaging,* 37 Journal of Human Evolution 191–223.

Rogers, Lesley J. 2002. *Lateralization in Vertebrates: Its Early Evolution, General Pattern, and Development, in* 31 Advances in the Study of Behavior 107–161 (Peter J. B. Slater et al. eds., San Diego, CA: Academic).

———. 1997. *Minds of Their Own: Thinking and Awareness in Animals* (Colorado: Westview).

Rogers, Lesley J., and Richard J. Andrew. 2002. *Comparative Vertebrate Lateralization* (Cambridge: Cambridge University Press).

Rogers, Lesley J., and Gisela Kaplan. 2003. *Spirit of the Wild Dog* (Sydney, Australia: Allen and Unwin).

———. 2000. *Songs, Roars and Rituals: Communication in Birds, Mammals and Other Animals* (Cambridge, MA: Harvard University Press).

Rumbaugh, Duane M. 1997. *Competence, Cortex, and Primate Models: A Comparative Primate Perspective, in* Development of the Prefrontal Cortex: Evolution, Neurobiology, and Behavior (Norman A. Krasnegor, G. Reid Lyon, and Patricia Goldman-Rakic eds., Baltimore, MD: Brookes).

Rumbaugh, Duane M., Michael J. Beran, and William A. Hillix. 2000. *Cause-Effect Reasoning in Humans and Animals, in* The Evolution of Cognition 221–238 (Celia Heyes and Ludwig Huber eds., Cambridge, MA: MIT Press).

Ruvinsky, Anatole, and Jeff Sampson. 2001. *The Genetics of the Dog* (Wallingford, England: CABI Publishing).

Sato, Akira, So Kanazawa, and Kazuo Fujita. 1997. *Perception of Object Unity in Chimpanzee (Pan troglodytes),* 39 Japanese Psychological Research 191–199.

Savage-Rumbaugh, Sue. 1994. *Kanzi: The Ape at the Brink of the Human Mind* (New York: Wiley).

Sawaguchi, Toshiyuki. 1992. *The Size of the Neocortex in Relation to Ecology and*

Social Structure in Monkeys and Apes, 58 Folia Primatologica 131–145.

Sekuler, Allison B., Jane A. J. Lee, and Sara J. Shettleworth. 1996. *Pigeons Do Not Complete Partly Occluded Figures*, 25 Perception 1109–1120.

Seyfarth, Robert M., Dorothy L. Cheney, and Peter Marler. 1980. *Vervet Monkey Alarm Calls: Semantic Communication in a Free-Ranging Primate*, 28 Animal Behavior 1070–1094.

Stanford, Craig B. 1995. *The Hunting Apes: Meat Eating and the Origins of Human Behavior* (Princeton, NJ: Princeton University Press).

Sternberg, Robert J., Elena L. Grigorenko, and Donald A. Bundy. 2001. *The Predictive Value of IQ*, 47 Merrill-Palmer Quarterly 1–41.

Suddendorf, Thomas, and Michael C. Corballis. 1997. *Mental Time Travel and the Evolution of the Human Mind*, 123 Genetics Society and Gen. Psychology Monographs 133–167.

Sugita, Yoichi. 1999. *Grouping of Image Fragments in Primary Visual Cortex*, 401 Nature 269–272.

Terrace, Herbert S. 1979. *Nim: A Chimpanzee Who Learned Sign Language* (New York: Knopf).

Tomasello, Michael, and Josep Call. 1997. *Primate Cognition* (New York: Oxford University Press).

Tomasello, Michael, Josep Call, and Brian Hare. 1998. *Five Primate Species Follow the Visual Gaze of Conspecifics*, 55 Animal Behavior 1063–1069.

Vallortigara, Giorgio. 2003. *Visual Cognition and Representation in Birds and Primates, in* Comparative Vertebrate Cognition: Are Primates Superior to Non-Primates? (Lesley J. Rogers and Gisela Kaplan eds., New York: Kluwer Academic).

Vallortigara, Giorgio, et al. 1998. *Delayed Search for a Concealed Imprinted Object in the Domestic Chick*, 1 Animal Cognition 17–24.

Vila, Carles, Jesus E. Maldonado, and Robert K. Wayne. 1999. *Phylogenetic Relationships, Evolution and Genetic Diversity of the Domestic Dog*, 90 Journal of Heredity 71–77.

Watanabe, S., and Y. Ito. 1991. *Discrimination of Individuals in Pigeons*, 9 Bird Behavior 20–29.

Wayne, Robert K., and E. A. Ostrander. 1999. *Origin, Genetic Diversity, and Genome Structure of the Domestic Dog*, 21 Bioessays 247–257.

Weiss, Daniel J., et al. 2002. *Specialized Processing of Primate Facial and Vocal Expressions: Evidence of Cerebral Asymmetries, in* Comparative Vertebrate Lateralization 480–530 (Lesley J. Rogers and Richard J. Andrew eds., New York: Cambridge University Press).

Wise, Steven M. 2002. *Drawing the Line: Science and the Case for Animal Rights* (Cambridge: Perseus).

Wrangham, Richard W., and Dale Peterson. 1996. *Demonic Males: Apes and the Origins of Human Violence* (Boston: Houghton Mifflin).

Wynne, Clive. 1999. *Do Animals Think? The Case against the Animal Mind*, 32 Psychology Today 50–53.

Zuberbühler, Klaus. 2000. *Referential Labeling in Diana Monkeys*, 59 Animal Behavior 917–927.

PART II

NEW
DIRECTIONS

9

DAVID J. WOLFSON AND MARIANN SULLIVAN

FOXES IN THE HEN HOUSE

Animals, Agribusiness, and the Law:

A Modern American Fable

The juxtaposition could not have been more telling. In the left column of the May 21, 2002, World Briefing section of the *New York Times* was a short story entitled "Germany: Equal Rights for Animals." The German lower house of Parliament, the *Times* declared, "has voted overwhelmingly to amend the Constitution to protect animals." If approved by the upper house, the amendment would include animals in a clause obliging the state to respect and protect their dignity. In the opposite column on the same page was a picture of a bald chicken next to the headline "Building a Better Chicken." The story described how scientists are developing a new breed of "featherless chicken" to allow farmers to produce birds faster and cut down on the processing of their bodies. The hope was that such chickens would grow faster, "save farmers money because less ventilation will be needed, be less fatty and will not have to be plucked after being killed."[1] Intentional or not, the presentation of these stories says much about our current legal treatment of farmed animals as compared to other animals.

There can be no doubt that change is in the air in relation to the legal status of animals. The philosophical debate is growing, and there is increased acceptance of the idea that the law must recognize that animals have intellectual, emotional, and physical attributes that entitle them to certain basic rights beyond protection from egregious cruelty. In the most scholarly annals of the law, there is serious discussion over whether animals should continue to be legally classified as property, whether animals should have legal standing to enforce the federal Animal Welfare Act, and even whether it is possible for a chimpanzee to appear in court on her own behalf or receive constitutional protection. Underlying this debate is a presumption that the law currently provides some basic legal protection for animals, even if there is skepticism about its effectiveness or enforcement. In fact, in the United States, this presumption is to a large extent false.

Legal scholarship has failed to recognize that only a tiny percentage of animals with whom humans interact are *not* raised for food, and that the legal status of farmed animals is dramatically different from that of other animals. While nonfarmed animals do have certain protections, albeit inadequate and poorly enforced, upon which future legal developments can be based, it is not unfair to say that, as a practical matter, farmed animals have no legal protection at all. As far as the law is concerned, they simply do not exist. One reason for this reality is the obvious fact that people do not like to think about how farmed animals are raised and killed. This natural reluctance has been used by the farmed-animal industry to perform an extraordinary legal sleight of hand: It has made farmed animals disappear from the law.

It is almost impossible to imagine the number of farmed animals. Approximately 9.5 billion animals die annually in food production in the United States. This compares with some 218 million killed by hunters and trappers and in animal shelters, biomedical research, product testing, dissection, and fur farms, *combined.* Approximately 23 million chickens and some 268,000 pigs are slaughtered every 24 hours in the United States. That's 266 chickens per second, 24 hours a day, 365 days a year. From a statistician's point of view, since farmed animals represent 98 percent of all animals (even including companion animals and animals in zoos and circuses) with whom humans interact in the United States, all animals are farmed animals; the number that are not is statistically insignificant.[2] (See figure 9.1, facing page)

Certainly, making this many animals disappear from the law is an enormous task. It has been accomplished, in significant part, through the efforts of the industry that owns these animals to obtain complete control, in one way or another, over the law that governs it. While this is not an unusual effort on the part of industry generally, the farmed-animal industry's efforts have been exceptionally successful. The industry has devised a legally unique way to accomplish its purpose: It has persuaded legislatures to amend criminal statutes that purport to protect farmed animals from cruelty so that it cannot be prosecuted for any farming practice that the industry itself determines is acceptable, with no limit whatsoever on the pain caused by such practices. As a result, in most of the United States, prosecutors, judges, and juries no longer have the power to determine whether or not farmed animals are treated in an acceptable manner. The industry alone defines the criminality of its own conduct.

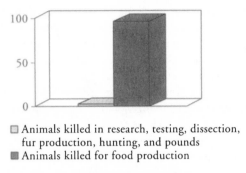

☐ Animals killed in research, testing, dissection,
    fur production, hunting, and pounds
■ Animals killed for food production

Figure 9.1. Percentage of animals killed in the United States in 2001.

The purpose of this chapter is to educate the reader as to the realities of farmed-animal law. It will demonstrate how farmed animals receive no effective legal protection in the United States and detail how the law has been altered to transfer the power to determine whether or not a farming practice is illegally cruel from the court to the farmed-animal industry. In addition, this chapter will briefly discuss customary farming practices and describe how many of such practices are not only outside the reach of courts in the United States, but cruel, as determined by an English court and European legislatures.

While the discussion of legal rights of animals is of undoubted importance, any discussion must take place with a clear understanding of a legal reality whereby nearly every animal in the United States has no real legal protection whatsoever, even though there is an assumption that such protection actually exists. There is a desperate need to focus on that simple fact, to look at where our feet are actually planted. The overwhelming majority of animals in the United States not only need viable legal rights, they need the most basic legal protection.

FEDERAL LAW

In the case of farmed animals, federal law is essentially irrelevant. The Animal Welfare Act, which is the primary piece of federal legislation relating to animal protection and which sets certain basic standards for their care, simply exempts farmed animals, thereby making something of a mockery of its title.[3] No other federal law applies to the *raising* of farmed animals, and, consequently, the U.S. Department of Agriculture has no statutory authority to promulgate regulations relating to the welfare of farmed animals on farms.

As a result, the Humane Slaughter Act is the primary federal legislation affecting farmed animals. It requires that livestock slaughter "be carried out only by humane methods" to prevent "needless suffering." Astoundingly, regulations promulgated pursuant to the statute exempt poultry, the result of which is that over 95 percent of all farmed animals (approximately 8.5 billion slaughtered per year) have no federal legal protection from inhumane slaughter. Even given its limited applicability, the Humane Slaughter Act would constitute a significant imposition on industry except for the fact that there are no fines available for violation of the statute and significant penalties are never imposed.[4] There can be little doubt that the act is not being effectively enforced. As Senator Robert Byrd (D-WV) recently stated on the floor of the Senate:

> The law clearly requires that these poor creatures be stunned and rendered insensitive to pain before this process [i.e., by which they are cut, skinned, and scalded] begins. Federal law is being ignored. Animal cruelty abounds. It is sickening. It is infuriating. Barbaric treatment of helpless, defenseless creatures must not be tolerated even if these animals are being raised for food—and even more so, more so.[5]

In 2002, Congress determined that the lack of enforcement was so problematic that it passed a resolution entitled Enforcement of the Humane Slaughter Act of 1958, whereby it stated that "it is the sense of the Congress that the Secretary of Agriculture should fully enforce [the act]" and that "it is the policy of the United States that the slaughtering of livestock and the handling of livestock in connection with slaughter shall be carried out only by humane methods, as provided in [the act]."[6] This may be one of the few occasions where Congress has felt the need to, in effect, reenact an existing statute, though it did not increase the likelihood of compliance by requiring fines or other significant penalties for violations. The whole affair brings to mind Robin Williams's comment on the ability of the British police to impact criminal behavior without carrying guns: "Stop! Or I'll say 'Stop' again!"

Finally, there is a little known statute entitled the Twenty-Eight Hour Law, enacted in 1877, which provides that animals cannot be transported across state lines for more than twenty-eight hours by a "rail carrier, express carrier, or common carrier (except by air or water)" without being unloaded for at least five hours of rest, watering, and feeding.[7] While on an initial reading the statute appears to be an attempt to limit farmed-animal abuse, the U.S. Department of Agriculture has determined that the statute and its regulations were "written to apply only to transport by a railcar . . . [and that] the Twenty-Eight-Hour Law does not apply to transport by trucks."[8] Of course, trucks are today's overwhelmingly preferred method of farmed-animal transport. The law is rarely, if ever, enforced, and even if a conviction occurs, the maximum penalty is only $500.

Given this ineffective federal legal protection, and the fact that no federal statute governs the treatment of farmed animals on the farm, the only hope for legal protection is at the state level. In this context, the only potential protection for farmed animals are criminal anticruelty statutes, which are intended to prohibit "unjustifiable" or "unnecessary" suffering to animals; in fact, many of such statutes were originally enacted to protect farmed animals. Thus, the question is simple: Do state criminal anticruelty statutes protect farmed animals from cruelty? The answer is no. Most important, while these laws have never worked well to protect farmed animals, there is a fast-growing trend to ensure that farmed animals are, as a practical matter, removed from the reach of these statutes entirely.

STATE CRIMINAL ANTICRUELTY STATUTES

State anticruelty statutes are criminal statutes that apply generally to all animals and not simply farmed animals.[9] Thus, they are usually worded in very broad and largely undefined terms, and do not specifically require affirmative acts, such as adequate exercise, space, light, ventilation, and clean living conditions and, where they do specify affirmative requirements, do not explain, in detail, what those requirements are. For many reasons, there are substantial problems inherent in the governance of an industry's conduct by means of a very general criminal statute, rather than a regulatory statute.

Contrary to regulatory schemes generally set up by legislatures to govern industry conduct, criminal anticruelty statutes which govern the farming industry's treatment of animals do not provide for the promulgation of specific regulations to govern animal welfare, and the farming industry is not subject to any sort of regulatory enforcement of farmed-animal welfare standards, does not undergo any inspections to determine whether farmed animals are being afforded appropriate treatment, and is not answerable to any governmental administrative agency (federal or state) on the subject of farmed-animal welfare. In addition, the burden of proof on the prosecution is very high, that is, beyond a reasonable doubt.[10]

Moreover, unlike regulatory statutes, criminal anticruelty statutes necessarily require that the prosecution demonstrate a mental state on the part of the defendant that may be hard to prove. Thus, a recent New Jersey conviction of an egg producer was vacated on appeal because the evidence failed to show that the company, which had been found guilty of cruelty for having discarded two sick, but living, hens in a garbage bin containing dead hens, had "knowingly" done so since, "keeping in mind someone is dealing with an awful lot of these chickens . . . I can perhaps see how it could have been overlooked" that the chickens were alive when they were discarded. The court went on:

> It's hard for this Court to determine whether there was an attempt at vertebrae dislocation [i.e., euthanization of the chickens by wringing their necks] which was unsuccessful or whether in fact perhaps vertebrae dislocation was negligently done or attempted in this case or

whether the employee in this case believed the chickens were even already dead and neglected to do it at all. And even if that was the case, I suppose it raises a doubt as to whether there was knowledge there necessary to establish beyond a reasonable doubt that there was cruelty.[11]

While regulatory schemes are generally enforced by governmental agencies with experience in the particular area, the enforcement of anticruelty statutes, like other criminal statutes, is left primarily to the police and public prosecutors, who have substantial other obligations to which they may assign a higher priority. While, in some states, limited enforcement powers are also granted to private Societies for the Prevention of Cruelty to Animals, such societies generally receive no public funding and do not view farmed-animal welfare as within their purview. To the extent that there is enforcement of these laws, it is largely directed at dogs, cats, and horses, rather than farmed animals. A New York court eloquently summarized this situation:

> The reluctance or inability on the part of the defendant ASPCA as set forth above, raises serious questions, vis-à-vis the effectiveness of our present procedure for dealing with allegations of cruelty to farm animals on the large scale. However, refinement or amendment of this procedure is in the province of the legislature rather than this court. . . . It's ironic that the only voices unheard in this entire proceeding are those of innocent, defenseless animals.[12]

Consequently, convictions are infrequent and generally limited to minimal fines; for example, Maine has a maximum fine of $2,500, Alabama and Delaware have a maximum fine of $1,000, and Rhode Island has a maximum fine of $500, for general cruelty to animals.[13] And while a great deal of attention has been placed on recently enhanced anticruelty statutes that have felony penalties, little has been written about the fact that only seven of the forty-one felony statutes enacted to date effectively apply to farmed animals.[14]

Even if the police and prosecutors were eager to enforce criminal anticruelty statutes, it is virtually impossible for enforcement agents to ascertain what occurs on the average farm because a farm is private property. Without any regulatory inspection powers, police and law enforcement officers associated with SPCAs and humane societies must demonstrate probable cause to obtain a warrant to search private property for evidence of abuse. Unless the agency is informed by someone "on the inside," it is extremely difficult for information to be discovered, and evidence obtained without a valid warrant will be suppressed.

In the unusual instance where a person willing to file a complaint of cruelty to farmed animals is in a position to observe it occur, the law does not necessarily encourage them to come forward. For example, in New York, a 2003 law (NY Education Law § 6714(2)) exempts veterinarians from liability for reporting, in good faith, their suspicions that the crime of animal cruelty has been committed, but such exemption applies only to cruelty against companion animals. The apparent implication is that veterinarians who have a good faith belief that criminal cruelty has been committed against a farmed animal are putting themselves at risk of liability should their complaint not ultimately result in a conviction.

In certain states, the obstacles are even greater; for example, in Tennessee, the anticruelty statute specifically states that although the SPCA is statutorily authorized to investigate animal abuse, it cannot do so in the case of farmed animals. Instead, law enforcement investigations relating to farmed animals, and entries onto farms, can only be conducted following an examination by "the county agricultural extension agent of such county, a graduate of an accredited college of veterinary medicine specializing in livestock practice or a graduate from an accredited college of agriculture with a specialty in livestock."[15] A small-animal veterinarian does not make the cut.

In the rare case when evidence of cruelty is nevertheless found, it does not mean that law enforcement will be eager to pursue charges. In 2003, until People for the Ethical Treatment of Animals (PETA) brought significant pressure on a local prosecutor, an Idaho sheriff had declined to pursue charges against a local dairy farmer in spite of a report by the Idaho Dairy Bureau that the dairy did not provide "reasonable care or sustenance to crippled or sick animals" and subjected cows to "needless suffering and inflicted unnecessary cruelty by dragging, lifting and burying live animals." The sheriff opined that farmed-animal cruelty cases cannot be prosecuted unless there are "a substantial number of witnesses." Since the lack of witnesses meant there was no actual proof that the dairy's owner was involved in or ordered the abuse, according to the sheriff, the evidence was insufficient to support a criminal prosecution.[16] This is particularly troubling given that the modern factory farm generally has an incredibly large number of animals managed by a remarkably small number of people, for example, 200,000 chickens may be monitored by only two people.[17]

Criminal anticruelty statutes are also generally worded in ways that leave the court extraordinary discretion. By including in the definition of *cruelty* the otherwise undefined requirement that the conduct must be unjustifiable or unnecessary, the law may invite the conclusion that a practice, though capable of causing great suffering, is not legally cruel if it is related, in any way, to food production. As one court stated:

> It must have come to the attention of many that the treatment of "animals" to be used for food while in transit to a stockyard or to a market is sometimes not short of cruel and, in some instances, torturable.
> Hogs have the nose perforated and a ring placed in it; ears of calves are similarly treated; chickens are crowded into freight cars; codfish is [*sic*] taken out of the waters and thrown into barrels of ice and sold on the market as "live cod"; eels have been known to squirm in the frying

pan; and snails, lobsters and crabs are thrown into boiling water. . . . still no one has raised a voice in protest. These practices have been tolerated on the theory, I assume, that, in the cases where these living dull and cold-blooded organisms are for food consumption, the pain, if any, would be classed as "justifiable" and necessary.[18]

Similarly, in 1963, an Oklahoma appellate court determined that the statute's use of the general word *animal* afforded it substantial discretion. As a result, the court determined that the legislature, in precluding cruelty to animals, did not intend to include "fowl" within that proscription, noting, inter alia, that fowl were referred to separately in Genesis 2:19 ("And out of the ground the Lord God formed every beast of the field and every fowl of the air"), and stating:

> Though we respect those courts that have held that various kinds of fowl fall within that category [i.e., "animals"], and likewise agree that the science of Biology holds them to be such; however, we are charged with the duty of concluding whether the man of "ordinary intelligence" would consider a rooster an animal. Surely, we would not expect a man of ordinary intelligence to fathom the law on the same footing as a learned Judge, or be as well versed in genetics as a student of biology. We feel that the Statute is not explicit, nor is it certain. And that persons of ordinary intelligence would have difficulty understanding what it attempts to prohibit.[19]

THE RISE OF THE CUSTOMARY FARMING EXEMPTION

While, for all of these reasons, it is hard to argue that state criminal anticruelty statutes present a significant obstacle for the farmed-animal industry in its pursuit of any practice that is economically expedient, the industry has, nevertheless, decided that these statutes are an unacceptable risk. In a rapidly growing trend, as farming practices have become more and more industrialized and possibly less and less acceptable to the average person, the farmed-animal industry has persuaded the majority of state legislatures to actually amend their criminal anticruelty statutes to simply exempt all "accepted," "common," "customary," or "normal" farming practices.[20] Since 1990, fourteen states have joined the growing majority of jurisdictions that have enacted such amendments. It is hard to imagine any reason for this aggressive legislative agenda on the part of industry other than a fear that it is using farming methods that might be considered illegal under prior criminal law. Farmed animals within these states do not have even the illusion of legal protection from institutionalized cruelty.

The overwhelming majority of such states simply prohibit the application of criminal anticruelty statutes to all customary farming practices. What is considered a customary practice? Most often there is no statutory definition, although Pennsylvania has provided the remarkably broad definition of "normal activities, practices and procedures that farmers adopt, use or engage in year after year in the production and preparation for market of poultry and livestock."[21] A practice will be considered customary if a majority, or perhaps even a significant minority, of the animal industry follows it. In Wisconsin, for example, the statute specifies with respect to shelter requirements that such shelter merely be of a type that is customary within the county.[22] Tennessee (which already limits cruelty investigations as described in the preceding section, and which also exempts customary farming practices) provides that a customary farming practice is whatever a "college of agriculture *or* veterinary medicine" says it is.[23]

North Carolina has a bizarre provision which exempts all "lawful activities conducted for . . . purposes of production of livestock [or] poultry" even though no other North Carolina statute forbids any farming practice on the basis of cruelty.[24] In the absence of any legal authority specifying what is or is not a "lawful activity," the circularity of the statute makes it impossible to understand whether the statute exempts everything or nothing. Georgia's criminal anticruelty statute creates similar confusion. The anticruelty statute does not apply to "conduct otherwise permitted under the laws of this state . . . including . . . animal husbandry . . . nor . . . limit in any way the authority or duty of the Department of Agriculture."[25] It is unclear what the consequences of this provision are given that Georgia's statutes do not provide any other guidelines as to farmed-animal welfare.

Certain states exempt only specific practices instead of all customary farming practices. This results in some surreal admissions. For example, Ohio exempts farmed animals from requirements for "wholesome exercise and a change of air," and Vermont exempts farmed animals from the section in its criminal anticruelty statute that deems it illegal to "tie, tether and restrain" an animal in a manner that is "inhumane or detrimental to its welfare."[26] One cannot help but assume that, in Ohio, farmed animals are denied wholesome exercise and a change of air, and, in Vermont, farmed animals are tied, tethered, or restrained in a manner that is inhumane or detrimental to their welfare. In California, if we step outside of criminal anticruelty statutes for a moment, there is a provision that live vertebrate animals in public elementary and high schools cannot, as part of a scientific experiment or for any other purpose, be experimentally medicated or drugged in a manner as to cause painful reactions or injury; these provisions, however, "are not intended to prohibit or constrain vocational instruction in the normal practices of animal husbandry."[27] And, in 2001, in an eyebrow-raising move, the legislature of Maine felt the need to exempt "normal and accepted practices of animal husbandry" from the bestiality provision of its criminal anticruelty statute; apparently, the farming community felt somewhat insecure about prosecutorial discretion in connection with a provision which prohibits the sexual stimulation of an animal by "any part of the person's body or an object."[28]

In an interesting twist, New Jersey amended its criminal anticruelty statute in 1995 to provide that the "raising, keeping, care, treatment, marketing and sale of domestic livestock" is legally presumed to not be cruel if farmed animals are kept in accordance with "humane" standards to be developed and adopted by the "State Board of Agriculture and the Department of Agriculture in consultation with the New Jersey Agricultural Experiment Station."[29] The legislature directed that the standards be promulgated within six months. Unlike all the other statutes described in this section, this statute, on its face, appears to promote humaneness, although whether by design or mistake is unknown. What is clear, however, is that the New Jersey Department of Agriculture had a difficult time producing a list of "humane" farming practices since, despite the statutory mandate to enact such standards within six months, the initial draft "humane" standards did not appear until 2003, following repeated requests from animal protection advocates. These draft "humane" standards authorize virtually every existing farming practice, including a number of farming practices that have been banned in Europe for humane reasons (such as the veal crate and the gestation crate).

As if the approval of such practices were not sufficiently problematic, the draft "humane" standards also permit all "routine husbandry practices . . . as long as all other State and Federal laws governing these practices are followed."[30] This ongoing endorsement of all "routine husbandry practices" without any analysis of whether such practices are cruel makes it hard to characterize the draft "humane" standards as anything other than deceptive. The supposed limitation that such "routine husbandry practices" are only permitted if they comply with "State and Federal laws" is particularly dishonest. As discussed earlier, there is no federal law governing the welfare of farmed animals on the farm. Moreover, the New Jersey anticruelty statute legalizes all practices permitted by the standards. And, as can be seen, the standards specifically allow all "routine husbandry practices." Thus, the phrase "as long as all other State and Federal laws governing these practices are followed" is illusory because there are, in fact, no "State or Federal laws" to "follow."

The draft standards received a number of critical comments from animal advocates and enthusiastic support from farmers. The standards have not been finalized at this time. In the meantime, New Jersey prosecutors have no guidance as to what is or is not an illegal farming practice.

The limited case law that has developed under these statutes reflects their extreme nature. In Pennsylvania, individuals accused of starving horses argued that the practice of denying nutrition to horses who were no longer wanted and were to be sold for meat was a "normal agricultural operation." The defendants elicited testimony from witnesses that it was normal "to neglect . . . horses for sale . . . for meat." Such horses, the defendants argued, are commonly denied veterinary care and sufficient nutrition, and are placed in so-called killer pens. Witnesses also stated that "various practices in the farming industry . . . might be considered cruel except for the fact that they are practices within the industry." While the court did convict the defendants of cruelty, it decided to do so only because the defendants failed to offer sufficient testimony as to the pervasiveness of the practice, and no testimony "indicat[ed] that in fact they were in the business of raising horses to be sold for dog food or that they had formed the definite intention of sending the horses in question to 'killer pens' for that purpose."[31]

The case highlights the ramifications of the exclusion of customary farming practices from criminal anticruelty statutes. If the defendants had successfully shown with additional testimony that the practice of starving horses was a normal business practice and that they were in that business, the criminal statute would not have applied to this act and the court could not have found the defendants criminally liable. The defendants' problem was not that they starved horses, but that they could not prove that enough people were doing the same thing. Clearly, if enough people do it, anything is possible under the new statutes.[32]

Ultimately, the impact of all this legislative maneuvering is a devastation of the existing, albeit weak, legal protection for farmed animals. State legislatures have endowed the farmed-animal industry with complete authority to define what is, and what is not, cruelty to the animals in their care. There is no legal limit to institutionalized cruel practices to farmed animals who live in states with customary farming exemptions, which constitute a growing majority of states; if a certain percentage of the farming community wants to institute a new method of raising a farmed animal, that is the end of the matter, and the hands of the judge, prosecutor, or local SPCA are tied. The customary farming exemptions are not only an example of a powerful industry evading a criminal law that applies to everyone else, they are a unique legal development in that they delegate criminal enforcement power to the industry itself. It is difficult to imagine another nongovernmental group possessing such influence over a criminal legal definition; for example, imagine a law that provided that chemical corporations have not polluted (and, consequently, violated criminal law) so long as they released pollutants in amounts "accepted" or viewed as "customary" by the chemical industry. In effect, state legislators have granted agribusiness a license to treat animals as it wishes.

Ironically, the current legal reality has allowed the industry to claim that it should not be accused of treating animals improperly since it is, in fact, in compliance with the law. For example, a letter issued by the Consumer Affairs Department of egg producer Foster Farms reassured a consumer troubled about animal welfare issues with the statement, "With regard to our poultry slaughtering practices, Foster Farms slaughters chickens and turkeys in accordance with all pertinent State and Federal Regulations."[33] Inasmuch as there are no federal regulations governing the welfare of chickens and turkeys during slaughter, and forty-seven states do not have any slaughter regulations that relate to chickens and turkeys, its compliance is presumably not overly burdensome.[34]

Similarly, according to the American Meat Institute, "Federal laws govern animal health and humane treatment of animals."[35] As noted, the only federal laws governing the humane treatment of farmed animals apply solely during shipment (but not by trucks) and at the slaughterhouse (but not chickens). Still, the American Meat Institute states:

> The government also plays a role in ensuring the humane treatment of animals. A federal animal welfare law passed in 1958 governs the U.S. meat industry and includes important rules that every meat plant must follow.

And:

> If you are one of the millions of people who enjoy our products, you should know that the meat industry, together with the government and academic researchers, are constantly seeking new ways to enhance animal welfare.[36]

The result of these obfuscations/legal deficiencies is not only a harsh reality for the animals themselves, but turns on its head one of the most fundamental purposes of the law: to set appropriate standards by which conduct may be judged. Supreme Court Justice Oliver Wendell Holmes described as "a commonplace of the law" the principle that "what usually is done may be evidence of what ought to be done, but what ought to be done is fixed by a standard of reasonable prudence, whether it usually is complied with or not."[37] Similarly, Justice Learned Hand, in determining whether a tugboat company had violated the law in failing to equip its tugboats with radios, responded to the argument that other companies had similarly failed:

> There are yet, no doubt, cases where courts seem to make the general practice of the calling the standard of proper diligence. . . . Indeed, in most cases reasonable prudence is common prudence; but strictly it is never its measure; a whole calling may have unduly lagged in the adoption of new and available devices. It may never set its own tests, however persuasive be its usages. Courts must in the end say what is required; there are precautions so imperative that even their universal disregard will not excuse their omission.[38]

In the area of farmed-animal law, which is predominantly criminal law, this is simply not the case. Courts are now irrelevant.

CUSTOMARY FARMING PRACTICES

Regardless of one's opinion as to whether or not customary farming practices are, or are not, cruel, the farming industry's control over criminal statutes is by itself cause for concern. The law, as it currently stands, allows the industry to create horrifyingly cruel farming practices without limitation if it so chooses. These legal developments have occurred in a cultural realm within which there is little public debate about the appropriate treatment of farmed animals and no apparent widespread awareness on the part of the public of the conditions under which animals are raised and slaughtered. As *The Economist* has noted: "It is all very well to say that individuals must wrestle with their conscience (but only if their consciences are awake and informed). Industrial society alas, hides animals' suffering. Few people would themselves keep a hen in a shoebox for her egg-laying life; but practically everyone will eat smartly packaged 'farm fresh' eggs from battery hens."[39]

It is also difficult to avoid the conclusion that, perhaps, the reason for all of the legal maneuvering described in this chapter is a fear on the part of the industry that the methods by which farmed animals are raised and slaughtered may not be acceptable to a significant percentage of people.

In fact, farmed animals live out their short lives in a shadow world. The vast majority never experience sunshine, grass, trees, fresh air, unfettered movement, sex, or many other things that make up most of what we think of as the ordinary pattern of life on earth. They are castrated without anesthesia, on occasion deliberately starved, live in conditions of extreme and unrelieved crowding, and suffer physical deformities as a result of genetic manipulation. Is this system cruel? Opinions vary. One Missouri legislator, in support of a bill that would make it a felony to enter a livestock facility without authorization and photograph the animals with the intent to harm the enterprise, said, "The [animals] never had it so good."[40] On the other hand, an Illinois legislator, confronted with videotapes of chickens on a modern egg farm, exclaimed, "It's incredible—if you see this—the hens are put into these positions, and there's seven or eight of them in these cages. It's dreadful."[41] In even greater detail, Senator Byrd declared:

> Our inhumane treatment of livestock is becoming widespread and more and more barbaric. Six-hundred-pound hogs—they were pigs at one time—are raised in two-foot-wide metal cages called gestation crates, in which the poor beasts are unable to turn around or lie down in natural positions, and this way they live for months at a time. On profit-driven factory farms, veal calves are confined to dark wooden crates so small that they are prevented from lying down or scratching themselves. These creatures feel; they know pain. They suffer pain just as we humans suffer pain. Egg-laying hens are confined to battery cages. Unable to spread their wings, they are reduced to nothing more than egg-laying machines.[42]

Intensive confinement systems such as those described by Senator Byrd have been instituted in every sector of the farmed-animal industry. The three specific practices that have been the subject of particular scrutiny are the ones to which he refers: the "battery cage" for laying hens, the "gestation crate" for breeding pigs, and the "veal crate" for calves. Every year, in the

United States, approximately 98 percent of egg-producing chickens live in battery cages; approximately two-thirds of breeding pigs (and over 90 percent of the 1.8 million breeding pigs kept by the ten top producers) are kept in gestation crates during pregnancy; and at least 40 percent of male dairy calves raised for veal are reared in veal crates.[43] These practices are only examples of what are perhaps some of the most egregious methods of intensive confinement of farmed animals. Other types of confinement systems are used throughout the industry, for example, for dairy cows, "broiler" chickens, and pigs generally.

The rather odd term "battery cage" is derived from the process of stacking cages one on the other, as in a "battery" of guns. It is standard practice to put eight hens in a cage that is approximately 20" by 19" though some suppliers put more.[44] The birds are unable to spread their wings. According to Dr. Joy Mench of the Department of Animal Science at the University of California, Davis:

> When there are eight birds in a cage this size, the bird barely has room to stand. And even then she's really compressed. There are a lot of birds pressing against her and turning around is really difficult. And a really important thing about this as well, probably one of the main reasons that crowded hens experience a lot of illness, is there's not enough space for all the birds to feed at the same time. If you're a low-ranking bird—low on the peck order—you tend to get pushed to the back during feeding and you can't get enough food. So often the lowest ranking bird in that cage gets sick and dies.[45]

In order to avoid the wounds that would be caused by the hens fighting, which, in these close conditions, is inevitable, their beaks are cut off. Mench states that the loss of the beak causes lifelong suffering to a hen, whose beak is her primary means of exploring her environment.[46]

The gestation crate is used to confine pregnant pigs. Pigs kept for breeding are impregnated continuously until their "production" drops off and they are sent to slaughter. The average life span of a breeding pig is about three years, which is significantly longer than that of other pigs who are generally slaughtered prior to maturity at four to six months.[47] The "crates" used to confine pregnant pigs are actually metal stalls, without any straw, lined up next to each other in large buildings with concrete floors. The pig can generally take no more than one step forward or back, and can never turn around. Shortly before giving birth, the pig is transferred to a different crate (the "farrowing crate"), which is similarly confining, where she gives birth and suckles her piglets until they are weaned at the age of approximately three weeks.[48] She is then impregnated again and transferred back to the gestation crate. Thus, in systems where the gestation crate is in use, the breeding pig spends the vast majority of her life intensively confined.[49]

Finally, perhaps the most well-known intensive confinement system is the veal crate. In this system, very young calves are confined in wooden stalls, which are, again, so small that the animal is unable to turn around. In order to maintain the whiteness of the flesh of the calves, thereby making it more marketable, the calves are often kept anemic through a diet deficient in iron.[50]

Not only are such practices legal in the United States, but the current legal framework prohibits U.S. courts from independently determining whether or not such practices are objectively cruel. Instead, in states with customary farming exemptions (i.e., the majority of states), a prosecutor's and judge's only role is to determine whether such practices are customary, which they all most certainly are. In states where there are no customary farming exemptions, on the rare occasion that a customary farming practice comes before a court, the legal focus is generally on whether such practices are "justifiable" or whether the worker acted with the appropriate state of mind or whether the animal was really an animal.

In the United Kingdom, however, due to a remarkable set of circumstances, a court was afforded a unique opportunity to examine customary farming practices and determine, for the first time, this exact point: whether, in the court's reasonable judgment, such customary farming practices are cruel.

McLIBEL

In the widely publicized "McLibel" case, McDonald's brought an action for defamation against a number of English political activists who helped hand out a pamphlet (of which no more than 1,000 or so copies had been distributed), which stated, among other things, that many customary farming practices were cruel and that McDonald's was responsible for such cruelty. The odds for McDonald's no doubt seemed favorable; the relatively impoverished defendants would defend themselves, and, most significantly, in the United Kingdom, in order to avail themselves of the absolute defense to defamation that their statements were true, the defendants bore the burden of proving such truth "on the balance of probabilities." This is in stark contrast to the law in the United States, where the plaintiff in a libel action bears the burden of establishing that the statements were false. But, surprisingly, two of the activists, Helen Steel and Dave Morris, decided to defend themselves, and the parties embarked on the longest civil trial in English history.[51]

At the outset, McDonald's argued the standard legal approach in the United States. The court, it stated, should decide whether or not a farming practice is cruel by looking at whether such farming practice is a typical farming practice, that is, the norm, and if it were, the court should conclude that such practice was "acceptable and not to be criticized as cruel." The court, however, clearly rejected this argument, stating that it "cannot accept this approach" because "to do so would be to hand the decision as to what is cruel to the food industry completely, moved as it must be by economic as well as animal welfare considerations."[52] This simple logical statement is an unequivocal rejection of the statutory reality in the majority of states in the United States.

McDonald's also asserted that the court should determine that a farming practice is cruel only when it contravenes governmental guidelines, recommendations, or codes; any practice which complies with the existing law or guidelines should be determined not to be cruel. But the court recognized that a farming practice can be cruel, within the ordinary meaning of the word, even if it is legal. Consequently, according to the court, while laws and government regulations are useful measures of animal welfare, neither is determinative of what is, or is not, a cruel practice. Instead, the court stated it would use its own judgment to "decide whether a practice is deliberate and whether it causes sufficiently intensive suffering for a sufficient duration of time to be justly described as cruel."[53]

While the court held a number of customary farming practices to be cruel, for the purposes of this chapter we will discuss only a few specific findings. Noting that "egg-laying hens . . . work for McDonald's," the court initially focused on the battery cage. Although the court believed the evidence presented by Steel and Morris failed to demonstrate that a chicken spending her whole life without sunshine or fresh air was cruel, it held that the severe restriction of movement caused by the battery cage for a chicken's whole life, which in the United Kingdom provides one bird "three-quarters of the area of a London telephone directory," was proven to be cruel.[54] As the court poignantly stated:

> It seems to me that even the humble battery hen probably has some sentience, some power of perception by its senses, of virtually total deprivation of all normal activities save eating, drinking, some minimal movement, defecating and laying eggs, and that the one in three or four of them which suffer broken bones on harvesting for slaughter must feel some significant pain. I conclude that the battery system as described to me is cruel in respect of the almost total restraint of the birds and the incidence of broken bones when they are taken for slaughter.[55]

In addition, in the context of chickens, the court held that calcium deficits in battery hens which result in osteopaenia (a leg problem leading to fractures), the severe space restrictions that meat-producing broiler chickens suffer in their last few days, and the standard practice in the egg industry of gassing male chicks (who are of no use in the egg industry) upon birth by carbon dioxide, were cruel.[56] Discussing the suffocating of chicks, the court stated:

> I bear in mind the danger of substituting one's own imagination of what it must be like to be gassed in this way. I bear in mind that a very

young chick's awareness must be limited. But as chickens are living creatures we must assume that they can feel pain, distress and discomfort in some form although we do not know exactly how they feel it. In my view chicks . . . do suffer significantly, albeit for a short period, when gassed by CO_2 and when an alternative method of instantaneous killing is available . . . I find the practice cruel.[57]

Finally, focusing on the gestation crate, the court concluded that while the defendants had not been able to prove that the lack of open air and sunshine was cruel, they had proven that the severe restriction of movement was. Thus, the court stated that "pigs are intelligent and sociable animals and I have no doubt that keeping pigs in dry sow stalls [gestation crates] for extended periods is cruel."[58]

No court in the United States has had the opportunity to determine whether such customary farming practices are cruel within the ordinary meaning of the word, nor is one likely to have a similar opportunity under the current state of the law. It does not seem probable that McDonald's, or any other facet of agribusiness, will make the mistake of initiating a defamation suit in the United States against individuals who claim they are responsible for cruel farming practices, particularly since, as stated above, Steel and Morris faced a number of legal disadvantages in the United Kingdom that they would not have faced in the United States. On the other hand, the one advantage Steel and Morris had was that the litigation took place in a cultural environment in which the subject of farmed-animal welfare has received serious societal and legislative consideration. An analysis of European legislation only further highlights the deficiencies of the legal approach taken in the United States.

EUROPE

European concern over the intensive farming of animals began to arise shortly after the publication of a book by Ruth Harrison entitled *Animal Machines* in 1964. The book prompted the British government, in 1965, to appoint a committee "to examine the conditions in which livestock are kept under systems of intensive husbandry and to advise whether standards ought to be set in the interests of welfare, and if so what they should be."[59] This committee, the Brambell Committee, set forth the "Five Freedoms" of movement: "In principal we disapprove of a degree of confinement of an animal which necessarily frustrates most of the major activities which make up its natural behavior. . . . An animal should at least have sufficient freedom of movement to be able without difficulty to turn around, groom itself, get up, lie down, stretch its limbs."[60]

While none of these recommendations were given the force of law at that time, their effect was significant. Specifically, in 1987, the Parliament of the

United Kingdom banned the veal crate and the anemic diet for veal calves.[61] This was followed by the Pig Husbandry Regulations enacted in 1991, which prohibited the gestation crate in the United Kingdom after 1999.[62]

Certain other individual European countries also made significant strides in the area of farmed-animal welfare at the same time as the United Kingdom. For example, in Switzerland, the Animal Protection Act banned all battery cages in 1991. The method of choice in Switzerland is now the aviary, "conceived in accordance with the natural behavior of fowl and based on installations and equipment such as nest boxes and scratching areas, or perches that enable birds to follow patterns of behavior specific to their species."[63] The Swiss Animal Protection Regulations of May 27, 1981, also provide that animals shall not be permanently tethered and that calves must receive sufficient iron in their feed.[64] In Sweden, Parliament enacted laws that require cattle to be permitted to graze if over six months old, banned the gestation crate, and required that cows and pigs have access to straw and litter in stalls and boxes. No drugs or hormones can be used on farmed animals, except to treat disease, and all slaughtering must be as humane as possible.[65]

The impact of such reforms led, in turn, to legislation by the European Union, which has significant consequences given that it is composed of such a large number of countries: Austria, Belgium, Denmark, Finland, France, Germany, Greece, Ireland, Italy, Luxembourg, the Netherlands, Portugal, Spain, Sweden, and the United Kingdom. In addition, Cyprus, the Czech Republic, Estonia, Hungary, Latvia, Lithuania, Malta, Poland, Slovakia, and Slovenia are all being considered for membership.

In 1999, the European Union prohibited all battery egg production from 2012. The system will be replaced by free-range farming, or the housing of hens in large, barnlike aviaries, or by "enriched" cages with at least 116 square inches of space per chicken (compared with the 70 square inches currently required by law in the European Union and the 48–59 square inches customarily used in the United States), a nesting area, litter, a scratching pad to sharpen claws, and a perch.[66] Germany has required that such prohibition take effect by 2007 and, simultaneously, banned cages entirely from 2012.[67] The European Union has also prohibited the veal crate from 2007, and the gestation crate (other than in the first four weeks of pregnancy) from 2013 and has enacted laws on slaughter which apply to all farmed animals, including poultry.[68] The prohibitions by the European Union discussed in this paragraph were all based on European scientific evidence that found such practices to be detrimental to animal welfare. Similarly, in light of scientific evidence that boredom in pigs can lead them to harm themselves and each other, the European Union now requires pigs to be provided with "manipulable material," such as hay, to satisfy natural rooting behaviors.[69] There are also relatively strong laws which limit the time periods for the continuous transport of farmed animals as well as a significant movement within the European Union to limit such transportation time periods to a maximum of eight hours.[70]

In another legal development, the Treaty of Rome, the founding document of the European Community, was recently amended to recognize that animals, including farmed animals, are sentient beings (it is unfortunate that the legal status of animals is such that it was considered necessary to pass a law declaring the truth of this thoroughly obvious statement and that its passage was regarded as such a profound event), and that all European Union legislation and member states must pay full regard to the welfare requirements of animals in the formulation and implementation of the community's policies on agriculture, research, and transport.[71]

Most fundamentally, from the viewpoint of a European farmed animal, a regulatory system has been initiated in Europe which prohibits a number of the most egregious intensive confinement farming practices. And, as the Supreme Court of Israel noted in August 2003, this European approach directly contradicts the approach in the United States. In an opinion declaring that, on the basis of a scientific report of the Council of Europe's Scientific Committee on Animal Health and Animal Welfare, the force-feeding of geese for foie gras caused suffering to the geese, and which then annulled regulations that permitted such practice (such ban to come into effect as of March 2005), Justice T. Strasberg-Cohen stated:

> Another question . . . is whether it is appropriate to . . . permit accepted farming practices to be defined as abuse? An examination of comparative jurisprudence reveals two basic tendencies concerning the applicability of cruelty to animals laws to farming practices. One tendency, dominant in the US and Canada, is to exempt accepted farming practices from the applicability of cruelty to animals laws. . . . Making regulations of this type in law suggests that if these regulations did not exist, those same "acceptable" and "reasonable" practices would be liable to be considered as abuse of animals. The difficulty with this approach is the fear that the law might provide immunity to cruel practices that are not for any worthwhile end or such as cause disproportionate suffering without fear of sanctions [citation omitted].

> Another tendency, dominant in Europe and other countries, puts the stress on animal welfare. According to it, farming practices are not exempt from the applicability of animal protection laws unless specific legislative arrangements are made that include rules on how various farming practices should be implemented.[72]

Justice Strasberg-Cohen concluded:

> As far as livestock is concerned, it would seem that the Israeli approach is closer to the European and New Zealand legislation than to the American-Canadian legislation. This approach does not ignore the need to provide for the protection and welfare of farm animals that are subject to farming practices, but sets clear limits on the activities of those engaged in raising livestock for food and gives the legislator flexi-

bility to adjust the rules and make changes in them as scientific knowledge accumulates and society's attitudes change.[73]

The European (and New Zealand and Israeli) approach to farmed animal welfare makes the following statement from the American Meat Institute particularly ironic:

> Caring for animals is an American value. In fact, few societies respect animals in the way Americans do. This value is shared by the meat industry, which has made animal well-being a high priority.[74]

INDUSTRY TO THE RESCUE?

Through a contrast of laws in the United States and Europe, one gains a true appreciation of the extent to which legislatures in the United States have abdicated their responsibilities. The failure of the law in the United States in this area is demonstrated perhaps most clearly by recent efforts on the part of fast food restaurants, supermarkets, and even animal industry groups, such as the United Egg Producers and the National Cattlemen's Beef Association, to pressure suppliers to treat animals less inhumanely.[75] These entities, the first of which to act was, interestingly enough, McDonald's, shortly followed by Wendy's, Burger King, and Safeway, have begun to develop standards, primarily in the area of slaughter and laying hens, that they will agree to impose on their suppliers.[76] In the case of restaurants and supermarkets, certain industry trade groups are preparing welfare guidelines and have set up third-party audit procedures to inspect animal facilities to see that such guidelines are being followed, though participation in the process remains voluntary.[77] While the standards that have been imposed to date are minimal, and far below what is to be required in the European Union, in light of the practices currently in place they are certainly a step forward, and all of the practices that they seek to affect are customary farming practices.

Such developments have come from these entities in the absence of a widespread public outcry, although certain companies such as McDonald's and Wendy's have been targeted by the late Henry Spira, working with Peter Singer, and People for the Ethical Treatment of Animals (PETA). In January 2003, PETA initiated a global boycott against KFC alleging that KFC had failed to respond to two years of negotiations in relation to the inhumane care and slaughter of chickens. While it is unclear whether KFC will be responsive to PETA's campaign, the willingness of retailers and industry groups to take on some responsibility for farmed-animal welfare is an obvious acknowledgment on their part that the situation is sufficiently negative that they need to get out ahead of the bad news. It is to be hoped that these initiatives will spur the government, at both the state and federal levels, to take a more active role. One obvious reason for the government to act is that these entities should not be the only ones with access to the animal facilities to determine whether their requirements are being met. It is inappropriate to rely on another (or in the case of the United Egg Producers or the National Cattlemen's Beef Association, the same) segment of the same industry to be the watchdog. Another reason that government action is needed is that certain suppliers will slip through the cracks because they do not do business with the companies that have agreed to impose the standards. Animals in the hands of those companies are no less deserving of humane treatment.

Most significantly, industry should not draft these standards. As noted, the standards are minimal and far weaker than those imposed in the European Union. They do not begin to compare to what has been required in particularly progressive European countries such as Germany, Sweden, Switzerland, and the United Kingdom. They are, nevertheless, being described as "humane" merely because they are better than what came before. Ultimately, standards set by industry will always run the risk of being the least that can be done in order to avoid public relations problems rather than what is necessary for the animals' well-being.

Nor can individual producers, by themselves, be expected to improve the conditions under which such animals are kept. Although measures which may be extremely deleterious to animals may shave only pennies from the cost of production, because of the economies of scale and the intensely competitive environment of the meat industry in the United States, producers who would prefer to treat their animals in a more ethical manner are severely constrained if they wish to compete. As a booklet published in 2003 by the National Pork Board stated:

> In a technologically complex world in which a producer's choices are sharply limited, it is no longer appropriate to place the entire burden of ethical responsibility on the shoulders of individual farmers. Above all, consumers must not expect individual farmers to undertake practices that will make them uncompetitive in the marketplace. Livestock producers will do what is necessary to compete, or else they will not be livestock producers for very long.[78]

Whatever the reason, there appears to be a substantial gap between the producer's view of an acceptable farming practice and what is considered acceptable by the public (once it is informed). This was clearly demonstrated by the success of a recent ballot initiative in Florida. In November 2002, more than 2.6 million Florida voters (55 percent of all votes cast) voted to amend the Florida constitution to ban the use of the gestation crate in the state.[79] The measure was placed on the ballot after more than 600,000 signatures were gathered, the vast majority of which were collected by unpaid volunteers. It seems clear that, at the citizen level, there is significant interest in the reform of laws that relate to the intensive confinement of farmed animals.

But while the Florida ballot initiative demonstrates growing support for such reform, state-by-state citizen ballot initiatives cannot be relied upon to resolve the deficiencies in the legal approach in the United States to farmed-animal welfare or to reform an entire industry. Ballot initiatives must necessarily focus narrowly on one specific practice at a time, are expensive and time consuming to pursue, and are not even permitted in twenty-six states.

Fundamentally, the United States has historically placed the role of protecting farmed animals with the government and, in particular, the courts. The first known statute ever to punish individuals for cruelty to animals was enacted in the Massachusetts Bay Colony in 1641 in order to protect farmed animals.[80] If a decision is to be made to abandon this principled tradition and place farmed animals beyond the law, it needs to be made with full awareness of all of the facts. Currently, there is still a basic belief on the part of the American public, and legal scholarship, that while all may not be right in the way we treat farmed animals, there are laws, albeit imperfect ones, that govern the industry. But, as has been demonstrated, this is simply not the case. The issue is not enforcement or effectiveness, it is jurisdiction.

Is our society really comfortable with removing judges, prosecutors, and juries from any role in the determination of what is or is not acceptable treatment of nearly every domesticated animal? Are we sufficiently aware of and comfortable with customary farming practices to simply allow the farmed-animal industry the power to do whatever it wants to animals? Should an industry be permitted to regulate itself? Is it right to proceed as if the law protects animals from cruelty when it does not?

NOTES

The views expressed by the authors in this chapter are solely their own.

The authors would like to thank Sara Amundson, Lydia Antoncic, Gene Bauston, Ellen Celnik, Len Egert, Kendra Fershee, Mary Finelli, Joseph S. Genova, Eva Hanks, Jane E. Hoffman, Michelle Jewett, Michael Markarian, Wayne Pacelle, Nancy Perry, Alan Rothstein, Peter Stevenson, Cass Sunstein, Amy Trakinski, Meredith Weisshaar, and Steven M. Wise for their support and their assistance in connection with the preparation of this chapter.

1. *N.Y. Times*, May 21, 2002, at A6.
2. In 2002, the U.S. Department of Agriculture's National Agricultural Statistics Service reported that approximately 8.9 billion animals were slaughtered for food in the United States: 36.6 million cattle and calves, 98 million pigs, 3.3 million sheep and lambs, 8.4 billion "broiler" chickens, 160 million laying hens and breeding chickens, 268 million turkeys, and 24.5 million ducks. In addition, an uncounted, but, at a minimum, 600 million farmed animals die annually in process before being slaughtered, e.g., approximately 210 million male chicks are killed at birth every year since they are of no use to the egg industry. These numbers do not include farmed fish. Although exact numbers are difficult to ascertain, it is believed that the number of animals killed in research in the United States ranges from 20–60 million per year, and an

additional 6 million animals per year are killed in teaching and education. Furthermore, approximately 8–10 million animals per year are killed for fur, 135 million animals per year are killed in hunting, and 5–7 million animals per year are killed in pounds. See *Introduction to Animal Rights: Your Child or the Dog?* Gary L. Francione, Temple University Press (2000); "Body Count: The Death Toll in America's War on Wildlife," April 2000, Fund for Animals, http://fund.org/library/documentviewer.asp?ID=85&leude=documents (October 18, 2003).

3. 7 U.S.C. §2132(g) (2003).

4. The harshest sanctions, which are rarely used, are that federal inspection can be suspended or withdrawn, thereby halting operations since the products cannot enter interstate or foreign commerce. The facility must be awarded a grant of inspection before it can resume operations. Recently, the USDA Food Safety and Inspection Service has directed its employees to place a "Reject Tag" on the equipment or area of the plant, thereby temporarily prohibiting its use, and to notify FSIS. 7 U.S.C. §§1901–1906 (2003); 9 C.F.R. §§301.2(qq), 500.1 et seq.; FSIS Directive 6900.2, October 7, 2003; U.S. General Accounting Office Report "Humane Methods of Slaughter Act," January 2004.

5. 147 Cong. Rec. S7310 (daily ed., July 9, 2001) (statement of Sen. Byrd). Subsequent to Senator Byrd's speech, Congress authorized some additional funding for increased enforcement of the Humane Slaughter Act.

6. Farm Security and Rural Investment Act of 2002 §10305.

7. 49 U.S.C. §80502 (2003).

8. 60 F.R. 48362, 48365.

9. Various categories of animals are often excluded from such statutes, e.g., animals who are hunted or used in research.

10. The 2003 decision of the Supreme Court of Israel invalidating regulations that permitted, under specified circumstances, the force feeding of geese for the production of foie gras, addresses the fundamental impossibility of dealing effectively with cruelty to farmed animals through a simple criminal anticruelty statute. Even the dissent, which found such force feeding to be cruel but did not find that the regulations were unacceptable, left no doubt that it agreed that detailed regulations were needed:

> It could be asked why the law in England and Israel should need provisions authorizing Ministers to make regulations concerning the conditions in which animals are kept. Are the criminal provisions not enough, not to mention the fact that some of them are broad enough in scope to ostensibly encompass many and varied agricultural practices? There are three reasons for this: first, it is difficult to accept that an existing practice that farmers have been engaged in for years should be considered a criminal offence with all that this implies. Secondly, the criminal offences are intended to define a minimum framework in respect of animal welfare. The authority vested in the Ministers is intended to lead to an improvement in animal welfare by imposing stricter conditions on the keeping of animals and their treatment. Thirdly, the authorization of Ministers makes it possible to deal with problems on a case-by-case basis, with more attention to detail, for example setting the minimum living space for each animal.

"Noah" The Israel Association of Organizations for the Protection of Animals v. Attorney General, In the Supreme Court sitting as a High Court of Justice,

High Court of Justice 9232/01; Dissenting opinion of Justice A. Grunis (translation on file with authors). An alternative English translation of this opinion is also available from CHAI—Concern for Helping Animals in Israel at www.chai-online.org/foiegras_verdict.htm (October 18, 2003).

11. State of New Jersey v. ISE Farms, Inc. (Sup. Ct. Warren Co., March 8, 2001 [John F. Kingfield, J.]) (unreported decision on the record).

12. County of Albany v. American Soc. for Prevention of Cruelty to Animals, 112 Misc. 2d 829 (Sup. Ct. Albany Co. 1982).

13. Ala. Code §§13A-11-14, 13A-5-12(2) (2003); Del. Code Ann. tit. 11, §1325 (2003); Maine Rev. Stat. Ann. tit. 7, §4016 (2003); R.I. Gen. Laws §4-1-2 (2002).

14. California, Delaware, Florida, New Hampshire, Massachusetts, Oklahoma, and Rhode Island.

15. Tenn. Code. Ann. §39-14-211 (2001).

16. Jennifer Sandman, "Dairy Investigation Reports Animal Cruelty: Officials Decide Not to Pursue Criminal Charges against Dairy Owner," *Times News,* Twin Falls, Idaho, January 30, 2003.

17. See State of New Jersey v. ISE Farms, Inc., supra note 11. See also *Dominion: The Power of Man, the Suffering of Animals, the Call to Mercy,* Matthew Scully, St. Martin's Press, 247 (2002). "Standing outside a factory farm, the first question that comes to mind is not a moral but a practical one. Where is everybody? Where are the owners, the farmers, the livestock managers, the extra hands, anybody? I have been driving around the North Carolina countryside on a Thursday afternoon in January 2001, pulling in at random to six hog farms, and have yet to find a single farmer or any other living soul. It is as if one of those vengeful hurricanes that pound the Carolinas has been spotted, and I am the only one who didn't get the word. Who runs these places? Why aren't they here? Who's looking after the animals?"

18. People ex. rel. Freel v. Downs, 136 N.Y.S. 444, 445 (N.Y. Magis. Ct. 1911).

19. Lock v. Falkenstine, 1963 Okla. CR 32, 380 P2d 238 (Okla. Ct. Crim. App. 1963).

20. The following states have exempted all customary farming practices: Arizona, Colorado, Connecticut, Idaho, Illinois, Indiana, Iowa, Kansas, Maryland, Michigan, Missouri, Montana, Nebraska, Nevada, New Mexico, North Carolina, Oregon, Pennsylvania, South Carolina, South Dakota, Tennessee, Texas, Utah, Washington, West Virginia, and Wyoming. In addition, South Carolina exempts fowl; Louisiana exempts fowl and the herding of domestic animals; New Jersey creates a legal presumption that certain practices to be specified by the Department of Agriculture are exempt; Ohio exempts farmed animals from requirements for wholesome exercise, a change of air, and shelter prior to slaughter; Vermont exempts farmed animals from its Animal Welfare Act and the provision in its anticruelty statute that makes it illegal to tie, tether, or restrain an animal in an inhumane or detrimental manner; Virginia exempts the dehorning of cattle; and Wisconsin requires farmed animals to be only provided with the types of shelter (or lack thereof) that are customary in the county.

21. Pa. Stat. Ann. tit. 18, §§5511(c),(q) (2001).

22. Wis. Stat. Ann. §951.14 (2001).

23. Tenn. Code Ann. §39-14-202 (e)(1) (2001).

24. N.C. Gen. Stat. §14-360(c)(2),(2A) (2001).

25. Ga. Code. Ann. §16-12-4 (2001).
26. Ohio Rev. Code Ann. §959.13(A)(4) (2001); Vt. Stat. Ann. tit. 13, §352(3) (2001).
27. Calif. Educ. Code §51540 (2001).
28. Maine Rev. Stat. Ann. tit. 17, §1031(I) (2001).
29. N.J. Stat. Ann. §4:22-16.1 (2001).
30. See, e.g., Section 2.6(f), Proposed New Regulations: N.J.A.C. 2:8 Humane Treatment of Domestic Livestock, Proposal Number: PRN 2003-168.
31. Commonwealth v. Barnes, 629 A.2d 123 (Pa. 1993).
32. In 1999 (North Carolina) and 2001 (Oklahoma), there were successful criminal state prosecutions for particularly heinous fatal beatings of pigs (and in the case of North Carolina, the skinning of a conscious sow) at farms or slaughterhouses. It appears that, in these cases, either the particular jurisdiction did not have a customary farming exemption, or no attempt was made to argue that these acts were customary farming practices. However, if they were shown to be common farming practices in a state with a customary farming practice exemption, the court would apparently have no choice but to acquit the defendant.
33. Letter on file with authors.
34. Only California, Indiana, and Utah have regulations which relate to the slaughter of poultry.
35. www.MeatAMI.com, American Meat Institute, http://www.meatami.com/Template.cfm?Section=AnimalWelfare&Template=/TaggedPage/TaggedPageDisplay.cfm&TPLID=2&ContentID=794 (October 18, 2003).
36. "Animal Welfare in the Meat Industry," January 2001, American Meat Institute, http://www.meatami.com/Template.cfm?Section=Brochuresand OtherPublications&CONTENTID=479&TEMPLATE=/Content Management/ContentDisplay.cfm (October 18, 2003).
37. Texas and Pacific Railway Company v. Behmeyer, 189 U.S. 468, 470 (1903).
38. T. J. Hooper et al. v. Same, 60 F.2d 737, 739 (1932).
39. "What Humans Owe to Animals," *The Economist*, August 19, 1995, at 12.
40. "Missouri House OKs Ban on Barn Photos," *Washington Post*, May 16, 2002.
41. A. Kovac, "Legislators Target Chicken Farms' Egg Production Practice," *Chicago Tribune*, February 14, 2002, at 5.
42. Byrd, supra, note 5.
43. Introduction to United Egg Producers, *Animal Husbandry Guidelines for U.S. Egg-Laying Flocks*, 2002 edition, United Egg Producers; *Swine 2000*, part I, *Reference of Swine Health and Management in the United States*, 2000, National Animal Health Monitoring System, USDA, August 2001; John J. McGlone, "The Crate (Stall, Case, Cage, Box, etc.): Its History and Efficacy," Pork Industry Institute, Texas Tech University, http://www.depts.ttu.edu/porkindustryinstitute/SowHousing_files/The%20Crate_files/frame.htm (October 18, 2003); L. Wilson et al., "Effects of Individual Housing Design and Size on Behavior and Stress Indicators of Special-Fed Holstein Veal Calves," *Journal of Animal Sciences*, June 1999; L. Wilson, C. Stull, and R. Warner, "Welfare Concerns of Special-Fed Veal in the United States," *Professional Animal Scientist* 10:53–58 (June 1994).
44. Battery cages may also be 16" by 20" (which typically hold between five and seven birds) or 24" by 20" (which typically hold between eight and ten birds).

A. Rahn, "Caged Laying Hen Well-Being: An Economic Perspective," Michigan State University, 2001, http://www.msu.edu/user/nrahn/Publications/NCADCPaper.pdf (October 18, 2003).

45. D. Zwerdling, "McDonald's New Farm: The Fast Food Industry and Animal Rights: Cracking Down on Egg Suppliers," American Radio Works, http://americanradioworks.org/features/mcdonalds/index.html (October 18, 2003).

46. Id.

47. "Nutrition of Piglets and Sows," American Soybean Association Technical Bulletin, 1999, htttp://www.asajapan.org/tech/animal_wiseman_e_52.html (October 18, 2003); "Swine 2000: Reference of Swine Health and Management in the United States," National Animal Health and Monitoring System (USDA), August 2001, http://www.aphis.usda.gov/vs/ceah/cahm/Swine/Swine2000/finalswoodes1.pdf (October 18, 2003).

48. Highlights of NAHMS, "Swine 2000," part I, August 2001, http://www.aphis.usda.gov/vs/ceah/cahm/Swine/Swine2000/swine1highlights.htm (October 18, 2003).

49. "Nutrition of Piglets and Sows," supra note 47; "Swine 2000," supra note 47; McGlone, supra note 43.

50. L. Wilson, Carolyn Stull, and R. Warner, supra note 43.

51. David J. Wolfson, "McLibel," 5 Animal L. 21 (1999). On March 31, 1999, an appeals court reversed the lower court and held in favor of Steel and Morris on several issues unrelated to animal cruelty. McDonald's had not appealed the findings of the lower court in relation to the animal cruelty discussed in this chapter. For a discussion of the extraordinary disadvantages faced by Steel and Morris in this case, including the fact that they represented themselves pro se, raised only $48,000 over six years (an amount McDonald's spent on legal fees in just one week), lost the right to a jury trial, and were denied access by McDonald's to any of its animal production or slaughter facilities in the United Kingdom, see David J. Wolfson, id.

52. Chief Justice Bell, Verdict Section 8, at 5, "The Rearing and Slaughtering of Animals," http:/www.mcspotlight.org/case/trial/verdict/verdict_jud2c.html (October 18, 2003).

53. Id. at 6.

54. Id. at 32.

55. Id. at 34.

56. Id. at 13.

57. Id. at 15–16.

58. Id. at 38.

59. Steven Wise, "Of Farm Animals and Justice," 3 Pace Entl. L. Rev. 191, 211 (1986).

60. Id. at 212.

61. Welfare of Calves Regulations No. 2021 (U.K. 1987).

62. Welfare of Pigs Regulations 1991; paragraphs 6 and 7 of schedule 6 to the Welfare of Farmed Animals Regulations 2000 (England).

63. Section 4, Article 25, www.animallaw.info/nonus/statutes/stchap01981.htm (October 18, 2003); "Swiss Ban on Battery Cages: A Success Story for Hens and Farmers," 44 Anml. Welfare Inst. Q., no. 1 at 10; "Laying Hens: 12 Years of Experience with New Husbandry Systems in Switzerland," Swiss Society for

the Protection of Animals. The Swiss laws were enacted in 1981 but came into effect in 1991.

64. Swiss Animal Protection Regulations, May 27, 1981, at 6; Chapter I, Article 1.3; Chapter II, Article 16, www.animallaw.info/nonus/statutes/ stchapo1981.htm, (October 18, 2003).

65. Swedish Animal Protection, cited in Swedish Ministry of Agriculture Press Release, May 27, 1998.

66. Article 5 of Council Directive 1997/74/EC of July 19, 1999.

67. "One Giant Leap for Animal Welfare," Press Release, Bundesministerium für Verbraucherschutz, Emährung und Landwirtschaft, October 19, 2001.

68. Article 3(3) of Council Directive 91/629/EEC of November 19, 1991 (as amended by Council Directive 97/2/EC of January 20, 1997); Article 3 of Council Directive 91/630/EEC of November 19, 1991 (as amended by Council Directive 2001/88/EC of October 23, 2001); Council Directive 93/119/EC of December 22, 1993.

69. "Pig Toy Tale 'Anti-Europe Rubbish,'" January 29, 2003, http://www.cnn.com/2003/WORLD/europe/01/29/uk.pigs.play/index.html (October 18, 2003).

70. Council Directive 91/628/EEC (as amended by Council Directive 95/29/EEC) on the Protection of Animals during Transport.

71. Treaty of Amsterdam, amending the Treaty on European Union: The Treaties Establishing the European Communities and Certain Related Acts, November 10, 1997.

72. Supra note 10, Opinion of Justice T. Strasberg-Cohen at Sections 13 and 14.

73. Id. at Section 15.

74. Supra note 36, www. MeatAMI.com, American Meat Institute.

75. A number of the standards relating to egg-laying hens are the result of guidelines prepared by the United Egg Producers (UEP) based on recommendations of a scientific advisory committee commissioned in 1999. The UEP guidelines include, among other things, increased cage space per hen and standards relating to "forced molting" (starving hens) and beak cutting of chicks. "UEP Animal Care Certification Logo," Egg Industry, October 2002. See also R. Hegeman, "Cattlemen Work on Animal Care Rules," Associated Press, December 25, 2002.

76. "Burger King Corporation Announces Industry-Leading Food Animal Handling Guidelines and Audits," June 28, 2001, http://www.prnewswire.com/cgi-bin/stories.pl?ACCT=105&STORY=/ www/story/06-28-2001/0001523576 (October 18, 2003); Zwerdling, supra note 45; Janet Adams, "PETA Withdraws Boycott of Safeway's," Contra Costa Times, May 16, 2002, http://www.bayarea.com/mld/cctimes/3273959.htm.

77. The National Council of Chain Restaurants and the Food Marketing Institute are preparing voluntary supplier guidelines setting uniform animal welfare standards and have established an audit program with a third-party verifier to enforce those standards. See "June 2003 Report: FMI-NCCR Animal Welfare Program," June 2003, http://www.nccr.net/newsite/download/0603_ report.doc. The guidelines have been produced in cooperation with industry trade groups, such as UEP, in an effort to produce uniform standards, though that effort has not always been successful. Id. The major criticisms leveled at the standards by animal protection advocates have been that they do not

adequately prevent cruel treatment of animals and that they remain purely voluntary. E. Weise, "Food Sellers Push Animal Welfare," *USA Today*, August 12, 2003, http://www.usatoday.com///news/nation/2003-08-12-animals-mainbar-usat_x.htm.

78. "Swine Care Handbook," National Pork Board, 2003, http://www.pork-board.org/docs/swinecarehandbook.pdf.
79. Animal Cruelty Amendment: Limiting Cruel and Inhumane Confinement of Pigs during Pregnancy:

> Inhumane treatment of animals is a concern of Florida citizens. To prevent cruelty to certain animals and as recommended by the Humane Society of the United States, the people of the State of Florida hereby limit the cruel and inhumane confinement of pigs during pregnancy as provided herein.
>
> a. It shall be unlawful for any person to confine a pig during pregnancy in an enclosure, or to tether a pig during pregnancy, on a farm in such a way that she is prevented from turning around freely.
> b. This section shall not apply:
>   1. When a pig is undergoing an examination, test, treatment or operation carried out for veterinary purposes, provided the period during which the animal is confined or tethered is not longer than reasonably necessary.
>   2. During the prebirthing period.
> c. For purposes of this section:
>   1. "enclosure" means any cage, crate or other enclosure in which a pig is kept for all or the majority of any day, including what is commonly described as the "gestation crate."
>   2. "farm" means the land, buildings, support facilities, and other appurtenances used in the production of animals for food or fiber.
>   3. "person" means any natural person, corporation and/or business entity.
>   4. "pig" means any animal of the porcine species.
>   5. "turning around freely" means turning around without having to touch any side of the pig's enclosure.
>   6. "prebirthing period" means the seven-day period prior to a pig's expected date of giving birth.
> d. A person who violates this section shall be guilty of a misdemeanor of the first degree, punishable as provided in s. 775.082(4)(a), Florida Statutes (1999), as amended, or by a fine of not more than $5000, or by both imprisonment and a fine, unless and until the legislature enacts more stringent penalties for violations hereof. On and after the effective date of this section, law enforcement officers in the state are authorized to enforce the provisions of this section in the same manner and authority as if a violation of this section constituted a violation of Section 828.13, Florida Statutes (1999). The confinement or tethering of each pig shall constitute a separate offense. The knowledge or acts of agents and employees of a person in regard to a pig owned, farmed or in the custody of a person, shall be held to be the knowledge or act of such person.

     e. It is the intent of this section that implementing legislation is not
       required for enforcing any violations hereof.

     f. If any portion of this section is held invalid for any reason, the re-
       maining portion of this section, to the fullest extent possible, shall
       be severed from the void portion and given the fullest possible force
       and application.

     g. This section shall take effect six years after approval by the electors.

80. Animal Welfare Institute, *Animals and Their Legal Rights: A Summary of
    American Laws from 1641–1990* 1 (1990).

10

DAVID FAVRE

A NEW PROPERTY STATUS FOR ANIMALS

Equitable Self-Ownership

AN INTRODUCTION TO THE FUTURE

There is presently a debate among legal writers about whether some, one, or all nonhuman animals should be accorded new legal rights. An assortment of arguments are used to support a higher level of recognition for animals in the legal arena, and this book contains a number of them. Assuming that some additional legal rights for animals are desired, this chapter addresses the more narrow topic of how might this be accomplished. We will also consider how it should not happen.

There has been considerable debate over the horrors of the property status of animals.[1] The following is one possible negative scenario of what might happen if those who wished to free animals from the shackles of property status got their wish.

> Excerpt from "History of the Animal Rights Movement within the United States"[2]
>
> While general history books refer to May 31, 2015, as "Animal Liberation Day," they also refer to the next 12 months as the "Year of Death for Animals." How something as positive as freedom and liberation

could turn into death is a fascinating tale of positive motivations gone amuck.

The story really starts about three years earlier when the optical fiber mogul Robert Kincade donated $50 million toward a campaign for the elimination of the property status of animals.[3] Five major animal rights organizations were able to set aside their usual friction and formed an umbrella organization, No Property Status (NPS), headed by the charismatic Peter Welling. These funds were used to realize the long-sought goal of freeing animals from their property status. With the sage advice of Animals Before the Law (ABL), they decided to seek a federal constitutional amendment. Their timing was good as the nation itself was weary of the Republican control of national politics and felt it was time to turn from allowing freewheeling capitalism to a concern for the humans and animals that capitalism had exploited. The language for the federal constitutional amendment was agreed upon by the end of 2012:

> No mammal, bird, fish, reptile or amphibian shall be property, but all shall have such legal status as to allow them to own property.[4]

Then began the political campaign . . . and the PR campaign with its many ads showing smiling animals in harmony with their human companions, or empty cages, and chains left on the ground. In two years, the amendment had been approved.

On the effective date of the amendment, not much happened, except for the human celebrations, as the animals themselves, of course, did not know what had happened. The next day, ABL filed a class action lawsuit against all horse race tracks and greyhound dog tracks demanding that as horses and dogs were no longer property they could not be used against their will to run races. A portion of the industrial chicken producers, seeing the handwriting on the wall, opened all their cages and shooed 15,000,000 chickens off their property. Within a month, a court in Maryland held that since dogs were not property, they could not be confined against their will. Immediately 1,000,000 dogs left human homes and sought to establish more natural territories. (On the flip side, 10,000,000 stayed with their human companions, knowing a good deal.) While it will never really be known how quickly the shakeout occurred, by the time fall arrived, half the dogs had died and most of the surviving dogs had formed packs of 4 to 10 animals. Besides the 325 humans that were killed that fall, these dogs consumed 95 percent of the chickens that had survived the first week of their freedom, most of the small mammals in the wild, and tens of thousands of the smaller dogs and cats that had strayed from home.

As animals could own property, courts upheld wills which left money and assets to pets. After about five years, it was estimated that 5 percent of the wealth of the United States was tied up with animal trusts. A new business quickly came into existence, mind readers for pets, to determine the investment preferences of various pets. While this seemed to work for mammals and birds, they were unsuccessful with fish and reptiles.

Perhaps the most ingenious actions brought by the ABL were after about ten years had passed. Based upon the concept of adverse possession, they were successful in convincing courts that since animals could own property they could obtain title by adverse possession. When they got another court to agree that having successive generations which shared the same land/habitat, without interruption from human owners could "tack" together their commutative [sic] years of possession, huge tracts of land began to go over to wildlife trusts. This land grab was also the beginning of the end of that phase of legal rights for animals. Loss of land ownership to nonhuman skunks, rats, and dog packs created a political groundswell that in a 13-month period resulted in the repeal of the Animal Property Amendment of the federal Constitution. It would be another twenty years before the next wave of change could begin to gather momentum.

Presumably, no one would wish a legal outcome that results in increased deaths of animals and harm to humans, but there is not clarity in the literature yet about exactly what ought to be the next step. One of the problems is that when speaking of new legal rights for animals, it is important to distinguish first steps of change within the legal system, where maximum consensus ought to exist, versus the ultimate destination of legal change. For example, wide support could be obtained for the proposition that when humans are having a divorce, and there is an issue about which human should obtain possession of the pet, that the law ought to give primary considerations to the interests of the pet, rather than who paid for the pet.[5] On the other hand, I suspect that there is not broad public support for the proposition that no mammal should be raised and killed for human food consumption. Agreement on the latter is not necessary for changing the legal system to realize the former.

It is a burden of the animal rights movement that so many of its leaders will support only the purest philosophical position, regardless of political feasibility. It must be realized by all that there is a key difference between personal philosophy and political reality. Many assume that the full legal implementation of their personal vegan philosophy is the immediate and only appropriate goal of legal change. And yet, such radical change in the short term is impossible in our legal system. It would be more realistic to be incremental, to begin the journey of change by modifying, but not eliminating, the existing property status of animals. The remainder of this chapter will consider the present possibility of moving toward the recognition of new rights for animals by awarding them the status of equitable self-ownership.

SELF-OWNERSHIP BY ANIMALS

It will be helpful for our discussion to use the following examples to delve into the present state of property jurisprudence. We will begin by placing an identification tag on a number of physical objects within the physical boundaries of the United States. Consider a rock (of considerable age), a newborn squirrel, a newborn cat, and a newborn human. Each has its own identification tag: *rock* R188A, located on land in Redford, Washington; *squirrel* S4444, born in the Yellowstone National Park; *cat* 54376 (referred to as Zoe for easy reference), born of Starburst and Big Bo in the house of Ralph and Penny Willard (humans); and a female *human*, 256,332,881, known as Susan, born of Donald and Cindy Greenberg of Lansing, Michigan. Having properly identified these items, the legal concepts of property law can now be used to define the legal status of these four objects.

As property laws are a human construct and not an inherent characteristic of physical objects, there is always conceptual space for innovation. One of the premises for our new animal property paradigm is that living objects have *self-ownership*. That is, unless a human has affirmatively asserted lawful dominion and control so as to obtain title to a living entity, then a living entity will be considered to have self-ownership. As will be shown, this is but a modest recasting of existing concepts, but one with significant consequences.

Our existing legal system does not now assert ownership in all physical things. Meteorites in the sky have no human-designated title, and particular molecules of water and air in their natural state have no human title constraining and defining them. Nor do newborn squirrels in the wilderness, or human babies in Lansing, Michigan, have human-based title claims against them.

For items not within the domain of human property law, our legal system does have a number of rules that allow humans to obtain ownership. Usually, as a prerequisite to title being acknowledged as held by a human, some assertion of possession and control over an object must be made by the person seeking title. This is logical, as the concept of *title* deals with the use and control of objects: Until an object is within the possession and control of some human, the law will be without effect, and there will be no reason to assert title over an object.

As a wild animal, the squirrel of Yellowstone is not yet human controlled; she retains self-direction, self-control, and self-ownership. It is a misperception of existing property law to say that title is in the state when wildlife exists in its natural environment. If no human or human substitute, like a government, has possession and control over a wild animal, there cannot be an assertion of title. The courts have long made it clear that using the word *title* as it relates to wildlife and state ownership issues is not title in the property sense. Rather, the word is being used as a surrogate for a different concept. The assertion of the common law is not that the state has title to the wild squirrel, but that it has the right to decide the conditions under which humans can obtain title to the squirrel.[6] Under these rules, if someone shows up in Yellowstone National Park and traps or shoots the squirrel, then the property rules of the state of Wyoming will decide if she becomes the owner of the squirrel, if she obtains "title" to the squirrel. Thus, the existing property rules relating to wild animals do not hinder assertions of self-ownership for wild animals.

Also, under existing property concepts, it is fair to state that the newborn human is self-owned.[7] Certainly in the negative sense, no one else is the owner of human Susan.[8] The extent to which state legislatures have sought to regulate the sale of human body parts is additional support for the conceptual existence of human self-ownership.[9] Susan's parents, while not having ownership of Susan, nevertheless have obligations toward Susan. While she is a minor, they certainly have physical possession and considerable control over Susan and what she experiences. But within the common law states today, these obligations do not rise to the level of having title in Susan, that is, the ability to use, kill, or transfer ownership to another. So our human child, like the squirrel, is not a being owned by a human and, therefore, must be considered to have self-ownership.

Our rock poses a different kind of problem. It has no "self" to which the concept of self-ownership can attach. It is not alive. Also, assuming that this rock, like all ageless rocks, is sitting on a tract of land, then property law dictates that the owner of the land has ownership of all the rocks located on, below, and above the land itself.[10] The rock is part of the land ownership.

Last, but certainly not least, is the cat Zoe. While Zoe has a set of self-interests to which can be attached the concept of self-ownership, title to her, unlike the Yellowstone squirrel, already rests in another: The human owner of the mother of Zoe is considered to be the owner of all offspring of the animal.[11] Title to Zoe rests with the Willards. This ownership is distinguished from the ownership of a rock primarily by the fact that prevention-of-cruelty laws apply to owners of pets but not to owners of rocks. Also, while rocks do not tend to harm humans of their own accord, animals can cause harm, and their owners may be liable for such harm. The Willards can sell the cat, give the cat away, put the cat in a trust, leave the cat by will to Aunt Mae, or kill the cat in a noncruel manner. In making decisions about the cat, the Willards may or may not adopt those courses of action which are in the best interest of the cat.

The focus of this discussion is to shift the nature of the relationship between the owner and the animal from that which is like the ownership of the rock to that which is more like, but not identical to, the custodial relationship of the human parent and the human child. The concept of equitable self-ownership is one useful construct toward this new view.

A CONTEXT FOR KNOWING WHAT DIRECTION
THE LAW SHOULD TAKE

Some continuation of the property status will be essential in the new animal paradigm, not only for the animals, but for the judges or lawmakers who take the next step on behalf of animals. Change in the legal system, because of its conservative structure, normally happens incrementally. Judges do not like to be put into positions where the consequences of their actions, by judgments, are not knowable in advance, and acceptable to them. If the next step for animal jurisprudence continues to be spoken in terms of traditional property concepts, then the judges and lawmakers will be more comfortable in pushing the process along.

The key question is: Can there be created a new property status that would allow animals to have rights? Well, first of all, it might be useful to acknowledge that animals presently have some legal rights, notwithstanding their existing property status. Zoe, just like a human child, has the right to be free from cruel treatment and to have an expectation of basic affirmative care.[12] These are rights not accorded to nonliving things such as chairs or televisions. These rights, however, are imperfect in that enforcement is limited to actions by the state in criminal court and in that large classes of animals, such as commercially raised chickens in battery cages, are exempted from the cruelty laws under most state laws. One group of animals has a set of federal rights which go beyond the cruelty laws of the state. Section 13 of the Animal Welfare Act (AWA) provides that anyone under the authority of the AWA who houses primates must take into account the psychological well-being of the animals.[13] This is the only known case where the law has demanded that the mental and social well-being of nonhumans be taken into account by those possessing them. Again, a significant limitation on the realization of this right is that enforcement is presently limited to the federal government.[14] But it does suggest that legal rights can coexist with property status. What is missing is the ability of the individual animal to act in the legal realm, as can a human, whether or not the government decides to take legal action.[15]

There are a few characteristics which will be critical to new legal rights for animals. First, the rights must be actionable, enforceable, by the animal him- or herself. The key limitation of the present right of animals to be free from cruel practices is that enforcement is restricted to legal actions filed by the state or local prosecutor. If the state decides not to act in a particular case, then the harmed animal is without remedy. With the new set of rights, this will be changed, so that the animal, through appointed counsel or guardians, may initiate legal action without state involvement. Second, a remedy must be made available which runs directly to the benefit of the animal whose interests have been or may be harmed or frustrated.

As an example, consider the case of Buster. He is a large dog of mixed breed, owned by Beer Belly. On a sunny Thursday afternoon, Buster is in the street in front of his house when Mr. Speedy, who is out for a ride on his new Cycle 2400, sees Buster and aims right for him. The dog tries to run, but Speedy hits him in the hind legs, crushing a hip. The state, through the local prosecutor, may or may not bring criminal charges for violation of the anticruelty laws. But, even if it does, no remedy, no money or benefit, will flow to Buster as a result of criminal legal action. Buster's owner may or may not do all that is necessary for the recovery of the dog. In fact, if it seems like too much of a bother, Beer Belly may have the dog euthanized. If the dog had the legal right to be free from the intentional infliction of bodily harm and pain, then the dog could have a suit filed on his behalf, and the remedy, in the form of money damages, could be awarded to and spent on behalf of the dog.[16]

So, what is needed is a way to establish a new status for animals without throwing away all of the past. To do this, we need only to add one more concept into this discussion, that of equitable title.

THE CONCEPT OF EQUITABLE TITLE FOR ANIMALS

For more than 500 years our inherited legal system, as practiced in England and then in the United States, has allowed the owner of property to divide the title of property into two elements: legal title and equitable title.[17] This is normally done when an owner of property wishes to separate the power to control the property from the person who should receive the benefits of the property. For example, consider the situation where an individual has children and wishes the children to have the benefits of ownership of the property without letting them have control over the right to sell the property. The owner of the property, S, could transfer the title of the property to party X, Bank Fifteen, for example. The instructions to X would be that he must manage the property and arrange for the benefits of the property to flow to A and B, the owner's children. The context for this change of title is primarily by the creation of a trust. The law will view X as having legal title and A and B as having equitable title. The laws of trust impose significant limitations on how X may exercise his power of ownership. X does not have total freedom to do as he might with the property. X's legal title, as a trustee, is encumbered with specific duties of loyalty toward S.[18]

An animal as property has title. This title, like any other title, can be divided into its legal and equitable elements. The final question to address is: Who may receive and hold either of the titles? Who is capable of holding a legal or equitable title? While historically only humans could hold title, is it not conceptually possible for other living entities to be holders of title, at least to the limited extent of holding their own equitable title? Could we not create a pattern where humans hold legal title to an animal while the animal holds his or her own equitable title: equitable self-ownership?

Presently, the private owner of an animal can do certain intentional acts that affect the title status of the animal beyond that of transferring it to another human. First, an owner can abandon his or her domestic animal. Abandonment is an intentional relinquishment of all title and interest in personal property, which should be shown by some explicit act.[19] It may be a criminal act to abandon an animal, but it can be effective in the property law realm so that the abandoned animal is without a human titleholder.[20] An abandoned domestic animal has his or her title (legal and equitable) go into "never-never" land. No one has it, but it is readily obtainable by another human taking dominion and control of the animal.[21] During this interim of no human having possession, perhaps it is useful to consider the animal itself as possessing his or her own title. A second pattern is where an owner of a wild animal can return title to a wild animal by releasing him back into his natural habitat. As a released wild animal regains self-control, it also regains self-ownership.

If the legal and equitable owner of an animal can change the title status completely by intentional acts, is there a policy reason to object to the titleholder returning a part of the title to an animal? The key public policy reason for allowing such a transfer is that now the animal would have a hybrid property status that differentiates it from other objects of property, and with this hybrid status the law can comfortably allocate new legal rights to such animals.

There are two methods by which a change of legal status might occur for nonhuman animals. The first is by the explicit private action of an existing titleholder. An example would be when an individual owner of an animal signs a carefully drafted instrument which transfers the equitable title of the animal to the animal.[22] The writing should be sufficient to make clear the owner's intention of creating a new legal status for his or her animal and the understanding that some legal consequences will follow from the action of signing the document.

Second, a legislature may find it appropriate to adopt legislation that would have the effect of causing the involuntary transfer of equitable ownership to a class or species of animals. For example, a legislature might decide that the scientific evidence of the nature of primates supports the proposition that every human owner of a primate should respect the nature of these primates and require, as a matter of law, that equitable self-ownership be acknowledged for all primates held by humans.[23]

Once the separation of legal and equitable title occurs for any one animal, then the attributes of legal ownership will change, as the legal titleholder must recognize and take into account the interests of the equitable titleholder. Part of the nature of this obligation can be found in the area of trust law. Human animal owners are presently subject to the restrictions of anticruelty and licensing laws, but this is a duty owed to the state, not to the animals. If an animal has equitable title, then a legal title owner would have obligations both to the state and to the equitable titleholder, the equitably self-owned animal.

HUMANS AS GUARDIANS

Having established the concept that an owner of an animal might have only the legal title, and thus be like a trustee, it is time for a modest word shift. While the term *trustee* was used in the prior analysis to build upon existing concepts in the law of trust, it is not the best term with which to proceed in the remainder of this chapter. The trust concept was used as a bridge concept, because it supports the idea of dividing the title of property into its two parts, and because the owner of the legal title has a legal duty to the equitable owner of the property.

Obviously, this new relationship is different in that the owner of the equitable title is also the subject matter of the legal title that is held by the human. An additional distinction between a traditional trust and the one suggested for animals is that a trustee is an individual with legal title and a financial accountability to another: the equitable owner. When the subject matter of the trust is nonliving property, this is fully appropriate. However, as this chapter seeks to establish that living beings are different from nonliving entities, the primary obligation of the legal titleholder will not be financial accountability, but "being" accountability. The holder of legal title to a self-owned animal should be judged more in the context of the responsibilities of a parent to a child than a bank to its customer. Such individuals may have some financial duties, like the parents of minor children, but the primary context for the judgment of legal duties will be that of the quality of life of the animal. Thus, henceforth, the holder of legal title will be referred to as the animal's *guardian*, while the holder of the equitable title will continue to be referred to as the equitably self-owned animal.

SOME INITIAL CONTOURS WITHIN
THIS NEW WORLD OF SELF-OWNERSHIP

Having created a new legal status for animals, it is important to develop some context in which to describe the contours and consequences of this new legal status. This topic will require books to be written in the future, but for now, a brief view upon opening the door should be sufficient to understand the potential dimensions of the concept. After the creation of this new property status, nothing changes about the nature or interests of the self-owned animals, as they have no knowledge of what property status we might impose upon them. The changes will arise in how we humans consider and relate to the animals in question. The nature of the duty toward the self-owned animal will arise out of two primary legal sources: anticruelty laws and the concepts developed for defining the parent-child relationship.

What interests of the self-owned animal will the guardian need to take into account? The focus should be on those fundamental to the individual, life-supporting, and species-defining activities.[24] Consider the example of a human infant who has an interest in receiving food so he or she can live and grow. It is an interest recognized by adult humans and easily asserted, such that if it is shown that humans with responsibility are ignoring this fundamental interest of an infant for which they have responsibility, then the courts may intervene and do whatever is required to fulfill that interest.[25] This can occur whether or not the infant has self-awareness of the interference with his or her self-interest. The parent may or may not have breached the duty to the state as set out in criminal law, but the court will certainly have the authority to make sure that the needs of the child are met.

It is equally clear that a dog, a horse, or a snake has an interest in living and that society presently expects those interests to be satisfied by the responsible human owner (keeper, trustee, or guardian). Thus, there have long existed the prohibitions or commands of criminal anticruelty law.[26] The difficulty, until now, has been in allowing anyone other than the state, through its prosecutors, to protect or assert the unfulfilled interests of nonhuman animals within either the civil or criminal side of the legal system. As it may now be asserted that the nonhuman animal has equitable self-interest within our new legal paradigm, civil equity courts should be available to hear claims of substantial interference with such fundamental interests. That a human recognizes the interference and asserts it on behalf of the self-owned animal does not diminish the legal vitality of the interest nor the ability of a court to address this interference.[27]

For example, consider if Zoe were owned by someone who enjoyed the infliction of pain by extinguishing lit cigarettes against the side of the cat. Today the state would have the right to bring a criminal action. But this would not help pay for the veterinary bills to help Zoe recover from the injuries. In our new property paradigm, Zoe could sue, certainly to obtain an injunction to stop the battery and additionally to recover at least actual damages in the form of veterinary care, if not also damages for intentional infliction of emotional distress, pain, and suffering.

While the civil protection of interests could be done by government agencies, just as they do today for the protection of the interests of human children, in the world of limited government resources, it is more likely that private parties will be called upon to protect and assert the interests of the self-owned animal. Today, the owners of equitable title in a trust may bring an action to question the actions or inaction of the legal titleholder of the trust property, the trustee. While this will require the appointment of an equitable guardian ad litem, this is a natural process that courts can easily handle, with or without additional legislation.

The closest parallel to the nature of equitable self-ownership and the relationship between legal and equitable ownership is that of minor children with their lawful guardians. It is the duty and right of the responsible adults to raise the children in a way they see fit, so long as certain critical interests of the child are met. Thus, the parent may discipline a child but may not abuse the child.[28] The parent must allow for the mental development of the child,[29] as well as the appropriate level of food, water, and shelter for the child.[30] The parent must also provide for medical assistance when the child has a need, even if it is against the religious beliefs of the parents.[31]

Likewise, there will have to be a balance between the desires and resources of the human legal titleholder, the animal guardian, and the interests and needs of the self-owned animal. Just as the parents of the child must sort out what is in the best interests of their child, so the animal's guardian must, in the first instance, decide what is in the best interests of the equitably self-owned animal for whom they are responsible. If Mr. and Mrs. Willard have responsibility for Zoe, and they find themselves in the circumstances of separating and divorcing, then the issue of what to do with Zoe must be addressed. The issue will not be resolved by reference to who wrote the check for Zoe or which human wants Zoe the most, but rather what is in the best interests of Zoe. If Mr. and Mrs. Willard cannot reach that decision mutually, then the courts are empowered to step in and make that decision.

The second category of relationships is between the self-owned animal and others besides the guardian. As entities with legally recognized interests, self-owned animals have sufficient status as juristic persons so as to be able to hold equitable interests in other property. Thus, a chimpanzee with self-owned animal status could have an equitable interest in a building or a bank account. Property could come to him or her by gift or will. The guardian of the self-owned chimpanzee will be a trustee for such assets with an obligation to use the assets for the interests of the equitable owner, the chimpanzee. The self-owned animal's interests will most likely be characterized as in the nature of a life estate or, perhaps, a fee tail. What if the self-owned animal should have assets at her death? As the possibility of an animal writing a will is not realistic, and some disposition of title is necessary, one possibility is to presume that the holder of the legal title of the property will obtain the equitable title, unless the prior owner of the asset has made other arrangements.

There are many possible topics of discussion once the issue of animals as juristic persons is taken under consideration. How can the legal system best accommodate, in an efficient manner, the protection of the interests of animals and the balancing of the interests of the self-owned nonhuman animal with those of the human animal?

CONCLUSION

Nonhuman animals by definition are not human, but neither are they in-animate objects. Presently, the law has only two clearly separated categories: property or juristic persons. But, by using existing concepts of property law, it is possible to construct a new paradigm that gives animals the status of juristic persons without entirely severing the concept of property ownership. It is a blending of the two previously separated categories. The new status can initially be created by the actions of individual humans, but in time the legislature may want to speak on the topic and regularize some of the rules and relationships. Creating this new status will impose duties upon the guardians. The scope of the potential legal duties can be ascertained by reference to our long-existing anticruelty laws and the obligations existing within the parent-child relationship. When these sources do not provide a sufficient answer, the powers of the court of equity can be tapped to resolve disputes. With these steps, the issue of justice for nonhuman animals can begin to be addressed.

APPENDIX

Below is some suggested language for a deed/contract which will create equitable self-interest in an animal. (Do not seek to implement without first discussing this with an attorney.)

I. Operative language for an adoption agreement from a humane society.

1. The parties agree that the dog, _____, is a unique form of property, and that as such, the dog, by the execution of this deed/contract, shall receive equitable title for him/herself. Legal title shall transfer to New Owner who shall be considered both legal titleholder and guardian of the dog. New Owner agrees that the Humane Society has the right to represent the interests of the dog should the New Owner fail in his or her guardian obligations toward the dog. New Owner also agrees that Humane Society shall receive information periodically from New Owner about the status and condition of the dog. The parties agree that the dog is a living animal in need of daily care by the New Owner/Guardian, and that the New Owner/Guardian has certain duties to provide care under this contract and under the laws of the state of _____.

2. List of duties

   A. The New Owner agrees that when making decisions which have an impact on the dog, the needs and interest of the dog shall be taken into account.

   B. . . .

3. In the event New Owner/Guardian shall fail to meet his or her obligations

under this contract, the Humane Society, on behalf of the equitable title-holder, shall have standing to bring an enforce action under the terms of this deed/contract in a court of law, including in case of a gross failure to provide adequate care, or the case of violation of the anticruelty laws the right to obtain the transfer of legal title to another human who is willing and able to meet the responsibilities of being an Owner/Guardian.

II. Operative language by which animal owners can create the new status for their animals.

I_____, owner of _____ a dog/cat/bird (hereafter, animal) and identified by _____, desirous of creating a new legal status for my animal, do hereby convey to this animal equitable title in him/herself while retaining for myself legal title. I understand that this transforms my relationship with the animal to one of a guardian, and that I will henceforth have the obligation of taking into account the needs and interests of the animal when making decisions about the animal. I hereby pledge to inform any subsequent owner of this changed legal status.

I acknowledge that if I fail in my obligations as a guardian, an appropriate court will have jurisdiction to impose equitable relief for the benefit of the animal.

NOTES

This chapter is based, in part, upon an article previously published in the *Duke Law Journal,* David Favre, "Equitable Self-Ownership for Animals," 50 Duke L.J. 473 (2000).

1. *See* Gary L. Francione, *Rain without Thunder: The Ideology of the Animal Rights Movement* 1–31 (Philadelphia: Temple University Press, 1996) (criticizing the animal welfare movement as advocating that animal exploitation be merely regulated rather than abolished); Thomas G. Kelch, *Toward a Non-Property Status for Animals,* 6 N.Y.U. Envtl. L.J. 531, 582 (1998) (arguing that animal rights should be teleologically based, rather than based on special characteristics, such as sensibility and identity over time, in order to protect a broader range of creatures).

2. Becky Lou Favre, at 207–210 (2057, Little Brown on the Green Web). While some reviewers are still skeptical of this author's independent judgment, given that she is the granddaughter of David Favre, most now accept her professional judgment and admire the access to material that her family relation allowed.

3. The full set of motivations for this donation will never be understood, but clearly his love of his two Irish Setters, and his romantic involvement with the executive director of Humans for Animals, were dominant in the donation.

4. In the first six months of the NPS, the issue of which animals to list almost caused a permanent split in the coalition, but $300,000 spent on surveys and focus groups made it clear that political support beyond this list did not exist, so the pragmatists won that round.

5. See Raymond v. Lachmann, 695 N.Y.S. 2d 308 (N.Y. App. Div. 1999): "Cognizant of the cherished status accorded to pets in our society, the strong emotions engendered by disputes of this nature, and the limited ability of the courts to resolve them satisfactorily, on the record presented, we think it best for all concerned that, given his limited life expectancy, Lovey, who is now almost ten years old, remain where he has lived, prospered, loved and been loved for the past four years."

One barometer of the accessibility of new ideas is their appearance in cartoons. A *Bizzaro* cartoon drawn by Dan Piraro, December 5, 2002, has two guys in ties next to the typical office water cooler, and one says to the other, "You think your divorce was bad—my wife and I got nothing. The judge gave everything to the dog." It's funny because within the social context that it was written, the cartoon is just on the other side of the possible/credible. It would not have made any sense nor be funny if the line had been "The judge gave everything to the computer."

6. *See* Walter B. Raushenbush, *Brown on Personal Property* §1.6 (3d ed.; Chicago: Callaghan & Co., 1975): "There are judicial and statutory statements to the effect that the state in its sovereign capacity has title to the game within its borders in trust for the benefit of its people. This is, however, not much more than a metaphor for the undoubted truth that the state may, by virtue of its police power, regulate hunting and fishing within its borders so as to preserve for the benefit of all the wildlife with which it has been endowed by nature." For a discussion of state regulations limiting the obtaining of title to wildlife, see David Favre and Peter L. Borchelt, *Animal Law and Dog Behavior* 38–42 (Tucson, AZ: Lawyers & Judges Publishing Co., 1999); *see also* Leger v. Louisiana Dep't of Wildlife & Fisheries, 306 So. 2d 391, 394 (La. 1975) (finding the state not liable for damages by wild animals because the state did not own the animal in its proprietary capacity, but only in its sovereign one).

7. The legal concepts are based upon philosophical precepts of self-ownership. Both natural rights theorists, such as Locke, and personalists, such as Hegel, presume that a property right in the human body exists. Locke begins with the premise that "every Man has a Property in his own Person." He continues, "The Labour of his Body, and the Work of his Hands . . . are properly his." Property is created when an individual expends labor on an object. For Locke, an individual's ownership of his body and labor is the postulate that enables man to own things external to himself. Only because people have physical ownership of their bodies do they have an ownership of their bodies' products. Michelle Bourianoff Bray, Note, *Personalizing Personality: Toward a Property Right in Human Bodies*, 69 Tex. L. Rev. 209, 212 (1990) (quoting J. Locke, *Two Treatises of Government* §27 [1698]) (internal citations omitted). *See*, e.g., Moore v. Regents of the Univ. of Calif., 249 Calif. Rptr. 494, 503–505 (1988), *aff'd in part, rev'd in part*, 793 P.2d 479 (Calif. 1990) (concluding that absent a lawful justification, such as consent or abandonment, a person has a property right in her own bodily tissues and organs).

8. *See*, e.g., United States v. King, 840 F.2d 1276, 1276 (6th Cir. 1988) ("The Thirteenth Amendment prohibits an individual from selling himself into bondage, and it likewise prohibits a family from selling its child into bondage. . . . Our law views the child as an individual with the dignity and humanity of other individuals, not as property").

9. In the absence of prohibitory or regulatory law, humans would have the ability to sell or transfer parts of themselves to others, and such physical transfers would also transfer title to the item. *See* National Organ Transplant Act (NOTA), 42 U.S.C. §§273–274 (1988) (establishing organ procurement organizations and network); Unif. Anatomical Gift Act (UAGA) §2 (1987), 8A U.L.A. 5 (Supp. 2000) (establishing procedures and criteria for organ gifts).

10. *See* Frank Hall Childs, *Principles of the Law of Personal Property* §2 (Chicago: Callaghan & Co., 1914) ("Real property is land, things therein, or annexed thereto, the space above the soil, and certain interests in any or all of these").

11. See Carruth v. Easterling, 150 So. 2d 852, 855 (Miss. 1963); West v. Ankney, 134 N.E. 2d 185, 192 (Ohio 1956); Kauffman v. Stenger, 30 A. 2d 239, 241 (Pa. 1943); Favre and Borchelt, *supra* note 6 at 25.

12. Anticruelty laws are a restriction on the conduct of humans. While they clearly apply to the owners of animals, they also apply to others who simply interact with animals. *See* Mich. Comp. L. §750.50(2) (1994) ("An owner, possessor, or person having the charge or custody of an animal shall not . . . cruelly drive, work, or beat an animal, or cause an animal to be cruelly driven, worked, or beaten"); David Favre and Murray Loring, *Animal Law* 123–144 (Westport, CT: Quorum Books, 1983). As rocks are not animals, comparable restrictions of human conduct vis-à-vis the rock do not exist. There is a second category of statutes applying to owners and possessors of animals. These statutes impose an affirmative duty of care on the human for the benefit of the animal. *See* Favre and Loring, *supra* at 144–148. For example, the Michigan code states: "'Adequate care' means the provision of sufficient food, water, shelter, sanitary conditions, exercise, and veterinary medical attention in order to maintain an animal in a state of good health." Mich. Comp. L. §750.50(1)(a) (1994).

13. 7 U.S.C. §2143. "Humane standards for animals transported in commerce [sec. 13]:
(a)(2)The standards described in paragraph (1) shall include minimum requirements . . . ; and (B) for exercise of dogs, as determined by an attending veterinarian in accordance with general standards promulgated by the Secretary, and for a physical environment adequate to promote the psychological well-being of primates."

14. For discussion of regulations, *see* Animal Legal Defense Fund v. Glickman, 204 F.3d 229 (D.C. Cir. 2000).

15. For the first case to allow standing for humans questioning the care of animals under the AWA, *see* ALDF v. Glickman, 154 F.3d 426 (D.C. 1998), which found that one plaintiff had sufficient standing to reach the merits of the claim and that the regulations adopted by the agency were an inadequate expression of the congressionally mandated language of the AWA.

16. This author proposed a new tort action for animals at a conference held at the Harvard Law School on September 30, 2002: "I urge for the adoption of a new tort—the intentional interference with the primary interests of a chimpanzee. This tort would allow for the resolving of conflicts between the competing interests of humans and chimpanzees by courts of law.
Under this cause of action the plaintiff must show the following elements:
    1. Assert the existence of an interest.
    2. Show that the interest is of fundamental importance to the plaintiff.

3. Assert that the being's interest has been interfered with or harmed by the actions or inactions of the defendant.

4. Show that the weight and nature of the interests of the chimpanzee plaintiff substantially outweigh the weight and nature of the interests of the defendant.

Multiauthored speech: *The Evolving Legal Status of Chimpanzees*, 9 Animal L. 1 (2003), Favre material at pp. 31–40.

17. See David Favre, "Equitable Self-Ownership," *supra* unnumbered note at pp. 484–487, for details of the history of the concept of equitable title and a full set of references.

18. The trustee owes a duty to the beneficiaries to administer the affairs of the trust solely in the interests of the beneficiaries and to exclude from consideration his own advantages and the welfare of third persons. This is called the *duty of loyalty*. If the trustee engages in a disloyal transaction, the beneficiary may secure the aid of equity in voiding the act of the trustee or obtaining other appropriate relief, regardless of the good faith of the trustee or the effect of the trustee's conduct on the beneficiary or benefit to the trustee. *See* George T. Bogert, *Trusts* 95 (6th student ed.; Boulder, CO: West Publishing Co., 1987). "A trust is a fiduciary relationship in which one person is the holder of the title to property subject to an equitable obligation to keep or use the property for the benefit of another." *Id.* at 1.

19. See Childs, *supra* note 10 at 435–437; Raushenbush, *supra* note 6 at §1.6.

20. See Raushenbush, *supra* note 6 at §1.6. The ability to claim ownership of an abandoned animal will depend upon the status of being a "finder." *See* Favre and Borchelt, *supra* note 6 at 28–29.

21. "Thus leaving it [abandoned personal property] to be acquired by any person who subsequently may choose to assert title by occupancy." Childs, *supra* note 10 at 436.

22. See appendix A for suggested language.

23. *See generally* Jane Goodall and Steven Wise, *Are Chimpanzees Entitled to Fundamental Legal Rights?* 3 Animal L. 61 (1997) (suggesting that chimpanzees might be entitled to legal rights, although not using the property law approach suggested by this chapter).

24. This should tie in with the tort described in note 16, *supra*.

25. "The statutes authorizing the involuntary termination of parental rights . . . enable the courts permanently to remove children from harmful parents or damaging environments." Homer H. Clark, Jr., *The Law of Domestic Relations in the United States* 631 (2d ed.; St. Paul, MN: West Publishing, 1987). The author details the considerable variability among the states as to circumstances justifying removal of children from their lawful parents. *Id.*

26. *See* David Favre and Vivien Tsang, *The Development of Anticruelty Laws during the 1800s*, Det. C.L. Rev. 1, 2 (1993). For a summary of existing anticruelty laws, *see*, generally, Pamela D. Frasch et al., *State Animal Anticruelty Statutes: An Overview*, 5 Animal L. 69 (1999).

27. An animal can have rights without possessing the ability to claim them: "Capacity for rights (legal personality) must be distinguished from capacity for legal transactions, . . . capacity for wrongs, . . . and capacity for crimes. . . . A person may have legal rights and yet be incapable of legal transactions, or incapable of incurring legal liability, or incapable of incurring

responsibility for what would otherwise be accounted crimes." Roscoe Pound, *The History and System of the Common Law* 180–181 (New York: Collier, 1939).

28. "Child abuse, at least where it is likely to be repeated or where the parents have not responded to counseling and assistance, clearly is and should be a ground for termination of parental rights." Clark, *supra* note 25 at 633.

29. "It therefore is more realistic to say that the parent has an interest in and responsibility for the education of his child." *Id.* at 573.

30. "The most obvious forms of child neglect occur when the parent fails to provide for the child's elementary needs . . . maintaining entirely inadequate or harmful living conditions." *Id.* at 639; State v. Bachelor (*In re* Interest of Bachelor), 508 P.2d 862, 866 (Kans. 1973) (citing a child's poor living conditions while in the custody of its parents as evidence of neglect).

31. See Jehovah's Witnesses v. King County Hosp. Unit No. 1, 278 F. Supp. 488, 504 (W.D. Wash. 1967) (upholding the declaration of Jehovah's Witnesses' children as wards of the court when their parents objected on religious grounds to proposed blood transfusions), *aff'd*, 390 U.S. 598 (1968); Sopar v. Storar (*In re* Matter of Storar), 420 N.E. 2d 64, 73 (N.Y. 1981) (stating in dicta that a state's interest in protecting a child's welfare overrules a parent's refusal, based on religious belief, to provide necessary medical assistance); Clark, *supra* note 25 at 582 (noting an Illinois case ordering a blood transfusion for a child of a Jehovah's Witness).

11

CASS R. SUNSTEIN

CAN ANIMALS SUE?

For those interested in expanding rights of any kind, there are two historically honored strategies. The first is to enlarge the category of rights beyond what the legal system now recognizes. This was the strategy used by Thurgood Marshall, the great civil rights lawyer who argued *Brown v. Board of Education*.[1] Of course Marshall was, in a sense, insisting on the implementation of the constitutional guarantee of "equal protection of the laws." But realistically, Marshall sought to alter the meaning of that guarantee, so as to enlarge the rights enjoyed by African Americans. Those who argue that animals should not be treated as property, or who seek to prohibit meat eating and scientific experimentation, are certainly seeking large-scale changes in existing understandings of animal rights. A second, more modest strategy is simply to try to ensure that the rights that are now on the books actually exist in the world. Much of the time, this was the strategy of Martin Luther King, Jr., who urged that his goal was to ensure that social practices would comport with existing law. With respect to animals, a great deal might be done in the Thurgood Marshall direction—expand the category of rights by ensuring, at a minimum, that animals are used less cruelly, or less frequently, as food, in entertainment, or in scientific experiments. But what I seek to explore here is the more modest strategy, that is, to see what might be done to try to ensure that such rights as are now recognized on paper are actually enjoyed by animals in the world. I will try to make a few suggestions for how a legal system might go about doing that.

My simplest suggestion is that private citizens should be given the right to bring suit to prevent animals from being treated in a way that violates current law. I offer a recommendation that is theoretically modest but that should do a lot of practical good: Laws designed to protect animals against cruelty and abuse should be amended or interpreted to give a private cause of action against those who violate them, so as to allow private people to supplement the efforts of public prosecutors. Somewhat more broadly, I will suggest that animals should be permitted to bring suit, with human beings as their representatives, to prevent violations of current law.

ANIMAL RIGHTS IN ACTION

Without much fanfare or advance foresight, U.S. law has come to recognize a wide array of protections for animals. Indeed, it would not be a gross exaggeration to say that federal and state laws now guarantee a robust set of animal rights. A major problem is that the relevant laws are rarely enforced. They exist, but for too many animals, they are worth little more than the paper on which they are written.

STATE LAW: CRUELTY, EXPANSIVELY CONSTRUED

The first animal protection law of the West apparently came from the Puritans of the Massachusetts Bay Colony, who enacted a "Body of Liberties" that prohibited "any Tirranny or Crueltie towards any bruite Creature which are usuallie kept for man's use." The common law has of course been superseded by state statutes, and every state now purports to provide significant safeguards against cruelty or mistreatment of animals. Hence it is now said, in many jurisdictions, that "animals have rights, which, like those of human beings, are to be protected."[2]

What is perhaps most striking is that the relevant statutes go well beyond prohibiting beating, injuring, and the like, and impose affirmative duties on people with animals in their care. Omissions may count as cruelty; so too for overworking or underfeeding animals, or for depriving them of adequate protection. Owners must offer adequate sustenance and shelter. Defenses and excuses are quite limited. Protection of life or property is a defense against a charge of unlawful killing of an animal, but there must be a reasonable proportion between the danger presented and the action taken; and anger, intoxication, and impulse provide neither defense nor excuse.

New York contains an illustrative representative set of provisions. Anyone who has impounded or confined an animal is obliged to provide good air, water, shelter, and food. Criminal penalties are imposed on anyone who transports an animal in a cruel or inhuman manner, or in such a way as to subject it to torture or suffering, conditions that can come about through neglect. People who transport an animal on railroads or in cars are required to allow the animal out for rest, feeding, and water every five hours. Those who abandon an animal, including a pet, face criminal penalties. A separate provision forbids people from torturing, beating, maiming, or killing any animal, and also requires people to provide adequate food and drink. Indeed it is generally a crime not to provide food, water, shelter, and protection from severe weather. New York, like most states, forbids overworking an animal, or using it for work when it is not physically fit. Compare in this regard the unusually protective California statute, which imposes criminal liability on negligent as well as intentional overworking, overdriving, or torturing of animals. *Torture* is defined not in its ordinary language sense, but to include any act or omission "whereby unnecessary or unjustified physical pain or suffering is caused or permitted."[3]

There are three noteworthy points about state prohibitions on cruelty to animals. First, enforcement can occur only through public prosecution; the state has a monopoly on implementation. The point is important because prosecution occurs only in a subset of the most egregious cases; there is a great deal of difference between what these statutes ban and what in practice is permitted to occur. Private enforcement would obviously make a great deal of difference. Second, duties to animals, and the rights of animals, exist largely by virtue of a particular relationship voluntarily assumed by human beings—that of owner, transporter, driver, and so forth. There are no obligations to animals not within one's domain or care. In these ways the network of duties to animals tracks the corresponding network of duties to human beings, many of which are enforced publicly rather than privately, and which generally do not include obligations of good samaritanship. Third, and perhaps most important, state law protections do not apply to the use of animals for medical or scientific purposes, nor do they address cruelty toward farm animals and the production and use of animals as food; here, cruel and abusive practices are generally unregulated at the state level.

It would be an overstatement to say that the relevant provisions are entirely symbolic. But they say much more than they do.

FEDERAL LAW: SPECIES, MAMMALS, HORSES, OTHERS

In the last several decades, a remarkable number of federal statutes have been enacted to protect species, animals, and animal welfare. More than fifty such statutes are now in place, and the number is growing. The most famous of these statutes is the Endangered Species Act, designed to protect against the extinction of threatened or endangered species, enforced publicly rather than privately, and raising a number of knotty legal problems. A great deal of litigation has involved the meaning of the Marine Mammal

Protection Act, which imposes a selective moratorium on the taking and importation of marine mammals and marine mammal products. The act outlaws commercial whaling and also requires the Secretary of the Interior to issue regulations to protect marine mammals from unlawful activity.

Federal law contains a number of more specialized provisions. An important statute is specifically designed to protect horses from cruel treatment and in particular to prevent the exploitation of injured horses. The key statute involving game parks provides, "No person shall kill any game in said park except under an order from the Secretary of the Interior for the protection of persons or to protect or prevent the extermination of other animals or birds."[4] Another statute is designed to protect migratory bird habitat and also to protect habitat for mammals, including bears, moose, and wolves. Federal law imposes a moratorium on the importation of raw and worked ivory, as a way of helping to protect the African elephant. It is a federal crime to shoot birds, fish, or mammals from an aircraft, or to use an aircraft to harass birds, fish, or animals. It is also a federal crime to kill or harass wild horses or burros and to possess, sell, buy, or transport any bald or golden eagle, alive or dead. The Secretary of Agriculture is charged with ensuring that slaughtering of animals must be "humane," and Congress lists two methods that are designed to ensure "rapid and effective" killing.[5]

A FEDERAL BILL OF RIGHTS FOR ANIMALS?

In terms of animal protection, by far the most important measure is the Animal Welfare Act, which imposes, on those who deal in or with animals, a wide range of negative constraints and affirmative duties.[6] The act begins with an elaborate statement of purposes, emphasizing the need for "humane care and treatment" in the exhibition of animals, transportation of animals, and "use" of animals "as pets." There is a flat ban on commercial ventures in which animals are supposed to fight. Licenses are required for all those who sell animals for exhibition or for use as pets. The secretary is also asked to issue "humane standards" with respect to "the purchase, handling, or sale of animals" by "dealers, research facilities, and exhibitors at auction sales."

A key provision of the statute requires the secretary to issue "standards to govern the humane handling, care, treatment, and transportation of animals by dealers, research facilities, and exhibitors." These are supposed to include "minimum requirements" governing "handling, housing, feeding, watering, sanitation, ventilation, shelter from extremes of weather and temperatures, adequate veterinary care."[7] A separate provision lists minimum requirements for "exercise of dogs" and "for a physical environment adequate to promote the psychological well-being of primates."[8] Animals in research facilities must be protected through requirements "to ensure that animal pain and distress are minimized." In "any practice which could cause pain to animals," a veterinarian must be consulted in planning, and tranquilizers, analgesics, and anesthetics must be used. An independent provision requires compliance by the national government with the secretary's standards. Breeders of dogs and cats must allow inspections and may not transport underage dogs. The act also contains a set of record-keeping requirements, designed to ensure that dealers, exhibitors, research facilities, and handlers provide records, evidently designed to allow federal monitoring of the treatment of animals.

By virtue of its scope, the Animal Welfare Act promises an ambitious set of safeguards against cruel or injurious practices. Taken together with other federal statutes, above all the Marine Mammal Protection Act, it suggests that national law is committed to something not so very different from a bill of rights for animals. But there are important limitations in the statute. Perhaps most important, it does not apply to the treatment of animals raised for food or clothing. In fact no federal statute regulates the treatment of animals raised for food or food production on farms, and states typically exempt farm animals from anticruelty statutes. In addition, the Animal Welfare Act has an odd pattern of inclusion and exclusion. There is a requirement for the exercise of dogs, but no such requirement for the exercise of horses, who have at least an equivalent need; the relevant physical environment must promote the psychological well-being of primates, but no comparable protections apply to dogs, cats, and horses.

Many people have also complained that the Animal Welfare Act has been indifferently or even unlawfully enforced, not least via regulations that do far less than the statute requires. The Department of Agriculture has hardly been eager to press the act on those who abuse animals. Here too there is a question whether statutory law is not largely expressive and symbolic, a statement of good intentions, delivering far more on paper than in the world. An important issue therefore becomes: Who has standing to bring suit to require compliance with laws governing animal welfare? Can animals sue to protect themselves? Can people sue on animals' behalf?

STANDING: HUMAN BEINGS, HUMAN RIGHTS, AND ANIMAL WELFARE

To answer these questions, it is necessary to understand some basic legal principles. You cannot bring suit in federal court simply because people have violated the law and you are upset about what they have done. As the Constitution is now understood, you must show that you have suffered an "injury in fact" as a result of the actions of the defendants. There are two other requirements that the law usually imposes, though Congress is permitted to override those requirements. First, you must show that your injury is "arguably within the zone of interests" protected or regulated by the statute in question.[9] Second, you must show that your injury is not widely generalized, that is, it must not be shared by all or most citizens.[10] Under what circumstances do these requirements permit or bar an action brought to prevent unlawful injury to an animal?

Existing Law: Informational Standing

It is now established that Congress can confer on citizens—even on citizens as a whole—a right to obtain information.[11] It is also established that Congress can give citizens—even all citizens—a right to bring suit to vindicate that interest. If Congress says that people have a right to information of a certain kind, and if that information is denied, Congress is permitted to say that the deprivation of information counts as an injury in fact, for which suit may be brought.

These points suggest the first route by which people might have standing to protect the rights of animals. Suppose, for example, that a statute obliges laboratories and zoos to provide to the government, or even the public at large, information about their treatment of animals within their care. Suppose that it is argued that under the government's unlawfully weak regulations, far less information is forthcoming than would be available under lawful regulations. If Congress has granted standing to "any person" to contest violations of this duty of disclosure, there should be no constitutional obstacle to the suit. The deprivation of the information counts as the injury in fact. Provisions of the Animal Welfare Act require public reports about the treatment of animals; if Congress grants citizens a right to obtain that information, standing should be available.

Human beings who seek information about the treatment of animals must also show that they are arguably within the zone of interests protected by the statute and that their injury is not too "widely generalized." Consider *Animal Legal Defense Fund v. Espy*.[12] There the Animal Legal Defense Fund and the Humane Society of the United States challenged what they saw as an unduly narrow definition of *animal* for purposes of the Animal Welfare Act, a definition that excluded birds, rats, and mice from the category "animal." The plaintiffs claimed injury because the narrow definition of animal undermined "their attempts to gather and disseminate information on laboratory conditions for those animals." With a broader definition, laboratories would be required to provide more information about their treatment of animals, and the plaintiffs contended that they would use that information in public education and rule-making proceedings. The narrow definition of animal also made it harder for plaintiffs to educate the laboratories about the "humane treatment of birds, rats, and mice."

It is clear that the plaintiffs would have had standing if Congress had expressly said that they had standing. But the court held otherwise. Its central claim was that the informational injury did not fall within the zone of interests of the Animal Welfare Act. The Animal Legal Defense Fund was not attempting to protect its members' own legal rights, but "simply to educate all those who desire to promote the statute's substantive purpose." According to the court, informational standing would require not merely a "general corporate purpose to promote the interests to which the statute is addressed" but also "a congressional intent to benefit the organization" or some evidence that the organization is "a peculiarly suitable challenger of administrative neglect."

The decision in *Espy* is probably wrong. The Supreme Court has made clear that the zone-of-interests test is not meant to be demanding, and if anyone is within the zone of interests of the act, members of the Animal Legal Defense Fund are within that zone. For present purposes, what matters is less the particular evaluation of *Espy* than the general suggestion that Congress can grant people standing to receive information relating to animal welfare if it wishes to do so.

Existing Law: Competitive Injuries

Suppose that certain companies care about the well-being of animals and are willing to sacrifice, financially, in order to ensure that animals are not injured or mistreated. Suppose too that other companies do not much care about animal well-being. Suppose finally that a law protects animals against suffering and injury, and in that way puts companies that care about animals on the same plane as companies that don't. If the latter companies mistreat animals in a way that violates the law, their competitors might well be able to sue.

As an example, consider a proposed legal ban on the importation of products made with dog or cat fur. That ban would plainly help companies that sell ordinary or synthetic fur coats. The companies that comply with the law should be fully entitled to sue to ensure that such laws are enforced. Their injury is competitive in nature, and the competitive injury counts as an injury in fact. It follows that a company that complies with the Animal Welfare Act (in testing pain-relief products, for example) would have standing to challenge governmental practices that allow its competitors to do whatever they wish.

Existing Law: Aesthetic Injuries

In many cases, people contend that the unlawful mistreatment of animals imposes some kind of aesthetic or recreational injury on them. In a number of these cases, standing is available. But there is considerable conflict in the lower courts, and the outcomes seem quite unruly and even odd. Let us begin with some simple examples.

NO INJURIES AND NO PLANS

Suppose that a citizen, activist, or researcher objects to the unlawful and inhumane treatment of animals in a certain facility; the facility may be a zoo or a laboratory engaged in experimentation. Suppose that the citizen, activist, or researcher attempts to bring suit. On the facts as stated, the outcome is clear: Standing is unavailable, for there is no injury in fact. The plaintiffs have only an ideological interest in the dispute, and they are attempting to enforce the law for its own sake.

Under current law, there is universal agreement on this point. The key decision is *Lujan v. Defenders of Wildlife*,[13] where the plaintiffs, including people interested in seeing and studying members of an endangered species, challenged a federal decision not to apply the Endangered Species Act extraterritorially. The court held that the plaintiffs lacked standing because they had no plan to visit the members of the species; whether they had a concrete interest of this kind was purely speculative. Thus, they failed to show an injury in fact. Along the same lines, consider *Animal Lovers Volunteer Association v. Weinberger*,[14] in which the plaintiffs sought to enjoin the aerial shooting of goats on a military enclave for which public access is unavailable. The court held that standing was unavailable because the members did not visit the enclave and hence lacked any concrete injury.

PLANS, SCIENTISTS, VISITORS

Now assume that certain scientists and researchers are attempting to see and study members of a particular species; that their desire to see and study the relevant animals is imminent and definite rather than conjectural; and that they challenge government action that, on their view, will reduce the supply of animals available for study. Under current law, the scientists, researchers, and visitors have standing to sue.

The key case is *Japan Whaling Assn. v. American Cetacean Society*.[15] There several wildlife conservation groups, including members who were committed to watching and studying whales, objected to the failure of the secretary of commerce to certify that people in Japan were endangering whales, thus diminishing the effectiveness of the International Convention for the Regulation of Whaling. In a brief discussion in a footnote, the court held that the wildlife organizations had standing. "They undoubtedly have alleged a sufficient 'injury in fact' in that the whale watching and studying of their members will be adversely affected by continued whale harvesting." Indeed, the same conclusion applies not only to scientists and researchers, but also to everyone with an interest in observing members of the relevant species, even if the interest is "for purely [a]esthetic purposes." Thus, in *Animal Welfare Institute v. Kreps*,[16] the court held that members of the Animal Welfare Institute had standing to challenge a waiver of the moratorium on marine mammal importation under the Marine Mammal Protection Act. The court referred to the ability of the members "to see, photograph, and enjoy Cape fur seals alive in their natural habitat under conditions in which the animals are not subject to excessive harvesting, inhumane treatment and slaughter of pups that are very young and still nursing."[17]

Now imagine that there is no argument that the species will dwindle in number, but that someone alleges that the difficult conditions faced by the animal will cause, to him, an injury in fact. Suppose, for example, that someone who visits a zoo, or a stable, objects to the cruel and unlawful treatment of an animal on the premises. An obvious oddity here is that the plaintiff is likely to be concerned ethically or morally, not "aesthetically"— at least if the notion of the "aesthetic" is taken to refer to judgments, neither ethical nor moral in character, about beauty or ugliness. Nonetheless, it is the aesthetic injury that courts recognize as the basis for the suit.

The most directly relevant decision is *Animal Legal Defense Fund v. Glickman*.[18] In that case, Marc Jurnove, an employee and volunteer for animal relief and rescue organizations, complained about what he believed to be the unlawful treatment of many animals at the Long Island Game Farm Park and Zoo. Jurnove contended that he had visited the park at least nine times between May 1995 and June 1996, and that the unlawful and inhumane treatment caused "injury to [his] aesthetic interest in observing animals living under humane conditions." Thus Jurnove did not urge that he had a special interest in the decent treatment of animals by virtue of his service as an employee and volunteer for animal relief and rescue organizations. What mattered was that he was a visitor to the zoo.

The court concluded that the aesthetic interest counted as an injury in fact and that Jurnove had "far more" than an abstract interest in law enforcement for its own sake. In the court's view, Jurnove established an aesthetic interest that he had repeatedly attempted to promote by "visiting a particular animal exhibition to observe particular animals there." Thus the court concluded that an injury in fact could be established "to a plaintiff's interest in the quality and condition of an environmental area that he used."

Do Animals Have Standing?

From the discussion thus far, we can see that human beings have standing to protect animals in federal court under three circumstances. The first is when they seek information about animal welfare—at least if that information must, under the law, be disclosed to the public. The second is when the government's failure to protect animals inflicts a competitive injury on the human plaintiff. The third is when a human being visits or works with animals that are threatened with illness, death, or other harm. But in some cases, no human being will be able to fit within any of these categories. This possibility raises an obvious question: Do animals have standing? To many people, the very idea seems odd. But several cases suggest that the answer might be yes.

In a remarkably large number of cases in the federal courts, animals appear as named plaintiffs.[19] In *Palila v. Hawaii Dept. of Land and Natural Resources*,[20] for example, the court said, "As an endangered species under the Endangered Species Act, . . . the bird (*Loxioodes bailleui*), a member of the Hawaiian honey-creeper family, also has legal status and wings its way into federal court as a plaintiff in its own right." But some courts have held that animals cannot bring suit in their own names.[21] It is important to be clear about the stakes here. No one makes the ludicrous suggestion that a bird or a dog would be able to make decisions about whether and how to sue. Any animals that are entitled to bring suit would be represented by (human) counsel, who would owe guardianlike obligations and make decisions, subject to those obligations, on their clients' behalf. The important point is that this type of proceeding is hardly foreign to our law; consider suits brought on behalf of children or corporations.

From the discussion thus far, it should be clear that the question of whether animals have standing depends on what the law is. If Congress has not given standing to animals, the issue is at an end. Generally, of course, Congress grants standing to "persons," as it does under the Marine Mammal Protection Act and the Endangered Species Act. Indeed, I have not been able to find any federal statute that allows animals to sue in their own names. As a rule, the answer is therefore quite clear: Animals lack standing as such, simply because no relevant statute confers a cause of action on animals.

It seems possible, however, that before long, Congress will grant standing to animals to protect their own rights and interests. Congress might do this in the belief that in some contexts, it will be hard to find any person with an injury in fact to bring suit in his own name. And even if statutes protecting animal welfare are enforceable by human beings, Congress might grant standing to animals in their own right, partly to make a public statement about whose interests are most directly at stake, partly to increase the number of private monitors of illegality, and partly to bypass complex inquiries into whether prospective human plaintiffs have injuries in fact. Indeed, I believe that in some circumstances, Congress should do exactly that, to provide a supplement to limited public enforcement efforts.

Suppose that Congress does grant a cause of action to animals directly, to allow them to prevent actions harmful to their interests, such as extinction or suffering. Is there anything problematic in this course of action? The only serious question is constitutional: whether the grant of standing would violate Article III's requirement of a "case or controversy." Nothing in the text of the Constitution limits "cases" to actions brought by persons, but perhaps it could be argued that Congress could not constitutionally confer standing on animals. To say the least, the founding generation believed that actions would be brought by human beings, and did not anticipate that dogs or chimpanzees could bring suit in their own names.

The central problem with this objection is that Congress is frequently permitted to create juridical persons and to allow them to bring suit in their own right. Corporations are the most obvious example. But plaintiffs need not be expressly labeled "persons," juridical or otherwise, and legal rights are also given to trusts, municipalities, partnerships, and even ships. In an era in which slaves were not "persons," let alone "citizens," it was entirely acceptable to allow actions to be brought on behalf of slaves. The fact that slaves

Sunstein vs. Wise (different)

did not count as persons was no barrier to the suit. This basic understanding seems to underlie the many cases in which animals or species are listed as named plaintiffs. In the same way, Congress might say that animals at risk of injury or mistreatment have a right to bring suit in their own names. So long as the named plaintiff would suffer injury in fact, the action should be constitutionally acceptable. The point is even simpler at the state level. In general, state legislatures have the power to give animals standing to sue, and they might well seek to do this if they want to ensure more enforcement of the anticruelty laws.

Let me conclude with a cautious recommendation. A serious problem under the principal national protection against animal suffering—the Animal Welfare Act—is that the Department of Agriculture lacks sufficient resources to enforce it adequately. At a minimum, the act should be amended so as to create a private cause of action by affected persons, allowing them to bring suit against those who violate the act. A serious problem with current animal welfare statutes, including the Animal Welfare Act, is an absence of real enforcement—a problem that stems partly from limited government resources. At least when a violation of the statute is unambiguous, private parties should be permitted to bring suit directly against violators. This system of dual public and private enforcement would track the pattern under many federal environmental statutes; it should be followed for statutes protecting animal welfare.

In the future, legislative decisions on such questions will have considerable symbolic importance. But they will not be only symbolic, for they will help define the real-world meaning of legal texts that attempt to protect animal welfare—statutes that now promise a great deal but deliver far too little.

NOTES

1. Brown v. Bd. of Educ. of Topeka, 347 US 483 (1954).
2. State v. Karstendiek, 22 So. 845 (1897); Hodge v. State, 79 Tenn. 528 (1883).
3. Calif. Penal Code 599b.
4. 16 U.S.C.A. 352.
5. 7 USC 1901 et seq.
6. 7 USC 2131 et seq.
7. 7 USC 2143(a)(2)(A).
8. 7 USC 2143(a)(2)(B).
9. See Clarke v. SIA, 479 US 388 (1987); Data Processing v. Camp, 397 US 150 (1970); National Credit Union Admin. v. First National Bank, 118 S. Ct. 927 (1998).
10. See FEC v. Akins, 118 S. Ct. 1777 (1998). There, the court held that Congress could give standing to "any person" to require disclosure of information about an alleged "political committee."
11. See FEC v. Akins, 118 S. Ct. 1777 (1998). For general discussion, see Cass R. Sunstein, "Informational Standing and Informational Regulation: Akins and Beyond," 147 U. Pa. L. Rev. 613 (1999).

12. 23 F.3d 496 (DC Cir. 1994).
13. 504 US 555, 558 (1992).
14. 765 F.2d 937 (9th Cir. 1985).
15. 478 US 221 (1986).
16. 561 F2d 1002 (DC Cir. 1977).
17. Id. at 1007. See also Alaska Fish & Wildlife Fed'n v. Dunkle, 829 F.2d 933 (9th Cir. 1987), granting standing to those "who wish to hunt, photograph, observe, or carry out scientific studies on migratory birds," in the context of a challenge to agreements that would permit the hunting of such birds in Alaska); Humane Society of the United States v. Hodel, 840 F.2d 45 (DC Cir. 1988) (allowing society members who visited wildlife refuges standing to challenge rulings expanding hunting, on the ground that members would be subjected to environmental degradation, fewer numbers of animals, and corpses).
18. 154 F.3d 426 (D.C. Cir. 1998).
19. See, e.g., Northern Spotted Owl v. Hodel, 716 F. Supp. 479 (WD Wash. 1988); Northern Spotted Owl v. Lujan, 758 F. Supp. 621 (WD Wash. 1991); Mt. Graham Red Squirrel v. Yeutter, 930 F.2d 703 (9th Cir. 1991).
20. 852 F.2d 1106, 1107 (9th Cir. 1988).
21. See Citizens to End Animal Suffering and Exploitation v. New England Aquarium, 836 F. Supp. 45 (D Mass. 1993).

12

CATHARINE A. MacKINNON

OF MICE AND MEN

A Feminist Fragment on Animal Rights

Nonhuman animals in man's society are more than things, less than people. If the father of all social hierarchies, or the mother of all social distinctions, is the animate-inanimate division, it is quickly followed by the human-animal dichotomy,[1] and then (for present purposes) the male-female line. When the three hierarchies are analyzed together—even tentatively and incompletely, as here—the ordering of humans over animals appears largely retraced within the human group at the male-female line, which retraces the person-thing dichotomy, to the detriment of animals and women. To unpack and pursue this analysis in the context of theorizing animal rights in law, the ways nonhuman animals are seen and treated by human animals is considered in gendered terms. Comparing humans' treatment of animals with men's treatment of women illuminates the way the legal system's response to animals is gendered, highlighting its response to women's inequality to men as well. How animals are treated like women, and women like animals, and both like things, are interrogated in search of reciprocal light.

Beneath the inquiry lurk large issues. Is the fact that, from the human side, the animal-human relation is necessarily (epistemically and ontologically) a relation *within* human society more problematic than it has been seen to be? Is the inquiry into what can be done for animals in human society and law limited when women's social and legal subordination to men is overlooked? Specifically, is missing the misogyny in animal use and abuse detrimental to gaining rights for animals? Under existing law, are animals in any respects treated better than women are? On these questions, the operative suspicion is yes. The resulting further suspicion is that the primary model of animal rights to date—one that makes animals objects of rights in standard liberal moral terms—misses animals on their own terms, just as the same tradition has missed women on theirs. If this is right, seeking animal rights on a "like-us" model of sameness may be misconceived, unpersuasive, and counterproductive.

I

People dominate animals, men dominate women.[2] Each is a relation of hierarchy, an inequality, with particularities and variations within and between them. Every inequality is grounded and played out and resisted in unique ways, but parallels and overlaps can be instructive. One prominent similarity between these two hierarchies is ideological: In spite of the evidence that men socially dominate women and people dominate other animals, the fact that relations of domination and subordination exist between the two is widely denied. More precisely, it is widely thought and practiced and said that people are "above" animals, while being commonly thought and practiced but denied that it is thought and practiced that men are "above" women. And while a hierarchy of people over animals is conceded, and a social hierarchy of men over women is often denied, the fact that the inequality is imposed by the dominant group tends to be denied in both cases. The hierarchy of people over animals is not seen as imposed by humans because it is seen as due to animals' innate inferiority by nature. In the case of men over women, it is either said that there is no inequality there, because the sexes are different, or the inequality is conceded but is said to be justified by the sex difference, that is, women's innate inferiority by nature. Religion often rationalizes both.

In place of recognizing the realities of dominance of humans over animals and men over women is a sentimentalization of that dominance, combined with endless loops of analysis of sameness and difference. We see denial that each hierarchy involves socially organized power, combined with justifications of why one group, because of its natural superiority, should have what is, in substance, power, dominion, and sovereignty over the other. The denial often takes the form of the assumption that the groups are equal just different, so their different treatment, rather than being a top-down ranking, is not unequal treatment but merely an appropriate reflection of their respective differences. It is as if we are confronting Aristotle's level line unequally divided, treating unlikes unalike—that is, equality.[3]

The denial of social hierarchy in both relations is further supported by verbiage about love and protection, including in what have been termed "the humane movements." The idea is, love of men for women or people for animals, motivating their supposed protection, mitigates the domination. Or, by benign motivation, it eliminates the dominance altogether. One recalls Justice Bradley's concurring language denying Myra Bradwell's petition to be admitted to the bar that permitted persons: "The humane movements of modern society, which have for their object the multiplication of avenues for women's advancement, and of occupations adapted to her condition and sex, have my heartiest concurrence."[4] Difference rationalized dominance despite support for movements for advancement. Organized attempts to prevent cruelty to animals or to treat them "humanely" echo a similar underlying top-down paternalism, most vividly in some social movements of the past to uplift prostituted women.[5] Neither with women nor animals has redress of abuses of power changed that power's underlying distribution. Loving women is an improvement over hating them, kindness to animals is an improvement over cruelty, but neither has freed them nor recognizes their existence on their own terms.

Women are the animals of the human kingdom, the mice of men's world. Both women and animals are identified with nature rather than culture by virtue of biology. Both are imagined in male ideology to be thereby fundamentally inferior to men and humans. Women in male-dominant society are identified as nature, animalistic, and thereby denigrated,[6] a maneuver that also defines animals' relatively lower rank in human society. Both are seen to lack properties that elevate men, those qualities by which men value themselves and define their status as human by distinction. In one vivid illustration that condescends to women and animals at once, James Boswell recounts Samuel Johnson saying, "Sir, a woman's preaching is like a dog's walking on his hind legs. It is not done well but you are surprised to find it done at all."[7] Using dogs imitating people as a simile for women speaking in public, a woman engaging in democratic discourse becomes as inept, laughable, unnatural, and imitative as a dog trying to walk upright. Qualities considered human and higher are denied to animals as qualities considered masculine and higher are denied to women.

In a related parallel, both animals and women have been socially configured as property (as has been widely observed), specifically for possession and use. Less widely observed, both women and animals have been status objects to be acquired and paraded by men to raise men's status among men, as well as used for labor and breeding and pleasure and ease. Compare beauty pageants with dog and cat shows. Men have also appointed themselves women's and animals' representatives without asking and have often defined both as to be protected by them. In law, this has often meant that injuries to animals and women—if seen as injuries at all as opposed to breaches of moral rules—are seen as injuries to their owners, like the seduction of a young woman (which was often rape) was legally considered an injury to her father.[8] In neither case has protection worked.

In a point of overlap and convergence between the two hierarchies, women have been dominated by men in part through the identification of their sexuality with their bodies and their bodies with nature, meaning with animals. Women are attributed "naturalness," hence proximity to supposedly lower life forms. When your name is used to degrade others by attribution, it locates your relative standing as well, as "girl" is an insult for boys. Animality is attached to women's sexuality; the most common animal insults for women are sexual insults. Women are called animal names— bunny, beaver, bitch, chick, and cow—usually to mark their categorically lesser humanity, always drawing on the assumption that animals are lower than humans.[9] In pornography, women are often presented as animals and mated with animals. The more denigrated the woman among women, prominently on racial grounds, the more and lower animal names she is called. This dynamic insults women, reinforces the notion that being like animals is a denigration, and denigrates animals.

Both women and animals are seen as needing to be subdued and controlled. Both are imagined as dangerously powerful so must be kept powerless; if not locked up and kept down and in place, and killed when they step out, they will take over, overrun civilization, make chaos, end the known world. They can be subjected to similar treatment, often by the same people in the same course of conduct, including torture, battering, terrorizing, taunting, humiliation, and killing.[10] Nowhere are the powerless as powerful as in the imaginations of those with real, not imaginary, power.

A related ideological parallel is the endless moralism of people with power in contending how good "we" are to be good to "them," surrounded by the resounding silence of the powerless. Consider the repeated retracing of the "as we treat them, so go we" trope.[11] We can tell how civilized we are by how well we treat our _____. Fill in the blank with the unfortunates, the lessers. Take Senator Jennings Randolph in congressional debate in 1963 over the Equal Pay Act: "Emerson wrote that one of the measures of a civilization is the status which it accords women."[12] Or Mahatma Gandhi: "The greatness of a nation and its moral progress can be judged by the way its animals are treated."[13] Treating the low well, raising up women and animals within their limits, shows how civilized and great humans and men are. The ranking of noblesse oblige, who and what matters, in whose eyes, who is great, civilized, and progressing could not be clearer or more self-referential.

Men's debates among themselves over what makes them distinctively human have long revolved around distinctions from women and animals. Can they think? Are they individuals? Are they capable of autonomous action? Are they inviolable? Do they have dignity? Are they made in the image of God? Men know they are men, meaning human, it would seem, to the degree that their answer to these questions is yes for them and no for animals and women. In response to this definition-by-distinction, many who seek rights for women and for animals have insisted that they do, too, have these qualities that men value in themselves. If men have dignity, women and animals have dignity. If men can think, women and animals can think.

If men are individuals, so are women and animals. That women are like men and animals are like people is thought to establish their existential equality, hence their right to rights.

So the question becomes: Are they like us? Animal experimentation, using mice *as* men (so men don't have to be), is based on degrees of an affirmative answer.[14] The issue is not the answer;[15] the issue is, is this the right question? If it is the wrong question for women—if equality means that women define the human as much as men do—it is at least as wrong for nonhuman animals.[16] It is not that women and animals do not have these qualities. It is why animals should have to be like people to be let alone by them, to be free of the predations and exploitations and atrocities people inflict on them, or to be protected from them. Animals don't exist for humans any more than women exist for men.[17] Why should animals have to measure up to humans' standards for humanity before their existence counts?

II

Bearing in mind the limitations of dominant standards, following Mari Matsuda's injunction to "ask the other question,"[18] the woman question can be asked of animals in the animal law area. Relatively little attention has been paid by animal law scholars to the sexual use and abuse of animals.[19] Most states have provisions against bestiality, which in substance are laws against doing sexually to animals what is done to women by men on a daily basis. These laws define it as immoral for men to treat animals as they treat women free of legal restraints.[20] To the degree an injured party is envisioned in bestiality laws, though, it is structurally imagined to be the human or the community. Only Utah categorizes the laws against sexual contact by humans with animals under cruelty to animals.[21]

Why do laws against sex with animals exist? Their colonial roots indicate a preoccupation with debasement of the self, a lowering of the human to the animal realm.[22] In contemporary times, these laws are barely enforced if they ever were. Commercial pornography alone shows far more sex with animals than is ever prosecuted for the acts required to make it. Much like laws on sodomy (not a random parallel; in some sodomy laws, gay men are *sub silentio* lumped in with beasts), so little is done with it, one wonders what the law is doing there. Moralism aside, maybe the answer is that people cannot be sure if animals want to have sex with us. Put another way, we cannot know if their consent is meaningful. Other than in some feminist work, the question of whether the conditions of meaningful consent to sex exist for women has not been seriously asked. Whether it is possible, under conditions of sex inequality, to know whether women fully and freely consent to sex, or comply with much sex without wanting to (not to mention whether they consent to other things, like the form of government they live

267

under), is a neglected question of inequality among people. So, too, it is neglected between people and animals, although the substance of the inequalities are not identical. Surely animals could be, and are, trained to make it appear that they enjoy doing what people want them to do, including have sex with people. Pornographers train dogs to sexually penetrate women on signal; other pimps train donkeys to have sex with women in stage shows. Pornographers joke that women would have more sex with animals in their films but that would be cruelty to animals; putting a mouse in a woman's vagina would be cruel to the mouse, ha ha. Now whose status is higher?[23]

Laws against "crush videos" illustrate the comparative public ethos on this point. In this genre of pornography, mice or other small rodents are "taunted, maimed, tortured and ultimately crushed to death under the heel of a shoe or bare feet of a provocatively dressed woman"[24] to make a fetish film. The sex in the movie centers on the slow killing of the animals, called "pinkies" when they are babies. Congress made crush videos a federal crime recently in a bill providing "punishment for depiction of animal cruelty."[25] It covers any visual or auditory depiction in which a living animal is "intentionally maimed, mutilated, tortured, wounded, or killed" if the conduct is illegal under federal law or the law of the state in which the "creation, sale, or possession" of such materials occurred.[26] There is no such law against depicting cruelty to women, a multibillion-dollar industry with considerable constitutional protection.

There was some dissent to the federal bill, largely by the American Civil Liberties Union on First Amendment speech grounds, and some opposition to it in committee. The essence of the objection: "Films of animals being crushed are communications about the act depicted, not doing the acts."[27] That it often takes the doing of the act to create the communication about the acts depicted is as obvious as the fact that the film itself is not the killing of the animal, although it would not usually exist without it. To the question "whether protecting animal rights counterbalances citizens' fundamental constitutional rights" to speech, the dissenters concluded that they did not.[28] But the bill passed. No prosecutions under it have yet been reported, so no occasion has arisen to consider any issues of freedom of expression further. There still is no equivalent statute prohibiting a depiction in which a living human is intentionally maimed, mutilated, tortured, wounded, or killed in order to make a film. The First Amendment–protected status of such films, including snuff films, in which a human being is murdered to make a sex film, remains contested even in theory, making it unclear whether such a statute would be found constitutional.

In California, a bill was introduced in February 2000 that would have prohibited both crush videos of animals and torture and snuff films of human beings. For animals, it sought to prohibit an "image that depicts . . . the intentional and malicious maiming, mutilating, torturing, or wounding of a live animal" or the similar "killing of an animal" when the "killing of an animal actually occurred during the course of producing the depiction and for the purpose of producing that depiction."[29] For humans, the bill defined as a felony "the intentional or malicious killing of, or intentional maiming, torturing, or wounding of a human being, and intentional killing or cruelty to a human being actually occurring in the course of producing the depiction and for the purpose of producing the depiction."[30] A massive public First Amendment hue and cry, principally by the ACLU, was raised about the human part of the bill only.[31] No part of the bill passed. However, the makers of a crush video were successfully prosecuted for the underlying acts under the California law this measure had sought to amend, a provision that prohibits malicious mutilation, torture, or killing of a living animal.[32] In the prosecution, the videotape—for which rats, mice, and baby mice were slowly killed "for sexual gratification of others and for commercial gain"[33]—was evidence.

Instructively, the joint crush/snuff bill had a consent provision only for people.[34] Welcome to humanity: While animals presumably either cannot or are presumed not to consent to their videotaped murder, human beings could have consented to their own intentional and malicious killing if done to make a movie, and the movie would be legal. Even that was not enough to satisfy the avatars of freedom of speech. One wonders anew if human rights are always better than animal rights. Many laws prohibit cruelty to animals, but no laws prohibit cruelty to women as such. There are prohibitions on behavior that might be said to be cruel that at times are applied to women, such as laws against battering and torture. And laws against cruelty to animals are not well enforced. But then again the laws against battering and torture of people are not well enforced either where women are concerned. Consider the outcry if California's criminal law against negligent and intentional "torture" of animals—defined as any act or omission "whereby unnecessary or unjustified physical pain or suffering is caused or permitted"—was sought to be extended to women.[35] One has to go to the Canadian criminal law on pornography to find a law against "cruelty" to women, sexual or otherwise.[36]

Having asked a woman question—sexuality—about animals, it is time to ask the animal question of animals. What is the bottom line for the animal-human hierarchy? I think it is at the animate-inanimate line, and Carol Adams and others are close to it: We eat them.[37] This is what humans want from animals and largely why and how they are most harmed. We make them dead so we can live. We make our bodies out of their bodies. Their inanimate becomes our animate. We justify it as necessary, but it is not. We do it because we want to, we enjoy it, and we can. We say they eat each other, too, which they do. But this does not exonerate us; it only makes us animal rather than human, the distinguishing methodology abandoned when its conclusions are inconvenient or unpleasant. The place to look for this bottom line is the farm, the stockyard, the slaughterhouse. I have yet to see one run by a nonhuman animal.

The main lesson I draw for theorizing animal rights from work on women's issues is that, just as it has not done women many favors to have those who benefit from the inequality defining approaches to its solution, the same might be said of animals. Not that women's solution is animals' solution. Just as our solution is ours, their solution has to be theirs. This recognition places at the core of the problem of animal rights a specific "speaking for the other" problem. What is called "animal law" has been human law: the laws of humans on or for or about animals. These are laws about humans' relations to animals. Who asked the animals? References to what animals might have to say are few and far between. Do animals dissent from human hegemony? I think they often do. They vote with their feet by running away. They bite back, scream in alarm, withhold affection, approach warily, fly and swim off. But this is interpretation. How to avoid reducing animal rights to the rights of some people to speak for animals against the rights of other people to speak for the same animals needs further thought.[38]

A related absence is the lack of serious inquiry into animal government, including political organization in the sense of patterns of deference and command, and who gets what, when, how, and why. Ethologists and animal behaviorists have provided observations that might be put into that category,[39] but lawyers have devoted little attention to the emerging rules and forms of governance in animal societies that might illuminate entitlement, ethics, justice. The point of this inquiry would not be to see how "they" are like "us" or different. One point is to see whether, not having made such a great job of it, people might have something to learn. Maybe hierarchy and aggression and survival of the fittest are systematically focused upon by people in animal studies because those dynamics are so central to the organization of human affairs by male humans. How animals cooperate and resolve conflicts within and across species might be at least as instructive. How do they define and distribute what we call rights, or is there some other concept? Do they recognize and redress injuries? While animals aggress, so far as I know, there has yet to be an animal genocide. This inquiry would be into animals' laws, not just what the two-leggeds say about the four-leggeds. Inventing what is not known across power lines has not worked well between men and women. I do not know why it would work any better between people and animals.

The question is (with apologies for echoing Freud's infamous question of women), what they want from us, if anything other than to be let alone, and what it will take to learn the answer. Instead of asking this question, people tend to remain fixated on what we want from them, to project human projects onto animals, to look for and find or not find ourselves in them. Some see economics. Some see Kant-in-the-making. Some see women. People who study animals often say more about themselves than about animals, leaving one wondering when the road kill will rise up off the page and say: Stop making me an object of your analysis. What it would do to the discussion if they spoke for themselves is the question. The animal communicators are working on it.[40] People joke about dolphins having discursive democracy but miss whether people will ever be able to communicate collectively as well as whales and blackbirds—who do not seem to have our collective action problems—do.

Women are doubtless better off with rights than without them. But having rights in their present form has so far done precious little to change the abuse that is inflicted on women daily, and less to alter the inferior status that makes that abuse possible. Like women's rights, animal rights are poised to develop first for a tiny elite, the direction in which the "like us" analysis tends. Recognizing rights for chimpanzees and bonobos,[41] for instance, would be like recognizing them for the elite of women who can preach in public—perhaps at the expense of, and surely in derogation of, the rights of that rest of women who are most women. Establishing animal individuality, agency, and rationality as a basis for their rights goes down that road.

Predicating animal rights on the ability to suffer is less likely to fall into this trap, as it leads more directly to a strategy for all.[42] Indeed, capacity to suffer may be closer to women's bottom line than liberal legal approaches to women's rights have yet reached. But women's suffering, particularly in sexual forms, has not delivered us full human status by law. It has gotten us more suffering. That women feel, including pain, has been part of stigmatizing them, emotions in particular traditionally having been relegated to the lower, animal, bodily side of the mind-body split. What will it do for animals to show that they feel?[43] Calculations of comparative suffering weighted by status rankings, combined with the inability to register suffering on the sufferer's terms, have vitiated the contribution Bentham's recognition might make. The ways women suffer as women have been denigrated and denied, and when recognized more often used to see us as damaged goods than as humans harmed. Fundamentally, why is just existing, being alive, not enough? Why do you have to hurt? Men as such never had to hurt or to suffer to have their existence validated and their harms be seen as real. It is because they are seen as valid and real to begin with that their suffering registers and they have rights against its harm.

Women have been animalized, animals feminized, often at the same time. If qualified entrance into the human race on male terms has done little for women—granted, we are not eaten, but then that is not our inequality problem—how much will being seen as humanlike, but not fully so, do for other animals? What law resists doing is taking anything they want away from those at the top of hierarchies. It resists effectively addressing the inequality's material bottom line.

III

Rereading Steinbeck's play *Of Mice and Men*[44] in this context—seeing mice as animals in the animal rights and crush video sense, and men as men in the sense of exercising gender dominance—offers insights in hierarchy, power, and love among people and between people and animals. Three interlocking hierarchies structure the play. Lenny, the slow, caring guy who doesn't know his own strength, is above animals. Curly, the boss's son, who only wants to have a level conversation with the boys in the bunkhouse, is above his recently wed young wife, initially a sexualized tart. George, Lenny's buddy, the guy's guy, is the smart one: Shutting Lenny up, he will speak for him, make everything come out right. You know Lenny cares about animals. You question if Curly cares about his wife. You never doubt that George, with condescension and comprehension, loves Lenny, who returns that love with unquestioning trust, adulation, and adoration.

With his love, Lenny kills the mice he dotes on, then the puppy his heart and hands adore; eventually, by accident and in panic, he kills Curly's wife. Curly's masculinity is desperate. The boss's son, he has to make himself a place among men. He is ultimately responsible for his wife's death, because he set her up for it: He stifled her, made her have to leave, run away, by depriving her of the ability to have her own life. He made Lenny rightly fearful of her making noise, of exposing her plans to flee, of them being together. Curly put her in the position where Lenny, always stronger than he knows, stifles her life out of her because he so loves her silky hair and to keep her leaving from being found out once she starts screaming. She is an animal to him. Once George realizes what Lenny has done, knowing Lenny will be hunted down like an animal and will not survive men's legal system, because he loves him, George kills Lenny himself. As we say of animals, including those who attack humans, he put him down.

On this reading, the play is about men's love: unknowing, gentle, soft, sensual love; sexual and explosive and possessive love; protectionist and "humane" love. Every relationship here is unequal: between humans and animals, between women and men, between some men and other men. It is about unequal love. In Steinbeck's context, one I am calling socially male, loving means death. Specifically, it makes murder.

Read this way, *Of Mice and Men* is a morality play about loving to death: the relation between affection and aggression. It shows the stifling lethality of protective love in society ordered hierarchically, where no one but George gets to be who he is without dying for it. In the interlocking connections among hierarchies among men, women and men, and people and animals, between love in its male-dominant form and death dealing, each man with the best of intentions kills what he loves most. Men's love did not save Curly's wife, the mice, or Lenny—quite the contrary. The good intentions of the powerful, far from saving the powerless, doom them. Unless you change the structure of the power you exercise, that you mean well may not save those you love. Animal rights advocates take note.

Central dilemmas in the use of law by humans to free women—men's pets, their beasts of burden, their living acquisitions—from male dominance have included analyzing structural power in intimate settings, meeting and changing standards simultaneously, redefining power while getting some, gaining protection without strengthening its arbitrary exercise,[45] and supporting caring and empathy while enforcing accountability. And we supposedly speak the same language. In the effort to use law to free animals from the species domination of human beings, the most socially empowered of whom are men, these and further challenges remain unmet.

NOTES

Special thanks go to Ryan Goodman, Cass Sunstein, Lisa Cardyn, Kent Harvey, and most of all Carol Adams for their helpful comments, and to the University of Michigan law library staff as always for their resourceful and responsive research assistance.

1. Recognizing that human beings are also animals, and the linguistic invidiousness that elides this fact of commonality, I sometimes here, for simplicity of communication, term nonhuman animals "animals," while feeling that this usage gives ground I do not want to concede.
2. One analysis and documentation of male dominance is Catharine A. MacKinnon, *Sex Equality* (New York: Foundation Press, 2001).
3. For discussion of this standard approach to equality, and a book full of examples of the problem discussed in this paragraph in the case of women, see MacKinnon, *Sex Equality*.
4. *Bradwell v. Illinois*, 83 U.S. 130, 142 (1872).
5. See, e.g., Mark Thomas Connelly, *The Response to Prostitution in the Progressive Era* (Chapel Hill: University of North Carolina Press, 1980); David J. Pivar, *Purity Crusade: Sexual Morality and Social Control, 1868–1900* (Westport, Conn.: Greenwood, 1973).
6. Carolyn Merchant, *The Death of Nature: Women, Ecology, and the Scientific Revolution* (1980); Josephine Donovan, "Animal Rights and Feminist Theory," 15 *Signs: Journal of Women in Culture and Society* 350 (1990), reprinted in Josephine Donovan and Carol J. Adams, eds., *Beyond Animal Rights: A Feminist Caring Ethic for the Treatment of Animals* (New York: Continuum, 1996); and Carol Adams, *Neither Man nor Beast: Feminism and the Defense of Animals* (New York: Continuum, 1994), have theorized this question.
7. James Boswell, I *Boswell's Life of Johnson* 266 (Mowbray Morris, ed., Crowell, 1922).
8. See Lea Vandervelde, "The Legal Ways of Seduction," 48 *Stanford Law Review* 817 (1996).
9. See Joan Dunayer, "Sexist Words, Speciesist Roots," in Carol J. Adams and Josephine Donovan, eds., *Animals & Women: Feminist Theoretical Explorations* 11 (1995) (hereafter Adams and Donovan).
10. The parallels are documented and analyzed in Carol Adams, *The Pornography of Meat* (New York: Continuum, 2003).
11. This may have begun with Fourier, to whom the insight is often credited, who said something somewhat different: "As a general proposition: *Social progress and changes of historical period are brought about as a result of the progress of*

women towards liberty; and the decline of social orders is brought about as a result of the diminution of the liberty of women. . . . To sum up, the extension of the privileges of women is the basic principle of all social progress." Charles Fourier, *The Theory of the Four Movements* 132 (Gareth Stedman Jones and Ian Patterson, eds., Cambridge: Cambridge University Press, 1996) (emphases in original). (The first edition published in the United States was in 1857.) He was making an empirical causal observation that the condition of women causes social progress and decline, not drawing the moral conclusion that one can tell if one's era is virtuous by how women are treated. Closer to the usual interpretation, Fourier also said that "the best countries have always been those which allowed women the most freedom," p. 130.

12. 109 Cong. Rec. 8915 (88th Cong., 1st sess., 1963). Probably Senator Randolph was referring to Emerson's statement, "Women are the civilizers. 'Tis difficult to define. What is civilization? I call it the power of a good woman." "Address at the Woman's Rights Convention, 20 September 1855," in 2 *The Later Lectures of Ralph Waldo Emerson, 1843–1871* 15, 20 (Ronald A. Bosco and Joel Myerson, eds., University of Georgia Press, 2001), which is something else again.

13. Mahatma Gandhi, quoted in Christopher C. Eck and Robert E. Bovett, "Oregon Dog Control Law and Due Process," 4 *Animal L.* 95 (1998).

14. As James Rachels puts it, "If the animal subjects are not sufficiently like us to provide a model, the experiments may be pointless. (That is why Harlow and Suomi went to such lengths in stressing the similarities between humans and rhesus monkeys.)" James Rachels, *Created from Animals: The Moral Implications of Darwinism* 220 (New York: Oxford University Press, 1990). Harlow and Suomi designed horrific aversive experiments in an unsuccessful attempt to create psychopathology in monkeys by depriving infant monkeys of loving mothers. They did, however, succeed in creating monstrous mothers through isolation and rape by a machine. See Harry Harlow and Stephen J. Suomi, "Depressive Behavior in Young Monkeys Subjected to Vertical Chamber Confinement," 80 *Journal of Comparative and Physiological Psychology* 11 (1972). As Rachels points out, if monkeys are sufficiently similar to people to make the experiments applicable to humans, ethical problems arise in using the monkeys, but if the monkeys are sufficiently different from people to make the experiment ethical, the results are less useful in their application to humans. Rachels does not analyze the common mother-blaming theory of child psychopathology that the experiments sought to test—an antifemale notion directed equally at humans and nonhuman animals—nor the misogyny of an experimental methodology that would, in an attempt to create a bad mother, place female monkeys in an isolation chamber for up to eighteen months after birth, so all they felt was fear, and then impregnate them with a device they called a "rape rack." With their multilayered sexism, these are experiments in the perpetuation of abuse.

15. Elizabeth Anderson productively explores answers in her essay in this volume.

16. Deep ecology makes a similar point on the existence of animals on their own terms. See Bill Devall and George Sessions, *Living as If Nature Mattered* (1985); Bill Devall and George Sessions, *Deep Ecology* (Salt Lake City, Utah: G. M. Smith, 1985); Alan Drengson and Yuichi Inoue, eds., *The Deep Ecology Movement: An Introduction* (North Atlantic Books, 1995); George Sessions, ed., *Deep Ecology for the Twenty-First Century* (New York: Random House, 1995).

However, deep ecology has been criticized as lacking awareness of gender issues. See Val Plumwood, *Feminism and the Mastery of Nature* (New York: Routledge, 1993); and Joni Seager, *Earth Follies: Coming to Feminist Terms with the Global Environmental Crisis* (New York: Routledge, 1993): "Despite its surface overtures to feminists, the transformation of deep ecology into an environmental force has been characterized by deeply misogynistic proclivities. . . . Despite their putative tilt toward feminism, deep ecologists are unwilling to include gender analysis in their analytical tool kit" (p. 230).

17. Alice Walker puts it: "The animals of the world exist for their own reasons. They were not made for humans any more than black people were made for whites or women for men." Alice Walker, preface to Marjorie Spiegel, *The Dreaded Comparison: Human and Animal Slavery* 10 (New Society Publishers, 1988).

18. "When I see something that looks racist, I ask, 'Where is the patriarchy in this?' When I see something that looks sexist, 'Where is the heterosexism in this?'" Mari J. Matsuda, "Standing beside My Sister, Facing the Enemy: Legal Theory Out of Coalition," in *Where Is Your Body?* 61, 64–65 (Boston: Beacon Press, 1996).

19. It figures little to not at all in the following large surveys: Gary L. Francione, *Animals, Property, and the Law* (1995); Pamela D. Frasch, Sonia S. Waisman, Bruce A. Wagman, and Scott Beckstead, *Animal Law* (Durham, N.C.: Carolina Academic Press, 2000); Keith Tester, *Animals and Society: The Humanity of Animal Rights* (1991); Emily Stewart Leavitt, *Animals and Their Legal Rights: A Survey of American Laws from 1641 to 1990* (1990); Daniel S. Moretti, *Animal Rights and the Law* (1984).

20. See, for example, Wisconsin Statutes, making "sexual gratification" a class A misdemeanor for anyone who "commits an act of sexual gratification involving his or her sex organ and the sex organ, mouth or anus of an animal." §944.17(2)(c).

21. 76 Utah Criminal Code §76-9-301.8; chapter 9 is Offenses against Public Order and Decency, of which part 3 is Cruelty to Animals.

22. People in colonial times apparently abhorred intercourse with animals because they thought it could produce progeny. On the race and gender axes, bestiality for white men was considered like interracial sex for white women, both in their unnaturalness and in the forfeiting of moral superiority and privileged status for the dominant group member. See Kirsten Fischer, *Suspect Relations: Sex, Race, and Resistance in Colonial North Carolina* 147–148, 156–157 (Ithaca, N.Y.: Cornell University Press, 2002).

23. It is often said that Hitler was a vegetarian, but some people say he ate sausages and squab and the notion he was a vegetarian is Nazi propaganda. It is also said that he was gentle and kind and solicitous to his dogs. Some men who abuse other people also abuse animals. See Carol J. Adams, "Woman-Battering and Harm to Animals," Adams and Donovan 55.

24. *People v. Thomason*, 84 Cal. App. 4th 1064, 1068 (Ct. App. 2d 2000).

25. 18 U.S.C. §48.

26. Id.

27. 145 Cong. Rec. H10,268 (daily ed., Oct. 19, 1999) (statement of Rep. Scott).

28. Id.

29. A.B. 1853, sec. 2, amending section 597 of the Penal Code at 597(g)(1). The

first conviction is a misdemeanor. The second is a felony. There is an exception for a serious constitutionally protected purpose.

30. A.B. 1853, sec. 1(a), amended in Assembly, Mar. 20, 2000.

31. The First Amendment double standard posed by those who oppose statutes against the harms of pornography but do not oppose laws against hunter harassment is explored by Maria Comninou, "Speech, Pornography, and Hunting," Adams and Donovan 126–148.

32. *People v. Thomason*, 84 Calif. App. 4th 1064 (2002).

33. Calif. App. 4th at 1067.

34. "It does not include conduct committed against a human being to which the human being has given his or her consent." A.B. 1853, sec. 1(a).

35. Calif. Penal Code §599b (West 1999).

36. Canada prohibits as obscene "any publication a dominant characteristic of which is the undue exploitation of sex, or of sex and . . . crime, horror, cruelty [or] violence." 163(8) Criminal Code (Canada).

37. Carol Adams, "Vegetarianism: The Inedible Complex," 4 *Second Wave* 36 (1976); Carol J. Adams, *The Sexual Politics of Meat: A Feminist-Vegetarian Critical Theory* (New York: Continuum, 1990).

38. This question is implicit in Cass. R. Sunstein, "Standing for Animals (with Notes on Animal Rights)," 47 *UCLA L. Rev.* 1333 (June 2000).

39. For an argument that rather than ethology, what is needed is an anthropology of animals that acknowledges them as subjects, see Barbara Noske, *Beyond Boundaries: Humans and Animals* (Montreal: Black Rose, 1997).

40. See, e.g., Amelia Kinkade, *Straight from the Horse's Mouth* (New York: Harper-Collins, 2001). One fictional description is contained in the portrayal of Elizabeth in Jane Smiley, *Horse Heaven* (2000).

41. See the work of Steven Wise in this volume and elsewhere.

42. This of course refers to Jeremy Bentham's famous repudiation of reason and speech as the bases for animal rights and invocation of suffering as its basis. See Jeremy Bentham, *Introduction to the Principles of Morals and Legislation*, ch. XVII n. 122 (Oxford: Clarendon, 1907 [1780]): "It may come one day to be recognized, that the number of the legs, the villosity of the skin, or the termination of the *os sacrum*, are reasons equally insufficient for abandoning a sensitive being to the same fate. What else is it that should trace the insuperable line? Is it the faculty of reason, or, perhaps, the faculty of discourse? But a full-grown horse or dog is beyond comparison a more rational, as well as a more conversable animal, than an infant of a day, or a week, or even a month old. But suppose the case were otherwise, what would it avail? the question is not, Can they *reason?* nor, Can they *talk?* but, Can they *suffer?*"

43. That they do is analyzed and documented in Jeffrey Moussaieff Masson and Susan McCarthy, *When Elephants Weep: The Emotional Lives of Animals* (New York: Delacorte, 1995).

44. John Steinbeck, *Of Mice and Men* (New York: Covici-Friede, 1937).

45. For an analysis of protectionism, see Suzanne Kappelar, "Speciesism, Racism, Nationalism . . . or the Power of Scientific Subjectivity," Adams and Donovan 320, 322.

13

ELIZABETH ANDERSON

ANIMAL RIGHTS AND THE VALUES OF NONHUMAN LIFE

ANIMAL WELFARE, ANIMAL RIGHTS, AND ENVIRONMENTALISM

I believe that animals have intrinsic value, that is, value in their own right, not derived from the ways they serve human welfare. Indeed, I believe that living things in general have intrinsic value, as individual organisms and as systematically related in ecosystems and the biosphere as a whole. Those who hold at least some nonhuman organisms or systems of organisms to be intrinsically valuable generally fall into one of three theoretical approaches: animal welfare, animal rights, and environmental ethics. These three perspectives differ in their criteria of intrinsic value. They therefore draw the lines of moral considerability—that is, the class of entities that should serve as ends, or that for the sake of which we ought to act—in different places.

Advocates for animal welfare hold that the fundamental criterion for moral considerability is sentience, or the capacity to suffer. This draws the line of moral considerability at least to include vertebrates, and arguably much further. Sentience generates a claim on moral agents to protect and promote the interests of those who have it. Peter Singer (1976, 152), the most prominent advocate of this view, believes that sentience qualifies an organism for equal consideration of its interests. According to this principle, moral agents should give equal weight to substantively equivalent interests, regardless of the species of the individuals whose interests they are. The animal welfare perspective does not ground rights, understood as claims that cannot be overridden simply by appeal to the greater aggregate interests of others. In accord with utilitarian logic, animals may be sacrificed to advance total welfare. Animals are fungible, to the extent that they will experience equivalent welfare levels.

Advocates of animal rights hold that the fundamental criterion for moral considerability (at least strong enough to ground rights claims) is subjecthood. To be a subject requires not simply sentience, but the capacity to have propositional attitudes, emotions, will, and an orientation to oneself and one's future (Regan 1983, 243). This more stringent criterion draws the line of rights bearers at least to include the great apes, dolphins, whales, dogs, pigs, and other highly intelligent mammals, and arguably includes all mammals and birds. Subjecthood generates rights not only against the infliction of pain but to the conditions for integrity of consciousness and activity, including freedom from boredom, freedom to exercise normal capacities, freedom of movement, and the right to life. The animal rights view embodies a strong claim of equality, namely, that animals with equivalent morally relevant capacities have equal rights, regardless of species membership. In accord with deontological moral theories, these rights cannot be overridden by the aggregate interests of humans or any other beings.

Advocates of environmental ethics (Callicott 1992) hold that the criterion of moral considerability is being alive, or more generally, a system of life, especially a "natural" one as opposed to part of the humanmade environment. Morally considerable entities generate claims to preservation and health. The environmentalist's object of concern is typically an aggregate or system: a species, an ecosystem, the biosphere. Organisms, from this perspective, are fungible, valued for their role in perpetuating the larger unit, but individually dispensable. Nonliving components of systems of living things, such as rivers and mountains, may also be valued for their role in sustaining the system, and so may be preserved at the expense of individual organisms. Sensitive to the destructive influence of human activity on natural ecosystems, environmentalists tend to focus their concern on wild animals and their habitats over domesticated animals and their habitats. They also value biodiverse and rare over degraded and common ecosystems.

These three views lead to conflicting prescriptions. The animal welfare perspective can countenance animal experimentation, provided that the gains for humans outweigh the losses to the animals. Thus, if dreadful experiments on a few thousand chimpanzees enable the development of drugs that save millions of humans from AIDS, animal welfare advocates should not object. Animal rights advocates do object. Beings with equal capacities have equal rights. Chimpanzees, they argue, have capacities at least equivalent to mentally retarded children. If using mentally retarded children for such experiments would violate their rights, then using chimps for these experiments equally violates the chimps' rights.

Animal rights and animal welfare advocates also disagree with environmentalism. Feral pigs, not native to Hawaii and reproducing rapidly in an environment without predators, are destroying the Hawaiian rainforest, threatening its unique biodiversity. Rabbits, not native to Australia, are similarly wreaking ecological havoc in the Australian outback. Environmentalists advocate hunting down the pigs and rabbits, even using germ warfare (myxomatosis virus) to control their populations. From an animal rights perspective, this violates the pigs' and rabbits' rights to life. Rabbits in Australia are also driving various species of plants to extinction. Environmentalists advocate sacrificing the rabbits for the sake of the plants. This is perverse from both an animal rights and animal welfare perspective: The animals have moral considerability, but the plants have no competing claims to consider (Regan 1983, 362). To take a more extreme case, Sapontzis (1987, 237) and Rakowski (1991, 363–367) defend an animal rights case for eliminating predators due to the suffering they inflict on their prey, if painless methods of limiting prey populations (e.g., contraception) could be implemented. From an environmentalist perspective, such wholesale destruction of species and interference with natural processes is morally wrong.

I find myself moved by some of the considerations advanced by all three perspectives. This puts me in a quandary. How can I do justice to the values upheld by all three, given their conflicts? I shall argue that, while each perspective has identified a genuine ground of value, none has successfully generated a valid principle of action that does justice to all the values at stake. The plurality of values must be acknowledged. I shall pay particular attention to a deeply entrenched style of argument in the animals rights/ animal welfare literature. This style infers principles of morally right action immediately from the possession of the morally relevant qualities, typically by drawing on an analogy with parallel principles of action that we already accept for human beings. I shall argue that this style of argument neglects certain background conditions, present in the human case but not always in the case of animals, that enable the principles in question to serve reasonable functions in the lives of human agents. I shall then suggest an alternative approach to understanding the evaluative claims of the three perspectives, drawn from what I have elsewhere (Anderson 1993) called a "rational attitude theory of value." Finally, I shall consider how this framework may guide us adjudicating the conflicts among them.

THE ARGUMENT FROM MARGINAL CASES

The central argument for the animal rights/animal welfare perspectives draws an analogy between animals and human beings who lack distinctively human capacities. It is known as "the argument from marginal cases," or AMC

(Dombrowski 1997). Most humans have morally relevant capacities, such as for autonomous action, that no animal has. Yet we do not treat possession of distinctively human capacities as a prerequisite for having rights or being entitled to equal consideration, for we acknowledge that infants, severely retarded and demented people, and other humans who do not have or cannot develop or recover such distinctively human capacities have rights and are entitled to equal consideration. All such humans have the rights not to be killed for food, imprisoned in a cage for human convenience, subjected to deliberately disabling experiments, and hunted down or tortured for entertainment or profit. These rights are grounded in their possession of morally relevant capacities, such as sentience and will, that nonhuman creatures also have. To be morally consistent, therefore, we must extend these same rights or consideration to any creature with equivalent capacities. As Dombrowski (1997, 31) asserts, describing Tom Regan's view, "If the relevant respects in which certain marginal humans possess capacities that merit rights also apply to certain animals, then these animals also merit the appropriate rights."

The style of argument embodied in the AMC generates principles of justice, defining what moral agents owe to individual, morally considerable creatures. Several features of this style of argument are worth noting. It has a striking simplicity, deriving principles of justice immediately from the possession of valuable capacities. It thereby assumes that such possession is a sufficient condition for entitlement to be treated in accordance with a certain principle of justice. It also assumes that species membership is a morally irrelevant feature of an animal.

If moral rights could be grounded so easily, then advocates of the AMC would be on strong ground in arguing that opponents of animal rights are guilty of "speciesism." This charge invokes an analogy with racism. The wrong of racism is commonly thought to consist in discrimination against people on account of a morally irrelevant trait. Similarly, the wrong of speciesism is thought to consist in discrimination against animals on account of the morally irrelevant fact of species membership.

I shall argue that the AMC fails to appreciate the rich complexity of both animal and human lives, and the ways this figures in rights claims. It also fails to appreciate the natural conditions under which, and the social relations within which, certain principles of justice make sense. Principles of justice cannot be derived simply from a consideration of the intrinsic capacities of moral patients. Their shape also depends on the nature of moral agents, the natural and social relations they do and can have with moral patients, and the social meanings such relations have. I shall expose the deficiencies of the AMC by presenting a series of test cases, considering where they go wrong, and what we can learn from the AMC's mistakes. In the following section, I will focus on some of the morally relevant differences that species membership makes. In the subsequent section, I will focus on the connections of rights with social membership, and in the next section, on the connections of rights to capacities for reciprocity.

THE MORAL SIGNIFICANCE OF SPECIES MEMBERSHIP

Animal rights advocates acknowledge that what species an animal belongs to makes a difference to its capacities. Newts can feel pain; sea anemones can't. Their point is that what really matters to an individual animal's moral entitlements is its capacities, not the normal capacities of its fellow species members. The analogy with racism helps make this point, for in that context we acknowledge the injustice of using average group capacities as a proxy for determining how an individual is to be treated. In this individualistic framework, individuals must earn entitlements on their own merits, independently of their membership in generally meritorious groups. Thus, infants, mentally retarded people, and demented people cannot claim rights on account of the rational capacities of the normal human. If they have rights, this must be because of intrinsic capacities they possess—which nonhuman animals equally well possess.

To see what is wrong with this way of thinking, consider the following case. There is some evidence that chimps and parrots can be taught a language, at least up to the linguistic level of a toddler. Let us suppose that this is so. There are some human beings whose potential for language development is limited to the level of the average toddler, and hence no greater than the potential for language possessed by chimps and parrots. It is evident that any human, even with such limited linguistic capacities, has a moral right to be taught a language. If the AMC is right in deriving moral rights from individual capacities, then chimps and parrots also have a moral right to be taught a language.

The conclusion is absurd. But it could be argued that the AMC requires only minor modification to get the case right. Moral rights aim to protect individual interests. Even where the linguistic capacities of a human and a parrot or chimp are identical, their interests in learning a language are not. It is no disadvantage to chimps or parrots that their potentials for language are so limited. For the characteristic species life of chimps and parrots does not require sophisticated linguistic communication. It is a grave disadvantage to a human being for its language capacities to be similarly limited, for the species life of humans does require language. Every human being therefore has a profound interest in learning a language. This interest is certainly strong enough to ground every human's right to be taught a language.

Of course, a chimp or a parrot may also have an interest in learning a language, in the sense that communicating with humans may be a good for them. I assume that it is, since chimps and parrots, once having learned to communicate with humans, seem to enjoy doing so even when it does not give them immediate material rewards, such as food. Nevertheless, chimps and parrots do not *need* to learn a language and are not harmed if they do not learn one. As species, they can get along perfectly well, probably even better, without us. But humans cannot get along without other humans. The AMC must therefore be modified, along the lines that Singer suggests:

What matters for moral claims is not equivalent capacities but equally important interests.

This answer is partly right. It acknowledges that what is in an animal's interests depends not only on its individual capacities, but on the normal life of its species. The significance of species membership to the good of an animal goes beyond this, however. Consider the evocative idea of "animal dignity" introduced by Martha Nussbaum (2000) as a contrast with Kantian dignity. Nussbaum argues that individual humans possess a form of dignity that attaches to their animal bodies, distinct from the one they claim in virtue of their rationality. She does not explain the content of this dignity. But I think the following is in the spirit of her suggestion. Her idea is not simply that human dignity calls for the protection and care of our bodies, insofar as this is needed to underwrite each individual's own rationality or self-concept. For humans have this "animal" dignity of the body even if they lack reason and self-understanding. Even a profoundly demented Alzheimer's patient, unable anymore to recognize herself or others, or to care about or for herself, has a dignity that demands that others care for her body. It is an indignity to her if she is not properly toileted and decently dressed in clean clothes, her hair combed, her face and nose wiped, and so forth. These demands have only partially to do with matters of health and hygiene. They are, more fundamentally, matters of making the body fit for human society, for presentation to others. Human beings need to live with other humans, but cannot do so if those others cannot relate to them as human. And this specifically human relationship requires that the human body be dignified, protected from the realm of disgust, and placed in a cultural space of decency.

If the relatives of an Alzheimer's patient were to visit her in a nursing home and find her naked, eating from a dinner bowl like a dog, they might well describe what shocks them by saying, "They are treating her like an animal!" The shock is a response to her degraded condition, conceived in terms of a symbolic demotion to subhuman animal status. This shows that the animal dignity of humans is essentially tied to their human species membership, conceived hierarchically in relation to nonhuman animals and independently of the capacities of the individual whose dignity is at stake. There is no way to place animals on an equal footing in this system of meanings. If we were to dress up and spoon-feed a dog as we would an Alzheimer's patient, such action would not dignify the dog, but make a mockery of it.

This is not to deny that animals have a dignity. Indeed, the fact that we can conceive of mocking a dog reflects our recognition that dogs have a dignity we ought to respect. We would rightly be outraged at some fool who turned a dog into a figure of ridicule by spray-painting graffiti on its fur. We could even say that such treatment violates the dog's *right* to dignified treatment. But the conceptual world in which this sort of moral claim makes sense is considerably more complex than the one in which the AMC, even as modified, has a home.[1] For the interests being protected by such a right are unintelligible apart from a system of meanings in which species membership per se has moral significance. It is a system of meanings in which humans qua human have a status—a form of dignity—higher than animals, even with respect to features they share with animals. The moral hierarchy implicit in this system is not designed to deny nonhuman animals moral standing. For the meanings in question endow animals with their own species-specific dignity. An animal's interest in its dignity exists only in relation to human beings. The dignity of an animal, whether human or nonhuman, is what is required to make it decent for human society, for the particular, species-specific ways in which humans relate to them. (This is not to say that animals don't have other values independent of relations to humans.) Finally, the rights at stake exist not only to protect the interests that the rights bearer has in relating to humans, but the interests humans have in decent relations to the rights bearer. They do not flow immediately from a creature's capacities, but make sense only within a complex system of social relations and meanings.

RIGHTS AND SOCIAL MEMBERSHIP

Let us explore the social conditions of a different sort of rights claim by considering the following case. There is evidence that sophisticated mammals, such as the great apes and dolphins, have intellectual, affective, and agentic capacities at least equal to that of toddlers. Let us suppose that this is so. Human toddlers have a moral right to have their needs for food, shelter, and love directly provided by humans in human society. It therefore follows from the AMC that each individual great ape and dolphin also has a moral right to have its needs directly provided by humans in human society.

This case might seem easily handled by the version of the AMC advanced by Singer, in which the animal's interests rather than its capacities make the morally relevant difference. Here, human provision may even be a positive harm to the animals, rather than just an unneeded benefit, as language learning was in the previous case. If humans provided the necessities of life to great apes and dolphins, the latter would lose some of their species-typical skills in providing for themselves. From an environmentalist point of view, this would be bad, because it would constitute a degradation of the animal from its valued wild state. I think it would also be bad *for* the animal, in the sense that this would make its life go less well. The exercise of species-typical skills and capacities is, in general, good for animals.[2] Here I endorse the theory of "behavioral needs."[3] According to this theory, the good of a scavenger, for instance, consists not only in getting adequate nutrition, but in foraging for its food. Bears, who scavenge for food, get profoundly bored in zoos, which rarely provide sufficiently complex environments for them to fully exercise their foraging skills. Even in the absence of mental suffering (such as boredom), I would argue that the deprivation of opportunities to exercise healthy species-typical behaviors, or even tempting them away from such exercise, is, other things being equal, bad for the animal. The rangers in Yellowstone National Park rightly stopped feeding grizzly bears in part for this reason.

Suppose, however, other things are not equal. Suppose a particular pod of dolphins in the ocean would starve if we did not feed them, due to a sudden collapse of their usual sources of food. Do they have a moral right to human provision? Let us distinguish this claim, based on the concept of moral rights, from other reasons we might have for feeding the dolphins. Environmentalists might take an interest in feeding the dolphins, to preserve a valuable participant in the oceanic ecosystem. But this is an attitude toward a collective (the whole pod) that does not necessarily extend to *each* dolphin in the pod. This would remain so even if we had a moral *obligation* to preserve the species, or the ecosystem of which they were a part. Out of sympathy, we might also want to feed the dolphins. But this is not the same as according each dolphin a specific moral right to our provision.

In general, individual animals living in the wild do not have a moral right to our direct protection and provision, even if they need it to survive. Nor do individual animals in the wild have a right to our assistance to protect them against animal predation. This is not, as Regan (1983, 285) asserts, because predators do no moral wrong to their prey in killing them. For we have a moral obligation to protect human children from predation, even though nonhuman predators do no moral wrong in killing *them*. The answer lies rather in the connection of rights to provision with membership in society. An essential commitment of any society is the collective provision of goods to its members. The possession of morally significant capacities alone does not make one a member of human society, with claims to social provision. Being born to a member of society does make one a member of that society, however. This is why infants and other humans without developed potential, or recoverable rationality have moral rights to provision. So here is a species-specific moral entitlement that humans have: *automatic* inclusion in human society, with the positive rights that accompany this. Why are individual moral rights to provision tied to social membership? Only social membership could vindicate these rights, by specifying who has the obligation to provide the necessities of life to which individuals. This contrasts with rights to nonaggression, which can be observed by everyone without collectively instituting a division of moral labor.

Thus, when the moral rights in question are rights to positive provision, only members of human society can claim them. This, of course, does not exclude all animals from claiming rights to provision. Two classes of animals have been incorporated into human society: domesticated animals, and captives from the wild (e.g., animals in zoos and marine parks). The fact of incorporation commits their owners or stewards to providing their protection and means of subsistence, since they have no alternative means of providing for themselves. To fail to provide is an act of cruelty, rightly condemned by society and rightly prevented by force of law. Domestic, zoo, and lab animals have more extensive rights than wild animals.

This is not because the former are thought to be morally superior, or to have more valuable intrinsic capacities, than wild animals. The AMC misleads, insofar as it assumes that the only way to ground a difference in moral rights is to assert a moral hierarchy. That would be true if all moral rights flowed directly from the estimability of the rights bearer's intrinsic capacities. But they don't. Consider, for example, that only house-trained pets have the right to freedom of the house. Other animals are either kept out of our homes, or caged. This is not because the capacity to regulate one's excretions is a criterion of moral superiority. It is due simply to the fact that we can't tolerate a fouled house. Only house-trained pets have the right to roam the house because only they are fit for intimate human society. Hence it is not just rights to provision, but rights constitutive of certain kinds of *social* standing, that depend on an animal's actual membership in human society.

RIGHTS AND RECIPROCITY

Skeptics about animal rights (if they are not simply skeptics about animal minds) tend to argue that animals cannot have rights because they lack the rational capacity to enter into reciprocal relations with other rational agents. The intuition behind this claim is contractualist. Moral rights are conceived as the product of some kind of rational agreement or convention, based on a negotiated balance of the interests of the parties, or reached through the reciprocal exchange of reasons. This thought can be expressed independently of any idea of a historical contract. On Kant's ([1785] 1981) view, only rational beings have rights because only they are "ends in themselves," or worthy of respect. This conclusion is entailed by Kant's conception of what respect consists in: being treated only in accordance with principles that one has sufficient reason to accept. Since only rational beings can have reasons to accept or reject principles of action, only they can be subjects of respect. Since all rational beings are subjects of respect, the only morally right principles of action are those that all rational beings have reason to accept. The concept of reciprocity is built into Kantian theories as in contractualist frameworks.

Against this argument, there are two possible responses. One is to deny the major premise, that only beings capable of entering into reciprocal relations can possess moral rights. This is the response offered by the AMC. Animal rights advocates observe that we extend moral rights to humans who do not and cannot exercise reason nor enter into reciprocal relations with others. Infants, severely retarded people, the insane, the demented all enjoy various rights, including the right to life. Since they cannot enjoy these rights in virtue of their rationality, they must enjoy them in virtue of some other capacity they possess—presumably, their sentience and emotional capacities. Whatever capacity one picks as the one that grounds rights, the AMC argues that there exist some animals that possess the same capacity. Therefore, at least some animals have the same rights as "marginal" human beings.

We have already exposed some weaknesses in this style of argument. Rights bearers enjoy some rights not in virtue of their intrinsic capacities, but in virtue of their membership in human society, the requirements of standing in a particular sort of relationship to humans, or the interests of other people in standing in a certain relationship to the rights bearer. It is not clear which rights are dependent on social relations in one of these ways. At least, the *immediate* derivation of rights from the bare possession of certain capacities or interests, without regard to the interests and capacities of the agents supposedly bound by those rights claims, or the relations of rights bearers to moral agents so bound, cannot withstand scrutiny.

A different response to the skeptic about animal rights is worth exploring. This is to deny the minor premise of the skeptical argument, that animals are incapable of entering into reciprocal relations with humans. Vicki Hearne, a philosophically sophisticated animal trainer, adopts this strategy. We can learn a lot about animals and about the importance of reciprocity from her accounts of animal training. Consider her account of how riders and horses come to communicate in a language expressed in the medium of touch:

> With horses . . . the handler must learn to believe, to "read" a language s/he hasn't sufficient neurological apparatus to test or judge, because the handler must become comprehensible to the horse, and to be understood is to be open to understanding. . . . [In] the plight of the fairly green rider mounted on a horse . . . every muscle twitch of the rider will be like a loud symphony to the horse, but . . . one that calls into question the whole idea of symphonies, and the horse will not only not know what it means, s/he will be unable to know whether it has meaning or not. However, the horse's drive to make sense of things is as strong as ours. . . . So the horse will keep trying but (mostly) fail to make sense of the information coming through the reins and the saddle. . . . The rider will be largely insensitive to the touch messages the horse is sending out, but because horses are so big, there will be some the rider will notice. . . . If the rider is working with the help of a good instructor and is very brave (smart), then out of this unlikely situation will come the conversation we call the art of horsemanship. (Hearne 1986, 107–108)

In Hearne's tale, the merging of wills that is horsemanship—a riding *together*, with consummate skill and grace, as a shared end, a joint, cooperative activity—is produced by the reciprocal attempts of rider and horse to make themselves understood to the other.

Properly trained dogs, too, are capable of reciprocal relations with humans, a capacity that entitles them to more and more rights, the more commands they understand and obey. The authority relation that competent owners have over their dogs is a relation that itself must be earned through the coherent and responsible assumption of command, including a commitment to respect the dog's "right to the consequences of its actions." One of these rights is to be disciplined, that is, for its misbehavior to be corrected, for only so can it learn the behaviors necessary for rights to freedom. The same is true of children, of course. Applying the AMC in a manner not found in the standard animal rights literature, Hearne observes that the same rights and conditions on rights apply to humans, when the rights in question are "civil," or pertaining to the entitlements of freedom in human society:

> We don't imagine we can grant civil rights to human beings without first assuming authority over them as teachers, parents and friends, but we have lately argued, strangely, that rights can be granted to animals without first occupying the ground of commitment that training them instances. . . . The mastery of the "okay" command is not an achievement of love but rather of the simultaneous granting and earning of some rudimentary rights—in particular, Salty's right to the freedom of the house, which, like my right to the freedom of the house, is contingent on making a limited number and kind of messes, respecting other people's privacy, refraining from leaping uninvited onto furniture and laps and making the right distinctions between mine and thine, especially in the matter of food dishes. . . . In most adult human relationships we don't have to do quite so much correcting in order to grant each other house privileges, but that doesn't mean that house privileges don't depend on the possibility of such corrections. (Hearne 1986, 49, 53)

Discipline ennobles the dog by establishing the reciprocal, *cooperative* relations through which it earns civil rights, and hence an entitlement to civil respect.

There are many lessons to be learned in Hearne's rich account of the connections among responsible authority, civil rights, communication, and reciprocal relationships. I want to focus on one: the connection between having rights and the capacity to engage in a mutual accommodation of interests, to adapt one's behavior in response to the claims, corrections, and commands of others. I think this, and not "reason" in the more demanding sense of autonomous reflection on the validity of claims, holds the key to understanding why reciprocity is so important to rights. (Possessing reason is of course a sufficient condition for the capacity for reciprocity, but as Hearne's cases demonstrate, it is not necessary.) It is not so much that the capacity for reciprocity commands our esteem and thereby obliges us to recognize rights (although this is an element). It is that to bind oneself to respect the putative rights of creatures incapable of reciprocity threatens to subsume moral agents to intolerable conditions, slavery, or even self-immolation. As it cannot be reasonable to demand this of any autonomous agent, it cannot be reasonable to demand that they recognize such rights.

To make this point vivid, consider the case of vermin, such as certain species of rats and mice, who have found their ecological niche inside human homes. Such creatures are human symbionts—they do not live in the "wild" and would die if expelled from human spaces into fields or forests. Rats and mice are certainly subjects, in Regan's sense. So by the standard reasoning accepted in the animal rights literature, they have a right to life. It follows that we violate their rights by exterminating them or expelling them from our homes.

Such reasoning fails to appreciate the implications of granting rights to creatures who implacably behave in ways hostile to human interests. Vermin, pests, and parasites cannot adjust their behavior so as to accommodate human interests. With them, there is no possibility of communication, much less compromise. We are in a permanent state of war with them, without possibility of negotiating for peace. To one-sidedly accommodate their interests, as animal rights theorists demand of moral agents with respect to rights bearers incapable of reciprocation, would amount to surrender.

Beings whose interests are so fundamentally and essentially antagonistic to humans cannot claim even negative rights against interference and aggression from us. At least, there must be some possibility of securing peace via avoidance before an animal can claim rights to anything except freedom from subjection to gratuitous cruelty. Vermin, pests, and parasites may be killed, deprived of subsistence, and driven out of their human niches, in ways that, if necessary, cause them great suffering, even if their innate intellectual and affective capacities are considerable. Indeed, we have an obligation to our fellow members of society (whether human or animal) to drive them out, whenever this is necessary to protect ourselves (Warren 1997, 116–117).

It could be argued that in such cases, the interests of humans simply outweigh the interests of vermin. But this thought is hard to credit. Except in plague conditions, most vermin do not threaten to kill us. What are rat feces in the bedroom to us, compared to a painful death for the rat? The animal welfare perspective, which eschews rights talk in favor of the principle of equal consideration of interests, is hardly better off. Someone committed to an impartial, nonspeciesist, nonanthropocentric consideration of interests would hardly find compelling the claim that a filthy house is worse than a painful death. Indeed, the animal welfare perspective, by lowering the bar of moral considerability down to mere sentience, makes the predicament even worse. There are strong evolutionary reasons for thinking that the capacities for locomotion, perception, and sentience evolved in tandem (Warren 1997, 55–56). This means that even insects can feel pain. (If you think you doubt this, consider your reaction to seeing children pull wings off flies.) Since the animal welfare position insists on cross-species mini-mization of pain, and insect pests are vastly more numerous than us, it isn't difficult to see how little human interests would figure, in aggregate, under the principle of equal consideration.

I am *not* claiming that we may treat vermin any way we please, say, by torturing them for fun. Even vermin have some degree of moral consider-ability. I am claiming that the level of moral considerability they "have" (that is, that humans owe them) is profoundly diminished by the joint oc-currence of two facts about them: the essential opposition of their interests to ours and their incapacity for reciprocal accommodation with us. Moral considerability is not an intrinsic property of any creature, nor is it superve-nient on only its intrinsic properties, such as its capacities. It depends, deeply, on the kind of relations they can have with us.

I conclude that the AMC misses out on the implicit social background requirements for rights, because it models animal rights claims on human rights claims, where these requirements can be taken for granted. Humans are by their species nature fit for living with one another in society. What-ever hostile relations exist among them are products not of their essential natures, but of contingent social identities (e.g., of Nazi and Jew, slave owner and slave) that can be, and ought to be, discarded. Animals, however, cannot discard their species nature at will. Some have the potential for living peacefully with humans; others do not. This species difference matters for the rights they can claim.

So, the AMC is mistaken in equating speciesism with racism. Species membership, over and above the intrinsic (nonrelational) features of animals, matters for the rights they can claim. Nevertheless, sensitivity to the social and natural conditions for grounding rights claims does not put all animals on the other side of the rights divide from us. Instead, these conditions require us to face up to a series of morally significant species distinctions. First, a condition on being a bearer of rights (beyond protec-tion from wanton cruelty) is that peace be *possible* between the animal and those supposed to be bound by rights claims. Such peace may be secured by cooperative living, captivity, or occupation of separate habitats. This con-dition places those human symbionts that are parasites and pests—living in human-created niches, or on human bodies, at human expense—on the other side of the rights divide, and domesticated animals, captives, and wild animals not living in human-created niches at our expense, on the other. Second, a condition on having rights to the positive provision of the means of life is that one *actually* be incorporated into human society. This condi-tion places wild animals on the other side of the positive rights divide, and domesticated animals and captives on our side. Third, a condition on hav-ing a right to be incorporated in human society is that life with humans is necessary to the animal. This places domesticated animals on the human side of the rights divide, and wild animals on the other side. Fourth, a con-dition on having a claim *against* being incorporated into human society is that such a life would be bad for the animal. This makes many wild animals eligible for a right that no human has.

These social conditions on animal rights are not simply dependent on the species nature of the animals themselves. They are also dependent on historically contingent facts about human beings. Humans, for most of their natural and social history, have had a necessarily antagonistic relationship to many animals. Hunter-gatherers could not have survived without hunting. Nomadic herders could not have survived without killing their animals for food. Jared Diamond (1997) persuasively argues that the rise of human civilization itself depended on the massive (and probably brutal) exploitation of animals for food, clothing, transport, and energy. During this lengthy period of human history, the social conditions for granting animals substantial moral rights did not obtain. Even today, many human societies have no other option than to rely on hunting and herding for a living. Even more have no other option for survival than to encroach upon wild animal habitats. It is no wonder, then, that old habits die hard. The possibility of moralizing our relations to animals (other than our pets) has come to us only lately, and even then not to us all, and not with respect to all animal species. But once it becomes possible, we have compelling reasons to do so.

THE MANY VALUES OF ANIMALS

The criticisms I have made of the AMC are not directed against the idea that animals have rights. They are directed against simplistic ways of justifying animal rights, and simplistic ways of defining their contents. My intent has not simply been critical, but also constructive. I hope to have shown that there is no single criterion of moral considerability, and that what rights should be extended to a creature depend not only on its individual intrinsic capacities, but on its species nature, its natural and social relations to the moral agents to whom rights claims are addressed, and the social and historical background conditions applicable to the moral agents themselves. Different rights emerge in different social contexts. There is no easy way to simplify the task, either by asserting the moral equality of species (which makes no sense of the distinctive content of human dignity, not even of our animal dignity), nor by arranging species in a single hierarchy of estimability (which makes no sense of important yet nonhierarchical distinctions, as between domesticated and wild animals). The themes I want to highlight are of the plurality of values associated with animals, and the contextual justification of moral claims concerning them.

The previous sections have said a lot about contextual justification, about the natural and social background contexts in which rights claims make sense. It is time to focus on pluralism. In previous work, I have argued that there is a plurality of qualitatively different values. All claims of value addressed to human beings are normative for some human response: They prescribe an "ought" for our feelings, deliberations, and actions. Different *kinds* of value are normative for different *kinds* of favorable responses or ways of valuing. A "way of valuing" here refers to a favorable attitude, which is a complex of emotional dispositions toward, beliefs about, and patterns of deliberation and action oriented to what is valued. In the case of animal rights, we are especially interested in ways of valuing animals *intrinsically*, where our valuation of the animal is not justified by appealing to the ways we care about ourselves. Examples of such favorable attitudes of intrinsic valuation include respect, love, admiration, and consideration.

An evaluative claim is valid when it is apt or rational for us to respond in the prescribed way. A type of attitude is rational if we subject it to normative standards and thereby exercise some reflective control over its responses. Given the principle that "ought" implies "can," evaluative prescriptions need to be sensitive to the contours of our actual affective, deliberative, and agentic capacities. At the same time, the fact that we engage in evaluation entails that we subject our responses to critical, reflective control (that is, to "reason"). So we don't simply take our actual responses as given, but ask whether they are rational, justified, or make sense. To the extent that we are rational, we modify our responses by reflecting on the answers to such questions. Thus, to be valuable is to be the proper object of a rational favorable attitude.

Against this theory, skeptics might claim that it is not irrational to take any attitude toward any object. Wholesale skepticism about rational constraints on affective responses is unintelligible, however. Some affective responses have constitutive objects. A standard case is fear. Fear takes as its constitutive object some danger or threat to the well-being of some person or creature one cares about. If there is no threat, or if the threat is to someone that one (rationally) doesn't care about, it is not rational to feel fear. Wherever feelings or attitudes have constitutive objects, they have rationality constraints. Let us turn our attention, then, to the various values of animals, that is, the variety of ways in which we rationally, favorably respond to them.

When animal welfare activists describe the miserable conditions of animals in ghastly experiments, such as LD50 tests (in which animals are exposed to noxious chemicals until half of them die), the response of any person of decent human feeling is *sympathy* for the animals. Sympathy takes as its proper object the suffering or disadvantage of another. All sentient beings are capable of suffering. So it is always rational to sympathize with a sentient being who is suffering. Sympathy therefore knows no inherent species boundary. In the light of sympathy, we view the relief and avoidance of suffering as reasons for action.

In *People of the Forest*, Hugo van Lawick's 1991 film based on Jane Goodall's research, we perceive the stunning aptness of applying an extraordinarily rich anthropomorphic vocabulary to describe the distinctive personalities and activities of the chimpanzees of Gombe. No thinner vocabulary can make sense of their behavior. Love, friendship, grief, and social ostracism are unmistakable phenomena, to which the different chimps respond in their own ways. Hearne (1986, 62) testifies to a similar individuality among dogs. Her playful Airedale, finding the retrieving dumbbell whimsically set on end instead of its usual position, "enjoyed the play on form" and "toss[ed] it in the air a few times on his way back with it, to show his appreciation for the joke." By contrast, a German Shepherd, full of rectitude, "glared disapprovingly at the dumbbell and at me, then pushed it carefully back into its proper position before picking it up and returning with it, rather sullenly." The apt response to these cases is the bracing recognition that one is confronting animals who have their *own* point of view, with its own independence and integrity. Any animal with perception has its own point of view, of course. But there is a difference in kind—in *integrity*—between an animal's discrimination among phenomena in a generic way (responding to a dumbbell as a thing to be retrieved, for instance),[4] and discrimination in a highly individualized way, reflecting the animal's distinctive, stable, unified character and personality (responding to the dumbbell's unusual position as a joke, or as an incompetent performance on the part of the trainer). This respectful recognition—a mixture of awe and attention—amounts to an acknowledgment that this independent point of view *makes its own claims*, and should be heeded. To heed this point of view in the case at hand means to continue to play jokes with the Airedale, but to play fetch straight with the German Shepherd. Kant thought that only rational beings commanded such respect, and in his technical definition of respect, this is true. But I do not see why we should be so stinting with our heeding of others' points of view, except, as argued above, in contexts of an antagonism of interests, where the lack of reason entails an incapacity for reciprocal accommodation. Respectful attention to the claims of animals is rational except in the latter context.

My 2002 World Wildlife Fund calendar features glossy photographs of a majestic breaching humpback whale; polar bear cubs cuddling up to their mother, who appears to be alert to the photographer's presence; a magnificent eagle skillfully capturing a fish while skimming the water; an inquiring giant river otter poking its head out of a stream; a splendid multicolored green-winged macaw; and much more. Superb individuals, all. Such representations appeal to a range of responses in us: our sense of beauty, curiosity about other minds, delight in the sheer glory and diversity of the animal kingdom. If one response stands out as most consistently apt, however, it is admiration. The proper object of admiration is excellence. Each animal depicted in the calendar manifests excellent qualities or capacities: beauty, intelligence, care for others, athleticism, and so forth. So, admiration is also a rational response to animals. Admiration makes us want to contemplate animals and also to preserve and protect their estimable qualities.

When I take my seven-year-old daughter to the Huron River in Michigan, or to the Atlantic Ocean in midcoast Maine, we spend endless hours together by the water, looking for shells, crawfish, crabs, fish, seaweed, and other living things. She speaks to me, wide-eyed, of how there must be a "kabillion" grains of sand on the beach. Her fine observational skills lead her to one discovery after another: minute, perfectly formed snail shells in unexpected locations, metallic green beetles and flies, an extraordinarily dense tangle of red worms under a rock in a tidal pool (we wonder how they can survive in the sharp sand, unlike slugs). She asks, and sometimes correctly answers, questions about how one creature is related to another: Do seagulls eat snails? What lives among the seaweed? Are those freshwater crawfish just little lobsters? Comparing the flora and fauna at the different locations, she grasps, at some level, that the living things she knows are part of one vast interconnected system. Our responses to the natural world around us on such occasions are wonder and awe. The proper object of awe is the sublime, that which is so grand that it gives us intimations of the infinite. The proper object of wonder is the wonderful, that which commands our contemplation and quest for understanding. Nature is both sublime and wonderful, so these responses are rational, too. They make us want to study nature, and also to preserve and protect it, in its full integrity and complexity.

With this much pluralism about the values of animals in place, we can now identify the origins of the three perspectives with which I opened this essay. The animal welfare perspective originates in our sympathetic reactions to animals. The animal rights perspective originates in our respect for animals, our sense that their independent perspectives make claims on us that we ought to heed. It also, although it does not want to admit it, trades on our esteem for animals. The environmentalist perspective originates in our wonder at and awe of nature, conceived as an interconnected system of organisms, as well as in our admiration for individual animals.

Because all of these responses are rational, we should try to find the proper place for each of these perspectives in our policies, to take seriously all of the reasons these attitudes make salient to us. Because the principles of action proposed by the advocates of these perspectives are rigidly uncompromising in relation to the competing claims of the others, none of them are eligible for unqualified or exclusive endorsement. We need to search harder for sensible policies in these areas.

NO EASY ANSWERS

It is common, in essays written by those who believe that animals have rights, to conclude by drawing up a bill of rights for animals. My initial response to this is: It depends on what is meant by a bill of rights. If what is meant is a sweeping set of categorical imperatives for animals, valid in all contexts for all creatures possessing some defined capacities, that trump all considerations other than competing rights, thereby relieving us of any responsibility for investigating and evaluating the consequences of obeying and enforcing these imperatives, I demur. But we might mean something more modest. John Stuart Mill (1957, 66) defined an individual's right to something as a claim on society to protect her possession of it, either by legal means or moral suasion. He thought that, in specific contexts, we knew enough about the consequences of alternative policies to know that enforcing certain rights would be a good idea. Believing that we must consider the consequences of enforcing rights does not commit one to a consequentialist moral theory. Kantian and contractualist views, too, insist on considering the consequences of different policies. Only they reject a purely aggregative function for weighing the consequences, due to the distributive nature of the demands of respect as something we owe to *each* morally considerable creature, not just something owed to an aggregate. It follows that on these views, too, the rights to which we are entitled are contingent on the circumstances.

There are ways of defining rights so that the countervailing considerations are necessarily outweighed by the interest that the right protects. Thus, it is uncontroversial, except among obtuse skeptics about animal minds, or people who think something suspiciously metaphysical is going on when we talk about rights, that all sentient animals, even vermin, have a moral right against the wanton or sadistic infliction of suffering. We have enough experience with the consequences of anticruelty laws to know that the consequences of legally enforcing such moral rights are acceptable. I also think animals have a right, which should be legally enforceable, against subjection to painful experiments merely to test cosmetics. Safe, nontested cosmetics are readily available, and the human interest in having novel cosmetics pre-screened for safety on animals is too trifling to count against horrors such as the Draize test (in which the cosmetic is applied to rabbits' eyes to test for inflammatory reactions).

But what about animal experimentation for medical purposes? Here the human interests at stake are profound. In my reading of the antivivisectionist literature, I have become convinced of two propositions. One is that there are lots of scientific experiments on animals that are monstrous, and of dubious scientific value. The other is that animal rights advocates, such as Francione (2000, 31–49), who categorically oppose animal experimentation, are ignorant of science. None of their general claims about the unreliability of animal models for understanding human disease, or the availability of scientific alternatives to animal testing, such as computer models, reflects a serious engagement with science. It is easy to pick and choose just those cases that prove one's point. But that is an unreliable way to make decisions. One of the purposes of scientific method, which seems lost on antivivisectionists, is to guard against such biases. I also do not trust the simplistic formulas for assessing the consequences advanced in the standard animal welfare and animal rights literatures—the equal consideration of interests, or rights as trumps—to yield morally reliable results (they certainly don't work even when only human interests are at stake). Here is an arena where it is literally dangerous to philosophize from an armchair. While we must recognize a powerful claim of animals against cruel treatment, even for compelling purposes, a responsible comparison of the interests on all sides requires far more empirical research into the consequences of alternative policies, and a far more nuanced moral theory. The latter is not something that can be pulled out of a hat via a four-line argument such as the AMC.[5]

Consideration of the values of ecosystems also makes me reluctant to endorse a general right to life for animals, even for highly intelligent mammals such as pigs. Ecosystems are wonderful and awe-inspiring. To take these responses seriously is to acknowledge reasons to protect and preserve the integrity of ecosystems. Ecosystems do not exist merely for the exploitation of humans, and not merely for the exploitation of other animals either. We have rightly enacted laws to protect the integrity and biodiversity of ecosystems and endangered plant and animal species. So we already acknowledge that we need not permit human beings to lay waste to the environment. Nor should we permit rabbits and pigs to do so, especially given the fact that it was our own wrongdoing that enabled their destructiveness in the first place. Again, the AMC offers little understanding of the moral issues at stake. Of course, we acknowledge a right of humans not to be killed for harming the environment. But that is because we can reason with one another and reach a reasonable accommodation of our interests in exploiting and preserving nature. (On the other hand, if a group of terrorists were determined to destroy an ecosystem, say by spreading nuclear waste, and we could only prevent this by killing them, the killing would be justified.) We cannot reason with feral pigs and Australian rabbits. So violent means are sometimes necessary to deal with their depredations (Warren 1997, 114–117).

I would, however, support a right of great apes against human predation. Here the distinction between generic and individualized points of view is morally significant. Ruminants and rodents have a point of view that is generic. While they may have an interest in continued life, one day is like the next, and a longer life does not add up to more than an accumulation of days. It is not evident to me that this sort of interest in continued life is important enough to be protected by a right.[6] By contrast, great apes are certainly among those creatures who have the kind of individuality, described above, that commands our respect. They have a *biography*. Their lives unfold as a development of personality in long-term intimate social relations with others. When they die, other members of their society grieve, and their social order goes into upheaval. Their deaths are therefore not merely unwanted, but *meaningful* from the perspective of the apes themselves. This kind of interest in continued life is compelling and deserves protection by a right. To hunt down great apes for sport or food violates that right.

Even here, we must not forget the calamitous fate of the Ik (Turnbull 1972). Their hunter-gatherer society disintegrated into a Hobbesian nightmare, partly due to the fact that they were prohibited from ranging into

their traditional hunting grounds, which had been turned into a nature preserve. Desperately poor miners today depend on chimpanzee bushmeat for
a substantial part of their diets. The hunting done to supply their demand
for meat probably poses the greatest current threat to the chimps' survival. It
is unlikely that the miners would suffer a fate as bad as the Ik's, were they to
be deprived of bushmeat. Yet those of us who care for the apes must heed
the demands of respect for the miners, by finding them some alternative
means of subsistence. We cannot justly enforce a right against hunting apes
while blithely leaving the costs of this prohibition to be borne by those least
able to afford them.

If there is a general conclusion to be drawn from this essay, it is that
there are no easy answers. Animals have rights, to be sure. But once we acknowledge the plurality of values, the inadequacy of simplistic moral formulas, the dependence of rights on the natural and social contexts, and the
consequences of their enforcement, we have quite a lot more work to do to
figure out what they are.

NOTES

I thank Stephen Darwall, Rachana Kamtekar, and David Velleman for helpful
conversations. After I drafted most of this essay, I came across Mary Anne
Warren's *Moral Status* (1997), which draws some of the same conclusions I do
about animal rights and moral considerability. I recommend it for those interested in a more extensive treatment of these issues.
1. Cora Diamond (1978) makes a similar point about the obtuseness of AMC arguments for vegetarianism. Dombrowski (1997, 42) suggests, for example, that
   if sentience or subjecthood are not sufficient grounds for a right not to be
   killed for food, then there can be no moral objections to killing mentally retarded children for food. Diamond observes that our moral objections to eating people have little to do with any such right, for we abhor eating human
   corpses, amputated human limbs, human blood, and so forth, even when the
   tissue is made available by means that don't violate anyone's rights. We mark
   what it means to be human in part by making cannibalism taboo. (Even in
   societies that practice it, the consumption of humans is always freighted with
   ritual significance; it is never just another food in the pantry.) I would add
   that it is hard to imagine how social relations could carry on if people knew
   that their companions were salivating at the prospect of gobbling them up.
   We find it difficult to carry on intimate, companionate relations with any
   creature whom we view as dinner. No wonder we extend the taboo against
   eating to *all* of our companions, including our pets.
2. This claim needs to be qualified. Evolutionary theory suggests that reproductive behaviors are those most likely to entail the sacrifice of the individual animal to the survival of its progeny. In addition, disease sometimes provokes
   animals into species-typical but self-destructive responses. Thus, my claim
   should be understood to exclude species-typical behaviors that tend to lead to
   the serious injury, sickness, or death of the individual.

3. Skeptics have questioned the experimental evidence that has been taken to confirm this theory. But some of the skepticism seems based on behaviorist presuppositions that have been discredited on other grounds. For a sensitive discussion of the theory of behavioral needs, the evidence for it, and its critics, see Young (1999).

4. Even this discrimination is a remarkable achievement, in that it represents the dog's recognition of *another's* intention, and a willingness to heed it, thereby making the intention shared. A better example of a manifestation of a merely generic point of view would be responding to a wall as an obstacle, or a lever in a behaviorist's experiment as what-needs-to-be-pushed-to-get-food.

5. For example, that humans have a right not to be caged for experiments does not easily translate to the animal case. Researchers don't *need* to cage human experimental subjects to be able to keep track of them, make sure they don't get lost, and prevent them from endangering the lives of other experimental subjects and fouling up the lab. Caging human subjects would be utterly gratuitous relative to the scientific purposes at stake. I am not saying that caging human subjects would be justified if humans could not be trusted to avoid these problems when at liberty. If humans, as a species, could not be trusted in these ways, we wouldn't have been capable of *conducting* science in the first place.

6. The AMC nags us with the question: Why, then, do we grant a right to life to demented Alzheimer's' patients, for whom continued life, if pleasant at all, is no more than this? For the same reasons that we also insist upon respecting their specifically *human* "animal" dignity.

REFERENCES

Anderson, Elizabeth. 1993. *Value in Ethics and Economics.* Cambridge, Mass.: Harvard University Press.

Callicott, J. Baird. 1992. "Animal Liberation: A Triangular Affair." In *The Animal Rights, Environmental Ethics Debate,* ed. Eugene C. Hargrove. Albany: State University of New York Press.

Diamond, Cora. 1978. "Eating Meat and Eating People." *Philosophy* 53:465–479.

Diamond, Jared. 1997. *Guns, Germs and Steel.* New York: Norton.

Dombrowski, Daniel A. 1997. *Babies and Beasts: The Argument from Marginal Cases.* Urbana: University of Illinois Press.

Francione, Gary. 2000. *Introduction to Animal Rights: Your Child or the Dog?* Philadelphia, Pa.: Temple University Press.

Hearne, Vicki. 1986. *Adam's Task.* New York: Vintage.

Kant, Immanuel. [1785] 1981. *Grounding for the Metaphysics of Morals.* Trans. James Ellington. Indianapolis, Ind.: Hackett.

Mill, John Stuart. 1957. *Utilitarianism.* New York: Liberal Arts Press.

Nussbaum, Martha. 2000. "The Future of Feminist Liberalism." *Proceedings and Addresses of the American Philosophical Association* 74:47–79.

Rakowski, Eric. 1991. *Equal Justice.* New York: Oxford University Press.

Regan, Tom. 1983. *The Case for Animal Rights.* Berkeley: University of California Press.

Sapontzis, Steve. 1987. *Morals, Reason, and Animals.* Philadelphia, Pa.: Temple

University Press.

Singer, Peter. 1976. "All Animals Are Equal." In *Animal Rights and Human Obligations*, ed. Tom Regan and Peter Singer. Englewood Cliffs, N.J.: Prentice-Hall.

Turnbull, Colin. 1972. *The Mountain People.* New York: Simon and Schuster.

van Lawick, Hugo, dir., Caracal Ltd., prod. 1991. *People of the Forest: The Chimps of Gombe.* Discovery Channel.

Warren, Mary Anne. 1997. *Moral Status: Obligations to Persons and Other Living Things.* Oxford: Clarendon; New York: Oxford University Press.

Young, Robert J. 1999. "The Behavioral Requirements of Farm Animals for Psychological Well-Being and Survival." In *Attitudes to Animals*, ed. Francine L. Dolins. Cambridge and New York: Cambridge University Press.

14

MARTHA C. NUSSBAUM

BEYOND "COMPASSION AND HUMANITY"

Justice for Nonhuman Animals

Certainly it is wrong to be cruel to animals. . . . The capacity for feelings of pleasure and pain and for the forms of life of which animals are capable clearly impose duties of compassion and humanity in their case. I shall not attempt to explain these considered beliefs. They are outside the scope of the theory of justice, and it does not seem possible to extend the contract doctrine so as to include them in a natural way.

—JOHN RAWLS, A Theory of Justice

In conclusion, we hold that circus animals . . . are housed in cramped cages, subjected to fear, hunger, pain, not to mention the undignified way of life they have to live, with no respite and the impugned notification has been issued in conformity with the . . . values of human life, [and] philosophy of the Constitution. . . . Though not homosapiens [*sic*], they are also beings entitled to dignified existence and humane treatment sans cruelty and torture. . . . Therefore, it is not only our fundamental duty to show compassion to our animal friends, but also to recognise and protect their rights. . . . If humans are entitled to fundamental rights, why not animals?

—*NAIR V. UNION OF INDIA*, Kerala High Court, June 2000

"BEINGS ENTITLED TO DIGNIFIED EXISTENCE"

In 55 B.C. the Roman leader Pompey staged a combat between humans and elephants. Surrounded in the arena, the animals perceived that they had no hope of escape. According to Pliny, they then "entreated the crowd, trying to win their compassion with indescribable gestures, bewailing their plight with a sort of lamentation." The audience, moved to pity and anger by their plight, rose to curse Pompey, feeling, writes Cicero, that the elephants had a relation of commonality (*societas*) with the human race.[1]

We humans share a world and its scarce resources with other intelligent creatures. These creatures are capable of dignified existence, as the Kerala High Court says. It is difficult to know precisely what we mean by that phrase, but it is rather clear what it does not mean: the conditions of the circus animals in the case, squeezed into cramped, filthy cages, starved, terrorized, and beaten, given only the minimal care that would make them presentable in the ring the following day. The fact that humans act in ways that deny animals a dignified existence appears to be an issue of justice, and an urgent one, although we shall have to say more to those who would deny this claim. There is no obvious reason why notions of basic justice, entitlement, and law cannot be extended across the species barrier, as the Indian court boldly does.

Before we can perform this extension with any hope of success, however, we need to get clear about what theoretical approach is likely to prove most adequate. I shall argue that the capabilities approach as I have developed it—an approach to issues of basic justice and entitlement and to the making of fundamental political principles[2]—provides better theoretical guidance in this area than that supplied by contractarian and utilitarian approaches to the question of animal entitlements, because it is capable of recognizing a wide range of types of animal dignity, and of corresponding needs for flourishing.

KANTIAN CONTRACTARIANISM: INDIRECT DUTIES, DUTIES OF COMPASSION

Kant's own view about animals is very unpromising. He argues that all duties to animals are merely indirect duties to humanity, in that (as he believes) cruel or kind treatment of animals strengthens tendencies to behave in similar fashion to humans. Thus he rests the case for decent treatment of animals on a fragile empirical claim about psychology. He cannot conceive that beings who (in his view) lack self-consciousness and the capacity for moral reciprocity could possibly be objects of moral duty. More generally, he cannot see that such a being can have dignity, an intrinsic worth.

One may, however, be a contractarian—and indeed, in some sense a Kantian— without espousing these narrow views. John Rawls insists that we have direct moral duties to animals, which he calls "duties of compassion and humanity."[3] But for Rawls these are not issues of justice, and he is explicit that the contract doctrine cannot be extended to deal with these issues, because animals lack those properties of human beings "in virtue of which they are to be treated in accordance with the principles of justice" (*TJ* 504). Only moral persons, defined with reference to the "two moral powers," are subjects of justice.

To some extent, Rawls is led to this conclusion by his Kantian conception of the person, which places great emphasis on rationality and the capacity for moral choice. But it is likely that the very structure of his contractarianism would require such a conclusion, even in the absence of that heavy commitment to rationality. The whole idea of a bargain or contract involving both humans and nonhuman animals is fantastic, suggesting no clear scenario that would assist our thinking. Although Rawls's Original Position, like the state of nature in earlier contractarian theories,[4] is not supposed to be an actual historical situation, it is supposed to be a coherent fiction that can help us think well. This means that it has to have realism, at least, concerning the powers and needs of the parties and their basic circumstances. There is no comparable fiction about our decision to make a deal with other animals that would be similarly coherent and helpful. Although we share a world of scarce resources with animals, and although there is in a sense a state of rivalry among species that is comparable to the rivalry in the state of nature, the asymmetry of power between humans and nonhuman animals is too great to imagine the bargain as a real bargain. Nor can we imagine that the bargain would actually be for mutual advantage, for if we want to protect ourselves from the incursions of wild animals, we can just kill them, as we do. Thus, the Rawlsian condition that no one party to the contract is strong enough to dominate or kill all the others is not met. Thus Rawls's omission of animals from the theory of justice is deeply woven into the very idea of grounding principles of justice on a bargain struck for mutual advantage (on fair terms) out of a situation of rough equality.

To put it another way, all contractualist views conflate two questions, which might have been kept distinct: Who frames the principles? And for whom are the principles framed? That is how rationality ends up being a criterion of membership in the moral community: because the procedure imagines that people are choosing principles *for themselves*. But one might imagine things differently, including in the group for whom principles of justice are included many creatures who do not and could not participate in the framing.

We have not yet shown, however, that Rawls's conclusion is wrong. I have said that the cruel and oppressive treatment of animals raises issues of justice, but I have not really defended that claim against the Rawlsian alternative. What exactly does it mean to say that these are issues of justice, rather than issues of "compassion and humanity"? The emotion of compassion involves the thought that another creature is suffering significantly, and is not (or not mostly) to blame for that suffering.[5] It does not involve the thought that someone is to blame for that suffering. One may have compassion for the victim of a crime, but one may also have compassion for someone who is dying from disease (in a situation where that vulnerability to disease is nobody's fault). "Humanity" I take to be a similar idea. So compassion omits the essential element of blame for wrongdoing. That is the first problem. But suppose we add that element, saying that duties of com-

301

passion involve the thought that it is *wrong* to cause animals suffering. That is, a duty of compassion would not be just a duty to have compassion, but a duty, as a result of one's compassion, to refrain from acts that cause the suffering that occasions the compassion. I believe that Rawls would make this addition, although he certainly does not tell us what he takes duties of compassion to be. What is at stake, further, in the decision to say that the mistreatment of animals is not just morally wrong, but morally wrong in a special way, raising questions of justice?

This is a hard question to answer, since justice is a much-disputed notion, and there are many types of justice, political, ethical, and so forth. But it seems that what we most typically mean when we call a bad act unjust is that the creature injured by that act has an entitlement not to be treated in that way, and an entitlement of a particularly urgent or basic type (since we do not believe that all instances of unkindness, thoughtlessness, and so forth are instances of injustice, even if we do believe that people have a right to be treated kindly, and so on). The sphere of justice is the sphere of basic entitlements. When I say that the mistreatment of animals is unjust, I mean to say not only that it is wrong *of us* to treat them in that way, but also that they have a right, a moral entitlement, not to be treated in that way. It is unfair *to them.* I believe that thinking of animals as active beings who have a good and who are entitled to pursue it naturally leads us to see important damages done to them as unjust. What is lacking in Rawls's account, as in Kant's (though more subtly) is the sense of the animal itself as an agent and a subject, a creature in interaction with whom we live. As we shall see, the capabilities approach does treat animals as agents seeking a flourishing existence; this basic conception, I believe, is one of its greatest strengths.

UTILITARIANISM AND ANIMAL FLOURISHING

Utilitarianism has contributed more than any other ethical theory to the recognition of animal entitlements. Both Bentham and Mill in their time and Peter Singer in our own have courageously taken the lead in freeing ethical thought from the shackles of a narrow species-centered conception of worth and entitlement. No doubt this achievement was connected with the founders' general radicalism and their skepticism about conventional morality, their willingness to follow the ethical argument wherever it leads. These remain very great virtues in the utilitarian position. Nor does utilitarianism make the mistake of running together the question "Who receives justice?" with the question "Who frames the principles of justice?" Justice is sought for all sentient beings, many of whom cannot participate in the framing of principles.

Thus it is in a spirit of alliance that those concerned with animal entitlements might address a few criticisms to the utilitarian view. There are some difficulties with the utilitarian view, in both of its forms. As

Bernard Williams and Amartya Sen usefully analyze the utilitarian position, it has three independent elements: *consequentialism* (the right choice is the one that produces the best overall consequences), *sum-ranking* (the utilities of different people are combined by adding them together to produce a single total), and *hedonism*, or some other substantive theory of the good (such as preference satisfaction).[6] Consequentialism by itself causes the fewest difficulties, since one may always adjust the account of well-being, or the good, in consequentialism so as to admit many important things that utilitarians typically do not make salient: plural and heterogeneous goods, the protection of rights, even personal commitments or agent-centered goods. More or less any moral theory can be consequentialized, that is, put in a form where the matters valued by that theory appear in the account of consequences to be produced.[7] Although I do have some doubts about a comprehensive consequentialism as the best basis for political principles in a pluralistic liberal society, I shall not comment on them at present, but shall turn to the more evidently problematic aspects of the utilitarian view.[8]

Let us next consider the utilitarian commitment to aggregation, or what is called "sum-ranking." Views that measure principles of justice by the outcome they produce need not simply add all the relevant goods together. They may weight them in other ways. For example, one may insist that each and every person has an indefeasible entitlement to come up above a threshold on certain key goods. In addition, a view may, like Rawls's view, focus particularly on the situation of the least well off, refusing to permit inequalities that do not raise that person's position. These ways of considering well-being insist on treating people as ends: They refuse to allow some people's extremely high well-being to be purchased, so to speak, through other people's disadvantage. Even the welfare of society as a whole does not lead us to violate an individual, as Rawls says.

Utilitarianism notoriously refuses such insistence on the separateness and inviolability of persons. Because it is committed to the sum-ranking of all relevant pleasures and pains (or preference satisfactions and frustrations), it has no way of ruling out in advance results that are extremely harsh toward a given class or group. Slavery, the lifelong subordination of some to others, the extremely cruel treatment of some humans or of nonhuman animals—none of this is ruled out by the theory's core conception of justice, which treats all satisfactions as fungible in a single system. Such results will be ruled out, if at all, by empirical considerations regarding total or average well-being. These questions are notoriously indeterminate (especially when the number of individuals who will be born is also unclear, a point I shall take up later). Even if they were not, it seems that the best reason to be against slavery, torture, and lifelong subordination is a reason of justice, not an empirical calculation of total or average well-being. Moreover, if we focus on preference satisfaction, we must confront the problem of adaptive preferences. For while some ways of treating people badly always cause pain (tor-

[margin note] Nassbaum's Complaints

ture, starvation), there are ways of subordinating people that creep into their very desires, making allies out of the oppressed. Animals too can learn submissive or fear-induced preferences. Martin Seligman's experiments, for example, show that dogs who have been conditioned into a mental state of learned helplessness have immense difficulty learning to initiate voluntary movement, if they can ever do so.[9]

There are also problems inherent in the views of the good most prevalent within utilitarianism: hedonism (Bentham) and preference satisfaction (Singer). Pleasure is a notoriously elusive notion. Is it a single feeling, varying only in intensity and duration, or are the different pleasures as qualitatively distinct as the activities with which they are associated? Mill, following Aristotle, believed the latter, but if we once grant that point, we are looking at a view that is very different from standard utilitarianism, which is firmly wedded to the homogeneity of good.[10]

Such a commitment looks like an especially grave error when we consider basic political principles. For each basic entitlement is its own thing, and is not bought off, so to speak, by even a very large amount of another entitlement. Suppose we say to a citizen: We will take away your free speech on Tuesdays between 3 and 4 P.M., but in return, we will give you, every single day, a double amount of basic welfare and health care support. This is just the wrong picture of basic political entitlements. What is being said when we make a certain entitlement basic is that it is important always and for everyone, as a matter of basic justice. The only way to make that point sufficiently clearly is to preserve the qualitative separateness of each distinct element within our list of basic entitlements.

Once we ask the hedonist to admit plural goods, not commensurable on a single quantitative scale, it is natural to ask, further, whether pleasure and pain are the only things we ought to be looking at. Even if one thinks of pleasure as closely linked to activity, and not simply as a passive sensation, making it the sole end leaves out much of the value we attach to activities of various types. There seem to be valuable things in an animal's life other than pleasure, such as free movement and physical achievement, and also altruistic sacrifice for kin and group. The grief of an animal for a dead child or parent, or the suffering of a human friend, also seem to be valuable, a sign of attachments that are intrinsically good. There are also bad pleasures, including some of the pleasures of the circus audience—and it is unclear whether such pleasures should even count positively in the social calculus. Some pleasures of animals in harming other animals may also be bad in this way.

Does preference utilitarianism do better? We have already identified some problems, including the problem of misinformed or malicious preferences and that of adaptive (submissive) preferences. Singer's preference utilitarianism, moreover, defining *preference* in terms of conscious awareness, has no room for deprivations that never register in the animal's consciousness.

But of course animals raised under bad conditions can't imagine the better way of life they have never known, and so the fact that they are not living a more flourishing life will not figure in their awareness. They may still feel pain, and this the utilitarian can consider. What the view cannot consider is all the deprivation of valuable life activity that they do not feel.

Finally, all utilitarian views are highly vulnerable on the question of numbers. The meat industry brings countless animals into the world who would never have existed but for that. For Singer, these births of new animals are not by themselves a bad thing: Indeed, we can expect new births to add to the total of social utility, from which we would then subtract the pain such animals suffer. It is unclear where this calculation would come out. Apart from this question of indeterminacy, it seems unclear that we should even say that these births of new animals are a good thing, if the animals are brought into the world only as tools of human rapacity.

So utilitarianism has great merits, but also great problems.

TYPES OF DIGNITY, TYPES OF FLOURISHING: EXTENDING THE CAPABILITIES APPROACH

The capabilities approach in its current form starts from the notion of human dignity and a life worthy of it. But I shall now argue that it can be extended to provide a more adequate basis for animal entitlements than the other two theories under consideration. The basic moral intuition behind the approach concerns the dignity of a form of life that possesses both deep needs and abilities; its basic goal is to address the need for a rich plurality of life activities. With Aristotle and Marx, the approach has insisted that there is waste and tragedy when a living creature has the innate, or "basic," capability for some functions that are evaluated as important and good, but never gets the opportunity to perform those functions. Failures to educate women, failures to provide adequate health care, failures to extend the freedoms of speech and conscience to all citizens—all these are treated as causing a kind of premature death, the death of a form of flourishing that has been judged to be worthy of respect and wonder. The idea that a human being should have a chance to flourish in its own way, provided it does no harm to others, is thus very deep in the account the capabilities approach gives of the justification of basic political entitlements.

The species norm is evaluative, as I have insisted; it does not simply read off norms from the way nature actually is. The difficult questions this valuational exercise raises for the case of nonhuman animals will be discussed in the following section. But once we have judged that a central human power is one of the good ones, one of the ones whose flourishing defines the good of the creature, we have a strong moral reason for promoting its flourishing and removing obstacles to it.

Dignity and Wonder: The Intuitive Starting Point

The same attitude to natural powers that guides the approach in the case of human beings guides it in the case of all forms of life. For there is a more general attitude behind the respect we have for human powers, and it is very different from the type of respect that animates Kantian ethics. For Kant, only humanity and rationality are worthy of respect and wonder; the rest of nature is just a set of tools. The capabilities approach judges instead, with the biologist Aristotle (who criticized his students' disdain for the study of animals), that there is something wonderful and wonder-inspiring in all the complex forms of animal life.

Aristotle's scientific spirit is not the whole of what the capabilities approach embodies, for we need, in addition, an ethical concern that the functions of life not be impeded, that the dignity of living organisms not be violated. And yet, if we feel wonder looking at a complex organism, that wonder at least suggests the idea that it is good for that being to flourish as the kind of thing it is. And this idea is next door to the ethical judgment that it is wrong when the flourishing of a creature is blocked by the harmful agency of another. That more complex idea lies at the heart of the capabilities approach.

So I believe that the capabilities approach is well placed, intuitively, to go beyond both contractarian and utilitarian views. It goes beyond the contractarian view in its starting point, a basic wonder at living beings, and a wish for their flourishing and for a world in which creatures of many types flourish. It goes beyond the intuitive starting point of utilitarianism because it takes an interest not just in pleasure and pain, but in complex forms of life. It wants to see each thing flourish as the sort of thing it is.

By Whom and for Whom? The Purposes of Social Cooperation

For a contractarian, as we have seen, the question "Who makes the laws and principles?" is treated as having, necessarily, the same answer as the question "For whom are the laws and principles made?" That conflation is dictated by the theory's account of the purposes of social cooperation. But there is obviously no reason at all why these two questions should be put together in this way. The capabilities approach, as so far developed for the human case, looks at the world and asks how to arrange that justice be done in it. Justice is among the intrinsic ends that it pursues. Its parties are imagined looking at all the brutality and misery, the goodness and kindness of the world and trying to think how to make a world in which a core group of very important entitlements, inherent in the notion of human dignity, will be protected. Because they look at the whole of the human world, not just people roughly equal to themselves, they are able to be concerned directly and nonderivatively, as we saw, with the good of the mentally disabled. This feature makes it easy to extend the approach to include human-animal relations.

Let us now begin the extension. The purpose of social cooperation, by analogy and extension, ought to be to live decently together in a world in which many species try to flourish. (Cooperation itself will now assume multiple and complex forms.) The general aim of the capabilities approach in charting political principles to shape the human-animal relationship would be, following the intuitive ideas of the theory, that no animal should be cut off from the chance at a flourishing life and that all animals should enjoy certain positive opportunities to flourish. With due respect for a world that contains many forms of life, we attend with ethical concern to each characteristic type of flourishing and strive that it not be cut off or fruitless.

Such an approach seems superior to contractarianism because it contains direct obligations of justice to animals; it does not make these derivative from or posterior to the duties we have to fellow humans, and it is able to recognize that animals are subjects who have entitlements to flourishing and who thus are subjects of justice, not just objects of compassion. It is superior to utilitarianism because it respects each individual creature, refusing to aggregate the goods of different lives and types of lives. No creature is being used as a means to the ends of others, or of society as a whole. The capabilities approach also refuses to aggregate across the diverse constituents of each life and type of life. Thus, unlike utilitarianism, it can keep in focus the fact that each species has a different form of life and different ends; moreover, within a given species, each life has multiple and heterogeneous ends.

How Comprehensive?

In the human case, the capabilities approach does not operate with a fully comprehensive conception of the good, because of the respect it has for the diverse ways in which people choose to live their lives in a pluralistic society. It aims at securing some core entitlements that are held to be implicit in the idea of a life with dignity, but it aims at capability, not functioning, and it focuses on a small list. In the case of human-animal relations, the need for restraint is even more acute, since animals will not in fact be participating directly in the framing of political principles, and thus they cannot revise them over time should they prove inadequate.

And yet there is a countervailing consideration: Human beings affect animals' opportunities for flourishing pervasively, and it is hard to think of a species that one could simply leave alone to flourish in its own way. The human species dominates the other species in a way that no human individual or nation has ever dominated other humans. Respect for other species' opportunities for flourishing suggests, then, that human law must include robust, positive political commitments to the protection of animals, even though, had human beings not so pervasively interfered with animals' ways of life, the most respectful course might have been simply to leave them alone, living the lives that they make for themselves.

The Species and the Individual

What should the focus of these commitments be? It seems that here, as in the human case, the focus should be the individual creature. The capabilities approach attaches no importance to increased numbers as such; its focus is on the well-being of existing creatures and the harm that is done to them when their powers are blighted.

As for the continuation of species, this would have little moral weight as a consideration of justice (though it might have aesthetic significance or some other sort of ethical significance), if species were just becoming extinct because of factors having nothing to do with human action that affects individual creatures. But species are becoming extinct because human beings are killing their members and damaging their natural environments. Thus, damage to species occurs through damage to individuals, and this individual damage should be the focus of ethical concern within the capabilities approach.

Do Levels of Complexity Matter?

Almost all ethical views of animal entitlements hold that there are morally relevant distinctions among forms of life. Killing a mosquito is not the same sort of thing as killing a chimpanzee. But the question is: What sort of difference is relevant for basic justice? Singer, following Bentham, puts the issue in terms of sentience. Animals of many kinds can suffer bodily pain, and it is always bad to cause pain to a sentient being. If there are nonsentient or barely sentient animals—and it appears that crustaceans, mollusks, sponges, and the other creatures Aristotle called "stationary animals" are such creatures—there is either no harm or only a trivial harm done in killing them. Among the sentient creatures, moreover, there are some who can suffer additional harms through their cognitive capacity: A few animals can foresee and mind their own deaths, and others will have conscious, sentient interests in continuing to live that are frustrated by death. The painless killing of an animal that does not foresee its own death or take a conscious interest in the continuation of its life is, for Singer and Bentham, not bad, for all badness, for them, consists in the frustration of interests, understood as forms of conscious awareness.[11] Singer is not, then, saying that some animals are inherently more worthy of esteem than others. He is simply saying that, if we agree with him that all harms reside in sentience, the creature's form of life limits the conditions under which it can actually suffer harm.

Similarly, James Rachels, whose view does not focus on sentience alone, holds that the level of complexity of a creature affects what can be a harm for it.[12] What is relevant to the harm of pain is sentience; what is relevant to the harm of a specific type of pain is a specific type of sentience (e.g., the ability to imagine one's own death). What is relevant to the harm of diminished freedom is a capacity for freedom or autonomy. It would make no sense to complain that a worm is being deprived of autonomy, or a rabbit of the right to vote.

What should the capabilities approach say about this issue? It seems to me that it should not follow Aristotle in saying that there is a natural ranking of forms of life, some being intrinsically more worthy of support and wonder than others. That consideration might have evaluative significance of some other kind, but it seems dubious that it should affect questions of basic justice.

Rachels's view offers good guidance here. Because the capabilities approach finds ethical significance in the flourishing of basic (innate) capabilities—those that are evaluated as both good and central (see the section on evaluating animal capabilities)—it will also find harm in the thwarting or blighting of those capabilities. More complex forms of life have more and more complex capabilities to be blighted, so they can suffer more and different types of harm. Level of life is relevant not because it gives different species differential worth per se, but because the type and degree of harm a creature can suffer varies with its form of life.

At the same time, I believe that the capabilities approach should admit the wisdom in utilitarianism. Sentience is not the only thing that matters for basic justice, but it seems plausible to consider sentience a threshold condition for membership in the community of beings who have entitlements based on justice. Thus, killing a sponge does not seem to be a matter of basic justice.

Does the Species Matter?

For the utilitarians, and for Rachels, the species to which a creature belongs has no moral relevance. All that is morally relevant are the capacities of the individual creature: Rachels calls this view "moral individualism." Utilitarian writers are fond of comparing apes to young children and to mentally disabled humans. The capabilities approach, by contrast, with its talk of characteristic functioning and forms of life, seems to attach some significance to species membership as such. What type of significance is this?

We should admit that there is much to be learned from reflection on the continuum of life. Capacities do crisscross and overlap; a chimpanzee may have more capacity for empathy and perspectival thinking than a very young child or an older autistic child. And capacities that humans sometimes arrogantly claim for themselves alone are found very widely in nature. But it seems wrong to conclude from such facts that species membership is morally and politically irrelevant. A mentally disabled child is actually very different from a chimpanzee, though in certain respects some of her capacities may be comparable. Such a child's life is tragic in a way that the life of a chimpanzee is not tragic: She is cut off from forms of flourishing that, but for the disability, she might have had, disabilities that it is the job of science to prevent or cure, wherever that is possible. There is something blighted and disharmonious in her life, whereas the life of a chimpanzee may be perfectly flourishing. Her social and political functioning is threatened by these disabilities, in a way that the normal functioning of a chimpanzee in the community of chimpanzees is not threatened by its cognitive endowment.

All this is relevant when we consider issues of basic justice. For a child born with Down syndrome, it is crucial that the political culture in which he lives make a big effort to extend to him the fullest benefits of citizenship he can attain, through health benefits, education, and the reeducation of the public culture. That is so because he can only flourish as a human being. He has no option of flourishing as a happy chimpanzee. For a chimpanzee, on the other hand, it seems to me that expensive efforts to teach language, while interesting and revealing, are not matters of basic justice. A chimpanzee flourishes in its own way, communicating with its own community in a perfectly adequate manner that has gone on for ages.

In short, the species norm (duly evaluated) tells us what the appropriate benchmark is for judging whether a given creature has decent opportunities for flourishing.

EVALUATING ANIMAL CAPABILITIES: NO NATURE WORSHIP

In the human case, the capabilities view does not attempt to extract norms directly from some facts about human nature. We should know what we can about the innate capacities of human beings, and this information is valuable, in telling us what our opportunities are and what our dangers might be. But we must begin by evaluating the innate powers of human beings, asking which ones are the good ones, the ones that are central to the notion of a decently flourishing human life, a life with dignity. Thus not only evaluation but also ethical evaluation is put into the approach from the start. Many things that are found in human life are not on the capabilities list.

There is a danger in any theory that alludes to the characteristic flourishing and form of life of a species: the danger of romanticizing nature, or suggesting that things are in order as they are, if only we would stop interfering. This danger looms large when we turn from the human case, where it seems inevitable that we will need to do some moral evaluating, to the animal case, where evaluating is elusive and difficult. Inherent in at least some environmentalist writing is a picture of nature as harmonious and wise, and of humans as wasteful overreachers who would live better were we to get in tune with this fine harmony. This image of nature was already very sensibly attacked by John Stuart Mill in his great essay "Nature," which pointed out that nature, far from being morally normative, is actually violent, heedless of moral norms, prodigal, full of conflict, harsh to humans and animals both. A similar view lies at the heart of much modern ecological thinking, which now stresses the inconstancy and imbalance of nature,[13] arguing, inter alia, that many of the natural ecosystems that we admire as such actually sustain themselves to the extent that they do only on account of various forms of human intervention.

Thus, a no-evaluation view, which extracts norms directly from observation of animals' characteristic ways of life, is probably not going to be a helpful way of promoting the good of animals. Instead, we need a careful evaluation of both "nature" and possible changes. Respect for nature should not and cannot mean just leaving nature as it is, and must involve careful normative arguments about what plausible goals might be.

In the case of humans, the primary area in which the political conception inhibits or fails to foster tendencies that are pervasive in human life is the area of harm to others. Animals, of course, pervasively cause harm, both to members of their own species and, far more often, to members of other species.

In both of these cases, the capabilities theorist will have a strong inclination to say that the harm-causing capabilities in question are not among those that should be protected by political and social principles. But if we leave these capabilities off the list, how can we claim to be promoting flourishing lives? Even though the capabilities approach is not utilitarian and does not hold that all good is in sentience, it will still be difficult to maintain that a creature who feels frustration at the inhibition of its predatory capacities is living a flourishing life. A human being can be expected to learn to flourish without homicide and, let us hope, even without most killing of animals. But a lion who is given no exercise for its predatory capacity appears to suffer greatly.

Here the capabilities view may, however, distinguish two aspects of the capability in question. The capability to kill small animals, defined as such, is not valuable, and political principles can omit it (and even inhibit it in some cases, to be discussed in the following section). But the capability to exercise one's predatory nature so as to avoid the pain of frustration may well have value, if the pain of frustration is considerable. Zoos have learned how to make this distinction. Noticing that they were giving predatory animals insufficient exercise for their predatory capacities, they had to face the question of the harm done to smaller animals by allowing these capabilities to be exercised. Should they give a tiger a tender gazelle to crunch on? The Bronx Zoo has found that it can give the tiger a large ball on a rope, whose resistance and weight symbolize the gazelle. The tiger seems satisfied. Wherever predatory animals are living under direct human support and control, these solutions seem the most ethically sound.

POSITIVE AND NEGATIVE, CAPABILITY
AND FUNCTIONING

In the human case, there is a traditional distinction between positive and negative duties that it seems important to call into question. Traditional moralities hold that we have a strict duty not to commit aggression and fraud, but we have no correspondingly strict duty to stop hunger or disease, nor to give money to promote their cessation.[14]

The capabilities approach calls this distinction into question. All the human capabilities require affirmative support, usually including state action. This is just as true of protecting property and personal security as it is of health care, just as true of the political and civil liberties as it is of providing adequate shelter.

In the case of animals, unlike the human case, there might appear to be some room for a positive-negative distinction that makes some sense. It seems at least coherent to say that the human community has the obligation to refrain from certain egregious harms toward animals, but that it is not obliged to support the welfare of all animals, in the sense of ensuring them adequate food, shelter, and health care. The animals themselves have the rest of the task of ensuring their own flourishing.

There is much plausibility in this contention. And certainly if our political principles simply ruled out the many egregious forms of harm to animals, they would have done quite a lot. But the contention, and the distinction it suggests, cannot be accepted in full. First of all, large numbers of animals live under humans' direct control: domestic animals, farm animals, and those members of wild species that are in zoos or other forms of captivity. Humans have direct responsibility for the nutrition and health care of these animals, as even our defective current systems of law acknowledge.[15] Animals in the "wild" appear to go their way unaffected by human beings. But of course that can hardly be so in many cases in today's world. Human beings pervasively affect the habitats of animals, determining opportunities for nutrition, free movement, and other aspects of flourishing.

Thus, while we may still maintain that one primary area of human responsibility to animals is that of refraining from a whole range of bad acts (to be discussed shortly), we cannot plausibly stop there. The only questions should be how extensive our duties are, and how to balance them against appropriate respect for the autonomy of a species.

In the human case, one way in which the approach respects autonomy is to focus on capability, and not functioning, as the legitimate political goal. But paternalistic treatment (which aims at functioning rather than capability) is warranted wherever the individual's capacity for choice and autonomy is compromised (thus, for children and the severely mentally disabled). This principle suggests that paternalism is usually appropriate when we are dealing with nonhuman animals. That conclusion, however, should be qualified by our previous endorsement of the idea that species autonomy, in pursuit of flourishing, is part of the good for nonhuman animals. How, then, should the two principles be combined, and can they be coherently combined?

I believe that they can be combined, if we adopt a type of paternalism that is highly sensitive to the different forms of flourishing that different species pursue. It is no use saying that we should just let tigers flourish in their own way, given that human activity ubiquitously affects the possibilities for tigers to flourish. This being the case, the only decent alternative to complete neglect of tiger flourishing is a policy that thinks carefully about the flourishing of tigers and what habitat that requires, and then tries hard to create such habitats. In the case of domestic animals, an intelligent paternalism would encourage training, discipline, and even, where appropriate, strenuous training focused on special excellences of a breed (such as the border collie or the hunter-jumper). But the animal, like a child, will retain certain entitlements, which they hold regardless of what their human guardian thinks about it. They are not merely objects for human beings' use and control.

TOWARD BASIC POLITICAL PRINCIPLES: THE CAPABILITIES LIST

It is now time to see whether we can actually use the human basis of the capabilities approach to map out some basic political principles that will guide law and public policy in dealing with animals. The list I have defended as useful in the human case is as follows:

The Central Human Capabilities

1. *Life.* Being able to live to the end of a human life of normal length; not dying prematurely, or before one's life is so reduced as to be not worth living.
2. *Bodily Health.* Being able to have good health, including reproductive health; to be adequately nourished; to have adequate shelter.
3. *Bodily Integrity.* Being able to move freely from place to place; to be secure against violent assault, including sexual assault and domestic violence; having opportunities for sexual satisfaction and for choice in matters of reproduction.
4. *Senses, Imagination, and Thought.* Being able to use the senses, to imagine, think, and reason—and to do these things in a "truly human" way, a way informed and cultivated by an adequate education, including, but by no means limited to, literacy and basic mathematical and scientific training. Being able to use imagination and thought in connection with experiencing and producing works and events of one's own choice, religious, literary, musical, and so forth. Being able to use one's

313

mind in ways protected by guarantees of freedom of expression with respect to both political and artistic speech, and freedom of religious exercise. Being able to have pleasurable experiences and to avoid non-beneficial pain.

5. *Emotions.* Being able to have attachments to things and people outside ourselves; to love those who love and care for us and to grieve at their absence; in general, to love, to grieve, to experience longing, gratitude, and justified anger. Not having one's emotional development blighted by fear and anxiety. (Supporting this capability means supporting forms of human association that can be shown to be crucial to our development.)

6. *Practical Reason.* Being able to form a conception of the good and to engage in critical reflection about the planning of one's life. (This entails protection for the liberty of conscience and religious observance.)

7. *Affiliation.* (A) Being able to live with and toward others, to recognize and show concern for other human beings, to engage in various forms of social interaction; to be able to imagine the situation of another. (Protecting this capability means protecting institutions that constitute and nourish such forms of affiliation, and also protecting the freedom of assembly and political speech.) (B) Having the social bases of self-respect and nonhumiliation; being able to be treated as a dignified being whose worth is equal to that of others. (This entails provisions of nondiscrimination on the basis of race, sex, sexual orientation, ethnicity, caste, religion, national origin.)

8. *Other Species.* Being able to live with concern for and in relation to animals, plants, and the world of nature.

9. *Play.* Being able to laugh, to play, to enjoy recreational activities.

10. *Control over One's Environment.* (A) Political. Being able to participate effectively in political choices that govern one's life; having the right of political participation; protections of free speech and association. (B) Material. Being able to hold property (both land and movable goods), and having property rights on an equal basis with others; having the right to seek employment on an equal basis with others; having the freedom from unwarranted search and seizure. In work, being able to work as a human being, exercising practical reason and entering into meaningful relationships of mutual recognition with other workers.

Although the entitlements of animals are species specific, the main large categories of the existing list, suitably fleshed out, turn out to be a good basis for a sketch of some basic political principles.

1. *Life.* In the capabilities approach, all animals are entitled to continue their lives, whether or not they have such a conscious interest. All sentient animals have a secure entitlement against gratuitous killing for sport. Killing for luxury items such as fur falls in this category, and should be banned. On the other hand, intelligently respectful paternal-

ism supports euthanasia for elderly animals in pain. In the middle are the very difficult cases, such as the question of predation to control populations, and the question of killing for food. The reason these cases are so difficult is that animals will die anyway in nature, and often more painfully. Painless predation might well be preferable to allowing the animal to be torn to bits in the wild or starved through overpopulation. As for food, the capabilities approach agrees with utilitarianism in being most troubled by the torture of living animals. If animals were really killed in a painless fashion, after a healthy and free-ranging life, what then? Killings of extremely young animals would still be problematic, but it seems unclear that the balance of considerations supports a complete ban on killings for food.

2. *Bodily Health.* One of the most central entitlements of animals is the entitlement to a healthy life. Where animals are directly under human control, it is relatively clear what policies this entails: laws banning cruel treatment and neglect; laws banning the confinement and ill treatment of animals in the meat and fur industries; laws forbidding harsh or cruel treatment for working animals, including circus animals; laws regulating zoos and aquariums, mandating adequate nutrition and space. Many of these laws already exist, although they are not well enforced. The striking asymmetry in current practice is that animals being raised for food are not protected in the way other animals are protected. This asymmetry must be eliminated..

3. *Bodily Integrity.* This goes closely with the preceding. Under the capabilities approach, animals have direct entitlements against violations of their bodily integrity by violence, abuse, and other forms of harmful treatment—whether or not the treatment in question is painful. Thus the declawing of cats would probably be banned under this rubric, on the grounds that it prevents the cat from flourishing in its own characteristic way, even though it may be done in a painfree manner and cause no subsequent pain. On the other hand, forms of training that, though involving discipline, equip the animal to manifest excellences that are part of its characteristic capabilities profile would not be eliminated.

4. *Senses, Imagination, and Thought.* For humans, this capability creates a wide range of entitlements: to appropriate education, to free speech and artistic expression, to the freedom of religion. It also includes a more general entitlement to pleasurable experiences and the avoidance of nonbeneficial pain. By now it ought to be rather obvious where the latter point takes us in thinking about animals: toward laws banning harsh, cruel, and abusive treatment and ensuring animals' access to sources of pleasure, such as free movement in an environment that stimulates and pleases the senses. The freedom-related part of this capability has no precise analogue, and yet we can come up with appropriate analogues in the case of each type of animal, by asking

what choices and areas of freedom seem most important to each. Clearly this reflection would lead us to reject close confinement and to regulate the places in which animals of all kinds are kept for spaciousness, light and shade, and the variety of opportunities they offer the animals for a range of characteristic activities. Again, the capabilities approach seems superior to utilitarianism in its ability to recognize such entitlements, for few animals will have a conscious interest, as such, in variety and space.

5. *Emotions.* Animals have a wide range of emotions. All or almost all sentient animals have fear. Many animals can experience anger, resentment, gratitude, grief, envy, and joy. A small number—those who are capable of perspectival thinking—can experience compassion.[16] Like human beings, they are entitled to lives in which it is open to them to have attachments to others, to love and care for others, and not to have those attachments warped by enforced isolation or the deliberate infliction of fear. We understand well what this means where our cherished domestic animals are in question. Oddly, we do not extend the same consideration to animals we think of as "wild." Until recently, zoos took no thought for the emotional needs of animals, and animals being used for research were often treated with gross carelessness in this regard, being left in isolation and confinement when they might easily have had decent emotional lives.[17]

6. *Practical Reason.* In each case, we need to ask to what extent the creature has a capacity to frame goals and projects and to plan its life. To the extent that this capacity is present, it ought to be supported, and this support requires many of the same policies already suggested by capability 4: plenty of room to move around, opportunities for a variety of activities.

7. *Affiliation.* In the human case, this capability has two parts: an interpersonal part (being able to live with and toward others) and a more public part, focused on self-respect and nonhumiliation. It seems to me that the same two parts are pertinent for nonhuman animals. Animals are entitled to opportunities to form attachments (as in capability 5) and to engage in characteristic forms of bonding and interrelationship. They are also entitled to relations with humans, where humans enter the picture, that are rewarding and reciprocal, rather than tyrannical. At the same time, they are entitled to live in a world public culture that respects them and treats them as dignified beings. This entitlement does not just mean protecting them from instances of humiliation that they will feel as painful. The capabilities approach here extends more broadly than utilitarianism, holding that animals are entitled to world policies that grant them political rights and the legal status of dignified beings, whether they understand that status or not.

8. *Other Species.* If human beings are entitled to "be able to live with concern for and in relation to animals, plants, and the world of nature," so

too are other animals, in relation to species not their own, including
the human species, and the rest of the natural world. This capability,
seen from both the human and the animal side, calls for the gradual
formation of an interdependent world in which all species will enjoy
cooperative and mutually supportive relations with one another.
Nature is not that way and never has been. So it calls, in a very general
way, for the gradual supplanting of the natural by the just.

9. *Play.* This capability is obviously central to the lives of all sentient animals. It calls for many of the same policies we have already discussed:
provision of adequate space, light, and sensory stimulation in living
places, and, above all, the presence of other species members.

10. *Control over One's Environment.* In the human case, this capability has
two prongs, the political and the material. The political is defined in
terms of active citizenship and rights of political participation. For
nonhuman animals, the important thing is being part of a political
conception that is framed so as to respect them and that is committed
to treating them justly. It is important, however, that animals have
entitlements directly, so that a human guardian has standing to go to
court, as with children, to vindicate those entitlements. On the material side, for nonhuman animals, the analogue to property rights is
respect for the territorial integrity of their habitats, whether domestic
or in the wild.

Are there animal capabilities not covered by this list, suitably specified?
It seems to me not, although in the spirit of the capabilities approach we
should insist that the list is open-ended, subject to supplementation or
deletion.

In general, the capabilities approach suggests that it is appropriate for
nations to include in their constitutions or other founding statements of
principle a commitment to animals as subjects of political justice and a
commitment that animals will be treated with dignity. The constitution
might also spell out some of the very general principles suggested by this capabilities list. The rest of the work of protecting animal entitlements might
be done by suitable legislation and by court cases demanding the enforcement of the law, where it is not enforced. At the same time, many of the issues covered by this approach cannot be dealt with by nations in isolation,
but can only be addressed by international cooperation. So we also need international accords committing the world community to the protection of
animal habitats and the eradication of cruel practices.

THE INELIMINABILITY OF CONFLICT

In the human case, we often face the question of conflict between one capability and another. But if the capabilities list and its thresholds are suitably

designed, we ought to say that the presence of conflict between one capability and another is a sign that society has gone wrong somewhere.[18] We should focus on long-term planning that will create a world in which all the capabilities can be secured to all citizens.

Our world contains persistent and often tragic conflicts between the well-being of human beings and the well-being of animals. Some bad treatment of animals can be eliminated without serious losses in human well-being: Such is the case with the use of animals for fur, and the brutal and confining treatment of animals used for food. The use of animals for food in general is a much more difficult case, since nobody really knows what the impact on the world environment would be of a total switch to vegetarian sources of protein, or the extent to which such a diet could be made compatible with the health of all the world's children. A still more difficult problem is the use of animals in research.

A lot can be done to improve the lives of research animals without stopping useful research. As Steven Wise has shown, primates used in research often live in squalid, lonely conditions while they are used as medical subjects. This of course is totally unnecessary and morally unacceptable and could be ended without ending the research. Some research that is done is unnecessary and can be terminated, for example, the testing of cosmetics on rabbits, which seems to have been bypassed without loss of quality by some cosmetic firms. But much important research with major consequences for the life and health of human beings and other animals will inflict disease, pain, and death on at least some animals, even under the best conditions.

I do not favor stopping all such research. What I do favor is (a) asking whether the research is really necessary for a major human capability; (b) focusing on the use of less-complex sentient animals where possible, on the grounds that they suffer fewer and lesser harms from such research; (c) improving the conditions of research animals, including palliative terminal care when they have contracted a terminal illness, and supportive interactions with both humans and other animals; (d) removing the psychological brutality that is inherent in so much treatment of animals for research; (e) choosing topics cautiously and seriously, so that no animal is harmed for a frivolous reason; and (f) a constant effort to develop experimental methods (for example, computer simulations) that do not have these bad consequences.

Above all, it means constant public discussion of these issues, together with an acknowledgment that such uses of animals in research are tragic, violating basic entitlements. Such public acknowledgments are far from useless. They state what is morally true, and thus acknowledge the dignity of animals and our own culpability toward them. They reaffirm dispositions to behave well toward them where no such urgent exigencies intervene. Finally, they prompt us to seek a world in which the pertinent research could in fact be done in other ways.

TOWARD A TRULY GLOBAL JUSTICE

It has been obvious for a long time that the pursuit of global justice requires the inclusion of many people and groups who were not previously included as fully equal subjects of justice: the poor; members of religious, ethnic, and racial minorities; and more recently women, the disabled, and inhabitants of nations distant from one's own.

But a truly global justice requires not simply that we look across the world for other fellow species members who are entitled to a decent life. It also requires looking around the world at the other sentient beings with whose lives our own are inextricably and complexly intertwined. Traditional contractarian approaches to the theory of justice did not and, in their very form, could not confront these questions as questions of justice. Utilitarian approaches boldly did so, and they deserve high praise. But in the end, I have argued, utilitarianism is too homogenizing—both across lives and with respect to the heterogeneous constituents of each life—to provide us with an adequate theory of animal justice. The capabilities approach, which begins from an ethically attuned wonder before each form of animal life, offers a model that does justice to the complexity of animal lives and their strivings for flourishing. Such a model seems an important part of a fully global theory of justice.

NOTES

This essay derives from my Tanner Lectures in 2003 and is published by courtesy of the University of Utah Press and the Trustees of the Tanner Lectures on Human Values.

1. The incident is discussed in Pliny *Nat. Hist.* 8.7.20–21, Cicero *Ad Fam.* 7.1.3; see also Dio Cassius *Hist.* 39, 38, 2–4. See the discussion in Richard Sorabji, *Animal Minds and Human Morals: The Origins of the Western Debate* (Ithaca, N.Y.: Cornell University Press, 1993), 124–125.
2. For this approach, see Martha C. Nussbaum, *Women and Human Development* (Cambridge: Cambridge University Press, 2000), and "Capabilities as Fundamental Entitlements: Sen and Social Justice," *Feminist Economics* 9 (2003): 33–59. The approach was pioneered by Amartya Sen within economics, and is used by him in some rather different ways, without a definite commitment to a normative theory of justice.
3. All references are to John Rawls, *A Theory of Justice* (Cambridge, Mass.: Harvard University Press, 1971), hereafter *TJ.*
4. Rawls himself makes the comparison at *TJ* 12; his analogue to the state of nature is the equality of the parties in the Original Position.
5. See the analysis in Martha C. Nussbaum, *Upheavals of Thought: The Intelligence of Emotions* (Cambridge: Cambridge University Press, 2001), ch. 6; thus far the analysis is uncontroversial, recapitulating a long tradition of analysis.
6. See Amartya Sen and Bernard Williams, introduction to *Utilitarianism and Beyond* (Cambridge: Cambridge University Press, 1982), 3–4.

7. See the comment by Nussbaum in *Goodness and Advice*, Judith Jarvis Thomson's Tanner Lectures (Princeton, N.J.: Princeton University Press, 2000), discussing work along these lines by Amartya Sen and others.

8. Briefly put, my worries are those of Rawls in *Political Liberalism* (New York: Columbia University Press, 1996), who points out that it is illiberal for political principles to contain any comprehensive account of what is best. Instead, political principles should be committed to a partial set of ethical norms endorsed for political purposes, leaving it to citizens to fill out the rest of the ethical picture in accordance with their own comprehensive conceptions of value, religious or secular. Thus I would be happy with a partial political consequentialism, but not with comprehensive consequentialism, as a basis for political principles.

9. Martin Seligman, *Helplessness: On Development, Depression, and Death* (New York: Freeman, 1975).

10. Here I agree with Thomson (who is thinking mostly about Moore); see *Goodness and Advice*.

11. Peter Singer, "Animals and the Value of Life," in *Matters of Life and Death: New Introductory Essays on Moral Philosophy*, ed. Tom Regan (New York: Random House, 1980), 356.

12. James Rachels, *Created from Animals: The Moral Implications of Darwinism* (New York: Oxford University Press, 1990).

13. Daniel B. Botkin, "Adjusting Law to Nature's Discordant Harmonies," *Duke Environmental Law and Policy Forum* 7 (1996): 25–37.

14. See the critique by Martha Nussbaum in "Duties of Justice, Duties of Material Aid: Cicero's Problematic Legacy," *Journal of Political Philosophy* 7 (1999): 1–31.

15. The laws do not cover all animals, in particular, not animals who are going to be used for food or fur.

16. On all this, see Nussbaum, *Upheavals of Thought*, ch. 2.

17. See Steven Wise, *Rattling the Cage: Toward Legal Rights for Animals* (Cambridge, Mass.: Perseus, 2000), ch. 1.

18. See Martha C. Nussbaum, "The Costs of Tragedy: Some Moral Implications of Cost-Benefit Analysis," in *Cost-Benefit Analysis*, ed. Matthew D. Adler and Eric A. Posner (Chicago: University of Chicago Press, 2001), 169–200.

BIBLIOGRAPHIC ESSAY

There is an extensive literature concerning animal rights and animal welfare. This brief note is not intended to offer a comprehensive bibliography of this literature, but only to provide an entry into that body of work.

Early discussions of the moral status of animals may be found in Humphry Primatt, *A Dissertation on the Duty of Mercy and Sin of Cruelty to Brute Animals* (1776), and Henry S. Salt, *Animals' Rights: Considered in Relation to Social Progress* (1892). Richard Sorabji presents an excellent discussion of the Western philosophical tradition as it concerns animals in *Animal Minds and Human Morals: The Origins of the Western Debate* (1993). *Animal Rights and Human Obligations* (Tom Regan and Peter Singer, eds., 2d ed. 1989) and *Political Theory and Animal Rights* (Paul A. B. Clarke and Andrew Linzey, eds., 1990) are collections of excerpts about the moral status of animals from a wide range of present and past philosophers and political theorists. A useful general reference work is *Encyclopedia of Animal Rights and Animal Welfare* (Marc Bekoff and Carron A. Meaney, eds., 1998).

In 1971, Stanley Godlovitch, Roslind Godlovitch, and John Harris edited a collection of essays entitled *Animals, Men and Morals: An Enquiry into the Maltreatment of Non-Humans* that may be regarded as inaugurating the modern period of philosophical scholarship on the topic. This was followed in 1975 by the influential *Animal Liberation: A New Ethics for Our Treatment of Animals*, in which Peter Singer elaborates on the position of Jeremy Bentham that the principle of equal consideration applies to animal interests in not suffering. Singer also argues that, for the most part, animals do not have an interest in their lives, that is, in continuing to live. Therefore, we may use animals for human purposes as long as we give equal consideration to animal interests in not suffering. Singer is a utilitarian and, like Bentham, eschews moral rights and maintains that animal (and human) interests may be sacrificed if to do so will promote overall social utility. In *The Moral Status of Animals* (1977), Stephen R. L. Clark argues that traditional liberal principles prohibiting unnecessary suffering are sufficient to conclude that much of our animal use is not morally justifiable.

The view that animals have moral rights and that their interests may not be sacrificed for consequential reasons is developed by Tom Regan in *The Case for Animal Rights* (1983). Regan's theory is, however, limited to those animals that have preference autonomy, meaning that they have preferences and are capable of acting on them, and does not extend to those that are merely sentient. Regan argues that all beings with preference autonomy have equal inherent value that precludes their being used exclusively as means to the ends of others. In *Introduction to Animal Rights: Your Child or the Dog?* (2000), Gary L. Francione presents a rights theory that applies to all sentient animals irrespective of their other cognitive characteristics. Francione maintains that if animals are to have any moral significance at all, they must be accorded one basic right: the right not to be treated as property. Like Regan, Francione concludes that all institutionalized animal exploitation must be abolished and not merely regulated. Evelyn B. Pluhar, *Beyond Prejudice: The Moral Significance of Human and Nonhuman Animals* (1995), also presents a theory that rejects Regan's limitation of rights to animals with preference autonomy but does not require the eventual demise of all practices involving domesticated animals.

Various theorists have attempted to bridge the gap between the utilitarian and rights-based approaches to animal issues. For example, in "Animal Welfare and Animal Rights" (13 J. Med. & Phil. 159 [1988]), L. W. Sumner presents a theory based on rule utilitarianism that provides rights-type protection for animal interests as a general matter, but allows these interests to be sacrificed for consequential reasons in certain circumstances. Others reject altogether the desirability or possibility of developing a unified moral theory concerning the human-animal relationship. For example, S. F. Sapontzis, *Morals, Reason, and Animals* (1987), criticizes the reliance on abstract moral norms and characterizes ethics as an activity that is grounded in cultural traditions that are neither exclusively rights based nor utilitarian, but that are capable of development within a tradition. Although the Western tradition has usually discounted animal interests, certain elements of that tradition, such as the development of moral virtues, the reduction of suffering, and the importance of fairness, all militate against our use of animals. Mary Midgley, *Animals and Why They Matter* (1983), argues that an emphasis on justice, equal consideration, rights, or utility result in an oversimplification of moral issues, including those involving animals. Midgley challenges the notion that animal interests are morally unimportant, but she maintains that a preference for our own species is acceptable under some circumstances. In *Taking Animals Seriously: Mental Life and Moral Status* (1996), David DeGrazia claims not to rely on rights or welfare theories, and argues that prevalent ethical attitudes about animals are simply incoherent.

Ecofeminists argue that theories involving rights or utility are hierarchical and patriarchal and that the human-animal relationship should be informed by an ethic of care. *See, e.g., Beyond Animal Rights: A Feminist Caring Ethic for the Treatment of Animals* (Josephine Donovan and Carol J. Adams, eds., 1996). Ted Benton, *Natural Relations: Ecology, Animal Rights and Social Justice* (1993); Jim Mason, *An Unnatural Order: Uncovering the Roots of Our Domination of Nature and Each Other* (1993); David Nibert, *Animal Rights/Human Rights: Entanglements of Oppression and Liberation* (2002); and Barbara Noske, *Beyond Boundaries: Humans and Animals* (1997), explore the moral status of animals as part of an overall discussion of social justice and a critique of capitalism. James Rachels, *Created From Animals: The Moral Implications of Darwinism* (1990); Rosemary Rodd, *Biology, Ethics, and Animals* (1990); and Bernard E. Rollin, *Animal Rights and Human Morality* (1992), emphasize the importance of modern science in assessing our moral obligations to animals. In "Animal Rights: The Need for a Theoretical Basis" (114 Harv. L. Rev. 1506 [2001]), Martha C. Nussbaum argues that our moral theories about animals are hopelessly deficient in various respects and a theoretical basis remains to be provided.

An early discussion concerning the legal status of animals may be found in John Hall Ingham, *The Law of Animals: A Treatise on Property in Animals, Wild and Domestic and the Rights and Responsibilities Arising Therefrom* (1900). In *Animal Law* (1983), David S. Favre and Murray Loring describe the various consequences of animal ownership, but apart from describing types of anticruelty laws, the authors do not discuss the jurisprudential issues raised by the legal status of animals as property. These issues are first discussed in Gary L. Francione, *Animals, Property, and the Law* (1995), in which Francione argues that the status of animals as property precludes their having respect-based rights and ensures that there will never be a meaningful balance of human and animal interests as is supposedly required by animal welfare laws. According to Francione, because animals are our property, the law will generally require their interests to be observed only to the extent that it facilitates their use. Animal welfare laws (with modifications) are defended by Mike Radford, *Animal Welfare Law in Britain: Regulation and Responsibility* (2001), and Robert Garner, *Animals, Politics and Morality* (1993). Christopher D. Stone, "Should Trees Have Standing?—Toward Legal Rights for Natural Objects" (45 S. Cal. L. Rev. 450 [1972]), argues that animals and the environment may coherently be regarded as possessing legal rights. In *Drawing the Line: Science and the Case for Animal Rights* (2002) and *Rattling the Cage: Toward Legal Rights for Animals* (2000), Steven M. Wise argues that animals that are cognitively similar to humans should be accorded legal rights. Wise's position is similar to that proposed in *The Great Ape Project* (Paola Cavalieri and Peter Singer, eds., 1993), which maintains that cognitive and genetic similarities to humans justify extending legal protection to the great apes. In "From Property to Person: The Case of Evelyn Hart" (11 Seton Hall

Const. L. J. 1 [2000]), Lee Hall and Anthony Jon Waters argue that the cognitive attributes of the great apes are sufficient for legal personhood, but that sentience is the only characteristic that should be regarded as morally necessary. The Animal Legal Defense Fund and the students at Lewis and Clark, Northwestern School of Law, produce an annual journal called *Animal Law*, which contains articles concerning animals and the law.

The topic of religion and animals is discussed by a number of scholars. For example, *Animal Sacrifices: Religious Perspectives on the Use of Animals in Science* (Tom Regan, ed., 1986) presents essays on animal use by theologians from different religious traditions. Andrew Linzey, *Christianity and the Rights of Animals* (1987), and Matthew Scully, *Dominion: The Power of Man, the Suffering of Animals, and the Call to Mercy* (2002), focus on Christianity, which has historically taken a particularly negative attitude toward according moral significance to animal interests.

There are numerous books that concern particular uses of animals. For example, historical discussions concerning vivisection may be found in Richard D. French, *Antivivisection and Medical Science in Victorian Society* (1975); Coral Lansbury, *The Old Brown Dog: Women, Workers, and Vivisection in Edwardian England* (1985); and Nicholas A. Rupke, *Vivisection in Historical Perspective* (1987). More recent discussions are presented in Andrew N. Rowan, *Of Mice, Models, and Men: A Critical Evaluation of Animal Research* (1984); Richard D. Ryder, *Victims of Science: The Use of Animals in Research* (2d. ed. 1983); *Animal Experimentation: The Consensus Changes* (Gill Langley, ed., 1989); and *Animals in Research: New Perspectives in Animal Experimentation* (David Sperlinger, ed., 1981). The use of animals for food is discussed in Michael Allen Fox, *Deep Vegetarianism* (1999); Jim Mason and Peter Singer, *Animal Factories* (1990); Bernard E. Rollin, *Farm Animal Welfare: Social, Bioethical, and Research Issues* (1995); and Orville Schell, *Modern Meat* (1984).

A number of modern theorists have been highly critical of the view that animals have any morally significant interests. Peter Carruthers, *The Animals Issue: Moral Theory in Practice* (1992); R. G. Frey, *Interests and Rights: The Case Against Animals* (1980); and Michael P. T. Leahy, *Against Liberation: Putting Animals in Perspective* (rev. ed. 1994), reject the fundamental premises of the animal rights position.

There are a number of books that focus on the animal rights/animal welfare movement in the United States and Great Britain. For example, Richard D. Ryder discusses the historical development of the movement in both countries in *Animal Revolution: Changing Attitudes Toward Speciesism* (rev. ed. 2000). Lawrence Finsen and Susan Finsen discuss the American animal protection movement in *The Animal Rights Movement in America: From Compassion to Respect* (1994). In *Animal Liberators: Research and Morality* (1988), Susan Sperling focuses on the American antivivisection movement. Gary L. Francione, *Rain Without Thunder: The Ideology of the Animal Rights Movement* (1996), argues that the prevailing ideology of the modern American animal rights movement actually rejects animal rights in favor of animal welfare.

INDEX

self-awareness and, 177
tool use by, 194
vocalizations, 188, 189
Bobbitt, Philip, 28
bodily integrity, 21, 35, 39, 40, 55, 157, 315.
    See also self-ownership
bonobos, 33, 51, 52, 128, 188, 271
Boswell, James, 265
Boudin, Michael, 73
bow hunting, 109
Bradley, Justice, 265
Bradwell, Myra, 265
brain, 14, 35, 129, 172, 177, 189–93
brain damage, 79, 94, 128
Brambell Committee, 221
Britain. See Great Britain
Bronx Zoo, 311
Brown v. Board of Education (1954), 59, 251
Burger King, 224
Burns, Robert, 102
Bush, George W., 163
Byrd, Robert, 208, 217

Cabanac, Michel, 35
California, 213, 229n.34, 253, 268–69
Call, Josep, 185
Callaghan v. Society for the Prevention of
    Cruelty to Animals (1885), 118
calves. See veal crates
Canada, 269
canids, 178
cannibalism, 95–96, 99, 296n.1
capabilities, 14–15, 300, 302, 305–19
Carruthers, Peter, 130
categorical harm principle, 157
cats, 3, 63
    ancient views of, 53
    autonomy and, 10
    declawing of, 315
    life expectancy, 73
    protective legislation, 162–63, 174, 210,
    255
cattle, 222, 226–27n.2
    dehorning of, 118, 228n.20
    fencing of, 146
    veal crates, 217–19, 221, 222
    See also meat eating
central nervous system, 129, 172
cetaceans, 190, 192

Chang, P. C., 91n.7
Chartists, 94
chickens. See poultry
child abuse, 250nn.28–31
children, 12, 31, 54, 55, 167, 247n.8
    cruelty to animals by, 77n.40, 103
    guardians of, 196, 244
    mental state attribution by, 181
    moral rights of, 283
    parental bonds with, 82–83, 243
    parental obligations to, 238, 243, 244
    proportional liberty rights and, 39
    teachings about animals and, 101, 103
    See also infants
chimpanzees, 65–66, 172–73, 179, 291–92
    episodic memory and, 184
    flourishing by, 309–10
    hunting by, 185–86
    killing among, 85
    language use, 188
    legal status of, 248–49n.16, 271
    mental disabilities compared with, 54,
    55, 65, 154–55, 278–79
    mental state attribution by, 181
    object recognition by, 187
    rights and, 12, 51, 52, 54–57, 59
    self-recognition by, 34, 176, 180
    sense of self and, 128
    tool use by, 194
Christianity, 23, 24, 53, 61
Cicero, Marcus T., 195–96, 300
circus animals, 5, 110, 300, 304, 315
civil rights, 164, 287
Clever Hans (horse), 188
cognitive capacity, 24, 128, 179, 308
    as animal rights basis, 12–14, 54–57,
    144, 154–55, 176, 195
    autonomy and, 34, 35, 40
    brain size and, 189–92
    computers and, 55, 56
    intelligence and, 178
cognitive ethology, 33, 128
Coke, Lord, 37
Colorado, 228n.20
common law, 28–29, 32, 37, 51–52, 57, 71,
    146, 252
Commonwealth v. Turner (1827), 123
communication, 34, 126, 128, 183–89, 286.
    See also language

egg industry, 220–21, 226–27n.2
Egypt, ancient, 53
elephants, 41, 178, 180, 195, 254, 299–300
Emerson, Ralph Waldo, 266
emotions, 5–6, 35, 38, 52, 126, 316
empathy, 66, 69, 70
Endangered Species Act of 1973 (U.S.),
    36, 253, 258, 259, 260
endorphins, 172
Enforcement of the Humane Slaughter
    Act of 1958, 208
enjoyment, capacity for, 94, 99
entertainment, animals as, 5, 7, 110, 116
entitlements, 55–56, 300–317
environmental ethics, 14, 62, 277–79, 283,
    284, 293, 310
environmental law, 36, 37
episodic memory, 183–84
Epstein, Richard, 13, 20, 143–58
equal consideration, 78–80, 94, 120–34,
    278, 280, 288–89
equality, 33, 39, 64, 278
    feminist hierarchy theory and, 263–67,
        269, 272
    as human natural right, 94, 138–39n.71,
        142n.97
    as legal principle, 29, 30, 55, 196
Equal Pay Act of 1963 (U.S.), 266
equitable guardians ad litem, 243–44
equitable self-ownership, 237–45
equitable title, 240–44
ethical argument, 66–68, 163
    capabilities and, 306–10, 319
    personhood and, 166
    Singer and, 78–90
    See also environmental ethics
ethics of care, 196
Europe, 7, 8, 36, 103
    anticruelty laws, 221–24
    See also specific countries
European Union, 222, 223, 224, 225
euthanasia, 315
evolution theory, 23, 35, 39, 61, 63, 82, 127,
    179, 194
Exodus, 146
experiment subjects. See scientific experi-
    ments
exploitation principle, 36
extended consciousness, 128, 130

extinction, 279, 308
eye gaze, 182–83

factory farming, 109
farmed animals, 117, 118, 120, 206, 207,
    212–16, 219, 223, 253, 255, 315
    customary practices, 212–24
    See also anticruelty laws; specific types
Favre, Becky Lou, 246n.2
Favre, David, 14, 234–45
fear, 157, 189, 316
Feinberg, Joel, 32
"fellow creatures" concept, 101–5
feminist theory, 68, 263–73
fencing, 146, 159n.14
fetus, 32, 56, 71, 166
First Amendment, 269
fish, 109, 128, 164, 174, 190
    protective laws, 36, 253–54, 255, 258
fish farming, 226–27n.2
"Five Freedoms" of movement, 221
Fletcher, Joseph, 166
Florida, 225, 232–33n.79
flourishing, 305–17, 319
foie gras, 223, 227n.10
food. See agriculture; farmed animals; fish
    farming; meat eating; vegetarianism
Food and Safety Inspection Service,
    227n.4
Food Marketing Institute, 231–32n.77
Foster Farms, 215
Fourier, Charles, 273–74n.11
fowl. See birds; poultry
France, 6, 85
Francione, Gary L., 13, 108–34, 143, 152,
    156, 294
freedoms, 196, 309, 315–16
free-range farming, 222
Frey, R. G., 26
Friedan, Betty, 68
friendship, 102
Fugitive Slave Act of 1850 (U.S.), 35–36,
    37
furs, 109, 110, 116, 227n.2, 314, 315, 318

Galileo, 23
Gallup, Gordon, Jr., 34, 172
game parks, 254
game ranches, 109

paganism, 53
pain, 57, 64, 121, 308
　animal capacity for, 80, 94, 111, 113, 127,
　　165, 171–72
　Bentham's concept of, 196
　experimentation and, 63, 111
　humancentricism and, 66, 67
　legal system and, 52, 115, 118–19
　moral standing and, 167, 169
　utilitarianism and, 59, 60, 152–53,
　　303–4
　See also suffering
Palestinians, 85–86
*Palila v. Hawaii Dept. of Land and Natu-
　ral Resources* (1988), 259
parenthood, 82–83, 238, 243, 244
parrots, 41, 56, 191, 194, 195
paternalism, 312–15
Patterson, Orlando, 22
Paul, St., 22–23
Pennsylvania, 213, 214–15, 228n.20
People for the Ethical Treatment of
　Animals, 5, 211, 224
People of the Forest (film), 291–92
People v. Voelker (1997), 119
personhood, 25, 41
　animals and, 11, 131–32, 244–45, 260–
　　61
　conditions for, 166
　legal systems and, 31–32, 149–50
　practical autonomy and, 39
pets (companion animals), 3, 10, 45n.78,
　　72–73
　bill of rights for, 254
　cruelty liability, 211
　divorce custody of, 236
　guardianship of, 196
　house-trained, 285
　ownership of, 6, 148, 238–39
　taboos against eating, 97, 99, 296n.1
　women as, 272
philosophy, 3–4, 31, 59–66, 97
　moral change theories, 68–69, 84–86
　moral standing theories, 164–66
　See also utilitarianism; *specific philoso-
　　phers*
pigeons, 109, 177, 178, 180, 187, 191
Pig Husbandry Regulations of 1991
　(G.B.), 222

pigs, 206, 217–18, 221, 222, 278, 279
　numbers slaughtered, 226–27n.2
Piraro, Dan, 247n.5
Pitt, William, 21
pity, 102–3, 106
planning, 183, 184–86
Plato, 68
pleasure, 59, 60, 65, 80, 111, 152–53, 303–4
Pliny, 299
Political Liberalism (Rawls), 320n.8
Pompey, 299–300
Poole, Joyce, 41
pornography, 266, 267, 268–69
Posner, Richard, 13, 30, 51–74
　Singer's response to, 78–90
potentiality, 32
poultry, 205, 215–18, 220–22, 239
　anticruelty exemption, 208, 212
　numbers slaughtered, 206, 226n.22
Pound, Roscoe, 22, 25
pounds, animal, 226–27n.2
Povinelli, Daniel J., 194
power, 8, 27, 264–65, 266
practical autonomy, 13, 27, 32–41
pragmatism, 59, 61–62, 72, 80, 87–88, 90
precautionary principle, 36–39
predation, 279, 311, 315
preference autonomy, 142n.98
preference utilitarianism, 304–5
prejudice, 79–80, 93–94
primates, 195, 239
　brains of, 190–93
　episodic memory and, 184
　as experiment subjects, 63
　eye gaze following by, 182
　mental representations and, 187
　object recognition by, 187
　protective legislation, 254, 255
Primatt, Humphry, 135n.12
"prior existence" view, 89
private property. *See* property status
problem solving, 34, 40, 188
product testing, 109, 116, 158, 294, 318
property status, 150, 210
　of animal offspring, 145, 159n.10
　of animals, 6, 11–13, 28–29, 59, 73, 90,
　　108, 111–12, 116–22, 125, 127, 131, 132,
　　136n.29, 144–45, 148–49, 237–44,
　　247n.6, 254, 265